Retirement Made Easy

King Edward VII's Hospital for Officers
Beaumont Street, W1N 2AA   Tel: (071) 486 4411
PATRON: HER MAJESTY THE QUEEN
No Public Funds – A Charity to Help

KING EDWARD VII's HOSPITAL FOR OFFICERS is an acute Hospital enjoying the services of Harley Street consultants and the highest standards of nursing. Well equipped and supported, its objective is to provide treatment primarily for officers, ex-officers and their dependants but also for civilians, at prices tailored to its patients' means. It receives no help from public funds and is able to operate its low-cost pricing policy, so important to the elderly and those who cannot afford to obtain medical insurance, only because of the generosity of its benefactors.

Details available from: The Appeals Secretary,
KING EDWARD VII's HOSPITAL FOR OFFICERS.
6, Buckingham Place, SW1E 6HR   (Tel: 071-828 4454).
Reg. Charity No. 208944

The St. Andrew Animal Fund Limited
SO MUCH HELP IS NEEDED BY ANIMALS!
WHAT CAN ONE PERSON DO?

By supporting this FUND help is encouraged for the proper understanding and appreciation of animals and wildlife, for prevention of cruelty and the exploitation of animals.

These would be impossible tasks for one person, but THE ST. ANDREW ANIMAL FUND can attempt to help where the need is greatest. The Fund can provide financial and other support for the welfare and protection of animals, including grants made for the development by scientists of humane methods of research. No task is too great–none too small.

PLEASE help with Legacies, Gifts, Donations and Deeds of Covenant.

The ST. ANDREW ANIMAL FUND LIMITED is a registered charity, 47073 (Scotland)
10 Queensferry Street, Edinburgh EH2 4PG   Tel: 031-225 2116

Retirement Made Easy

Rosemary Brown

The Shortened 'Good Retirement Guide'

ENTERPRISE DYNAMICS

KOGAN PAGE

All rights reserved; no part of this publication may be
reproduced, stored in a retrieval system, or transmitted in any
form or by any means, electronic, mechanical, photocopying or
otherwise, without the prior written permission of the Publisher.

This edition first published 1993

Copyright © by Enterprise Dynamics Ltd 1993

Kogan Page Ltd, 120 Pentonville Road, London N1 9JN

British Library Cataloguing in Publication Data
A CIP record for this book is available from the British Library.

ISBN 0-7494-0807-3

Typeset by Saxon Graphics Ltd, Derby.
Printed and bound in Great Britain by
Clays Ltd, St Ives plc

REAL PAIN RELIEF
WITHOUT DRUGS

FROM ARTHRITIS, HEADACHES, ASTHMA, MIGRAINES AND PAIN IN GENERAL

The Healthpoint unit is a safe and gentle treatment for use in the home which gives effective relief from:
- ★ Arthritis ★ Back Problems
- ★ Shoulder Problems
- ★ Stress & Anxiety
- ★ PMS ★ Insomnia
- ★ Smoking ★ Headaches
- ★ Migraines
- ★ Sporting Injuries
- ★ Sinusitis ★ Asthma

and hundreds of other ailments

HEALTHPOINT ▶
TOTAL PAIN RELIEF

Now, you too, can join the many thousands of ordinary people, both young and old, as well as Doctors, hospitals and physiotherapists who are daily experiencing how fast and effective electro stimulation treatment is in the fight to relieve the crippling symptoms of many common ailments.

For an information pack – **Telephone 0606 854684** *or write to*
DOVE HEALTHCARE LTD FREEPOST (CW460) NORTHWICH CHESHIRE CW8 1BR

Leukaemia CARE

Registered Charity no. 259465

Last year Leukaemia CARE **helped** 1200 families by providing:
- 250 Financial Assistance Grants
- 270 Caravan Holidays
- 60,000 'Befriending hours'

This year Leukaemia CARE **will be asked to help** even more families. **We** can only **help them** if **you** will **help us**.
A donation or covenant now and a legacy later will make it possible.

**14 Kingfisher Court (2931), Venny Bridge, Pinhoe, Exeter, Devon EX4 8JN.
Tel: Exeter (0392) 64848 Fax: Exeter (0392) 460331**

THE DEPAUL TRUST
Housing Homeless Youth

The Depaul Trust aims to bridge the gap between the street and resettlement for young homeless people aged 16-25 who are trapped in a cycle of homelessness – no money means no accommodation – no accommodation means no job.

We need your support to help us prove that **HOMELESSNESS** need not equal **HOPELESSNESS**

Send your donation to The Director, THE DEPAUL TRUST, 247 Willesden Lane, NW2 5RY.   Tel: 081 459 4188

QUEEN ELIZABETH'S FOUNDATION FOR DISABLED PEOPLE

The Foundation works with disabled people to build confidence and train them to live as normal and fulfilling a life as their disabilities allow. The Foundation has eight operational units. A residential Training College, Hostel & Arts Centre, a Sheltered Industry, a Holiday Home, A Day Care/Resource Centre, a Mobility Centre, Assessment & Further Education Centre and an Information Service. We help some 2,000 people per year and give information to a further 10,000.

ACQUIRE THE DREAM... NOT THE NIGHTMARE!!

The Daily Telegraph
GUIDE TO LIVING AND RETIRING ABROAD

'The least expensive way to avoid being caught in the rain'
MONEY WEEK

Full of essential information, practical advice and handy hints for anyone planning a move abroad.

TELEPHONE YOUR CREDIT CARD DETAILS

on 071-278 0433 (24 hour) or send a cheque/po made payable to Kogan Page for £8.99 (£1 p&p) to Kogan Page, 120 Pentonville Rd, London N1 9JN.

A Legacy of Healthcare

NUFFIELD HOSPITALS is an independent British charity which, in the course of helping to preserve the health and well-being of local communities, offers both freedom of choice and an unsurpassed standard of treatment. In response to appeals from these communities for independent healthcare facilities, the charity has harnessed local financial support to provide 32 hospitals nationwide. All enjoy a high staff/patient ratio and include equipment that is the most advanced in its field.

It is in the latter area where charitable help is most needed. Ever more intricate treatment requires ever more sophisticated and expensive equipment. For this, NUFFIELD HOSPITALS relies heavily on donations and legacies – the annual need for renewals and other improvements exceeds £11 million.

Would you please remember NUFFIELD HOSPITALS when you are making your Will? You can nominate the Nuffield Hospital of your choice for a commemorative bequest linked either to a room or item of new equipment. For further details contact Bob Russell, Head of Fund Raising, Nuffield Hospitals, Nuffield House, 1-4 The Crescent, Surbiton, Surrey, KT6 4BN. Tel: 081-390 1200.

Nuffield Hospitals
Registered Charity Number 205533

Royal Society of Medicine

Charity Registration No. 206219

1 Wimpole Street, London W1M 8AE
Tel. 071-408 2119
Telex 298902 ROYMED G
Fax. 071-355 3196

PATRON: Her Majesty the Queen

President
Sir George Pinker KCVO FRCOG

Executive Director
Robert N Thomson MA

 The Royal Society of Medicine was founded in 1805 "for the cultivation and promotion of physic and surgery and of the branches of science connected with them." In the last 180 years, the Society has grown into an international organisation with more than 19,000 members worldwide. The original aims are pursued today in a variety of ways, including the following: by the organising and hosting of over 500 medical meetings each year; through the maintenance of one of Europe's major medical libraries with more than 500,000 volumes; by the publication of the proceedings of medical conferences and the production of both a monthly journal for members and a quarterly journal for doctors working in isolation in developing countries; and by providing a forum for specialists from different fields and for lay people to meet to discuss current medical issues of vital concern.

If you wish your donation to contribute to the advancement of medical knowledge as a whole, the Royal Society of Medicine is the nearest thing we have in the United Kingdom to a national academy of medicine.

This tragic sight is not uncommon in the Middle East today. Each week the Brooke Hospital for Animals gives free treatment to hundreds of suffering animals, and saves many more from years of crippling work. If you would like either to receive more information or to support our work, please simply fill out the coupon below and send it to:
Brooke Hospital for Animals, Dept GRG, 21 Panton Street, London SW1Y 4BR. Or call us on 071-930 0210.

How you can help the Brooke Hospital for Animals

I would like to know more about the Brooke Hospital for Animals (Charity No. 207869)

NAME: Mr/Mrs/Miss ....
ADDRESS...
.... POSTCODE .... GRG

They depend on us — we depend on you

THE PRINCE AND PRINCESS OF WALES HOSPICE

- Provides a free service to the terminally ill and their families in Glasgow.
- Patients can be cared for in their own homes by doctors, Macmillan nurses and a social worker.
- Respite care and symptom control, available in the Inpatient Unit, plays an important part too.
- And the Day Centre offers a relaxing and non-clinical atmosphere, in which counselling, occupational therapy, pain relief advice and social contact helps patients.
- Please help us to maintain this vital support for people involved in the stresses of dying.

Dr Anne J J Gilmore Founder and Chief Executive
The Prince and Princess of Wales Hospice 73 Carlton Place, Glasgow G5 9TD
Telephone: 041-429 5599

wish you were here?

John is 8 years old. He's never seen the sea. He's never built a sandcastle. Without your help, he never will.

Every summer the majority of Britons look forward to a relaxing fortnight in the sunshine. Yet there are millions of underprivileged families – imprisoned in squalid housing conditions by poverty, unemployment, ill-health or disability – who have no prospect of ever 'getting away from it all'.

For these people, the Family Holiday Association represents a lifeline. It is the only national charity which specialises in awarding holiday grants to deprived UK families, giving them the break they so desperately need.

Please send a donation or write for information on leaving a legacy of sunshine to:
FHA Freepost, London N3 3BR

the Family Holiday Association

Contents

Introduction   *xxv*

1. Looking Forward to Retirement   1

   Pre-retirement courses   5

2. Money in General   10

   Doing the sums   10
   Possible ways of boosting your retirement income   14
   Spending now for saving later   17
   Cherished plans, if affordable   19
   Cheques Act 1992   20
   Extra income   20

3. Pensions   21

   State pensions   21
   Your right to a State pension   21
   How your pension is worked out   23
   Working after you start getting your pension   27
   Private pensions   29
   Questions on your pension scheme   35
   What to do before retirement   37
   Self-employed and personal pension schemes   39
   A lump sum?   46
   Pension rights if you continue to work after retirement age   48
   Pensions for women   48

OUR CONCERN IS HEARING IN BRITAIN

- *Our expert technological committees encourage Government and manufacturers to intensify hearing aid research and improve telecommunications.*
- *We provide trained volunteers to give in-the-home support to help new sufferers, especially the elderly.*
- *Our Association has a Young Adults Hard Of Hearing section (YAHOH) and runs Noise Awareness Campaigns.*
- *We are developing a new, larger national centre for hearing concern in Britain.*

REG. CHARITY NO: 223322

THE BRITISH ASSOCIATION OF THE

HARD OF  HEARING

IF YOU SUFFER FROM HEARING IMPAIRMENT OR KNOW ANYBODY WHO DOES, YOU CAN HELP BY JOINING OUR ASSOCIATION, BY DONATION, OR BY REMEMBERING US IN YOUR WILL.

PLEASE CONTACT:
THE DIRECTOR OF APPEALS, BAHOH,
PO BOX 18, NEWPORT, ISLE OF WIGHT, PO30 4QD.

CAMPAIGNING FOR ALL SUFFERERS OF THE INVISIBLE HANDICAP

CARERS' NATIONAL ASSOCIATION
29 Chilworth Mews, London W2 3RG
Tel: 071-724 7776
Registered Charity No 246329

Carers' National Association supports and campaigns for people who lead a restricted life because of the need to care for a relative or friend, of any age, who is mentally ill or handicapped, physically disabled or frail.

Throughout the U.K. an estimated six million carers are suffering emotional and physical stress because of caring and yet are often unrecognised by health and social services.

We provide information and advice to carers and support through out network of branches and groups. We are supported by a Government grant but are heavily dependent on legacies and donations.

MACA

*meets mental health needs
where it matters most...*

- in the community

We provide a wide range of services for individuals and their families — and we know we're effective. But the needs keep growing — so do the costs. By sending a donation, or making a legacy, Will or codicil in our favour, you'll be helping us to complete the picture for many more people.

To send a donation or obtain more information, please write to: The Director, The Mental After Care Association, Bainbridge House, Bainbridge Street, London WC1A 1HP

MACA

COMPLETES THE PICTURE

Contents

4. Tax 55

Income tax 55
Tax allowances 56
Tax relief 59
Post-war credits 64
Capital gains tax (CGT) 65
Inheritance tax 68
Independent taxation 69
Value added tax (VAT) 70
Corporation tax 70

5. Investment 73

Sources of investable funds 73
Annuities 74
National Savings 75
Variable interest accounts 77
Fixed interest securities 80
Equities 82
Long-term lock-ups 86
Investor protection 90

6. Financial Advisers 94

Choosing an adviser 95
Accountants 96
Banks 97
Insurance brokers 100
Other pension advisers 103
Solicitors 105

7. Budget Planner 111

xi

HAVE YOU THE WILL TO HELP HER?

Mitzi is just one of thousands of animals – pets, livestock, wildlife and birds – helped by the Scottish SPCA each year. Our achievements last year were outstanding.

46 trained Inspectors, stationed throughout Scotland, responded to 73,000 calls for help in the course of their cruelty prevention work.

10 Animal Welfare Centres provided refuge for almost 9,000 cruelly treated and abandoned animals.

6 Education Officers visited schools and spoke to over 27,000 young people on all aspects of animal welfare.

In the UK and Europe, Society members and supporters participated in campaigns for new and improved welfare legislation.

Please help the Scottish SPCA continue its fight against animal abuse.

Scottish Society for the Prevention of Cruelty to Animals
Dept. GRG, 19 Melville Street, Edinburgh EH3 7PL.
Telephone: 031-225 6418.

8. Your Home — 118

Staying put *118*
Moving to a new home *119*
Moving in with family or friends *122*
Sharing with friends *123*
Retirement housing and sheltered accommodation *123*
Improvement and repair *130*
Safety in the home *135*
Home security *137*
Insurance *139*
Raising money on your home *140*
Letting rooms in your home *142*
Housing benefit and community charge benefit *144*
Council tax *145*
Useful organisations *149*

9. Leisure Activities — 153

Adult education *154*
Arts *155*
Music and ballet *156*
Crafts *160*
Dance/keep-fit *161*
For people with disabilities *162*
Games *163*
Gardens and gardening *163*
History *164*
Hobbies *166*
Museums *167*
Nature and conservation *168*
Public library service *169*
Sport *170*
Other information *176*

10. Looking for Paid Work 178

Assessing your abilities *180*
Job counselling *181*
Training opportunities *181*
Help with finding a job *182*
CV writing *183*
Interview technique *184*
Part-time openings *185*
Openings via a company reference *185*
Public appointments *186*
Market research *186*
Paid work for charities *187*
Sales *188*
Jobs in tourism *189*
Teaching and training skills *189*
Working in the Third World *190*
Caring for other people *191*
Cashing in your home interests *193*
Pubs and paying guests *194*
Agencies and other useful organisations *195*

11. Voluntary Work 202

General *203*
Animals *205*
Bereavement *205*
Children and young people *206*
Conservation *208*
The elderly *209*
The family *211*
Health and handicapped people *212*
Heritage and the arts *216*
The needy *216*
Offenders and victims of crime *218*

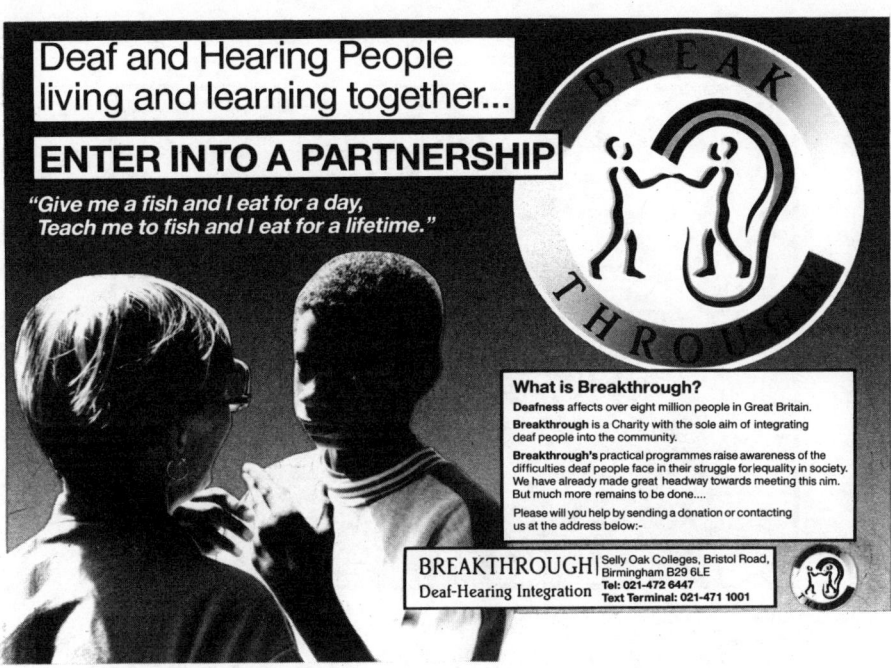

Deaf and Hearing People living and learning together...
ENTER INTO A PARTNERSHIP

"Give me a fish and I eat for a day, Teach me to fish and I eat for a lifetime."

What is Breakthrough?

Deafness affects over eight million people in Great Britain.

Breakthrough is a Charity with the sole aim of integrating deaf people into the community.

Breakthrough's practical programmes raise awareness of the difficulties deaf people face in their struggle for equality in society. We have already made great headway towards meeting this aim. But much more remains to be done....

Please will you help by sending a donation or contacting us at the address below:-

BREAKTHROUGH
Deaf-Hearing Integration

Selly Oak Colleges, Bristol Road, Birmingham B29 6LE
Tel: 021-472 6447
Text Terminal: 021-471 1001

A gift in your Will today could provide a lifetime of care for even more dogs like Jake and Ben.

Since its foundation in 1891, The National Canine Defence League has provided thousands of abandoned, stray and cruelly treated dogs like Jake and Ben with the comfort and care they need.

But sadly, the number of puppies and dogs brought into our thirteen Rescue Centres increases every year.

And the cost of caring for them until loving new homes can be found increases too, as no healthy animal is ever destroyed.

As a registered charity, we depend upon the generosity of fellow dog-lovers to continue our vital work.

And you can help today and in the years ahead, by leaving a Legacy to the NCDL in your Will. This is one of the most valuable and far-reaching ways that you can help us save even more dogs like Jake and Ben from cruelty, abandonment or even death.

Please do consider supporting the NCDL in this special way.

For more details about leaving a gift in your Will, please write to: The Secretary, National Canine Defence League, 1, Pratt Mews, London, NW1 0AD or telephone: 071 388 0137.

A DOG IS FOR LIFE ...

Registered Charity No: 227523

'I'll never stop caring for animals'

'I've loved and looked after animals all my life. Suki – that's her in the picture with me – is just the latest in a long line. I'll even be caring for animals after my days are over. How? I've left a legacy to the BUAV, of course.

'I hate to think of all the dreadful things they do to those poor animals in laboratories – a legacy to the BUAV is my way of helping to stop their suffering.'

The British Union for the Abolition of Vivisection (BUAV) leads the movement to end animal experiments, and our campaigns are making great headway. For our free booklet, *How to make a will and help animals at the same time*, please write to: Mr A.B. Burder, BUAV, 16a Crane Grove, London N7 8LB, or phone 071-700 4888. We'll be delighted to hear from you.

12. Health — 224

    Keeping fit *225*
    Sensible eating *226*
    Food safety *227*
    Drink *228*
    Smoking *229*
    Aches, pains and other abnormalities *230*
    Health insurance *230*
    Hospital cash plans *233*
    Eyes *237*
    Feet *239*
    Hearing *239*
    Teeth *240*
    Personal relationships *240*
    Depression *241*
    Some common afflictions *243*
    AIDS *246*
    Disability *247*

13. Holidays — 256

    Art appreciation *257*
    Arts and crafts *258*
    Coach holidays *259*
    Field studies *259*
    Historical holidays *260*
    Language courses *261*
    Other people's homes *262*
    Overseas travel *263*
    Retreats *265*
    Saga – in a class of its own *266*
    Self-catering and other low-budget holidays *266*

Will you enjoy life after retirement?

You probably already know that the prospects of doing so will be improved by sensible financial planning. But, like most people, you may not be aware of how to go about it.

If this is the case, our new booklet 'Enjoying Life After Work' will be of great help to you. It takes a refreshingly unbiased look at all the main financial aspects of retirement planning, tells you about the dos and don'ts and draws your attention to such issues as:

- Why 'independent' advice may not necessarily be unbiased

- Why some income-producing 'investment bonds' have to run very hard merely to stand still

- Why cash on deposit can never truly be described as a real investment

... and many more.

For your free copy please write to us using the coupon below.

To Alun Evans, W I Carr (Investments) Limited, No 1 London Bridge, London SE1 9TJ. Telephone: 071-378 7050.
Please send me a copy of 'Enjoying Life After Work'

Name_____

Address_____

_____

_____Postcode_____

W·I·CARR
Banque Indosuez Group

W I Carr (Investments) Limited is a member of the Securities and Futures Authority and the London Stock Exchange.

GRG 93

Special interest *269*
Sport *271*
Wine tasting *273*
Working holidays *273*
Holidays for singles *274*
Holidays for those needing special care *275*
Tourist boards *278*
Insurance *278*
Travel and other concessions *281*
Health tips for travellers *282*

14. Caring for Elderly Parents   284

Ways of adapting a home *284*
Alarm systems *287*
Main local authority services *288*
Key voluntary organisations *290*
Other sources of help and advice *292*
Transport *293*
Temporary living-in help *294*
Nursing care *295*
Emergency care for pets *296*
Practical help for carers *296*
Holidays *297*
Benefits and allowances *298*
Financial assistance *301*
Special accommodation *302*
Some special problems *311*

The Greeks had a word for it.

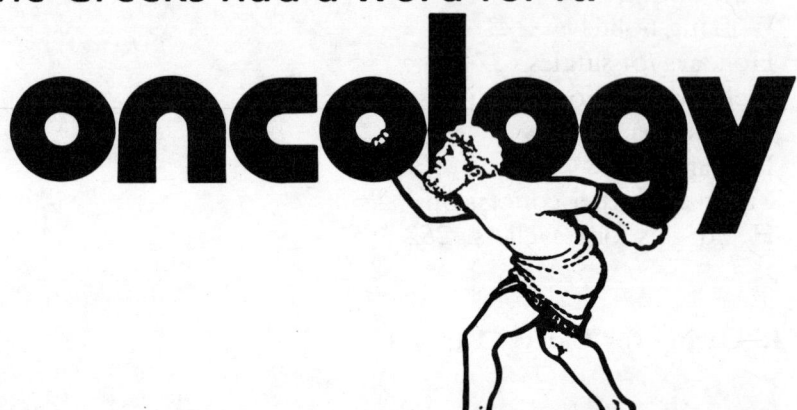

The campaign has undertaken to fund five new institutes for Cancer Research at the Universities of Leeds, Sheffield, Hull, York and Bradford...

...whilst maintaining its existing commitments to finance cancer research in all the Universities and Teaching Hospitals of Yorkshire.

CLINICAL ONCOLOY
'Clinical' means working with patients: 'Oncology' comes from the Greek word '*onkos*' meaning bulk or tumour and '*logos*' meaning science. So quite literally 'Clinical Oncology' is the science of studying tumours (mainly cancers) in patients.

YORKSHIRE CANCER RESEARCH CAMPAIGN

£3,500,000 needed per annum

Legacy income has always been a vital factor in financing the Campaign's work. Your continuing support by bringing to the notice of your clients this special appeal for extra funds will be of even greater value than in the past.

Please write to the Campaign's Secretary for further information and a copy of our 'Oncology' booklet and the annual report and accounts

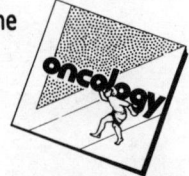

Mrs Maureen Smalley, Secretary, Yorkshire Cancer Research Campaign, 39 East Parade, Harrogate, North Yorkshire. HG1 5LQ.
Registered Charity No. 516298.

15. No One is Immortal   **315**

    Wills *315*
    Making a Will *315*
    Money worries – and how to minimise them *318*
    What to do when someone dies *324*
    Organisations that can help *327*

Index   *341*

List of Advertisers   *362*

List of Chapters

Introduction

1. Looking Forward to Retirement — 1
2. Money in General — 10
3. Pensions — 21
4. Tax — 55
5. Investment — 73
6. Financial Advisers — 94
7. Budget Planner — 111
8. Your Home — 118
9. Leisure Activities — 153
10. Looking for Paid Work — 178
11. Voluntary Work — 202
12. Health — 224
13. Holidays — 256
14. Caring for Elderly Parents — 284
15. No One is Immortal — 315

Index — 341

List of Advertisers — 362

THE ROYAL SCOTTISH AGRICULTURAL BENEVOLENT SOCIETY

Fighting Rural Hardship

The Royal Scottish Agricultural Benevolent Institution is dedicated to the relief of hardship in Scotland's rural community. It provides assistance to the aged, infirm, disabled and distressed whose roots are in the Scottish countryside. Anyone who has worked or is working in agriculture, aquaculture, forestry, horticulture and rural estate work and their dependants, may be eligible for help. Each case is sympathetically viewed and assistance is given in the form of single or annual grants and/or help in kind. The RSABI is entirely dependant for its resources on voluntary donations, legacies, etc.

Further information, application forms, etc from:
The Director, RSABI, Ingliston, Edinburgh EH28 8NB.
Tel: 031 333 1023.

A MATTER OF LIFE OR DEATH!

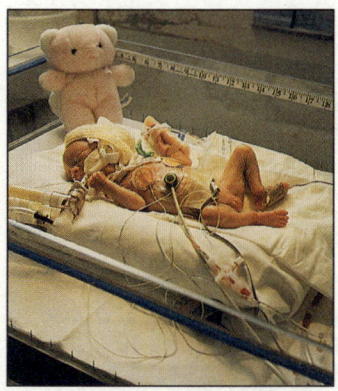

Many babies start their lives like this one. Whereas only a few years ago this premature baby would have died, today he will almost certainly grow up to be a normal, healthy child. This is due to the advances which have been made in paediatric medicine as a result of research funded by charities such as ours. He is being kept alive in a Children Nationwide neonatal intensive care unit at one of the hospitals which we support.

Donations to our research fund will enable more babies, either simply born prematurely like this one, or born with a serious disease or condition, to survive. Please send donations or requests for further information to Francesca MacArthur at the address below.

Chief Medical Adviser
Sir Raymond Hoffenberg, PRCP
(Past President of the Royal College of Physicians, London)
Honorary Medical Director
Sir Eric Stroud FRCP
Emeritus Professor of Child Health
Kings College Hospital, London

CHILDREN NATIONWIDE
MEDICAL RESEARCH FUND
Registered under Charities Act 1960 289600

NICHOLAS HOUSE · 181 UNION STREET · LONDON SE1 0LN · TELEPHONE: 071-928 2425

Let us take you on a holiday experience of a lifetime

- AUSTRALIA
- USA · CANADA
- SOUTH AFRICA
- NORWAY · ISRAEL
- EGYPT & GREECE
- NILE CRUISE · PORTUGAL
- NEW ZEALAND
- SOUTH OF FRANCE

Our service makes a world of difference... and that starts from the moment we collect you locally for the holiday of a lifetime. With over 15 years experience of catering for British tastes, the holidays we organise have been meticulously researched. All our tours have a properly balanced itinerary, with a complete range of excursions, covering all the major attractions, included. With the high quality of hotels we use along with our special flair for creating the big occasion our clients are promised the time of their lives.

At the airport our friendly staff are there to take care of check-in arrangements ready for your SCHEDULED flight aboard the world's leading Airlines DIRECT to your destination.

Send for our free detailed brochure(s) and see for yourself the super value for money and quality of service that makes Titan Travel the First Choice for Escorted Tours.

TITAN TRAVEL LIMITED GUARANTEED NO SURCHARGE

We also arrange special tailor made escorted tours for small or large groups.

Local departures from over 700 points in the U.K.

CALL OUR 24hr BROCHURE HOTLINE 0737 760033

ABTA No. 68982 TITAN TRAVEL LTD ARE FULLY BONDED MEMBERS OF ABTA – YOUR GUARANTEE OF QUALITY AND RELIABILITY

TITAN TRAVEL LTD, HiTOURS HOUSE, 28-30 HOLMETHORPE AVENUE, REDHILL, SURREY RH1 2NL

Introduction

Some people are never happier than when retired. Others seem to have the cares of the world on their shoulders.

The purpose of this book is to try to help ensure that you are among the lucky ones for whom retirement is genuinely fulfilling and fun.

Part of the secret is advance planning, so that when the times comes for leaving your job: (1) you are not worrying unnecessarily about money and (2) you have already lined up a host of activities on which to get started.

The key to getting it right is having the information you need at your fingertips. Whatever your interest – whether you are looking for a new focus, pondering decisions to do with your home or seeking a low cost adventure holiday – you will almost certainly be amazed at how many choices you have.

Sadly, too many people are still in the dark and so are missing out on opportunities. Just as some men and women are bored because they never realised the vast range of exciting outlets available to them, others worry about problems that need never have existed had they known earlier where to turn for advice. Likewise, many people are more hard up than they need be, either because they are paying more tax than necessary or because they are failing to take advantage of all the benefits to which they are entitled.

We have tried to include the answers to all the questions we thought you would be most likely to ask; or alternatively to suggest where you might go to get expert advice. In turn, if you have any tips to pass on to other readers or ideas for us on improving next year's edition, please write and let me know.

STOP PRESS. News has just come in of the new pension and benefit up-ratings – payable from April 1993. Among the highlights:

- The basic pension for a single person goes up to £56.10 a week; for a married couple, to £89.90
- Sickness benefit rises to £42.70 for those under pension age and to £53.80 for those over pension age.
- Attendance allowance is increased to £30 at the lower rate; and to £44.90 at the higher rate.

Retirement Made Easy

- Invalidity benefit goes up to £56.10.
- The basic adult income support allowance rises to £44 for a single person and to £69 for a married couple. People over pension age receive more.

I should like to thank everyone who has contributed to the launch of *Retirement Made Easy*. Literally hundreds of people have generously given their time in helping us to check the information. Their assistance is hugely appreciated.

My special thanks are due to the several officials at the Inland Revenue, DSS and other Government departments for their invaluable help and unfailing good humour.

I am also most grateful to our publishers Kogan Page for their enthusiastic backing for this new book.

Finally, a great big thank you to my assistant, Jean Rosete, who is quite simply a marvel.

Retirement Made Easy is dedicated to you, our readers, in the hope that you can look forward to many healthy, happy and satisfying years. With my very best wishes.

Rosemary Brown
November 1992

EVERY YEAR WE TAKE MORE PEOPLE UNDER OUR WING

Be they aircrew or ground staff. Be they ex-RAF or serving RAF members. Be they their spouses or their dependent children.

We help them overcome financial difficulties caused through no fault of their own.

Last year we helped in 16,000 ways to the tune of an average of over £21,000 for every day of the year, including Christmas day. This amounts to £7.99 million. This year, we'll need to be there for many more people and even more next year.

By sending us a donation now and by remembering us in your Will you will help ensure that we are.

COMRADES IN ARMS SHOULD BE COMRADES IN ALMS

To: The Royal Air Force Benevolent Fund, 67 Portland Place, London W1N 4AR. Tel: 071-580 8343. Ext 257. Or in Scotland: 20 Queen Street, Edinburgh EH2 1JX

☐ I would like to make a donation of £_____ by postal order/cheque (delete as applicable)
☐ Please charge my Access/Visa/American Express/Diners Club Number
☐☐☐☐☐☐☐☐☐☐☐☐☐☐☐☐ Expiry date ___/___
☐ Please send details of making a legacy/covenant
☐ Please send information on making a Will

NAME
ADDRESS
POSTCODE
SIGNATURE

MRG92

Charity Reg No. 207327

THE ROYAL AIR FORCE BENEVOLENT FUND

GIVE GENEROUSLY TO SAVE SIGHT

Every year in the U.K. thousands of people go blind. Successful eye research can save sight. In 1991, the sight of 2,000 people was saved as a result of successful corneal transplant operations using corneas from our Eye Bank.

Your legacy or donation can help run the Eye Bank and develop much needed research into the causes and treatment of eye diseases and the prevention of blindness.

Sight is precious, please be generous.

NATIONAL EYE RESEARCH CENTRE
Bristol Hospital, Lower Maudlin Street, Bristol BS1 2LX. Tel: 0272 290024
(Registered Charity 294087)

HALCYON DAYS or HARD TIMES?

A happy and fulfilling retirement, as opposed to a bleak and uncertain future, is the result of careful and accurate financial planning.

Boyton Financial Services Limited (BFS) has developed a highly refined and comprehensive service that will quickly highlight potential shortfalls in your current arrangements.

And, BFS is one of the few independent firms of advisers that only operates on a time spent, fee charging basis.

It is never too late for you to seek our professional advice – we could make a considerable difference to your life style in the years ahead.

Telephone or write to:
BOYTON FINANCIAL SERVICES LIMITED, PO BOX 14, HALSTEAD, ESSEX, CO9 4DY.
TELEPHONE: 0787 61919

BOYTON FINANCIAL SERVICES LTD
Member of the Financial Intermediaries and Brokers Regulatory Association.

When you're dying the last thing you want is excuses

working for *your* rights — your right to treatment — **your right to live**

NATIONAL KIDNEY FEDERATION
caring for kidney patients

6 Stanley Street, Worksop S81 7HX
Tel: 0909 487795 Fax: 0909 481723
Registered Charity No 278616
DONATIONS AND BEQUESTS MOST GRATEFULLY RECEIVED

IT'S MIGHTIER THAN THE SWORD.

Erskine Hospital needs to raise more than £1 million in public donations every year to provide medical care and special facilities for our many disabled residents.

That's why it's so important that people remember us when they make a will.

Legacies or bequests should be made available to The Princess Louise Scottish Hospital (Erskine Hospital), Bishopton, Renfrewshire. Correspondence to Treasurer I.W. Grimmond, B.Acc, C.A. at the hospital.
Telephone 041-812 1100.   **ERSKINE**

WHEN A DEAF CHILD TALKS, OUR WORK SPEAKS FOR ITSELF

The **ELIZABETH FOUNDATION** Family Centre in Portsmouth provides vital early detection of deafness, as well as education and support, for both parents and their deaf children. This help is also given to parents Nationally through our Correspondence and Advisory Course. All our services are FREE to parents of deaf children and are funded from voluntary donations.

WE are special.

YOU can do something special.

Remember **US** in your will.

THE ELIZABETH FOUNDATION FOR DEAF CHILDREN

Dept. GRG Southwick Hill Road Cosham PORTSMOUTH PO6 3LU
Tel: (0705) 372735 Fax: (0705) 326155
Registered Charity No. 293835

THE ROYAL SCHOOL FOR DEAF CHILDREN MARGATE

200th ANNIVERSARY 1792 - 1992

Patron: Her Majesty Queen Elizabeth the Queen Mother

A proper start in life . . .

We are more than just a school for the deaf – nearly half of our pupils have other handicaps too. Hearing children know hundreds, perhaps thousands of words when they start school. At Margate the children are lucky if they know a few dozen. They are profoundly deaf – to most noises, to almost all speech. A proper start in life for those youngsters would be cheap at any price.

We also have a unit that caters especially for the multiple handicapped profoundly deaf and the deaf/blind.

There are two units outside the main school that are for the over 16 year olds. These cater for work and life skills programmes and training in independent living. A third unit of six self-contained flats allows some to experience independence whilst help is near at hand.

To continue providing these specialised facilities requires a constant income from donations and legacies. Please help us to help them gain a PROPER START IN LIFE.

Registered Office: Victoria Road, Margate, Kent CT9 1NB.
Telephone: Thanet 227561
REGISTERED CHARITY No: 325109

Leave a legacy to The Salvation Army

Every day, we care for more than 10,000 people in the UK alone. We are a friend to the helpless, the lonely and the desperate.

We provide comfort and <u>practical support</u> worldwide – community centres, homes for children and the elderly, and essential emergency services.

If you are making a will, please think of the needy, and the vital help The Salvation Army can give to them.

Thank you

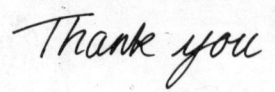

H1

The Salvation Army, Dept. LA20, 101 Queen Victoria Street, London EC4P 4EP. Telephone 071-236 5222.

*Retirement
Made Easy*

Get your brain into gear!

Make the most of your retirement and join the thousands of people from all walks of life who have discovered the rewards to be gained from studying with the Open University - wider horizons, personal satisfaction, greater self-confidence and sheer enjoyment.

Choose from courses and study packs in the Arts, Social Sciences, Science, Technology, Education, Mathematics, Computing and the Environment.

For your free copy of our introductory brochure *Studying With the Open University*, please telephone 0908 653231 (quoting code number A924B) or write to us at: C.E.D.S. (A924B), PO Box 625, The Open University, Milton Keynes MK1 1TY

British Veterinary Association

Animal Welfare Foundation

- Educating
- Informing
- Investigating

Founded by the British Veterinary Association to utilise veterinary knowledge and expertise in the cause of animal welfare, the BVA Animal Welfare Foundation:–

- established the world's first Chair of Animal Welfare at Cambridge University.
- funds scientific investigations and education projects aimed at improving the welfare of animals.
- runs Symposia and workshops to exchange information on welfare issues.

Bequests and donations are needed to further our professional, scientific and humane approach to animal welfare.

BVA Animal Welfare Foundation,
7 Mansfield Street, London W1M 0AT.

Reg. Charity 287118

Chapter 1

Looking Forward to Retirement

Just as there are some people who become engaged within three hours of meeting and live happily ever after, there are others who without any apparent planning enjoy a totally fulfilled retirement, clearly relishing everything it has to offer.

But for most of us life does not work like that. Important events require some preparation if we are to make the most of them and arguably this is more true of retirement than of any other stage.

A majority of people retiring today are fitter, more skilled and better off financially than any previous generation. Also, with early retirement increasingly becoming the norm, a great many of us can realistically look forward to 25 years or more of active life ahead. As a result, planning the future has become even more critically important. This guide is not designed to offer you a ready-made philosophy or a few rose-tinted blueprints on the theme 'Life Begins in Middle Age'. Its sole aim is to set you thinking along constructive lines, to indicate what is possible, to advise on the best sources of information and to help you avoid the pitfalls that can trap the unwary.

Key concerns are likely to be the question of money and how you will occupy your time. Others may well include: where you live, how best to keep fit, the effect of your retirement on close personal relationships and perhaps new responsibilities such as the care of elderly parents.

You do not need to be an accountant to know that once you stop earning your income will drop. However, if you complete the Budget Planner (see pages 112-117), you may be pleasantly surprised to find that the difference is far less than you had feared. On the plus side, you will be saving on travel and other work-related expenses as well as enjoying a welcome reduction in tax.

As with all questions affecting retirement, it is sensible if possible to plan ahead. Assess your likely savings including the lump sum from your pension and any insurance policies you may have. Then draw up a plan as to how you can maximise their value. Should you invest your money in a building society, PEP scheme, TESSA, unit trust, stocks and shares or government securities? Does it make sense to buy an annuity? What are the tax angles for someone in your position? Should you consider consulting a good accountant or other professional adviser? If you are unsure of some of the answers, then the Investment chapter may help to clarify your thinking.

Your retirement income may well depend on whether you start a new career. We are not pretending this is easy, but a great many men and women do in fact find rewarding work when they are well into their sixties. While some individuals turn their talents to something entirely new, others go freelance or become consultants in their existing area of expertise.

A worthwhile alternative to a new career could be to devote your energies to voluntary work. There are literally scores of opportunities for retired people to make a valuable contribution within their own community. You might visit the elderly in their own homes, drive patients to hospital, run a holiday playscheme, help out in your Citizens' Advice Bureau or become a Samaritan. Other ideas which might appeal are conservation work or playing a more active role in politics by joining your local party association. Whether you can only spare the occasional day or are prepared to help on a regular basis Chapter 11, Voluntary Work, lists a fund of suggestions you might like to consider.

A prime requirement, whether you are thinking of paid or unpaid work, or for that matter simply planning to devote more time to your hobbies, is to remain fit and healthy. Good health is the most valuable possession we have. Without it, energy is lacking, activities are restricted and the fun goes out of life. No amount of money can compensate for being bedridden or a semi-invalid.

While anyone can be unfortunate enough to be struck down by an unexpected illness, your future good health is largely in your own hands. The reason why the seventies are so often dogged by aches and pains is that sufficient care has not been taken during the fifties and sixties.

As well as all the obvious advice about not smoking, becoming too fat or drinking to excess, there is the important question of exercise. While you could of course do press-ups and go for walks, you will probably have a much better time if you join the new keep-fit brigade.

Thanks to the Sports Council there are opportunities around the country for almost every kind of sport, with 50-plus beginners especially welcome. Additionally, dancing, yoga, keep-fit-to-music and relaxation classes are readily available through most local authorities as well as being offered by the many specialist bodies listed in both the Health and Leisure Activities chapters.

The only problem is likely to be fitting everything in. The choice of organised leisure pursuits is little short of staggering. If you have ever wanted to learn about computers, take a degree, join a choir, become proficient in a craft, play competitive Scrabble, start coin collecting or become a beekeeper, you will find an organisation that caters for your enthusiasm.

The type of activities you enjoy could be an important consideration in choosing where you will live. Because we are conditioned to thinking of retirement as a time for settling into a new home, many people up sticks without perhaps giving enough thought to such essentials as proximity to family and friends and whether a different area would provide the same scope for pursuing their interests.

A fairly common mistake is for people to retire to a place where they once spent an idyllic holiday, perhaps 15 or 20 years previously, with only a minimum of further investigation. Resorts that are glorious in mid-summer can be bleak and damp in winter as well as pretty dull when the tourist season is over. Equally, many people sell their house and move somewhere smaller without taking account of the fact that when they are spending more time at home they may actually want more space, rather than less. This is particularly true of anyone planning to work from home or who has a hobby such as carpentry which requires a separate workroom.

While moving may be the right solution, especially if you want to realise some capital to boost your retirement income, there are plenty of ways of adapting a house to make it more convenient and labour-saving. Likewise, you may be able to cut the running costs, for example with insulation. These and other possibilities, including taking in a lodger and creating a granny flat, are explored in Chapter 8, Your Home.

On the subject of granny flats, if you are caring for elderly parents there may come a time when a little bit of outside help could make all the difference. The range of organisations that can provide you with back-up is far more extensive than is generally realised. For single women especially, who may feel that they have to give up a career, knowing what facilities are available could prove a veritable godsend.

While there may be pressure if a parent, however much loved, requires an undue amount of attention, a more commonplace problem is the effect of retirement on a couple's relationship.

Many husbands are puzzled, and sometimes hurt, by their wife's attitude to the event. For years she has been complaining 'I never see anything of you, darling' and 'Why can't you spend a little more time with the family?' – so naturally he expects her to be delighted to have him at home. But according to some husbands, the enthusiasm may seem less than wholehearted. As one recently retired 62-year-old put it: 'I had hardly had a chance to enjoy a couple of days pottering in the garden for the first time in years, when my wife was nagging me to go out and find something to do. She was the one who wanted me to take early retirement. Now she is wishing that I was back at work.'

The reverse situation can also apply, especially if the wife had a high-powered career. Although in general the evidence suggests that it is usually the man's retirement that provokes most friction, this may change as more of today's working wives turn 60 and find themselves facing the same need to make difficult adjustments.

Either way, the point is that after years of seeing relatively little of each other, retirement suddenly creates the possibility of much more togetherness. Put in blunt terms, many wives grumble that having a husband at home during the day means an extra meal to cook and inevitable disruption to their normal routine. And while this may not apply in an 'equal opportunity' marriage, where the domestic jobs are shared equally between husband and wife, in a majority of households women still do the lion's share of the cooking and cleaning. So, if he stays in bed longer in the morning, the chores will be finished later which can be an irritation. But an even greater cause for resentment is that she may feel guilty about meeting her friends or pursuing her usual weekday activities unless her partner is also busy.

If she is still at work, the situation can be even more fraught as, apart from the extra housework, she may find her loyalties uncomfortably divided. Furthermore, quite irrationally, some retired husbands begin to harbour dire suspicions about their wives' working colleagues, imagining romantic entanglements that had never crossed their minds before.

Sometimes too, retired people subconsciously label themselves as 'old' and start denying themselves and their partner the pleasures of a happily fulfilled sex life. It is difficult to know whether this is more ludicrous or tragic. As studies in many parts of the world show, the sexual satisfaction of both partners continues in a high proportion of cases long after the age of 70 and often well into the eighties. A welcome book which discusses the subject frankly is published by Age Concern. Called *Living, Loving and Ageing*, it costs £4.95 and is available from most bookshops or directly from Age Concern.

Usually, problems that coincide with retirement can be fairly simply overcome by willingness to discuss them frankly and to work out a solution that suits both partners. The situation is very much easier today than even ten years ago when male/female roles were far more stereotyped and many couples felt that they had to conform to a set pattern for the sake of convention.

Despite the impression given by some articles, marriage is not the only relationship and many non-marrieds equally find that adjusting to retirement is not always that easy. Relatives may impose new pressures once you are no longer at work. Likewise, close friendships sometimes alter when one friend retires – and not the other. Additionally, many single people admit that they had not realised before how much they relied on their job for companionship and sometimes, even for part of their week-end social life.

Pre-retirement courses

Talking to other people to find out how they plan to tackle the challenges as well as the opportunities of retirement can be immensely helpful. Many companies recognise this need by providing pre-retirement courses. If you are unlucky enough to be in a firm where this is not yet done, or if you are self-employed, there are a number of organisations to which you can turn for advice and help.

Before deciding on a particular course, it is worthwhile giving a little thought to the best time to go and the subjects which the counselling should cover. The traditional view is that the ideal time is somewhere between one and two years before you are due to retire. While this is probably true for most people, it is also important to remember that preparing for retirement really has to be a staged process. Some financial decisions, such as those affecting company or personal pension planning, need to be taken as early as possible. Others, such as whether to move house, can probably only be made much later.

The basic subjects that the best courses address are: finance, health, activity, leisure, housing and the adjustments which will need to be made by both you and your family when you retire.

The crucial test, however, is not the amount of factual information that is contained but the extent to which the course helps to focus and stimulate your own thoughts on the various issues and to lead to discussion with your partner and others in the same situation.

The following organisations should be able to advise you about courses available in your area.

The Pre-Retirement Association of Great Britain & Northern Ireland, Nodus Centre, University Campus, Guildford, Surrey GU2 5RX. T:0483 39323. The PRA is the national body for retirement counselling.

Retirement Made Easy

Their courses are independent, free from commercial bias and partners are encouraged to attend. A day's course at Sion College, in Central London, costs £95 plus £70 for the participant's partner. A weekend course at Stanford Hall in Leicestershire is offered four times a year for about £188 (including VAT). Week-long retirement planning holiday courses are run at Barton Hall Chalet Hotel, near Torquay, in the spring and autumn. Price is about £255 which includes full board, accommodation and evening entertainment. Details from Bill Tadd, PRA Holiday Courses, 78 Capel Road, East Barnet, Herts EN4 8JF. T:081-449 4506.

Throughout the UK some of the 40 affiliated local organisations of the PRA arrange their own pre-retirement courses, often in collaboration with other educational authorities. Details of these, as well as of many other courses, are listed in the PRA's annual *Directory of Pre-Retirement Courses*. Price £7.50; £6.50 for PRA members; regional offprints are available for £1.50 (including postage). Contact the PRA at the Guildford address above.

Scottish Retirement Council, Alexandra House, 204 Bath Street, Glasgow G2 4HL. T:041-332 9427. Runs courses in various regions of Scotland. These are normally held over six days and prices range from about £18 to £40. Courses in the Strathclyde area are free of charge.

Adult Education Centres. See local telephone directory under your local council listing. A growing number of Adult Education Centres are running both day and evening retirement courses. Standards vary but you should be able to get a good idea of the approach from the syllabus.

Workers' Educational Association, Temple House, 17 Victoria Park Square, Bethnal Green, London E2 9PB. T:081-983 1515. Many of the 900 branches of the WEA run local courses. Check your telephone directory for the nearest branch or contact the London HQ for further information.

Open University, Learning Materials Service Office, The Open University, PO Box 188, Milton Keynes MK7 6DH. T:0908 652185 or 0908 653338 (after office hours). The OU produces a study pack called 'Planning Retirement' (P941) which covers all the important areas and provides a useful starting point for thought and discussion. The price, which includes an audio cassette, is £28. This can be supplemented by written exercises which will be computer assessed at an extra cost of £15.

Looking Forward to Retirement

New focus for the retired

Over the past couple of years, a number of organisations have been launched offering services and facilities to people in the 50-plus age group. While their aims and activities differ slightly, all are clubs in the sense of recruiting members and most provide a variety of discount opportunities. Two of the best known are listed below.

ARP Over 50, (Third Floor), Greencoat House, 5 Francis Street, London SW1P 1DZ. T:071-828 0500. ARP Over 50 is a membership association for individuals and couples aged 50-plus which believes in improving opportunities for pre-and post-retired people. Local Friendship Centres offering various social events exist around the country. There are two 24-hour emergency helplines, plus another giving legal advice. Among other facilities, members receive the quarterly *O50 Magazine*; there is a project called Age Works to help with job-hunting; and additionally, members have access to a range of discounts including favourable travel and insurance rates. Membership costs £12 a year (or £10 by direct debit).

50-Forward, The Manor House, 46 London Road, Blackwater, Camberley, Surrey GU17 0AA. T:0276 34462. Members receive a quarterly magazine together with details of discounts on various goods and services including holidays, entertainment and high street purchases. Membership costs £9.50 a year.

Big Savings on Insurance For The Over 50s

Answer 'Yes' and you could save £££'s on motor insurance

	Yes	No
Car is driven by you and your wife/husband only.	☐	☐
Both drivers are between 50-70 years of age and live at the same address (not available in N. Ireland).	☐	☐
Both drivers hold a full driving licence free of conviction.	☐	☐
Both drivers free of disability and infirmity.	☐	☐
Neither driver has had an accident in the past 3 years.	☐	☐
Neither driver has been declined or refused insurance nor had special terms imposed.	☐	☐
Car is a family model (e.g. not a sports or high performance car).	☐	☐
Car is owned by you and kept at your home address.	☐	☐
Car is used for social, domestic, pleasure and/or personal business purposes only.	☐	☐

9 'Yes' Answers? DON'T DELAY

Plus great Savings on Home Contents Insurance.

CALL FREE NOW ON (0800) 01-01-99
Mon-Fri 8am-8pm; Sats 9am-Noon

COMMERCIAL UNION
General Insurance

We won't make a drama out of a crisis.

GRG 93

"It simply isn't cricket not to make a Will."

Send now for your free copy of this booklet.

"Far too few of us make Wills. In fact only one in three leaves a record of their wishes. The trouble is that the two who don't may seriously increase the distress of those near and dear to them by adding insecurity to sorrow at the time of their death.

"If you haven't yet made a Will, or wish to change one, you may need some helpful advice on how best to go about it. The RLSB's booklet, *"Making a Will"*, is full of common sense, it's written in plain English, and it explains what to do next.

"Don't be caught out! Send for the free booklet today."

Complete and return this coupon to: GRG
Brian Johnston, c/o Royal London Society for the Blind,
105 Salusbury Road, London NW6 6RH
Please send me _____ *copies of "A Simple Guide to Making a Will"*

Name (Mr/Mrs/Ms) _____

Address _____

_____

Town _____ Postcode _____

The Royal London Society for the Blind

Chapter 2

Money in General

For most people approaching retirement, the major concern is money. Some individuals have no worries; they have planned the event for years, made maximum pension contributions, carefully invested their savings, covered themselves and family in insurance policies, budgeted ahead and can even gleefully tell you about the exotic round-the-world trip they intend to take just as soon as their new life begins.

But for a majority of people, however, it is not like that. After years of hardly giving a thought to their pension, panic suddenly sets in as they consider the prospect of no longer drawing a regular salary. The fact that most of their friends who have already retired seem to manage pretty well is of little comfort. Even quite wealthy individuals confess to conjuring up images of going cold and hungry.

Happily, the reality is far rosier than many people imagine. For a start, those retiring today are better off financially than any previous generation. Equally to the point, the spectre of drastic economies that haunts so many men and women is often the result of their having only the haziest idea as to their likely income and expenditure.

Doing the sums

Knowing the facts is the first priority. To make a proper assessment, you need to draw up several lists:

- Expected sources of income on retirement
- Unavoidable outgoings
- Normal additional spending (including holidays and other luxuries).

Stage two, you need to consider a number of options under the following headings:

- Possible ways of boosting your retirement income

Money in General

- Spending now for saving later
- Cherished plans, if affordable.

Most difficult of all, you will require a third list of variables and unknowns which, while impossible to estimate accurately, must as a matter of prudence be taken into account in any long-term budget planning. The two most important are tax and inflation. Additionally, there are all the possible emergency situations, such as your health, for which, if this were ever to become a problem, you might want to make special provision. Your life expectancy is another consideration, as is that of your partner and any dependants.

Ideally, you should start thinking about at least some of these points, especially those that relate to your pension and to any savings or investment plans, five or even ten years before you retire. When doing the sums, aim to be realistic. Many people make the mistake of basing their calculations on their current commitments and expenditure, without properly realising that some of their requirements will change. To get the figures into perspective, it is a good idea to imagine yourself already retired. The good news is that, while some items will probably take a heftier slice of your budget, others will certainly be cheaper or no longer cost you anything at all.

Possible savings and extra outgoings are discussed below. The most practical way of examining the list is to tick off the items in each column that you expect definitely to apply and, where possible, to write down the expenditure involved in the adjacent box (see Budget Planner, pages 111-117). While inevitably this will be a somewhat rough-and-ready exercise – and obviously there will be gaps – the closer you are to retirement, the more worthwhile it will be.

Possible savings
Going out to work generally involves a fair number of expenses. When you leave your job, you will probably save at least several pounds a week. Items for which you will no longer have to pay include: your travelling costs to work, bought lunches, special clothes; plus all the out-of-pocket incidentals such as drinks with colleagues, trade magazines and collections for presents or the Christmas party.

You will not have to pay any more national insurance contributions and, unless you choose to invest in a private plan, your pension payments will also cease. Additionally, when you retire, you may be in a lower tax bracket.

At the same time you may have reached the stage when your children are now independent, your mortgage is substantially paid off and you have stopped subscribing to a life assurance policy. Moreover, one of the gratifying aspects of attaining state retirement age is that you become eligible for a variety of benefits, for example: concessionary travel, free national health service prescriptions, cheaper theatre and cinema tickets (usually matinees), reduced entrance charges for exhibitions and a wide choice of special holiday offers.

Another point worth remembering is that many insurance companies give substantial discounts to mature drivers. With motor insurance zooming in cost, this could give you a valuable saving. In some instances, discounts apply to those aged 50; other companies restrict eligibility to those aged 55 or even 60. Normally, but again this varies, the scheme is terminated when the policy holder reaches 75. Most companies, but not all, extend the cover to a spouse or other named person with a good driving record. As to the discounts, these appear to range in generosity from 5 per cent to over 60 per cent. Best advice is first approach your existing insurance company and ask what terms they will give you. If these appear dullish, it could pay to shop around. Among those that offer special rates for mature drivers are: Commercial Union Assurance, Sun Alliance, the Royal, the Provincial, Guardian Royal Exchange and Legal & General.

Extra outgoings

There is no escaping the fact that when you retire some of your expenses will be heavier than at present.

Firstly, you will probably be spending more time at home, so items like heating and lighting are liable to be costlier.

If you received any perks with your job, such as a company car or health insurance, then unless you have a very generous employer these will have to come out of your own pocket in future. Equally, any business entertaining you enjoyed will largely cease, so any free lunches and the like will have to be paid for instead from the domestic housekeeping.

Another very important consideration is your extra leisure. With more time available, you will understandably be tempted to spend more on outings, your hobbies and on longer holidays from home. To avoid having to stint yourself, these need to be budgeted for in advance. Most people say that in an ideal world they would assume to be spending roughly double on entertainment of all kinds, compared with when they were working. Even voluntary activity is not without its hidden expenses, for example: more use of the telephone, petrol costs, raffle tickets, support of fund-raising occasions and so on.

Looking ahead, as you get older you may want more home comforts.

Money in General

Likewise, you may have to pay other people to do some of the jobs, such as the decorating, that you previously managed yourself.

Anticipating the areas of additional expenditure is not to be pessimistic. On the contrary, it is the surest way of avoiding future money worries. Moreover, when you have sat down and worked out your retirement income in detail, you may even be pleasantly surprised.

Expected sources of income on retirement
Your list will include at least some of the following. Once you have added up the figures in the budget planner, you will have to deduct income tax to arrive at the net spending amount available to you.

- State basic pension
- State graduated pension
- SERPS
- Occupational pension
- Personal pension
- State benefits.

Additionally, you may receive income or a capital sum from some of the following:

- Company share option scheme
- Endowment policy
- Investments (stocks and shares, building society etc.)
- Bank deposit account
- National Savings interest
- Other existing income (from a trust, property, family business)
- Sale of business or personal assets.

You might also be in receipt of income from an annuity. However, since at this stage you will be unlikely to have purchased one, this really belongs in the category of investment decisions.

Unavoidable outgoings
One person's priority is another person's luxury – and vice versa. For this reason, the divide between 'unavoidable' and 'normal additional spending' (see section following) is fraught with obvious difficulty. For example, readers who do not possess a pet would never include pet food among the essentials, whereas a dog or cat owner unquestionably would.

Almost everyone will want to juggle some of the items between the two lists; or add their own particular commitments or special enthusiasms, omitted by us.

Our suggestions are simply intended as memory joggers – and emphatically not as a guide to what should, or should not, constitute a luxury. What matters is the basic principle behind the exercise. If at some stage budgeting choices have to be made, decisions will be very much easier if you already know: your total outgoings, what you are spending on each item individually and those you variously rate as important or marginal.

Whatever your own essentials, some of the following items will certainly feature on your list of unavoidable expenses:

- Food
- Rent or mortgage repayments
- Community charge/council tax
- Repair and maintenance costs
- Heating
- Lighting and other energy
- Telephone
- TV licence/rental
- Household insurance
- Clothes
- Domestic cleaning products
- Laundry, cleaners' bills, shoe repair
- Miscellaneous services, e.g. plumber, window cleaner
- Car, including licence, petrol, AA, etc.
- Other transport
- Regular savings and life assurance
- HP/other loan repayments
- Outgoings on health.

Normal additional expenditure
This may well include:

- Gifts
- Holidays
- Newspapers/books
- Drink
- Cigarettes/tobacco
- Hairdressing
- Toiletries/cosmetics
- Charitable donations
- Entertainment (hobbies, outings, video purchase/rental, home entertaining etc.)
- Miscellaneous subscriptions/membership fees
- Expenditure on pets
- Other.

Work out the figures against these lists. Then in order to compare your expenditure against likely income, jot them down on the Budget Planner (see pages 112-117).

Possible ways of boosting your retirement income

Other than luck - winning the football pools or coming into a legacy – there are three main possibilities for providing you with extra money: your home, work and investment skill.

Your home
Your home offers several different options.

Moving somewhere smaller. You could sell your present home, move into smaller accommodation and end up with the double bonus of pocketing a lump sum and reducing your running costs.

Leaving aside such considerations as whether you would still be able to have your grandchildren to stay and looking at the matter strictly in financial terms, it is as well to realise from the outset that the cash difference on the exchange – in other words, your profit – will invariably be less than you expect. What with removal charges and lawyers' fees, moving home is a very expensive business. Additionally, you will probably have some decorating expenses and there is bound to be a period of overlap when you will be paying two lots of telephone rental, extra electricity bills and so on.

This is not to say that moving may not be an excellent decision; simply that, if money is the main criterion, you need to be thoroughly realistic when calculating the gains.

An important new factor which has upset many people's sums over the past couple of years has been the state of the property market. There are two aspects to the problem. Firstly, if, as they have been, house sales are still sticking when you come to sell, you may have to accept a lower price than you had hoped to get (although, of course, you may also be able to buy your new property more cheaply). Rather more serious, if you buy a new home before selling your existing one, you could be faced by a bridging loan problem, which with today's high interest rates could soon eat into any profits you hope to realise on the exchange. Ideally, you should try to dovetail selling and buying at the same time. If this is not possible (and it usually isn't), the golden advice at the present time must be to sell first rather than risk lumbering yourself with the crippling expense of having to borrow for several months or possibly longer.

If you do decide to move, you should consider transferring an existing mortgage to your new property or getting a new one up to £30,000, even if you could afford to buy the property outright. Too old? Not at all. In contrast to 15 years ago, mortgages are commonly available to people over retirement age. However, especially with interest rates still relatively high, there may be reasons why a mortgage would not be sensible for you. You will need to do the sums carefully to see whether there is any real gain. If in doubt, consult an accountant or solicitor who will help you work out the various after-tax and other angles.

Taking in lodgers. If your children have left home and you have more space than you need, you could consider taking in lodgers, either as paying guests or, if your property lends itself to the creation of a separate flatlet, in a tenancy capacity.

When assessing the financial rewards, it is wise to assume that there will be times when the accommodation is empty – so you will not be receiving any rent. The good news is that you may be able to keep more of any earnings you make.

Until recently, *any* money you received in rent was counted as part of your taxable income. However, since the start of the tax year in April 1992, people letting out rooms in their home can claim tax relief of up to £62.50 a week (or £3,250 during the year). Any excess rental over £3,250 will be assessed for tax in the normal way. The relief only applies to accommodation that is 'part of your main home', so if you are thinking of creating a *separate flatlet*, you will need to take care that this qualifies and that it is not at risk of being assessed as a commercial let. Since the dividing line is somewhat hazy, check with your architect or other professional adviser that he/she fully understands the technical requirements.

Raising money on your home. A third option is to part-sell your home either for a capital sum or regular payments, under a home income plan, and continue to live in it for as long as you wish. Sounds wonderful? There are both attractions and drawbacks which need to be considered carefully and you would be strongly advised to discuss the matter with a solicitor.

All these possibilities are explored in greater detail in Chapter 8, Your Home. If you think any of the ideas sound interesting, see sections as follows: 'Moving to a new home', 'Letting rooms in your home' and 'Raising money on your home'.

Work
If you would like to continue working, arguably the easiest solution if your employer is agreeable is for you to remain where you are and to defer your pension. See 'Deferring your pension', in Chapter 3.

Alternatively, as many people do, you may look on retirement as the opportunity for a job switch (with perhaps a reduction in hours) or the chance you have always wanted of setting up on your own. When assessing your budget plans, it is as well to err on the cautious side as regards the additional income you will be likely to earn as – although this has been improving – many so called 'retirement jobs' are notoriously badly paid.

If instead of paid work, you are thinking of becoming self-employed or setting up a business, you will not only have the start-up costs but, as you are probably well aware, very few new enterprises make a profit during the first two or three years.

On the other hand – again, just looking at the economics – while you are working, you will not be spending money on entertainment. Also, particularly if you are self-employed or own a business, there may be certain tax advantages as well as possible scope for improving your pension. Lastly, of course, you may be one of the lucky ones for whom work after retirement really pays. Quite apart from the money, work can be thoroughly enjoyable and rewarding in its own right. For ideas and information, see Chapter 10, Looking for Paid Work.

Investment

Contrary to what some people believe, you do not need to be very rich; nor for that matter is it too late to start thinking about investing once you are over the age of 55.

As you will see from Chapter 5, investment can take many different forms and among the list of different options there should be something to suit almost everyone. Although you may consider this to be specialist reading, we do suggest that you at least look at it, since maximising your income in retirement could make all the difference between being able to enjoy life or worrying about money.

Spending now for saving later

Although you may normally take the view that there is never a best time for spending money, retirement planning is different in that sooner or later you will need, or want, to make certain purchases – or pay off outstanding commitments, such as a mortgage. Most people's basic list – at least to think about – under this heading includes one or more of the following:

- expenditure on their home
- the purchase of a car
- the termination of HP or other credit arrangement.

Additionally, there may be a number of general domestic or luxury items which you had been promising yourself for some time and the only question is one of actual timing, i.e. determining the right moment to buy. Typical examples might include: a duvet, gardening equipment, a video recorder, a home computer, hobby materials and so on.

To help you decide whether a policy of 'spending now' is sensible, or possibly self-indulgent, there are two very simple questions you should ask:

- Can I afford it more easily now – or in the future?
- By paying now rather than waiting, shall I be saving money in the long run?

True, the issue may be complicated by tax and other considerations but for most choices this very basic analysis helps greatly to clarify the financial arguments on both sides.

Home improvements. If you plan to stay where you are, the likelihood is that at some point you will want to make some changes or improvements: install central heating, insulate the loft, modernise the kitchen or perhaps convert part of the house to a granny flat for an elderly parent who is becoming too frail to live alone.

Conventional wisdom has it that any significant expenditure on your home is best undertaken several years prior to retirement. However, in our experience the matter is less clear-cut and what is right for some is not the solution for others.

As with many other important decisions, the question largely depends on individual circumstances. Some people find it easier, and more reassuring, to pay major household bills while they are still earning. Others specifically plan to use part of the lump sum from their pension to create a dream home.

To arrive at the answer that makes best financial sense, present commitments have to be weighed against likely future expenditure (together with what money you will have available). Equally, as with insulation for example, you will need to work out what long-term savings you could effect by taking the plunge now. There is also the safety aspect: if you have bad lighting or dangerously worn carpet on part of the staircase, waiting for a few years to tackle the problem because it is all part of the grand plan could prove very false economy indeed.

Another very important consideration is how certain you are that you intend to stay in your present home. Investing a fortune and then upping sticks a couple of years later is generally a recipe for being out of pocket. Despite what one or two people may have told you, it is very unusual to recoup all your expenditure by reaping a vast profit when you come to sell.

Though it involves a few minutes' paperwork, a worthwhile exercise is to jot down your own personal list of pros and cons, under the headings: 'spending now' and 'spending later'. If still in doubt, then waiting is normally the more prudent course.

Purchasing a car. There could be two good reasons for buying a new car ahead of your retirement. One is that you have a company car that you are about to lose. The other is that your existing vehicle is on the old side and is beginning (or will probably soon start) to give you trouble. If either of these apply, then it probably makes sense to buy a replacement while you are still feeling relatively flush.

However, on the principle of 'look before you leap', company car owners should first check whether they might be entitled to purchase their present car on favourable terms: over the past few years, the number of employers allowing this has been on the increase. Also, dreary though the suggestion sounds, if economies look like being the order of the day, two-car families might assess whether, come retirement when perhaps husband and wife will be doing more things together, two cars are really such an essential as before.

Paying off HP and similar. In general, this is a good idea since delay is unlikely to save you any money – and may in fact actually cost you more. The only precaution is to check the small print of your agreement, to ensure that there is no penalty for early repayment.

A further exception to the rule could be your mortgage. As already discussed, there could be tax advantages in retaining a mortgage. Since quite a lot of money may be involved, you would be well advised to consult an accountant: or, if you are thinking of moving (and the issue is really whether to transfer an existing mortgage – or possibly acquire a new one), include this among the points to raise with a solicitor.

Cherished plans, if affordable

The Budget Planner (pages 112-117) may help you to work out whether the various luxuries and plans of which nearly all of us dream could be affordable or are destined to remain as fantasies.

Fun as it might be to imagine what a 'top 20' list might include, there would be little real purpose in discussing the practicalities, or otherwise, of going on a cruise, owning a race horse, buying a caravan, flying Concorde or whatever, since not only – even among married couples – would there be wide variations in choice but more particularly, since normal budget wisdom does not apply, any advice would risk being grossly misleading. This does not mean that you should promptly forget the whole idea of noting items which come into this category; but that, as this is such a very personal decision area, only you can really make the assessments.

As a general point, however, if you plan your finances with a specific objective in view, you may find that against expectations a notion that first seemed impossible is actually affordable. Or possibly, when you really think about the choices, some of your earlier priorities will seem less important.

Cheques Act 1992

Over the past year or so, there has been growing concern about the number of cheques being stolen in the post. The risks have been somewhat reduced thanks to the 1992 Cheques Act which shifts responsibility to the banks provided all safeguards have been taken.

If you write the words 'Account Payee Only' between the crossings on the cheque, you can be certain that the cheque can only be banked by the person to whom you made it out. If your cheques say 'or order', cross these words out and initial the amendment.

Extra income

There are a great many state benefits and allowances available to give special help to people in need. Definition of need covers a very wide range and applies, among others, to problems connected with: health, housing, care of an elderly or disabled relative, as well as widowhood and problems encountered by the frail elderly who for example may require extra heating during the winter.

While many of these benefits are 'means-tested', in other words are only given to people whose income is below a certain level, some, such as disability living allowance, are not dependent on how poor or how wealthy you are. Moreover, even when 'means-testing' is a factor, for some of the benefits income levels are nothing like as low as many people imagine. Because this information is not widely enough known, many individuals or families are not claiming help to which they are entitled and for which in many cases they have actually paid through their national insurance contributions.

The main benefits and allowances are listed in their appropriate chapters: for example, housing benefit appears in Chapter 8, Your Home; invalidity benefit is briefly described in Chapter 14, Caring for Elderly Parents. For further information about these and some others, such as criminal injuries compensation, obtain a copy of DSS booklet FB2, *Which Benefit?*, available from any Social Security office. Alternatively, telephone DSS freephone number 0800 666 555.

Chapter 3

Pensions

Next to your home, your pension is almost certainly your most valuable asset. It is therefore important to check all the angles well ahead of time to ensure that when you retire you receive the maximum benefit.

State pensions

You can get a pension if you are a man of 65 or a woman of 60, provided you have paid (or been credited with) sufficient national insurance contributions.

Some time in the future, at least one of these ages is likely to change as the Government is planning to equalise the State pension age between men and women. However, for most readers this is hardly a cause for concern. The expectation is that any changes would be phased in over ten years or longer and that in any case people currently in their mid-fifties would not have to postpone their retirement.

Your right to a State pension

Your right to a State pension depends on your (or your spouse's) national insurance contributions. Most people have to pay contributions into the national insurance scheme while they are working.

If you are an employee, your employer will have automatically deducted Class 1 contributions from your salary, provided your earnings were above a certain limit (currently £54 a week).

If you are self-employed you will have been paying a flat-rate Class 2 contribution every week and possibly the earnings-related Class 4 contributions as well.

You may also have paid Class 3 voluntary contributions at some point in your life in order to maintain your contributions record.

If you are over pension age (65 for men and 60 for women) you do not need to pay national insurance contributions.

There may have been times during your working life when you have not, either knowingly or unwittingly, paid national insurance contributions. If you have not paid sufficient NI contributions to qualify for a full rate basic pension you may be entitled to a reduced rate of pension. *However, your NI contributions record will have been maintained in the following circumstances:*

If you have lived outside Great Britain. If you have lived in Northern Ireland or the Isle of Man, any contributions paid there will count towards your pension.

If you have lived in a European Community country or any country whose social security system is linked to Britain's by a reciprocal agreement, contributions or residence there may be counted towards your pension depending on the country concerned. If you have any doubts, you should enquire what your position is at your local Social Security office.

If you have received Home Responsibilities Protection (HRP). This would be likely to apply if, since 1978, you had to give up work for some time to care for a child or for a sick, or elderly, person. For further information, see page 50.

If you have been in any of the following situations, you will have been credited with contributions (instead of having to pay them):

- if you were sick or unemployed (provided you sent in sick notes to your Social Security office or signed on at the Unemployment Benefit office);
- if you were a man aged 60-64 and not working (from 1983);
- if you were entitled to maternity allowance, invalid care allowance or unemployability supplement;
- if you were taking an approved course of training (see leaflet NI 125 from your Social Security office);
- when you left education but had not yet started working.

Married women and widows who do not qualify for a basic pension in their own right may be entitled to some pension on their husband's contributions (see 'Pensions for women' at the end of the chapter).

Reduced rate contributions note. Many women retiring today may have paid a reduced rate contribution at some time. Sadly (see page 49) this *does not count* towards your pension.

Pensions

How your pension is worked out
Your total pension can come from three main sources: the basic pension, the additional pension and the graduated pension. There can also be additions, i.e. invalidity addition and age addition.

Anyone wanting to work out what they are due can write to their local Social Security office for a 'pension forecast'. This is normally expressed in percentage terms so, for instance, someone with full contributions will get 100 per cent of pension. You can also get a forecast of the additional earnings-related pension to which you are entitled. To obtain a forecast complete Form BR 19.

It is worth getting an early estimate of what your pension will be, as it may be possible to improve your national insurance contribution record by making additional Class 3 voluntary contributions. These can, however, only be paid for six years in arrears, so this concession may not help if you think about it too late.

Basic pension
The full basic pension for a man or woman (April 1992/93) is £54.15 a week, £86.70 for a married couple (unless your spouse is entitled to more than the £32.55 spouse's addition on his/her own contributions, in which case you will receive more). Pensions are uprated in April each year. Up-to-date rates are contained in leaflet NI 196, obtainable from your local Social Security office and main post offices.

All pensions are taxable other than one or two special categories, such as war widows and the victims of Nazism. If, however, your basic pension is your *only* source of income, you will not have to worry as the amount you receive is below the income tax threshold.

The rate of basic pension depends on your record of NI contributions over your working life. To get the full rate you must have paid (or been credited with) NI contributions for roughly nine-tenths of your working life, although widows can also be entitled to a full basic pension on their husband's contributions. If you are divorced, you may be able to use your former spouse's contributions to improve your own pension entitlement, provided that you have not remarried before reaching pension age.

Your working life, for this purpose, is normally considered to be 44 years for a woman and 49 years for a man (i.e. age 16 until pension age), but it may be less if you were of working age but not in insurable employment when the National Insurance Scheme started in 1948.

Reduced rate pension
If you do not have full contributions but have maintained your contribu-

tions record for between a quarter and nine-tenths of your working life, you may get a pension at a reduced rate. The amount is calculated according to the number of years for which you have paid contributions. However, to get any basic pension you must satisfy two conditions. Firstly, you must actually have paid enough full-rate contributions in any one tax year, from 6 April 1975, for *that* year to count as a qualifying year; or have paid 50 flat-rate contributions, in any one year, before 6 April 1975. Secondly, your total contributions must be enough to have entitled you to at least 25 per cent of the full basic rate.

Additional pension

This is also known as SERPS, short for the State Earnings Related Pension Scheme. It is worked out on earnings since April 1978 on which you have paid Class 1 contributions as an employee. It is not applicable to the self-employed.

Class 1 contributions are paid as a percentage of earnings between a 'lower' and an 'upper' limit (currently £54 and £405 a week respectively). The lower earnings limit is the same level as the basic retirement pension.

How much additional pension you get depends on the amount of your earnings over and above the lower earnings limit for each complete tax year since April 1978. The earnings for each tax year are then increased in line with the rise in national average earnings and added together to produce the total earnings figure on which your additional pension depends.

Since the scheme only started in 1978, the current maximum amount of additional pension to which you would be entitled is £66.97 a week. For details on how to apply for a statement of your current savings in SERPS, see Form BR 19 *Pension Forecast Application Form*, obtainable from any Social Security office. Full details and examples of how the additional pension is worked out can be found in leaflet NP 46 *A Guide to Retirement Pension*.

Although there are plans to scale down the additional pension, this will not affect anyone retiring before 1998 and will only marginally affect those retiring by 2009.

As you will probably know, if you think you can do better by making independent provision, you are not obliged to remain in SERPS but instead can invest in a personal pension. For details, see 'Personal pensions' further in the chapter.

If you are a member of a contracted-out occupational pension scheme, you are legally entitled to a guaranteed minimum pension which must be broadly the same as you would have got under the State scheme (i.e. the additional pension).

Graduated pension
This pension existed between April 1961 and April 1975. The amount you receive depends on the graduated NI contributions you paid during that period. Anyone over 18 and earning more than £9 a week at that time will probably be entitled to a small graduated pension. This includes married women and widows with reduced contribution liability. A widow or widower whose spouse dies when they are both over pension age can inherit half of the graduated pension based on their late spouse's contributions.

Other additions
Invalidity addition. Your pension will automatically be permanently increased if you were getting invalidity allowance with invalidity benefit within eight weeks before reaching retirement age. The amount you get will be the same as the invalidity allowance you are already receiving (lower rate £3.60; middle rate £7.20; higher rate £11.55) but any additional pension (SERPS) and/or occupational pension will be subtracted from your invalidity allowance with only the balance (if any) being paid to you as invalidity addition.

Age addition. Your pension will be automatically increased when you are aged 80 or over. The current rate is 25p a week.

Other ways to increase your pension
Deferring your pension. Your pension may be increased if you delay claiming it and instead continue working after normal retirement age. This applies between the ages of 65 and 70 for a man and from 60 to 65 for a woman. For every year that you defer retirement, approximately another 7.5 per cent a year will be added to your pension. This extra pension is paid either when you claim your pension or when you reach 70(65), regardless of whether you have retired from work or not.

An exception to the age rule sometimes applies in the case of a married woman over 65 whose pension is based on her husband's contributions. Her pension can continue to increase until such time as her husband gets his pension or reaches the age of 70, whichever is sooner.

For further details obtain leaflet NI 92 *Giving Up Your Retirement Pension to Earn Extra.*

Warning. If you plan to defer your pension, you should also defer any graduated pension to which you may be entitled – or you risk losing the increases you would otherwise obtain.

Increases for dependants. Your basic pension may be increased if you are supporting a dependent spouse or children. Most typically, this applies in respect of a non-working wife (or one whose earnings are very low) who is under 60 when her husband retires. However, this also applies for a retired wife supporting a husband dependent by reason of invalidity. The current rates are £32.55 a week for a spouse, £9.75 for the first child and £10.85 each for any other dependent children. The definition of dependent child is one for whom you are receiving child benefit. See leaflet NI 196 obtainable from your local Social Security office.

Income support

If you have an inadequate income, you may qualify for income support which is designed to provide those without sufficient means with enough money to live on. There are special premiums (i.e. additions) for lone parents, disabled people, carers and pensioners.

As a single retired person, you can claim income support to bring your total income to £57.15 a week; for married couples, the amount is £88.95 (April 1992/93 rates). These totals exclude mortgage interest and disregarded income, for example, attendance allowance. Higher sums apply for disabled pensioners, for individuals over the age of 75 and for people living in residential care or nursing homes.

A condition of entitlement is that you should not have capital, including savings, of more than £8,000. People with higher savings, however, receive less: for every £250 of capital over £3,000, individuals are deemed to be getting £1 a week income – so the actual amount of benefit will be reduced accordingly.

Additionally, those entitled to income support receive full help with their rent and up to 80 per cent assistance with their community charge. See 'Housing benefit and community charge benefit', in Chapter 8, Your Home. Even better, once the new council tax is introduced in April 1993, people on income support should normally have nothing to pay. See 'Council tax' in the same chapter.

If your only source of income is your basic State pension, you are likely to be entitled to income support. For more information, together with a claim form, see leaflet IS 1 *Income Support*, obtainable from any Social Security office or post office.

Social Fund. If you are faced with an exceptional expense you find difficult to pay, you may be able to obtain a Budgeting or Crisis Loan, or

Funeral Payment, from the Social Fund. Ask at your local Social Security office.

Working after you start getting your pension

This used to be a problem for many people as a result of the Earnings Rule. However, as you probably know, the Earnings Rule was abolished in October 1989. Until then, men between the ages of 65 and 69 and women between the ages of 60 and 64 who earned more than £75 a week had their basic State pension reduced. Happily, this does not apply any more and today there is no longer any limit to the amount pensioners can earn.

If you are among the many pensioners who had their pension deferred (in other words you put off receiving it) as a means of escaping the Earnings Rule, you have the choice whether to start claiming your pension or to continue deferment. If you continue deferment, which as a woman you can do until 65 and as a man until 70, you will earn what are known as 'increments' and your pension will be bigger when you receive it.

Early retirement and your pension

Because so many people now retire early, there is a widespread belief that it is possible to get an early pension. While the information is correct as regards a growing number of employers' occupational pension schemes, *it does not apply to the basic State pension.*

If you take early retirement before the age of 60, it may be necessary for you to pay voluntary Class 3 national insurance contributions in order to protect your contributions record for pension purposes. If you are a man over 60, however, you will automatically get contribution credits from the tax year in which you reach 60.

How you get a pension

You should claim your pension a few months before you reach State pension age. The Department of Social Security (DSS) should send you a claim form (BR 1) at the proper time but if this does not arrive, then it is your responsibility to contact them. Remember they will send the claim form to the last recorded address they hold for you, so if you have moved and not informed them do make sure they have your new address. You should apply for the form about four months before you are due to retire. If you claim your pension late, you could lose some of the money.

After you claim, you are told in writing exactly how much pension you will get. You will also be told what to do if you disagree with the decision.

The information you are given should include the name and address of the organisation responsible for paying you any guaranteed minimum pension.

How your pension can be paid
If you live in the UK, you can choose to have your pension paid either by credit transfer or in order book form.

Credit transfer. This method gives you the choice of having your pension paid direct into a bank or National Giro account; or, alternatively, into an investment account with either the National Savings Bank or with most building societies. Payment will be made in arrears every four weeks or quarterly, whichever you prefer.

Order book. You receive a book of orders (or pension book) which you can cash at a post office of your choice. Each order is your pension entitlement for one week and is valid for 12 weeks after the date shown on the voucher. If it is difficult for you to get to the post office, the coloured pages in the book explain how someone else can draw the payment for you.

Other situations. If your pension is £2 a week or less, it will normally be paid once a year in arrears by a crossed order which you can pay into a bank or building society account. Payment is made each year shortly before Christmas.

Pensions can be paid to an overseas address, if you are going abroad for three months or more. Contact your local Social Security office. For further details see leaflets NI 38 *Social Security Abroad* and SA 29 *Your Social Security and Pension Rights in the European Community*. If you are planning to retire abroad and have any queries about your pension, contact the DSS Overseas Branch at Newcastle Central Office, Longbenton, Newcastle upon Tyne NE98 1YX.

If you are in hospital, your pension can still be paid to you. You will receive a reduced amount if you are in hospital for more than six weeks. Leaflet NI 9 *Going Into Hospital* (obtainable from your local Social Security office) provides full information.

Christmas bonus
Pensioners usually get a small tax-free bonus shortly before Christmas each year. The amount and due date will be announced in advance. For the last few years the sum has been £10. The bonus is combined with your normal pension payment for the first week in December, so if you

have not received it by the end of that month ask at your local Social Security office.

Advice

If you have any queries or think that you may not be obtaining your full pension entitlement, you should contact your local Social Security office as soon as possible. If you think a mistake has been made, you have the right to appeal and can insist on your claim being heard by an independent Social Security Tribunal. Before doing so, you would be strongly advised to consult a solicitor at the Citizens' Advice Bureau or the Welfare Advice Unit of your local Social Security office. Some areas have special Tribunal Representation Units to assist people to make claims at Social Security Tribunals.

If you are writing to your local Social Security office with a query you should quote either your national insurance number (or your spouse's) or your pension number if you have already started receiving your pension.

For free advice on your pension, dial DSS freephone: 0800 666 555.

For further information about pensions, see leaflet FB 6 *Retiring?* and booklet NP 46 *A Guide to Retirement Pension* obtainable from any Social Security office.

Private pensions

The importance of persuading individuals to save for their own pension instead of just relying on the State has been recognised by successive governments. Encouragement has been made through tax incentives, so that pension savings are now one of the most tax effective investments available.

- You get income tax relief on contributions at your highest tax rate.
- The pension fund is totally exempt from income tax and capital gains tax.
- Part of the pension can be taken as a cash sum when you retire and that too is tax free.

Private pension schemes fall into two broad categories: those arranged by employers, e.g. company pension schemes, and those you can arrange for yourself.

Company pension schemes

Around half of all people at work are participating in company schemes.

While these can vary considerably, the following basic features apply to all of them.

Pension fund. Pension contributions go into a pension fund which is quite separate from your employer's company. It is set up under trust and run by trustees, appointed from management and sometimes from staff. It is the job of the trustees to manage the fund and its investments and to ensure that the benefit promises are kept.

Payments into the fund. Your scheme may or may not ask for a contribution from you. For this reason, schemes are known as 'contributory' or 'non-contributory'. If (as is normally the case) you are required to make a contribution, this will be deducted from your pay before you receive it.

Your employer's contributions to the scheme represent the money he is setting aside for your pension and other benefits. The amount needed is estimated by the scheme actuary and this can vary from year to year, according to how much money is accumulated and how much the scheme is likely to have to pay out in benefits.

Benefits from the scheme. All pension scheme members should normally be given a booklet describing how the scheme works, what benefits it provides, the names of the trustees and other information including the address of the Pensions Ombudsman. If you do not receive one, you should ask the person in the company responsible for the pension scheme – this is often the personnel manager – to supply you with a booklet. You can also ask to see a copy of the trust deed as well as the latest annual report and audited accounts.

The key benefits applicable to most pension schemes include:

- A pension due at whatever age is specified by the scheme, usually somewhere between 60 and 65 (although there is a growing trend for companies to offer early retirement provision)
- Death benefit (sometimes known as lump sum life assurance), paid out if you die before retirement age
- A widow/widower's pension paid for life no matter when you die.

Benefit limits. The Inland Revenue sets limits on pension benefits which members of company schemes can receive. The main ones are:

- The maximum pension you are allowed is two-thirds of your final pay (excluding state pension).
- If you die, the pension can be passed on to someone else but no one beneficiary can receive more than two-thirds.

- The tax-free lump sum, if you choose to take it, cannot be more than one and a half times salary.

Since the 1989 Budget, the above figures have become governed by a ceiling, currently based on £75,000 earnings a year. In other words, the maximum figure allowed for two-thirds of final salary is £50,000 a year; and the maximum tax-free lump sum allowed is £112,500.

Types of scheme
There are four main types of scheme, as follows:

Final salary scheme. This is the most common. Your pension is calculated as a proportion of your final pay, which could mean literally the last year you work or the average of three consecutive years during the last ten.

The amount you receive depends on two factors: the number of years you have worked for the organisation plus the fraction of final pay on which the scheme is based, typically 1/60th. So if you have worked 30 years for a company that has 1/60th pension scheme, you will receive 30/60ths of your final pay – in other words, half.

Final pay schemes can be contracted into or out of SERPS. If a scheme is contracted out of SERPS, it must provide a guaranteed minimum pension that is at least as good as its SERPS equivalent.

Money purchase scheme. This has been greatly increasing in popularity in recent years and, according to all the forecasts, looks set to become even more widespread. Unlike the other three types of scheme, the amount of pension you receive is not based on a fixed formula but (within Inland Revenue limits) is dependent on the investment performance of the fund into which your own and your employer's contributions on your behalf have been paid.

Although there is a slight element of gamble with money purchase schemes, in that no one can forecast with certainty how well or badly a pension fund might do, in practice most trustees act very conservatively.

Different schemes have different ways of determining how members' pension entitlements are calculated. You should enquire what the rules are and additionally, to give you a better idea of what size pension you might realistically expect, you could ask for some practical examples – say, over the last five years – of retired individuals in a similar earnings bracket to your own.

Average earnings scheme. This is based on your average earnings over the total period of time that you are participating in the scheme. Every year, an amount goes into the scheme on your behalf, calculated in accordance with your level of earnings. As your salary increases, so too do your potential benefits. Each year, your 'profits' from the scheme are worked out from a formal table and the total of all these annual sums constitutes your pension.

Flat rate pension scheme. Your level of pay is not a factor. Instead, the same flat rate applies to everyone, multiplied by the number of years in which they have been participants of the scheme. So, for example, if the flat rate is £200 a year of pension and you have been a member of the scheme for 20 years, your pension will be £4,000 a year.

Additional or other schemes. There may be one scheme that applies to everyone in the organisation or there may be a variety of schemes for different grades of employees. For example, there may be a works scheme and a staff scheme operating side by side. It is also quite common for there to be a special pension scheme for executives and directors.

Additional voluntary contributions (AVCs)

If, as you approach retirement, you become aware that you are not going to have a big enough pension to live as comfortably as you would like, you might seriously consider the possibility of making additional voluntary contributions. AVCs are a very attractive way of making extra savings for retirement for two special reasons. Firstly, AVCs – as well as the growth of the plan – enjoy full tax relief, so for basic rate tax payers the Inland Revenue is in effect paying £25 for every £100 you invest. A further key advantage for many people is that AVCs allow you to purchase 'added years', to make up any shortfall in your entitlement to benefit under a company scheme.

There is now also an option, known as 'free-standing AVCs'. As the name implies, these are not linked to a company scheme but can be purchased independently from: insurance companies, building societies, banks, unit trusts and friendly societies. You are allowed to contribute both to company AVCs and to a free-standing plan or plans. If you wish, you can purchase a new free-standing policy every year, so building up a spread of investments.

The total of all your AVCs plus other contributions to the pension plan is not allowed to exceed 15 per cent of your earnings. In the event of over-funding occurring, whether from a free-standing or company AVC, the surplus will simply be refunded to you in cash, minus the tax relief involved.

Individuals paying less than £2,400 a year in free-standing AVCs will not normally need to involve their employer but just have to certify that they are not paying more than 15 per cent of their earnings in total contributions. Where larger amounts are concerned, the employer will need to become involved but this should not deter you if you believe that the purchase of free-standing AVCs is in your best long-term interest.

Recent rule changes. There are two fairly recent rule changes of which you should be aware.

- Under the old AVC rules, individuals had to make a commitment to pay regular contributions for a period of at least five years. This requirement has now been abolished and (provided the actual scheme rules permit) both the amount and timing of payments can be varied to suit each member according to their personal circumstances.
- The other important rule change is that whereas prior to 8 April 1987 AVC plans could be used towards funding an individual's lump sum, this is no longer permitted. Instead the contributions can only be used for boosting the actual pension itself. These arrangements, however, only affect policies that were applied for after the April 1987 deadline. All policies, where a contract had already been entered into, are exempt from the 'no commutation' rule.

For most people, the only real problem with AVCs is the sheer enormity of choice. As with any other important investment decision, you would be well advised to take your time, do some basic research into the track record of any policies you might be considering (specialist magazines such as *Money Management* provide a useful starting point) and on no account sign any document without first being absolutely certain that you fully understand all the terms and conditions including the administrative charges. As general wisdom, these are likely to be higher with free-standing contracts than for a collective AVC scheme offered by an employer.

Finally, if you are already subscribing to company AVCs, before investing in a new plan check on your present level of contributions and the benefits that these are expected to yield. Your company pension adviser should be only too happy to answer any questions.

Early leavers

In the past, the big problem, as everyone knows, was that early leavers tended to do very badly, due to the heavy financial penalties of withdrawing from a scheme in mid-term. In recent years, however, the Government has introduced new rules which help considerably.

For example, employers are now permitted to pay full pension at any age between 50 and 70, provided an employee has completed 20 years' service with the organisation. That said, most employers still apply actuarial reductions (although these are sometimes waived in special cases such as redundancy) so, if you are thinking of taking early retirement it is advisable to work out very carefully how this might affect your pension.

Another very important change concerns what are known as your *preserved rights* – in other words, your financial rights with regard to your pension. Previously you only qualified if you had been in an employer's scheme for at least five years. This has now been shortened to two years. If you leave the scheme earlier, your employer might still be willing to return the contributions you paid. But, as you will realise, the amount of money involved is not likely to be very large. There are three choices available to people with preserved rights who leave a company to switch jobs.

Leaving the pension with the scheme. Whereas previously most pensions got frozen, new legislation obliges companies to increase all your accrued pension rights by 5 per cent a year or the rate of inflation, whichever is lower. If you choose to stay in the scheme, you may also share in its benefits – such as any additional increases that may be given.

Taking your pension to a new scheme. You do not have to make an immediate decision. You can transfer your pension scheme at any time, provided you do so over a year before you retire. If you wish to switch to a new scheme, this could either be to another company scheme or to a personal pension. Personal pensions are described a couple of pages further along, so if you are interested in taking advantage of this option you should read the section carefully. Here, we explain the various possibilities if you wish to join a scheme run by your new employer.

Early leavers now have the right to move their pension – or more precisely, its transfer value – to a new employer's scheme willing to accept it. The transfer value is the cash value of your current pension rights. Calculating this, however, is fraught with difficulties and early leavers are usually at a disadvantage compared with those who remain in the scheme. For example, if the job change has meant a salary increase, the new scheme will probably be more expensive to buy into as the likelihood is that it will be earnings-related. Any added years will also be calculated in relation to your new salary, so these too will be more expensive.

Your new employer might appear to place a disconcertingly low valuation on your old company pension rights. However, even if 10 years' worth of rights from an old company pension scheme are commuted to no more than two years' worth in your new one, it could still be worth accepting, particularly if your new job is likely to produce rapid pay rises.

Taking your pension to an insurance company. If neither of the two previous options appeal, or your new company will not accept your old pension value into its own scheme, you can go independent and have the transfer value of your pension invested by a life company into a personal scheme – normally either a Section 32 buy-out or a protected rights personal pension. Such contracts are in fact very similar to self-employed pension plans, with the same choice of vehicles: unit linked, deposit administration, with profits and non-profit. These are described on page 45 under 'Types of investment policy'.

Advice. Deciding on your best option is not easy, so before taking action you should at least consult your company pension scheme manager to give you an assessment of the likely value of your pension if you leave it in the scheme. As a result of the improved revaluation changes, explained earlier, this option could be considerably more attractive than it would have been a couple of years ago.

If you are planning to switch, you will need to decide between a Section 32 buy-out or a protected rights personal pension. Although for a majority of employees a protected rights contract is usually likely to offer a higher return, there are certain limitations and the accepted wisdom seems to be that the older the employee and the larger the transfer value, the more attractive a Section 32 buy-out becomes. Because this is a complex area – and making the wrong decision could prove expensive – independent expert advice is very strongly recommended.

Becoming self-employed
If, as opposed to switching jobs, you leave paid employment to start your own enterprise, you are allowed to transfer your accumulated pension rights into a new fund. For most people the choice will be either to invest their money with an insurance company, as mentioned above; or to take a personal pension.

A third possibility which might be more attractive if you are fairly close to normal retirement age is to leave your pension in your former employer's scheme. See page 34, 'Leaving the pension with the scheme'.

Questions on your pension scheme
Most people find it very difficult to understand how their pension scheme works. However, your pension may be worth a lot of money and, especially as you approach retirement, it is important that you should know the main essentials, including any options that may still be available to you.

If you have a query (however daft it may seem) or if you are concerned in some way about your pension, you should approach whoever is responsible for the scheme in your organisation.

The sort of questions you might ask will vary according to circumstance, such as: before you join the scheme, if you are thinking of changing jobs, if you are hoping to retire early and so on. You will probably think of plenty of additional points of your own. The questions listed are simply an indication of some of the key information you may require in order to plan sensibly ahead.

Before you join the scheme

- As a basic point, you should enquire whether the scheme is contracted in or out of SERPS and whether the intention is that it should remain so in the future.
- If it is contracted out, how do you qualify to become a member? For example, there may be different conditions for different grades of staff. There may be an age ceiling for new entrants. Sometimes too, although this is becoming less common, there is a minimum period of service required before you can join.
- Over the past few years, many companies have set up contracted-out money purchase schemes – or COMPS, as they are known for short – which operate on a different principle from final salary schemes. You should enquire what type of scheme it is that you would be joining and if it is a money purchase one, how in particular members' entitlements are calculated. (See 'Money purchase scheme' page 31.)
- If it is a final salary scheme, what is the exact definition of 'final salary'? This could be very important if the organisation offers phased retirement or the opportunity of a sponsorship in the voluntary sector and, as some employers do, adjusts your remuneration to take account of a shorter working week or less onerous responsibilities.
- Another point, if it is a final salary scheme, is whether guaranteed pension increases are given and, if so, whether these are 5 per cent increases (or higher or lower)?
- Is anything deducted from the scheme to allow for the State pension?
- At what age is the pension normally paid?
- What is payable if you die within the next year?
- Is there a widow/widower's pension and does it get contractual increases?

If you want to leave the organisation to change jobs

- Can you have a refund of contributions if you were to leave within two years?
- How much will your deferred pension be worth?

If you leave for other reasons

- What happens if you become ill – or die – before pension age?
- What are the arrangements if you want to retire early? Most schemes allow you to do this if you are within about 10 years of normal retirement age *but* your pension may be reduced accordingly.
- What are the rules/options regarding pension age for women if, as is increasingly becoming the case, this has recently been raised to bring it in line with male pension age?

If you stay until normal retirement age

- What will your pension be on your present salary? And what would it be assuming your salary increases by, say, 5 or 10 per cent before you eventually retire?
- What spouse's pension will be paid? Can a pension be paid to other dependants?
- Is there any contractual increase to reduce the effect of inflation? If not, ask what the history of discretionary increases has been (both for members' own pension and for spouses).
- What happens if you continue working with the organisation after retirement age? Normally, any contributions you are making to the scheme will cease to be required and your pension (which will not be paid until you retire) will be increased to compensate for its deferment.

What to do before retirement

In addition to understanding your current pension scheme, you may also need to chase up any previous schemes of which you were a member. This is well worth pursuing as you could be owed money from one or more schemes, which will all add to your pension on retirement day.

You may be able to get the information from your previous employer(s). Or, if your previous employer has gone out of business, the **Occupational Pensions Advisory Service (OPAS)** – see page 38 – may be able to tell you who took over the responsibility for payment of pensions.

Additionally, the Occupational Pensions Board manages a pensions registry and tracing service to assist individuals who need help in tracing their pension rights. All occupational and personal pension schemes including free-standing AVC (FSAVC) schemes are required to register. While only recently introduced, the service is already proving very successful. Applicants can either write to the Registrar giving as much essential detail about the scheme as possible; or alternatively can request a trace application form (PR4) to complete. This is a free service. The address to write to is: **Registrar of Pension Schemes**, Occupational Pensions Board, PO Box 1NN, Newcastle upon Tyne NE99 1NN.

Other help and advice

If you have any queries or problems to do with your pension, in addition to the registry there are three main sources of help available to you. These are: the trustees or managers of your pension scheme; OPAS; the Pensions Ombudsman.

Trustees or managers. These are the first people to contact if you do not properly understand your benefit entitlements or if you are unhappy about some point to do with your pension. The scheme booklet should give you the names of the individuals and advise you how they can be reached.

Occupational Pensions Advisory Service (OPAS). This is an independent voluntary organisation with a network of 360 advisers which can give help and advice about any type of pension scheme – except State schemes. The service is available to anyone who thinks they have pension rights including scheme members, existing pensioners, those with deferred pensions and dependants.

The usual way of contacting OPAS is via your local CAB. Equally, if you prefer, you can write direct to: **OPAS**, 11 Belgrave Road, London SW1V 1RB. T:071-233 8080.

Pensions Ombudsman. You would normally only approach the Ombudsman if neither the pension scheme trustees/managers nor OPAS are able to solve your problem. The Ombudsman can investigate: (1) complaints of injustice caused by maladministration by the trustees or managers of an occupational or personal pension scheme (2) disputes of fact or law with the trustees or managers.

He cannot, however, investigate a complaint that is already subject to court proceedings, one that is about a State social security benefit or a dispute that is more appropriate for investigation by another regulatory body. There is also a time limit for lodging complaints which is normally within three years of the act, or failure to act, about which you are complaining.

Provided the problem comes within the Ombudsman's orbit, he will look into all the facts for you and will inform you of his decision, together with his reasons.

There is no charge for the Ombudsman's service. The address to write to is: **The Pensions Ombudsman**, 11 Belgrave Road, London SW1V 1RB. T:071-834 9144. This is the same address (but different telephone number) as OPAS.

New protection for pension scheme members

Thanks to new legislation, pension scheme members can look forward to enjoying more protection in the future.

Since 1991 early leavers now get their entire frozen pension uprated and not just, as had been the case, benefits earned after 1985.

Also, in the wake of the Maxwell disaster, the government has published regulations restricting self-investment by occupational pension funds to 5 per cent (a transitional period could be allowed). A further welcome measure is that in the event of a scheme in deficit being wound up, the deficiency becomes a debt on the employer which the trustees can pursue.

New measures have also been introduced to protect pension scheme members in the event of a company take-over or proposed bulk transfer arrangement.

On a more technical note, since August 1990 pension schemes which are in surplus over the Inland Revenue limit (5 per cent) are no longer allowed to have the money returned to the company unless pension scheme members are first guaranteed certain benefits, namely: pension increases of either 5 per cent a year or the rate of inflation – whichever is lower. The jargon term for these increases is LPI, short for Limited Price Indexation.

In time, all company pension schemes will be required by law to provide LPI. The 'Appointed Day' marking the start date for LPI has not yet been announced but hopefully this will be soon.

Companies do not of course have to wait until the Appointed Day. Indeed, many pension schemes are already giving these increases on a guaranteed basis. Where this is the case, their members will not be affected and cannot expect to receive anything extra as a result of LPI.

Self-employed and personal pension schemes

Everyone – whether self-employed or working for an employer – has the choice of continuing with their present pension arrangements or switching instead to a personal pension.

Although, in general, individuals who have reached their fiftieth birthday are less likely to be tempted than younger people, if you are moving to a new job, are ineligible to join your company pension scheme or are thinking of becoming self-employed, one of the options described below may offer you an attractive solution.

Self-employed pensions

The terminology is a bit confusing. Firstly, because self-employed pensions have long also been called personal pensions – or, to use the former technical jargon, Section 226 policies. Next, because while they apply primarily to those who work on their own account, they may equally be used by employees who work for companies which do not have a pension scheme or which have a scheme for which they, as individuals, are not eligible.

If you have an existing Section 226 policy (or retirement annuity contract, as it is sometimes also called), then, as you will know, it is an insurance policy designed to invest money for your retirement. Under Inland Revenue rules, you are allowed to invest, up to 17.5 per cent of your relevant earnings tax free in the policy (with higher limits, rising to 27.5 per cent, if you are over 60). In accordance with the terms of the contract, you can choose to retire at any time after the age of 60, when the policy will buy you a regular pension plus the option of taking part of the money as a tax free lump sum.

Changes. In July 1988, the rules for self-employed pension plans were altered to bring them in line with other personal pensions. In particular, Section 226 policies ceased being available for purchase.

In practical terms, this change is unlikely to affect many people. For a start, anyone with an existing Section 226 policy has no need, unless they wish to alter their arrangements, to do anything at all. They can continue contributing to the policy on exactly the same terms and conditions as before. As general wisdom, the view in the pensions industry is that for most people in this situation there would be little point in changing – and for some, it could be positively detrimental. However, as with most decisions there are arguments on either side so it is important that you should at least know what the choices are.

There are four main differences between Section 226 policies and personal pensions. These concern: the age of retirement, the method of calculating the lump sum, allowable contributions into the plan and the possible size of your pension allowed for tax relief.

- *Age of retirement.* Under a Section 226 policy, retirement cannot be taken before the age of 60. With a new personal pension, you can retire at any time between 50 and 75.
- *Method of calculating the lump sum.* Under Section 226 contracts, this is expressed as three times pensionable earnings. The PP rules define the amount as 25 per cent (or a quarter) of the total fund excluding your protected rights.
- *Allowable contributions.* A Section 226 policy limits you to a maximum of 27.5 per cent of your earnings. For personal pensions, individuals over the age of 50 can contribute up to 30 per cent, rising (depending on their age) to a maximum of 40 per cent.
- *Size of pension.* For high earners, the £75,000 cap is probably the strongest argument for hanging on to an existing Section 226 policy, since such policies are not affected by the earnings' limit. A new personal pension on the other hand would stand to be affected.

Personal pensions for employees

A main aim behind the new personal pensions is to give people working for an employer the same freedom as the self-employed to make their own independent pension arrangements, should they wish to do so.

Virtually everyone who pays national insurance contributions is now entitled to acquire a personal pension. Although some people may not realise it, if they are paying NI contributions they are almost certainly already contributing towards an additional pension: either to the State scheme, known as SERPS; or to a contracted-out company pension scheme.

Since July 1988, you have the right to take a personal pension in place of SERPS; or alternatively, in place of your employer's scheme. Membership of your employer's scheme is no longer, as it was in many companies, a compulsory condition of employment.

There is in fact a third option. Members of a contracted-in occupational scheme may contract out of SERPS through a PP, while remaining in the occupational scheme (a solution not all that different from buying free-standing AVCs with the added benefit of extra tax relief advantages).

A major advantage of a personal pension is that if you change jobs you can take it with you without penalty. There are attractive tax relief benefits. The pension is protected against inflation after you retire. You will have real choice as to how your pension payments are invested. And if you change your mind after having taken a personal pension, you can switch back into SERPS; or, if the scheme rules allow it, you can transfer your payments into a company contracted-out scheme.

The big potential drawback of a personal pension, particularly for an older person, is that it may not offer you such attractive benefits as your present pension arrangements. You will need to consider, not just your future retirement income, but also any extras that may be part and parcel of your existing company scheme: an early retirement option; a pension before normal age were you to become ill; protection for your dependants should you unexpectedly die.

A further problem could be the sheer plethora of choice when selecting a pension plan. Knowing what to choose, assessing one policy against another, weighing up the risk factor as well as trying to estimate what this will mean in terms of your standard of living after you retire could be a bit of a gamble even for a financial expert.

Although as a breed pension providers act very conservatively, no one can forecast with total confidence how well or otherwise any particular investment will do. When taking a decision about personal pensions you should obtain as much information as possible. Herewith some of the basics you will need to know.

Starting date. You can decide to start a personal pension at any time you want and then, in order to receive all the DSS minimum contributions that will be paid into your pension plan, backdate it to the start of the tax year on April 6. The formalities involved are very easy.

Contributions into your pension plan. There are four possible ways of building up savings in your pension plan.

- *Minimum DSS contributions.* These will be paid into your new scheme automatically. They are worked out according to the level of national insurance contributions that both you and your employer are required to pay by law. Instead of going into either SERPS or a contracted-out company pension scheme, they will be paid directly into your personal pension plan.
- *Special incentive payments.* These come to an end after April 1993.
- *Extra contributions made by you.* You can make extra contributions into your pension plan. If you do so, you will not only build up more savings for your retirement but you also enjoy full tax relief on these contributions.

    A further advantage is that you will have more flexibility as to when you can retire. If only the minimum DSS contributions are paid, you will have to wait until the normal state retirement age. If

Pensions

you make extra contributions, you can use them to retire whenever you like between 50 and 75.
- There are Inland Revenue rules as to the amount you can invest, which varies according to your age.
  — If you are aged 35 or under, you can pay up to 17.5 per cent of your earnings into a personal pension.
  — For ages 36 to 45: the maximum is 20 per cent.
  — For ages 46 to 50: 25 per cent.
  — For ages 51 to 55: 30 per cent.
  — For ages 56 to 60: 35 per cent.
  — If you are over 60, you are allowed to invest up to 40 per cent of your earnings.

Ages are calculated at the beginning of the tax year.

Relating back. Thanks to a little known rule, individuals are allowed to 'relate back' personal pension premiums. This means that a premium paid during a tax year is treated as if it had been paid during the previous tax year; or the tax year before that, if there were no relevant earnings in the previous year. *So if a premium is paid before 6 April 1993*, it may be treated as having been paid during 1990/91. It is also possible to carry forward unused relief. Your financial adviser will be able to explain how you apply.

- *Voluntary contributions by your employer*. Your employer might decide that he wishes to help you improve your pension by making contributions over and above the statutory national insurance contributions into your pension plan. If you are considering leaving a company pension scheme, this could be one of the questions you should ask as a means of comparing the value of a personal pension against your existing scheme. The Inland Revenue limits described above include any contributions made by your employer, so the total must therefore not exceed the allowed amount.

Your pension receipts. As with all money purchase schemes, the amount of pension you eventually receive will depend on two main factors: the size of the fund you have been able to build up and the fund's investment performance. As general wisdom, the longer you have been saving towards a personal pension and the bigger the total contributions paid, the larger your pension will stand to be. You have a great deal of choice in the matter but there are also certain rules designed to protect you.

A basic rule concerns what are known as your *protected rights*. These are the DSS minimum contributions including the value of the special 2 per cent incentive payment and tax relief you may have received – together with their accumulated investment growth.

Your protected rights can only be invested in a single contract, in contrast to your/your employer's extra or voluntary contributions which can be invested in as many different personal plans as you please.

A further point is that your protected rights must be used to purchase the annuity which will pay for your annual pension when you retire; they cannot be used as a contribution towards your lump sum.

Your lump sum derives from the extra contributions that you and perhaps also your employer have made including (as from the 1989 Budget) the value of dependants' benefits. You can take up to 25 per cent (or a quarter) of this part of the fund. The remainder will be added to your protected rights to purchase a better annuity.

Choosing a pension plan. Personal pensions are offered by insurance companies, banks, building societies, unit trusts and friendly societies. Before you make up your mind, you should aim to look at a variety of plans. Furthermore, you should not hesitate to ask as many questions as you want about any points that are unclear or any technical term that you do not fully understand – including in particular any questions you may have about the level of charges.

Although all life and pension policy providers are now required by law to state their charges in writing, it is often extremely difficult for a lay person to work out exactly what is involved; or to make meaningful comparisons between one organisation's charges and another's. Probably the best common yardstick is what is known as 'the reduction in yield'; in other words, what charges cost as a percentage reduction in the rate of investment return.

Because choosing both the right type of investment and the particular institution with which you are likely to feel happiest is such an important decision, even after you have chosen a scheme you will have a *14-day cooling off period* that gives you a chance to change your mind.

Is a personal pension a wise decision? This is a question that only you, or an adviser who knows your personal circumstances, can answer. Most pension experts advise that most people over 40 in a good company pension scheme would not be recommended to switch.

The key issue, however, is how your existing pension arrangements compare with the alternatives. You will therefore need to know what the value of your pension would be if you stay in SERPS or your company scheme, whichever is applicable.

For information about the value of your SERPS rights, complete Form

BR 19 *Pension Forecast Application Form* obtainable from your local Social Security office.

In the case of an employer's scheme, ask the pensions department or the person responsible for pensions to provide you with full information about your pension and future benefits.

Other points you will need to consider include: what type of investment policy would suit you; what size contributions (within Inland Revenue allowed limits) you could realistically afford; and what, after deduction of administrative and other charges, your plan might be worth when you come to retire.

When doing the sums, remember that the special incentive payments given by the government to mark the launch of personal pensions are due to end by April 1993.

This is not to say that taking a personal pension is either a right or a wrong decision. Simply that you need to be aware of all the various factors before opting out of your present arrangements.

For further information about personal pensions, ask your local Social Security office for a copy of leaflet NP 41 *New Pension Choices for Employees.* Also obtain a copy of leaflet IR 78 *Personal Pensions* from any tax office.

Types of investment policy

There are four different types of investment policy: with profits, unit linked, deposit administration and non-profit policies. Brief descriptions of each follow.

With-profits policies. These are one of the safest types of pension investments. They guarantee you a known minimum cash fund and/or pension on your retirement and, while the guaranteed amount is not usually very high, bonuses are added at regular intervals, according to how the investments in the fund perform. Additionally, a terminal (or final) bonus is given when the pension policy matures. An important feature is that once bonuses are given, they cannot later be withdrawn or put at risk due to some speculative investment.

Unit-linked policies. These are less safe than with-profits policies but they offer the attraction of potentially higher investment returns. Because they are more risky, many advisers recommend that their clients swop their unit-linked policies to the with-profits type about five years before they retire.

The decision as to what is best will very much depend on timing – and the future outlook for stock market investments. Another factor that will need to be taken into account is the prevailing level of interest rates, since these affect annuity rates.

Deposit administration policies. These lie somewhere between with-profits and unit-linked policies in terms of their risk/reward ratio. They operate rather like bank deposit accounts, where the interest rate is credited at regular intervals.

Non-profit policies. These have lost favour in recent years. Although they provide a guaranteed pension payment, the return on investment is usually very low. As a rule, they tend only to be recommended for people starting a plan within five years of their retirement.

Choosing the right policy. This is one area where it really pays to shop around. Great care is needed when choosing the organisation to invest your pension savings. Once you have committed yourself to a policy, you will not usually be able to move your money without considerable financial penalty.

As a general rule, it is sensible to select a large, well-known company that has been in the market for a long time. Before deciding, you should compare several companies' investment track records. What you should look for is evidence of good, *consistent* results over a period of 10 to 20 years.

An important point to be aware of is that insurance and other financial companies may give illustrative projections of their investment performance. Projections, however, even when these take account of possible inflation, are not the same as guarantees and if, in the event, the results are disappointing you are most unlikely to have any claim.

A further fundamental consideration is the administrative and other charges you will have to pay. Many people do not realise just how much they are being charged as most financial advisers make their money via commission, which is normally obscured, so making it difficult to work out what the true cost is.

You should aim at very least to talk to two or three financial institutions or other specialists such as insurance brokers and make it clear to all of them that you are doing so. If you need further advice, there could be a strong argument for consulting an independent financial adviser who charges fees rather than earns commission. For further information see Chapter 6, Financial Advisers. You might also like to read the section on investor protection at the end of Chapter 5.

A lump sum?

Members of company pension schemes and people with individual pension policies are allowed to take a lump sum of money tax free when they retire. The greatest amount normally permitted is one-and-a-half times your average final salary.

Taking a lump sum reduces the pension you receive but, on the other hand, if you invest the money wisely, you could end up with a higher income. Alternatively, of course, as many people do, you could use the capital for a worthwhile project such as improving your home; or, if you were planning to give something to your grandchildren, this could be an opportune time to settle it on them. The first priority, however, is to ensure that you will have enough income for your own needs.

If you take a lump sum, the amount by which your pension will be reduced is mainly determined by your age. The younger you are, the smaller the reduction. Another consideration is your tax status. Since the lump sum is tax free, as a general rule the higher your top rate of tax after retirement, the greater the advantage in opting for a lump sum. Your life expectancy can also be an important factor. The shorter this is, the more sense it makes to take the lump sum, rather than deny yourself for a longer-term pension that you will not be around to enjoy. If you come from a long line of octogenarians, then clearly you will need to work out the sums on the basis of the next 20 years or longer.

Contrary to what some people believe, it is not an 'all or nothing' decision. You have considerable flexibility and can choose between: not taking a lump sum, taking the maximum amount allowed or taking a portion of it only (whatever sum you decide).

Often the deciding factor when choosing whether to take a lump sum is the problem of investing it. If you have never had to think of it before, the prospect of what to do with several thousand pounds can seem a very daunting challenge. It could be prudent to 'invest' some of it in good financial advice.

Before consulting an expert, it would be helpful to both of you if you could work out – at least in very general terms – what your financial priorities are. The sorts of questions your adviser will ask are: whether you are investing for income now or capital growth in the future; whether you need to go for absolute security with every penny you have or whether you can afford slightly more risky investments in the hope of making more money in the long run; what other sources of income you have, or might expect to receive.

As is normal conservative practice, you will probably find that you will be recommended to spread your lump sum across a mixture of investments. Depending on your circumstances, these might be long- or short-term investments, income or capital producing, or quite likely, a combination of all of them.

An outline of the different types of investment is given in Chapter 5.

Pension rights if you continue to work after retirement age

When you reach normal retirement age, you will usually stop making contributions into your company pension scheme, even if you decide to carry on working. Your employer would, of course, have to agree to your continuing to work, which he is under no compulsion to do. Indeed, some organisations have fixed rules about retirement age and do not allow any exceptions.

If, however, you are allowed to remain, you probably have three options:

- You can leave your pension in the fund where it will continue to earn interest until you retire. In most private schemes, you can expect to receive an extra 9 per cent for every year that you delay retirement. If you continue working, say for an additional five years, your pension will then be 45 per cent higher than if you had started taking it at the normal age. You will also have been earning a salary meanwhile, so you are likely to be considerably better off as a result.
  Unfortunately, this opportunity (see also paragraph below) no longer applies to individuals joining a new scheme after 13 March 1989; or an existing scheme after 1 June 1989.
- You can leave your pension in the fund, as described above, and additionally contribute to a personal pension, provided your contributions do not exceed the allowed Inland Revenue limit, i.e. two-thirds of final salary (or whatever is allowed according to the rules of the scheme).
- You can continue working, draw your company pension and put some of your earnings into a separate scheme. Once you are over 60, the Inland Revenue allows you to invest up to 40 per cent of your earnings tax free into a pension plan.

Pensions for women

Women who have worked all their adult lives and paid full Class 1 contributions should get a full basic pension in their own right at the age of 60. The current amount is £54.15 a week. This is up-rated each year in April.

Women who have only worked for part of their adult lives may not have enough contributions to get a full basic pension on their own record. Instead, they may receive a reduced pension or one based on their husband's contributions; or one topping up the other. A wife entitled to a reduced pension on her own contributions can claim it at 60, regardless of whether or not her husband is receiving his pension.

Married women who have never worked are also entitled to a pension on their husband's contributions. In money terms, the value is about 60 per cent of the level of basic pension to which their husband is entitled. There are several important conditions, however.

Firstly, women can only receive a pension based on their husband's contributions if he himself is in receipt of a basic pension. He will have to have reached 65 and must have retired. Additionally, the wife herself must be over 60 to qualify.

If she is still under 60 when her husband claims his State pension and does not work or her earnings do not exceed £43.10, *he* should be able to obtain a supplement of around £32.55 to his pension, on the grounds of having a wife to support. If the couple are living apart, the earnings limit for the wife is £32.55. Your local Social Security office will be able to advise.

In contrast, if a wife has had her sixtieth birthday but her husband has not yet reached 65 (or has decided to defer his retirement), she must wait until her husband retires to receive her share of the married couple's pension.

An important point to note is that since the introduction of independent taxation, a married woman is entitled to have her section of the joint pension offset against her own personal allowance instead of it being counted as part of her husband's taxable income. For many pensioner couples, this should have the happy result of reducing their tax liability.

If a wife who formerly worked is over 60 and retired but cannot yet get a basic pension on either her own or her husband's contributions, she may be able to qualify for an additional or graduated pension based on her own contributions. These are described a little further on.

But first a word about three other important matters: reduced rate contributions, abolition of the half test and Home Responsibilities Protection.

Reduced rate contribution
Many women retiring today have paid a reduced rate of NI contribution, also known as 'the small stamp'. This option was given to working wives in 1948 and withdrawn in 1978 but women who had already chosen to

pay the reduced rate were allowed to continue, provided they did not take more than a two-year break from employment after 1978. If you have never paid anything but reduced rate contributions, you are not entitled to a basic pension in your own right but instead must rely on your husband's contributions for the married couple's pension.

Abolition of the half test
Until a few years ago, married women had to have paid full NI contributions for half the time they were married and working to get anything at all in their own right. This rule, known as the 'half test', has now been abolished. If you were born before 6 April 1919 and were a married woman when you reached age 60, having paid full NI contributions while working, you should contact your local Social Security office.

Home Responsibilities Protection (HRP)
Men and women whether single or married who have been unable to work regularly because they have had to stay at home to care for children and/or a disabled or elderly person may be able to safeguard their pension by claiming Home Responsibilities Protection. This is a very important benefit, especially for the many single women in their fifties who are sacrificing their career to look after an elderly parent. This measure was introduced in 1978 and protection only applies therefore from this date. The person you are caring for must come into one of the following categories:

- A child under 16 for whom you are getting child benefit
- Someone whom you are looking after regularly for at least 35 hours a week, who is in receipt of attendance allowance, constant attendance allowance (or the new disability living allowance)
- Someone – for example, an elderly person – for whom you have been caring at home and in consequence have been getting income support (or supplementary benefit in the past)
- A combination of the above situations.

A married woman or widow cannot get HRP for any tax year in which she was only liable to pay reduced rate national insurance contributions. HRP can only be given for complete tax years (6 April to 5 April), so if you simply gave up work for a few weeks in order to help out, you would be unlikely to qualify. Additionally, HRP cannot be used to reduce your total working life to below 20 years. To obtain a claim form, you should ask your local Social Security office for leaflet NP 27.

Since 1978, anyone in receipt of child benefit, supplementary benefit or income support who is caring for someone in one of the eligible categories listed opposite is automatically credited with HRP. All other claimants should obtain Leaflet NP 27 from their local Social Security office.

Graduated pension

This scheme operated between April 1961 and April 1975. Anyone earning over £9 a week and over age 18 at the time would probably have paid graduated contributions and be due a pension. You can only get a graduated pension based on your own personal contributions. However, the pension from the graduated scheme is likely to be small. Further, women were penalised because their pension was calculated at a less favourable rate than for men on account of their longer life expectancy.

Additional pension

The scheme, which is commonly known as SERPS (or State Earnings Related Pension Scheme) started in 1978. Contributions are earnings related, paid by both employer and employees, as are the pension payments. Women in contracted-out pension schemes get a guaranteed minimum pension, which must be at least as much as the pension they would have received from SERPS.

Divorced wives

If you have a full basic pension in your own right, this will not be affected by divorce. However, if, as applies to many women, despite having worked for a good number of years you have made insufficient contributions to qualify for a full pension, you should contact your local Social Security office, quoting your pension number and national insurance number. It is possible that you may be able to obtain the full single person's pension, based on your ex-husband's contributions.

Your right to use your ex-husband's contributions to improve or provide you with a pension depends on your age and/or whether you remarry before the age of 60. As a general rule, you can use your ex-husband's contributions towards your pension *for the years you were married* (i.e. until the date of the decree absolute). After that, you are expected to pay your own contributions until you are 60 unless you remarry.

If you are over 60 when you divorce, whether you remarry or not, you can rely on your ex-husband's contributions. If you remarry before the age of 60, you cease absolutely being dependent on your former husband and instead, your pension will be based on your new husband's contribution record.

N.B. The same rules apply in reverse. Although it happens far less frequently, a divorced man can rely on his former wife's contribution record during the years they were married to improve his basic pension.

Graduated or additional pensions are of no help to a divorced partner of either sex, as these are earnings related and, therefore, only benefit the individual who has earned and paid for them.

For further information, ask your local Social Security office for leaflet NI 95, *National Insurance for Divorced Women*. You should also read leaflet NP 46 *A Guide to Retirement Pension*.

Separated wives

Even if you have not lived together for several years, from a national insurance point of view you are still considered to be married. The normal pension rules apply including, of course, the fact that, if you have to depend on your husband's contributions, you will not be able to get a pension until he is both 65 and in receipt of his own pension.

If you are not entitled to a State pension in your own right, you will receive the dependant's rate of benefit, i.e. about 60 per cent of the full rate (or less if your husband is not entitled to a full pension). In such a case, you can apply for income support to top up your income.

Once you are 60, you can personally draw the wife's pension of £32.55 a week, without reference to your husband.

If you are under 60 but your husband has reached 65 and is retired, he may be able to claim a dependency addition of £32.55 for you, provided he pays it to you or is maintaining you to an equivalent amount. He will not be able to claim dependency addition if you are earning more than £32.55 a week.

If your husband dies, you will be entitled to widows' benefit in the same way as any other widow. If there is a possibility that he may have died but that you have not been informed, you can check by writing to or visiting St. Catherine's House, where the indexes of registered deaths are filed. The address is: St. Catherine's House, 10 Kingsway, London WC2B 6JP. T:071-242 0262.

Widows

There are three important benefits to which widows may be entitled: widows' payment, widows' pension and widowed mother's allowance. To claim these, fill in Form BW1, obtainable from any Social Security office. You will also be given a questionnaire (BD 8) by the Registrar. It is important that you complete this, as it acts as a trigger to help speed up payment of your benefits. For more information, see leaflet NP 45 *A Guide to Widows' Benefits*. See also Chapter 15, *No One is Immortal*,

Pensions

where we have described all three benefits in detail. Widows' pension is explained immediately below.

Widows' pension. There are various levels of widows' pension: the full rate and age-related widows' pension. As with widows' payment, receipt is dependent on sufficient NI contributions having been paid.

Full-rate widows' pension is paid to widows between the ages of 55 and 59 inclusive. The weekly amount is £54.15, which is the same pension as that received by a single person. Prior to April 1988, younger widows from the age of 50 qualified for the full rate. If you were already receiving this, your benefits will not be affected by the age change and you can continue claiming the full benefit even though you may not yet be 55.

Age-related widows' pension is for younger widows, who do not qualify for full rate. It is payable to a widow who is between 45 and 54 inclusive when her husband dies; or when she ceases to receive widowed mother's allowance. Rates depend on age and vary from £16.25 for 45 year olds to £50.36 for those aged 54.

As with the standard rate widows' pension, the qualifying ages were changed in April 1988. Widows already receiving age-related pension are not affected. For further information, see leaflet NP 45.

Widows' pension is normally paid automatically once you have sent off your completed form BW 1, so if for any reason you do not receive it you should enquire at your local Social Security office. In the event of your being ineligible, due to insufficient NI contributions having been paid, you may still be entitled to receive income support, family credit, housing benefit or a grant or loan from the social fund. Your Social Security office will advise you.

Widows who remarry, or live with a man as his wife, cease to receive widows' pension unless, that is, they are aged 60 or over in which case they may continue to receive their pension.

A widow who has cohabited and loses her entitlement to widows' pension will, if the cohabitation ends, be entitled to claim it again.

Retirement pension. Once a widow reaches age 60, she has the choice of claiming retirement pension or of continuing with widows' pension (until 65, when she no longer has a choice and will receive retirement pension).

If she is over 60 when her husband dies, she will usually receive a retirement pension rather than a widows' pension.

If at the time of death the couple were already receiving the State retirement pension, the widow will continue to receive her share. An important point to remember is that a widow may be able to use her late husband's NI contributions to boost the amount she receives. See leaflet FB 6 *Retiring? Your Pension and Other Benefits*.

Other important points. Separate from the basic pension, a widow may also receive money from her late husband's occupational pension, whether contracted in or out of SERPS. She may also get half of any of his graduated pension.

Chapter 4

Tax

Unfortunately, much as we should like to leave this out, the taxman never seems to retire!

Unless you are on a very low income, you will almost certainly be paying income tax and possibly one or two other varieties of tax as well. Paradoxically, however, although over the years you may have been contributing many thousands of pounds to the Inland Revenue, in practice you may have had very little direct contact with the tax system.

The accounts department will have automatically deducted – and accounted for – the PAYE on your earnings as a salaried employee. So unless you have been self-employed or have had other money not connected with your job, you may never really have needed to give the question very much thought.

Come retirement, even though for most people the issues are not particularly complex, a little basic knowledge can be invaluable. Firstly, it will help you to calculate how much money (after deduction of tax) you will have available to spend: the equivalent, if you like, of your take-home pay. At a more sophisticated level, understanding the broad principles could help you save money, by not paying more in taxation than you need.

If you are lucky enough to be fairly wealthy or if some of the points mentioned in connection with recent Budget changes give you cause to wonder whether you are managing your money as tax-efficiently as you might, you should talk to an accountant.

Income tax

This is calculated on all (or nearly all) your income, after deduction of your personal allowance; and in the case of a married man and/or sometimes wife, the married couple's allowance. The reason for saying 'nearly all' is that some income you may receive is tax free: types of income on which you do not have to pay tax are listed a little further on.

Most income, however, counts and you will be assessed for income tax on: your pension, interest you receive from most types of savings, dividends from investments, any earnings (even if these are only from casual work) plus rent from any lodgers, if the amount you receive exceeds £3,250 a year. Many social security benefits are also taxable.

The tax year runs from 6 April to 5 April the following year, so the amount of tax you pay in any one year is calculated on the income you receive (or are deemed to have received) between these two dates.

There are three different rates of income tax: the new 20 per cent rate introduced in the 1992 Budget which applies to the first £2,000 of your taxable income; the 25 per cent basic rate tax which applies to the next slice of taxable income between £2,000 and £23,700; and the 40 per cent higher rate tax which is levied on all taxable income over £23,700.

All income tax payers will pay the 20 per cent rate on their first £2,000 of taxable income. Or put another way, for every £100 of your income that counts for income tax purposes up to £2,000, you have to pay £20 to the Exchequer – and are allowed to keep the remaining £80. If you are a basic rate taxpayer, the amount you have to pay the Exchequer increases (after the first £2,000) to £25; and if you are a higher rate taxpayer, it goes up to £40 for every £100 of your taxable income over £23,700.

The different rates sometimes change or, as in the 1992 Budget, a new rate may be introduced. Any changes, whether reductions or increases, are invariably announced in the Budget.

Tax allowances

Personal allowance
Income tax is not levied on every last penny of your money. There is a certain amount you are allowed to retain before income tax becomes applicable. This is known as your personal allowance. Therefore, when calculating how much tax you will have to pay in any one year, you should first deduct from your total income the amount represented by your personal allowance (plus any additional or other tax allowance to which you may be entitled, see sections following). If your income is no higher than your personal allowance (or total of these allowances), you will not have to pay any income tax.

Everyone receives the same basic personal allowance, regardless of whether they are male, female, married or single; and regardless of whether any income they have comes from earnings, an investment, their pension or other source.

Tax

- The basic personal allowance (1992/93) is £3,445.

People aged 65 and over may be entitled to a higher personal allowance, by virtue of their age. Those aged 75 and above may receive even more generous treatment.

The full amount is only given to people whose income does not exceed £14,200. People with higher incomes will have their age allowance reduced by £1 for every £2 of income above the income limit. But however large your income, your personal allowance can never be reduced below the basic personal allowance.

For those aged 65 (or due to reach 65 before 5 April 1993) to 74:

- Personal allowance is increased to £4,200.

For those aged 75 (or due to reach 75 before 5 April 1993) and older:

- Personal allowance is increased to £4,370.

N.B. Extra allowance linked to the age is *normally given automatically.* If you are not receiving it but believe you should be doing so, you should write to your local tax office (see under Inland Revenue in the telephone directory) stating your age and, if married, that of your partner. If you have been missing out, you may be able to claim back anything you have lost for up to six years and should receive a tax rebate. The amounts as well as qualifying ages have been altered several times since 1986/87, so any rebate would only apply to allowances that would have been due to you at the time.

Married couple's allowance

The married couple's allowance replaced the married man's allowance when independent taxation was introduced in April 1990. All married couples, provided they live together, are entitled to claim.

At time of writing the allowance would normally go to the husband unless, that is, he has a low income and cannot use all or part of the allowance – in which case, he can transfer the unused part to his wife in order not to lose the tax benefit.

After April 1993, couples will have greater freedom to decide how they wish the allowance to be split. They will be able to choose to divide it equally or, instead, to allocate the whole allowance to the wife. The wife, if she so wishes, will be able to claim half the allowance as of right. The rules apply to the basic married couple's allowance and also to the age-related addition. Couples who wish all or part of the allowance to go to the wife will need to arrange the transfer through their tax ofices, by completing Form 18. This will need to be done before the start of the tax year, i.e. before 6 April. For the address of your tax office, see Inland Revenue in the telephone directory.

As with the personal allowance, older people enjoy a more generous married couple's allowance. Increases are given when the husband or wife reaches 65, with a bigger increase still at 75.

Similar to (age-related) personal allowance, the married couple's age-related increases are subject to a couple's income so it is possible that they might get less than the full addition – or maybe nothing extra at all.

The current (1992/93) married couple's allowance, together with the ceiling limits for the higher allowance, are as follows:

- The basic married couple's allowance is £1,720.
- When the husband or wife reaches 65 (or is due to become 65 before 5 April 1993), the allowance is increased to £2,465.
- When the husband or wife reaches 75 (or is due to become 75 before 5 April 1993), the allowance is increased to £2,505.

N.B. Additions for age are normally given automatically. If couples are not receiving any extra but believe they should be, the husband should write to their local tax office stating their ages. If there has been a mistake, he will be given a rebate.

Useful reading
For more detailed information about tax allowances and other changes due to independent taxation, see the following Inland Revenue leaflets obtainable free from any tax office (see under Inland Revenue in the telephone directory).

- *IR 80 Income Tax: A Guide for Married Couples*
- *IR 81 Independent Taxation: A Guide for Pensioners*
- *IR 82 Independent Taxation: A Guide for Husbands on Low Income*
- *IR 90 Independent Taxation: A Guide to Tax Allowances and Reliefs*
- *IR 91 Independent Taxation: A Guide for Widows and Widowers*

Widow's bereavement allowance. This is an extra allowance, worth £1,720 a year at current rates, specially given to widows to assist them over the first difficult period. The only qualification is that a widow's late husband must have been entitled to the married couple's allowance at the time of his death. The allowance is given from the date of bereavement to the end of that tax year, and for the following year so long as she has not remarried by the start of that year.

As with other tax allowances, this is not a cash benefit that can be claimed at the post office. It is an offset against income, before calculation of tax. A widow would therefore be entitled to £5,165 (the total of her personal allowance and widow's bereavement allowance) before her income would start to be assessed for tax. She would also be entitled to any unused portion of the married couple's allowance in the year her husband dies. If a widow is aged 65 or over, she may also be able to claim the age-related addition (see 'Personal allowance' page 56).

Other tax allowances. Extra tax reliefs can also be claimed in a couple of other circumstances.

Additional personal allowance (single parent's allowance). This can be claimed by any parent bringing up dependent children on their own. The current value of the allowance is £1,720 a year. N.B. A married man whose wife is totally incapacitated can also claim this allowance, in addition to the married couple's allowance, if he has dependent children living at home.

Registered blind people can claim an allowance of £1,080 a year. If both husband and wife are registered as blind, they can each claim the allowance. It is called the Blind Person's Allowance.

If you think you might be entitled to either of the above, you should write to your local tax office (see under Inland Revenue in the telephone directory) with full relevant details of your situation. As with age-related additions, if you were entitled to receive the allowance earlier but for some reason missed out doing so, you may be able to obtain a tax rebate.

Tax relief

Separate from any personal allowances, you can obtain tax relief on the following:

- Interest payments on the first £30,000 of a mortgage paid on your own home (the relief only applies to basic rate tax – see note below)
- A covenant for the benefit of a charity; or donation under the Gift Aid Scheme
- Contributions to occupational pensions, self-employed pension plans and other personal pensions
- Some maintenance payments, if you are divorced or separated
- Private medical insurance for those aged 60 and over
- Rental income of up to £3,250 a year from letting out rooms in your home.

Mortgage interest relief. Tax relief on mortgage interest payments is now restricted to the basic rate of income tax; all higher-rate relief was withdrawn in the 1991 Budget. The change affects both existing and new loans used for home purchase. It also affects loans secured on an older person's (65 years or over) home which are used to purchase a life annuity.

No one loses their right to tax relief on borrowings up to £30,000 for these purposes. It is only the amount of relief granted that changes, with higher rate taxpayers now treated identically to everyone else.

Self-employed and other personal pension plans. According to your age, you can pay the following amounts into a pension scheme and obtain tax relief:

- if you are aged 35 or under, 17.5 per cent of your earnings (up to a ceiling of £75,000)
- between the ages of 36 and 45, 20 per cent of your earnings
- between the ages of 46 and 50, 25 per cent
- between the ages of 51 and 55, 30 per cent
- between the ages of 56 and 60, 35 per cent
- ages 61 and over, 40 per cent.

Ages are calculated at the beginning of the tax year.

Maintenance payments. The rules were considerably simplified in the 1988 Budget, and, except for previous maintenance arrangements, are now as follows:

- Individuals *receiving* payments are exempted from income tax
- Individuals *paying* maintenance receive tax relief on the first £1,720 of payments to a divorced or separated spouse; other maintenance payments, including any to children, do not qualify for tax relief.

Maintenance arrangements existing prior to the 1988 Budget remain largely unaffected, other than that *payments received* by divorced or separated spouses are exempt from tax on the first £1,720.

Private medical insurance. People over the age of 60 are able to get tax relief on private medical insurance. This operates in the same way as the Miras scheme for mortgages, with relief given at the basic rate by deduction at source. Where relief is due at the higher rate, it is given by the subscriber's tax office (e.g. by adjusting the PAYE code).

Relief is available whether premiums are paid by the insured person or paid by someone else (for example a relative) on their behalf. In the latter case, the rate of relief is the marginal rate of the person who pays the premium.

For further information, see leaflet IR 103 *Tax Relief for Private Medical Insurance* available from any tax office.

Tax

Tax-free income
Some income you may receive is entirely free of tax. It is not taxed at source. You do not have to deduct it from your income, as in the case of personal allowances. Nor do you have to go through the formality of claiming relief on it.

If you receive any of the following, you can forget about the tax angle altogether – at least as regards these particular items:

- Disability living allowance
- Invalidity pension
- Industrial injuries disablement pension
- Income support (in some circumstances, e.g. when the recipient is also getting unemployment benefit, income support benefit would be taxable)
- Housing benefit
- Community charge benefit/Council tax benefit (from April 1993)
- Any extra which may be added to your State pension if you support children under 16
- All pensions paid to war widows (plus any additions for children)
- Pensions paid to victims of Nazism
- Certain disablement pensions from the armed forces, police, fire brigade and merchant navy
- Annuities paid to the holders of certain gallantry awards
- £10 Christmas bonus (paid to pensioners)
- National Savings Premium Bond prizes
- SAYE bonuses
- Winnings on the football pools and on other forms of betting.

Other tax-free money
The following are not income, in the sense that they are more likely to be 'one off' rather than regular payments. However, as with the above list they are tax free:

- Virtually all gifts (in certain circumstances you could have to pay tax if the gift is above £3,000 or if, as may occasionally be the case, the money from the donor has not been previously taxed).
- Redundancy payment, or a golden handshake in lieu of notice, up to the value of £30,000.
- Lump sum commuted from a pension with (1992/93) a maximum figure of £112,500 allowed.
- A matured endowment policy.
- Accumulated interest from a Tax Exempt Special Savings Account (TESSA) held for five years.

- Dividends on investments held in a Personal Equity Plan (PEP).

Income tax on investments

For most investments on which you are likely to receive interest or dividends, basic rate tax will already have been deducted before the money is paid to you.

If you are a basic rate taxpayer, the money you receive will be yours in its entirety and you will not have to worry about making deductions for tax.

If you only pay tax at the new 20 per cent rate, you will be able to claim a repayment from the Inland Revenue.

If you pay tax at the higher rate, you will have to pay some additional tax and should allow for this in your budgeting, as its deduction is not automatic. Normally, you will receive a tax demand for the extra tax owing after the end of the year.

Exceptionally, there are one or two types of investment where the money is paid to you gross – without the basic rate tax deducted. These include National Savings income bonds, deposit bonds, capital bonds, the NS Investment account and also certain specialist types of gilts. As with higher rate taxpayers, you will receive a tax demand for the amount owing.

Abolition of composite rate tax. Since April 1991, non-taxpayers (people whose taxable income is less than their allowances) can request institutions such as banks and building societies to pay any interest owing to them gross, without deduction of tax at source. This is already benefiting several million people, including in particular many married women and pensioners, who although not liable for tax, were losing money through the composite rate tax system.

In order to receive payments gross, anyone who qualifies should request form R85 from the institution in question, which they will then need to complete. People with more than one bank or building society account will need a separate form for each account. Forms are also included in the Inland Revenue explanatory leaflet IR 110 *Can You Stop Paying Tax on Your Bank and Building Society Interest?*, obtainable from any tax office or from your bank/building society.

By now people who have filled in an R85 should be automatically receiving their interest gross. However, some account-holders have not completed the form and have still been receiving interest from which tax has been deducted. Anyone in this situation can reclaim the tax from their tax office after the end of the tax year in April.

Since abolition, people who are liable for basic rate tax suffer deductions at the normal 25 per cent, instead of the more favourable composite rate level of 22 per cent.

Useful reading
IR leaflet 110 *Can You Stop Paying Tax on Your Bank and Building Society Interest?*; IR leaflet 111 *How to Claim a Repayment of Tax on Bank and Building Society Interest*; and IR leaflet 112 *How to Claim a Repayment of Income Tax*, obtainable from any tax office.

Reclaiming tax overpaid

If your income consists mainly of taxed investments, then you can set your personal allowances against the income. This will normally mean that you are entitled to a tax rebate. To allow for this, there is a special tax form for retired people to reclaim any tax they have overpaid on investment income.

If you think this might apply to you, you should obtain Tax Claim Form R40 from your local tax office (see under Inland Revenue in the telephone directory). Complete the form and return it to the tax office, together with the tax vouchers concerned. For further information, obtain IR leaflet 112 *How to Claim a Repayment of Income Tax.*

In particular it is estimated by the Inland Revenue that there may be 2½ million married women who may be able to claim a repayment of tax on dividend income. Married women who are claiming a repayment for the first time should fill in form R95 (D) attached to leaflet IR 112 and send it to their local tax office. A repayment claim form will then be sent to them. The completed claim form should be returned with the certificates showing the amount of tax deducted.

Mistakes by the Inland Revenue

The Inland Revenue sometimes also makes mistakes. Normally, if they have charged you insufficient tax and later discover the error, they will send you a supplementary demand requesting the balance owing. However, under a provision known as the 'Official Error Concession', allowances are sometimes made and it is possible that you may not have to pay the full amount.

This is more likely if you have a modest income. Extra leniency is sometimes also shown to widows and the retired. The limits governing the definition of 'modest income' were fairly recently increased to, at their most generous, £35,300 in respect of taxpayers over 65.

Tax rebates

When you retire, you may be due for a tax rebate. If you are, this would

Retirement Made Easy

normally be paid automatically, especially if you are getting a pension from your last employer. The matter could conceivably be overlooked: either if (instead of from your last employer), you are due to get a pension from an earlier employer; or if you will only be receiving a state pension – and not a company pension in addition.

In either case, you should ask your employer for a P45 Form. Then, either send it – care of your earlier employer – to the pension fund trustees; or, in the event of your only receiving a State pension, send it to the tax office together with details of your age and the date you retired. Ask your employer for the address of the tax office to which you should write. If the repayment is made to you more than a year after the end of the year for which the repayment is due – and is more than £25 – the Inland Revenue will automatically pay you (tax free!) interest. The Revenue call this 'Repayment Supplement'.

Useful reading

For further information about income tax, see the following Inland Revenue leaflets, available from any tax office:

- IR 93 *Income Tax – Separation, Divorce and Maintenance Payments*
- IR 92 *Income Tax: A Guide for One-Parent Families*
- IR 34 *Income Tax – Pay As You Earn*
- IR 65 *Giving to Charity – How Individuals Can Get Tax Relief*
- IR 86 *Independent Taxation: A Guide to Mortgage Interest Relief for Married Couples.*

Post-war credits

Post-war credits are extra tax that people had to pay in addition to their income tax between April 1941 and April 1946. The extra tax was treated as a credit to be repaid after the war. People who paid credits were given certificates showing the amount actually paid.

Repayment started in 1946, initially only to men aged 65 or over and to women aged 60 or over, but the conditions for claiming varied over the years until 1972 when it was announced that there would be a 'general release' and that all credits were to be repaid without any further restrictions. In 1972 people who could produce at least one of their post-war credit certificates were invited to claim.

In cases where the original credit holder has died without claiming repayment and the Post-War Credit certificate is still available, repayment can be made to the next of kin or personal representative of the estate.

Interest is payable on all claims at a composite rate of 38 per cent. The interest is exempt from income tax.

Tax

All claims should be sent to the **Special Post War Credit Claim Centre** at: Inland Revenue, HM Inspector of Taxes – PWC Centre V, Ty Glas, Llanishen, Cardiff CF4 5TX.

Capital gains tax (CGT)

You may have to pay capital gains tax if you make a large profit on the sale of a capital asset, for example: stocks and shares, jewellery, any property that is not your main home and other items of value.

CGT only applies to the actual profit you make, so if you buy shares to the value of £25,000 and sell them later for £35,000 the taxman will only be interested in the £10,000 profit you have gained.

Not all your profits are taxable. There is an *exemption limit of £5,800 a year:* so if during the year your total profits amount to £12,000, tax would only be levied on £6,200. Additionally, certain items are free altogether of capital gains tax; and others, such as the sale of a family business, get special treatment. Details are given a little further on.

A very important point for married couples to know is that as a result of independent taxation each partner now enjoys his/her own annual exemption of £5,800 instead of, as before, their gains being aggregated (i.e. added together) for tax purposes. This means in effect that, provided both partners are taking advantage of their full exemption limit, a couple can make gains of £11,600 a year free of capital gains tax. However, under the new rules it is no longer possible to use the losses of one spouse to cover the gains of the other.

Transfers between husband and wife remain tax free, although any income arising from such a gift will of course be taxed. Income would normally be treated as the recipient's for tax purposes unless, that is, the donor has the right to get the asset back in the future or retains some control over it – in which case the *donor* would be liable for any tax.

Since 1982, the burden of CGT has been eased by the welcome introduction of *index-linking*. This means that any part of an asset's increased value, from 1982 or its subsequent purchase to its disposal, which is due to inflation is not counted for CGT purposes.

A further major reform was introduced in the 1988 Budget, namely: any disposals on or after 6 April 1988 will be rebased to March 1982, so that only gains or losses accrued since that date will be brought into account.

Gains are treated as a person's 'top slice' of income and are accordingly taxed at: 20 per cent (the new lower rate), 25 per cent (basic rate), 40 per cent (higher rate) or a mixture of two rates, i.e. in instances where a gain, or gains, pushes part of an individual's income into a higher rate bracket.

Free of capital gains tax

The following assets are not subject to capital gains tax and do not count towards the £5,800 profits you are allowed to make:

- Your main home (but, see note below)
- Your car
- Personal belongings up to the value of £6,000 each
- Proceeds of a life assurance policy (in most circumstances)
- Profits on British Government stocks
- National Savings Certificates
- SAYE contracts
- Building society savings
- Futures and options in gilts and qualifying corporate bonds
- Personal Equity Plan scheme
- Premium Bond winnings
- Football pool and other bettings winnings
- Gifts to registered charities
- Small part disposals of land (limited to 5 per cent of the total holding, with a maximum value of £20,000).

Your home. Your main home is usually exempt from capital gains tax. However, there are certain 'ifs and buts' which could be important.

If you convert part of your home into an office or into self-contained accommodation on which you charge rent, that part of your home which is deemed to be a 'business' may be separately assessed – and CGT may be payable when you come to sell it. (CGT would not apply, if you simply take in a lodger who is treated as family, in the sense of sharing your kitchen or bathroom).

If you physically vacate your home and let it for profit – perhaps because you have decided to live permanently with a friend – under tax law, the property would be treated as an investment and subject to certain exemptions would be assessed for CGT when it was sold.

Part of the argument hinges on *owner occupation.* If you are not living in the property (or a part of it which you have let out for rent), then the house – or that section of it – is no longer considered to be your main home. People who are liable for CGT in these circumstances can apply for special relief of up to £40,000.

If you leave your home to someone else who later decides to sell it, then he/she may be liable for CGT when the property is sold (although only on the gain since the date of death). There may also be inheritance tax implications, so if you are thinking of leaving or giving your home to someone, you are strongly advised to consult a solicitor or accountant.

If you own two homes, only one of them is exempt from CGT, namely the one you designate as your 'main residence'. An exception was sometimes allowed if a second home was occupied by a dependent relative, who lived in it rent free.

This concession was abolished as from 6 April 1988. However, anyone who had a dependent relative living in a second home before that date will continue to enjoy capital gains tax relief. But the relief only applies while the dependant is actually inhabiting the property. If he/she moves to more sheltered accommodation and you keep the property as an investment, it will be assessed for capital gains tax purposes from the date of your relative's departure.

Selling a family business. If you sell all or part of your business when you retire, you may not have to pay tax on the first £150,000 of capital gain with a further exemption allowed of one-half of gains between £150,000 and £600,000. Relief is on a sliding scale and to get maximum relief, you must be aged at least 55 and when selling shares must have owned 25 per cent as a working director for 10 years. (Lower share ownership is allowed if, together with your immediate family, you collectively own 50 per cent of the business.)

If you are forced to retire early through ill health, you may be entitled to more generous relief than would otherwise normally be the case.

There are also certain provisions for what is termed 'semi-retirement', which are hedged around with important rules.

Since this is a very complex field, before either retiring or selling shares, you are strongly recommended to seek professional advice.

Selling shares for gain should not be confused with *giving* part of your family business to the next generation, which was made easier a few years back under the inheritance tax rules. However, the advice about seeking professional help still applies.

Useful reading
For further information about capital gains tax, see the following booklets, available from any tax office:

- CGT 4 *Capital Gains Tax - Owner-Occupied Houses*
- CGT 6 *Capital Gains Tax - Retirement Disposal of a Business*
- CGT 11 *Capital Gains Tax and the Small Businessman*
- CGT 13 *The Indexation Allowance for Quoted Shares*
- CGT 14 *An Introduction to Capital Gains Tax*
- CGT 15 *Capital Gains Tax - A Guide for Married Couples*

- CGT 16 *Capital Gains Tax - Indexation Allowance*

Inheritance tax

Inheritance tax applies to money and/or gifts with a capital value passed on at time of death (or sometimes before).

The first £150,000 of an individual's estate is tax free. Amounts over this are taxed at a single rate of 40 per cent. However, before any tax is calculated, there are a number of exemptions and other concessions of which perhaps the most important is that there is no tax on gifts or inheritance between spouses. Additionally, most family-owned businesses are exempted from inheritance tax; as are most life-time gifts, provided certain important conditions are met.

For exemption on life-time gifts to apply, *the gift must have been made at least seven years before the donor's death* and moreover, it must have been unconditionally given; or to use the jargon, 'without reservation'. A gift in which the donor retains an interest or some direct control – for example, a house 'given' to his children in which the parent continues to live – does not qualify for exemption.

The seven-year period is not totally inflexible, in that (as well as a £3,000 annual exemption) there is *taper relief*: in other words, a tapering rate of tax, according to how close to the seven-year limit the death of the donor occurred. Gifts made within three years of death do not qualify for any relief and the tax will have to be paid in full. For gifts made more than three years before death, the rates are as follows:

- Death between 3 and 4 years of gift 80%
- Death between 4 and 5 years of gift 60%
- Death between 5 and 6 years of gift 40%
- Death between 6 and 7 years of gift 20%

Other than the exemptions described above, tax has to be paid on any capital gain that has built up on an asset you give away during your lifetime. As with capital gains tax, appreciation is only calculated from 1982 or subsequent year of purchase and any part of the asset's increased value due to inflation is not counted for tax purposes. Moreover, not surprisingly perhaps, tax specialists say that there are legitimate ways of minimising the liability. Since this is a fairly complex matter, professional advice is essential.

Another important consideration that should not be overlooked is the need to make a will. The rules of intestacy are very rigid and neglecting to make a proper will can have serious consequences for those whom you might wish to benefit. For further information, see 'Making a will' (page

315). Likewise, if you have already written a will, it is strongly recommended that you have this checked by a professional adviser to ensure that you do not give money unnecessarily to the taxman.

For further information about inheritance tax, see booklets IHT 1 *Inheritance Tax* and IHT 3 *An Introduction to Inheritance Tax*, obtainable from any tax office.

Independent taxation

As most readers will know, independent taxation was introduced on 6 April 1990. Throughout this chapter and elsewhere in the book, the key changes have been described as and where relevant, in particular under the headings 'Personal allowance', 'Married couple's allowance' and 'Capital gains tax'. However, because this is such a fundamental change, one or two of the essentials are worth repeating.

The switch to independent taxation affects nearly all married couples. As well as allowing married women privacy over their own financial affairs, another major gain is that many couples – especially retired people – are better off financially.

In contrast to the old system, whereby a married woman's income was treated as belonging to her husband for taxation purposes, both husband and wife are now taxed independently on their own income. Each has their own personal allowance and rate band; and each pays their own tax and receives their own tax rebates.

Most previous tax allowances have disappeared (the single person's allowance, wife's earned income allowance and married man's allowance) and have been replaced by a new personal allowance and a new married couple's allowance. Everyone, whether male or female, single or married, now receives their own personal allowance, which can be set against any income including savings or a pension as well as earned income. For many couples, this represents a real saving in tax, in consequence of a wife's income no longer being aggregated with that of her husband.

Moreover, independent taxation applies equally to the age-related additions (formerly known as age allowance) and both husband and wife are now eligible for their own higher tax allowance from the age of 65 (and more generous still after age 75).

Another welcome gain is that if a husband's income is too low for him to use all or part of the married couple's allowance, he can request that the unused part be transferred to his wife – thus reducing his wife's tax bill. As from April 1993, even more flexibility will be allowed with couples able to choose whether all the tax relief should go to one partner (husband or wife) or whether to split it on a 50-50 basis.

A further important point for many couples is that independent taxation does not simply apply to income tax but applies equally to both capital gains tax and inheritance tax. As a result, both husband and wife enjoy their own capital gains tax exemption (£5,800 in the 1992/93 tax year) and their own exemption from inheritance tax (£150,000 in the 1992/93 tax year).

Useful reading
For further information about independent taxation, see the following Inland Revenue booklets, available from any tax office:

- IR 80 *Independent Taxation: A Guide for Married Couples*
- IR 81 *Independent Taxation: A Guide for Pensioners*
- IR 82 *Independent Taxation: A Guide for Husbands on a Low Income*
- IR 86 *Independent Taxation: A Guide to Mortgage Interest Relief for Married Couples*
- IR 90 *Independent Taxation: A Guide to Tax Allowances and Reliefs*
- IR 91 *Independent Taxation: A Guide for Widows and Widowers*

Value added tax (VAT)

Unless you are thinking of starting a business or already run one, you do not require any special information about VAT. You pay it automatically on most goods and services, at the flat rate of 17.5 per cent. As a general rule, if you purchase a tangible object, it will be included in the price. For most services, including restaurant bills, it is itemised separately. Small firms that are not registered for VAT naturally do not charge it. However, even for very small enterprises, there may be definite advantages in registering. If you are planning to become self-employed or start a business after you retire, you should ask an accountant for advice.

Corporation tax

This is a business tax and unless you are involved in running a company, there is nothing you need to know. If you are already engaged in running a small business, you will probably hardly need reminding that the small companies' rate of corporation tax is 25 per cent (instead of the 33 per cent standard rate for larger concerns). The lower and upper limits for the application of marginal relief are £250,000 and £1,250,000 respectively.

Tax

Useful reading

Inland Revenue booklets which could be helpful, especially if you are interested in the possibility of becoming self-employed or starting your own business include:

- IR 28 *Starting In Business*
- IR 52 *Your Tax Office - Why It Is and Where It Is*
- IR 53 *Thinking of Taking Someone On?*
- IR 56/NI 39 *Employed or Self-Employed*
- IR 57 *Thinking of Working for Yourself*

UK pensions paid abroad

- Any queries about your pension should be addressed to the DSS Overseas Branch at Newcastle Central Office, Longbenton, Newcastle upon Tyne NE98 1YX.
- Technically your state pension could be subject to income tax, as it derives from the UK. In practice, if this is your only source of UK income, tax would be unlikely to be charged.
- If you have an occupational pension, UK tax will normally be charged on the total of the two amounts.
- Both state and occupational pensions may be paid to any country. (If you are planning to retire to Australia, Canada, New Zealand or Norway, you would be advised to check on the up-to-date position regarding any annual increases you would expect to receive to your pension. Some people have found the level of their pension 'frozen' at the date they left Britain.)
- If the country where you are living has a double tax agreement with the UK, as previously explained your income *may* be taxed there – and not in Britain. Britain now has a double tax agreement with most countries. For further information, check the position with your local tax office.
- If your pension is taxed in the UK, you will be able to claim part of your personal allowance as an offset. A married man living with his wife may also be able to claim part of the married couple's allowance.

HOW CAN YOU SPREAD YOUR RISK BY BUYING SHARES IN A SINGLE COMPANY?

::::: If you buy shares in a single Investment Trust company, your risk will be spread across as many as 200 companies.

Investment Trust managers have the skill, the expertise and the research back-up to pick winners both at home and overseas. As a result your investment has an excellent chance of keeping well ahead of inflation.

As public companies, Investment Trusts are quoted on the Stock Exchange. And, since most of them are listed on the share pages, you will be able to watch the progress of your investment.

Different Investment Trusts specialise in many different areas of investment, but they all allow you to buy into a spread of shares at low cost.

For more information please send for 'Buying Shares in Investment Trust Companies'. It's free and produced by AITC, the Association that speaks for Investment Trust companies.

Fill in the coupon or call us on 071-588 5347.

THE ASSOCIATION OF INVESTMENT TRUST COMPANIES

To Ian Cox, Association of Investment Trust Companies, Park House, 6th Floor, 16 Finsbury Circus, London EC2M 7JJ.

Please send me a free information pack.

☐ I am a private investor   ☐ I am an independent financial adviser   *Please Tick*

(Mr/Mrs/Miss) _____ Initials _____ Surname _____
BLOCK CAPITALS PLEASE
Address _____
_____
_____ Postcode _____   GR01012A

Please note that the value of and income from shares may fall and you may not get back the amount you have invested. This advertisement has been approved by AITC Services Limited. (FIMBRA)

Chapter 5

Investment

Investment is a subject for everyone. One of your single most important aims must be to make your existing money work for you so you will be more comfortable in the years ahead. The younger you start planning the better. If you are already 65 or over, there is still plenty you can do.

Many articles written on the subject of financial planning for retirement concentrate almost exclusively on ways of boosting your immediate income to compensate for your loss of earnings. Frankly, this is very misleading and short-sighted advice. An equally if not even more critical consideration must be to safeguard your long-term security, even if this means some minor sacrifice to your current standard of living.

The likelihood is that you will live for 20 years or longer after you retire and your partner may live longer still. Your investment strategy must therefore be aimed not just for your sixties but also for your eighties.

Inflation is another essential factor that must be taken into account since, unless you plan carefully, this could dramatically affect your standard of living after a few years.

Sources of investable funds

You do not need to be in the director league to have money for investment. Possible sources of quite significant capital include:

- *Commuted lump sum* from your pension
- *Insurance policies*, designed to mature around your retirement
- *Profits on your home*, if you sell it and move to smaller, less expensive accommodation
- *Redundancy money*, golden handshake or other farewell gift from your employer
- *Sale of SAYE and other share option schemes*

General investment strategy

Investments differ in their aims, tax treatment and the amount of risk involved. One or two categories are only suitable for the very rich, who can afford to take more significant risks. Others, such as certain types of National Savings, are only really suitable for those on a very low income.

These two groups apart, the aim for most people should be to acquire a balanced portfolio: in other words, a mix of investments variously designed to provide some income to supplement your pension and also some capital appreciation to maintain your standard of living long term.

Except for annuities and National Savings, which have sections to themselves, the different types of investment are listed by groups, as follows:

- Variable interest accounts
- Fixed interest securities
- Equities
- Long-term lock-ups.

As a general strategy, it is a good idea to aim to choose at least one type of investment from each group.

Annuities

Definition. An annuity is a very simple investment to understand. You pay a capital sum to an insurance company and in return are guaranteed a fixed income for life. The money is paid to you at fixed intervals and will remain exactly the same year in, year out. Payments are calculated according to life expectancy tables and for this reason an annuity may not really be a suitable investment for anyone under 70. Other than your age, the key factor affecting the amount you will receive in payments is the level of interest rates at the time you buy: the higher these are, the more you will receive.

An annuity would probably give you more immediate income than any other form of investment. But whether you actually get good value depends on how long you live. When you die, your capital will be gone and there will be no more payments. So if you die a short while after signing the contract, it will represent very bad value indeed. On the other hand, if you live a very long time, you may more than recoup your original capital.

As a precaution against early death, it is possible to take out a capital protected annuity or one guaranteed for a number of years: in other words, an annuity that runs for a specified period. Should you die before the end of the contract, the payments will go to your partner or other beneficiary. The major drawback to this arrangement is that if you outlive the contract, you will not receive any more annuity income and your capital will have gone along with your security.

There are also other types of annuity, such as capital and income plans (or temporary annuities, as they are sometimes called) which pay you a small income, say, for a 10-year period, at the end of which your capital is returned. These are sometimes taken out, as a kind of holding operation, by people who are too young to obtain sufficiently attractive terms on a normal life annuity. You have to assess whether you could get a better return from another fixed interest security.

Tax. Income tax is relatively low, as part of the income is allowed as a return on capital which is not taxable.

How to obtain. You can buy an annuity either direct from an insurance company or via an intermediary. But shop around, as the payments vary considerably. To find an insurance broker, contact the **British Insurance and Investment Brokers Association**, BIIBA House, 14 Bevis Marks, London EC3A 7NT (see Chapter 6, Financial Advisers).

Assessment. Safe. Attractive if you live to a ripe old age. But highly vulnerable to inflation. Sacrifice of capital that might otherwise benefit successors.

National Savings

It is extremely easy to invest in National Savings, as all you need do is go to the post office. Most types of investment it offers are broadly similar to those provided by banks and other financial bodies. So rather than explain in detail the exact terms and conditions of, say, a National Savings Investment Account, it is easier to suggest that you pick up the relevant leaflet at the post office counter; or telephone the numbers shown a little further down.

The main investments offered by National Savings are:

- *Ordinary account.* Pays a fairly low rate of variable interest. You can invest between £5 and £10,000. The first £70 of interest each year is free of tax (£140 for joint holdings). Ask for leaflet DNS 700 at your post office.
- *Investment account.* Pays an attractive rate of interest. You must give one month's notice if you wish to withdraw money. You can invest between £5 and £25,000. Interest is taxable but paid in full without deduction of tax at source. Ask for leaflet DNS 701.
- *Income bonds.* Pay an attractive rate of interest. Interest is taxable, but paid in full without deduction of tax at source. Three months'

notice of withdrawal is necessary. You can invest between £2,000 and £50,000. Ask for leaflet DNS 709.
- *39th (current) issue of National Savings Certificates.* Offers an attractive rate of fixed interest that is tax free. You can invest from £100 to £5,000. For maximum benefit, you must hold the certificates for five years. Ask for leaflet DNS 703.
- *Index-linked certificates (5th issue).* You can invest from £25 to £10,000. Interest is 4.5 per cent plus the increase in the Retail Prices Index but, to obtain this rate, certificates must be retained for five years. Interest is tax free. You can buy up to an additional £10,000 if you wish to reinvest earlier certificates held for at least five years. Ask for leaflet DNS 704.
- *Yearly plan.* Produces a tax-free return, paid at a fixed rate over five years. You can invest from £20 to £400 per month. Ask for leaflet DNS 705.
- *Gilts.* Can be bought through the National Savings Stock Register. Ask for leaflet DNS 708.
- *Capital Bonds.* These offer a guaranteed interest rate provided you do not withdraw your money before five years. The one big drawback is that tax on the interest has to be paid annually – with higher bills every year as the interest grows – until you actually receive any money. However, for non-taxpayers especially, it offers a very attractive investment as well perhaps as an ideal gift for grandparents to give children. Minimum purchase is £100 and Capital Bonds can be bought over the counter at post offices. Ask for leaflet DNS 717.
- *Children's Bonus Bond.* Bonds are sold in multiples of £25 and the maximum total purchase per child is £1,000. Both interest and bonus, which will be paid after five years, are free of income tax and need not be declared to the Inland Revenue. Interested parents and grandparents should ask for leaflet DNS 723 at their local post office.
- *FIRST Option Bond.* New guaranteed growth bond, offering a 12-month fixed rate of interest provided the money is not withdrawn earlier. Come the anniversary date, investors can leave the money in the bond (after deduction of basic rate tax) for a further 12 months – at the then prevailing fixed interest rate – or terminate the arrangement. You can invest between £1,000 and £250,000. Ask for leaflet DNS 724.

The National Savings Sales Information Units offer help during normal office hours. For information about buying National Savings products, telephone:

South	LONDON:	071-605 9461
North East	DURHAM:	091-374 5023
North West	BLACKPOOL:	0253 715666
Scotland	GLASGOW:	041-636 2950

Variable interest accounts

Recent changes. Over the past few years, many of the banks and building societies have introduced interest-bearing current accounts, as well as having made it easier to run small overdrafts (i.e. with a typical ceiling of £100 to £500). Although an improvement on the standard current account, these do not qualify in anyone's language as a vehicle for investment and are not suitable for keeping large savings for more than a short time. If you are tempted to switch to one of the new current accounts, you should check very carefully what charges apply if you dip into overdraft. You should enquire whether you are being offered 'tiered rates' – those paying the top rate of interest applicable on all your funds; or the less attractive 'banded rates' – those with two levels of interest, with a lower amount paid on, say, the first £500 or £1,000 and the higher rate only on funds above that amount.

A further point to investigate is whether there is a fixed monthly or other charge. This can sometimes change without customers always being properly informed. You should check your monthly statement carefully and consider moving your account if you are dissatisfied.

Definition. Other than the new style current accounts described above, these are all *deposit accounts* (share accounts in building societies) of one form or another, arranged with banks, building societies, the National Savings Bank and with some financial institutions that operate such accounts jointly with banks. They include among others: basic deposit accounts, high interest accounts and fixed-term deposit accounts, and also TESSAs.

Your money collects interest while it is on deposit, which may be automatically credited to your account or for which you may receive a regular cheque. Some institutions pay interest annually, others – on some or all of their accounts – will pay it monthly. If you have a preference, this is a point to check. The rate of interest will vary, up or down, according to the level of national interest rates. While you may get a poor return on your money if interest rates drop, your savings will nearly always be safe as you are not taking any kind of investment risk.

Access. Access to your money depends on the type of account you choose: you may have a cheque book and withdraw your money when you want; you may have to give a week's notice or slightly longer; or if you enter into a term account, you will have to leave your money deposited for the agreed specified period. In general, accounts where a slightly longer period of notice is required earn a better rate of interest.

Sum deposited. It is not usually sensible to consider a deposit account unless you have a minimum of £100. For certain types of account, the minimum investment could be anything from £500 to about £5,000. The terms tend to vary according to how keen the institutions are, at a given time, to attract small investors.

Tax. With the exception both of TESSAs, which are tax free, and of the National Savings Bank, where interest is paid gross, tax is deducted at source – so you can spend the money without worrying about the tax implications. However, you must enter the interest on your tax return; and if you are a higher rate taxpayer, you will of course have additional liability.

Anyone not liable to tax, including many pensioners, can arrange to have their interest paid in full by completing a certificate which enables the financial institution to pay the interest gross.

Choosing a deposit account

There are two main areas of choice: the type of deposit account and where to invest your money. The basic points to consider are as follows:

Basic deposit account. This attracts a relatively low rate of interest. But it is both easy to set up and very flexible, as you can add small or large savings when you like and can usually withdraw your money without any notice. It is a much better option than simply leaving your money in a current account and is an excellent temporary home for your cash if you are saving short term for, say, a holiday. However, it is not recommended as a long-term savings plan.

High interest deposit account. Your money earns a higher rate of interest than it would on an ordinary deposit account. However, to open a high interest account you will need to deposit a minimum sum, which could be of the order of £500 to £1,000. While you can always add to this amount, if your basic deposit drops below the required minimum, your money will immediately stop earning the higher interest rate. If you frequently dip into overdraft, a high interest deposit account is worse than useless.

Fixed-term deposit account. You deposit your money for an agreed period, which can vary from a few months to over a year. In return for this commitment, you will be paid a relatively star rate of interest.

As with high interest accounts, there is a minimum investment: roughly £1,500 to £5,000. If you need to withdraw your money before the end of the agreed term, there are usually hefty penalties. Before entering into a term account, you need to be sure that you can afford to leave the money on deposit. Additionally, you will need to take a view about interest rates: if they are generally low, your money may be better invested elsewhere.

A further important point is that you should keep a note of the date when the agreement expires. As a rule, your money will no longer earn preferential rates after the term has come to an end (unless of course you renew the agreement). The bank or other institution may not notify you in advance and may, quite legitimately, simply credit you with the normal interest rates after the contract's expiry.

Tax Exempt Special Savings Account (TESSA). TESSAs are special deposit accounts, designed to encourage saving, which, provided you leave the capital untouched for five years, allow you to keep all the interest free of tax. They are widely available from banks and building societies and work as follows.

The maximum amount you are allowed to put into the scheme is £9,000 over a five-year period. This can either be paid in regular monthly amounts, of up to £150, or savings can be paid in annual sums, as follows: year one, a maximum of £3,000; years two, three and four, up to £1,800 each year; year five, up to £600.

The gross interest earned on the money is credited to the account each year. The capital (i.e. the savings you pay into the account) cannot be withdrawn until the expiry of the scheme at the end of year five, otherwise you lose the tax advantage. People who need some money are, however, allowed to withdraw part of the interest less basic rate tax without penalty – other than the obvious one that if they reduce their 'savings pot', they will lose the extra tax-free interest that could have been generated.

For most people paying tax who can afford to save for five years, TESSAs are an attractive investment. The only point to watch is that, as with any deposit account, interest rates tend to vary from one bank and building society to another, so the usual advice about shopping around applies.

Information. Leaflets, describing the different accounts on offer, should be available at all bank and building society branches.

The **Building Societies Association** at 3 Savile Row, London W1X

1AF offers a free range of helpful leaflets and information sheets, including: *Taxation of Building Society Interest* and a factsheet describing the protection scheme which guarantees individual investors with 90 per cent of their investment up to a ceiling of £20,000. A *Directory of Members*, giving head office addresses and telephone numbers is also available.

Complaints. As with banks and insurance companies, building societies now also have an Ombudsman (or more precisely, three Ombudsmen). Individual members of building societies who have a complaint can appeal to them direct to investigate the matter, provided that the complaint has already been taken through the particular society's own internal disputes procedure and the matter is within the scope of the Ombudsmen Scheme. Broadly speaking, there are five areas where the Ombudsmen can intervene: the operation of share and deposit accounts; all kinds of loans and credits; banking services; trusteeship; and executorship. The Ombudsmen are able to make awards of up to £100,000. The address to contact is: **The Office of the Building Societies Ombudsmen**, Grosvenor Gardens House, 35-37 Grosvenor Gardens, London SW1X 7AW. T:071-931 0044.

Details of the Banking Ombudsman are given in the section headed 'Banks' in Chapter 6, Financial Advisers.

Fixed interest securities

In contrast to variable interest accounts, fixed interest securities offer a fixed rate of interest which you are paid, regardless of what happens to interest rates generally. If you buy when the fixed rate is high and interest rates fall, you will nevertheless continue to be paid interest at the high rate specified in the contract note. However, if interest rates rise above the level when you bought, you will not benefit from the increase. As a generalisation, these securities give high income but only modest, if any, capital appreciation.

The list includes: high interest gilts, permanent interest bearing shares, local authority bonds and Stock Exchange loans, debentures and preference shares.

Since most are only suitable for those who can afford riskier investments, we only describe gilts as these are obtainable through National Savings.

Gilt-edged securities
Definition. Usually known as 'gilts', these are stocks issued by the

Investment

government which guarantees both the interest payable and the repayment price which is promised on a given date.

The maturity date varies and can be anything from a few months to 20 years or longer. Accordingly, stocks are variously known as: short-dated, medium-dated and long-dated. A further category is undated. Additionally, there are index-linked gilts.

Prices for gilts are quoted per £100 of nominal stock. For example, a stock may be quoted as: 10 per cent *Treasury Stock* 1997, 99½ – 100¼. In plain English, this means the following:

- 10 per cent represents the interest you will be paid. The rate is fixed and will not vary, whatever happens to interest rates generally. You will receive the interest payment twice yearly, 5 per cent each time.
- You are buying Treasury Stock.
- The maturity date is 1997.
- To buy the stock, you will have to pay £100.25p (i.e. 100¼).
- If you want to sell the stock, the market price you will get is £99.50p (i.e. 99½).

In addition, when buying or selling, regard has to be given to the accrued interest which will have to be added to or subtracted from the price quoted.

Gilts are complicated by the fact that you can either retain them until their maturity date, in which case the government will return the nominal value in full. Or you can sell them on the Stock Exchange at market value. This accounts for the different buying and selling prices that may be quoted.

Prices are affected by current interest rates. If interest rates are at 7 per cent, a gilt with a guaranteed interest payment of 10 per cent is a very attractive buy – so the price will rise. Conversely, if interest rates are 15 per cent, a guaranteed interest payment of 10 per cent is a poor proposition, so there will not be many buyers and the price will drop. Because gilts are so closely tied to interest rates, the price can fluctuate daily, often by quite big jumps.

Index-linked gilts, while operating on the same broad principle, are different in effect. They are designed to shield investors against inflation: they pay very low interest but are redeemable at a higher price than the initial purchase price, as their value is geared to the cost of living. They are most valuable when inflation is high but are even more sensitive than other gilts to optimum timing when buying or selling.

Tax. Income tax is normally deducted at source. However, this does not apply if you buy gilts on the National Savings Stock Register (NSSR), when instead the interest will be paid to you gross. This does not mean that you avoid paying it, simply that you must allow for a future tax bill before spending the money.

A particular attraction of gilts is that no capital gains tax is charged on any profit you may have made. But equally, no relief is allowed for loss.

How to buy. You can buy gilts through banks, building societies, a stockbroker, financial intermediary or through National Savings via your post office. In all cases, you will be charged commission. Prices of gilts are published every day in all the quality newspapers under the heading 'British Funds'.

With National Savings you buy and sell by post, so by the time purchase is made for you the price may have changed. Also, although it may be cheaper, you will not get advice as you would from a financial adviser. It is, however, extremely easy. All you need to do is complete an application form DNS 400 and send it with your cheque in the special green envelope DNS 450 to the Bonds and Stock Office. Forms, envelopes and a leaflet, *Buying Gilts on the National Savings Stock Register*, are available from most post offices. Alternatively, you can address any queries to the **Bonds and Stock Office**, Blackpool, Lancs FY3 9YP; or telephone 0253 766151.

Assessment. Gilts normally pay reasonably good interest and offer excellent security, in that they are backed by the government. You can sell at very short notice and the stock is normally accepted by banks as security for loans, if you want to run an overdraft. This may not apply if you purchase through the NSSR.

However, gilts are not a game for amateurs as, if you buy or sell at the wrong time, you could lose money; and if you hold your stock to redemption, inflation could take its toll on your original investment.

Gilt plans. This is a technique for linking the purchase of gilt-edged securities and with-profit life insurance policies to provide security of capital and income over a 10 to 20 year period. It is a popular investment for the commuted lump sum taken on retirement. These plans are normally obtainable from financial intermediaries, typically members of FIMBRA or LAUTRO, (see Chapter 6, Financial Advisers).

Equities

These are all stocks and shares, purchased in different ways and involving varying degrees of risk. They are designed to achieve capital appreciation as well as give you some regular income. Most allow you to get your money out within 30 days or less. In the past, equities were by and large only considered suitable for a privileged minority. Today, there are an estimated 10 million shareholders and the number is rapidly increasing. One reason is that, as the flotation of British Telecom demonstrated, equities can be excellent money-spinners. Another is that over the last few years, investment has become very much easier, largely as a result of the growth in the unit trust movement.

Whatever people say, equities are always risky. But for those who believe in caution, the gamble can be substantially reduced by avoiding obviously speculative investments. Equities include: ordinary shares, unit trusts and personal equity plans.

Unit trusts
Definition. Unit trusts offer an alternative to buying shares on the Stock Exchange. Your money is pooled in a fund, run by professional managers, who invest the proceeds in a wide range of shares and other securities. The advantages are that: it is usually less risky than buying individual shares; it is very simple; you get professional management and there are no day-to-day decisions to make. Additionally, every trust is required by law to have a trustee to protect investors' interests.

The minimum investment in some of the more popular trusts is £500; in others, it can be as high as £10,000. Some trusts allow you to purchase units for smaller amounts on a regular monthly plan.

There is a front-end fee of around 5 to 6 per cent to join the trust and there is also an annual management charge.

Investors' contributions to the trust are divided into units, and proportionate to the amount they have invested, all unit holders receive an income distribution – normally paid every six months – or can choose to have their income reinvested.

As with ordinary shares, you can sell all or some of your investment by telling the unit trust managers that you wish to do so. The price you will receive is called 'the bid price'. This is published daily, in respect of all the main unit trusts, in the financial pages of the quality newspapers.

How to obtain. Units are purchased from the management companies, which can be: banks, insurance companies, stockbrokers, financial intermediaries or specialist unit trust management groups. Some advertise direct in the national newspapers and financial magazines. Some use salesmen or financial intermediaries. The bigger groups tend to use all these techniques.

For a complete list of unit trusts, you can look in the *Financial Times*. Or alternatively, write to the **Unit Trust Association**, 65 Kingsway,

Retirement Made Easy

London WC2B 6TD. T:071-831 0898. (Enclose A4 sized sae.) The Association publishes several free items of information. These include two booklets, *Details of Unit Trusts* and *Unit Trust PEPs*, and a quarterly performance report on the median funds in each UTA performance sector.

Tax. Identical to ordinary shares (see next section).

Assessment. An ideal method for smaller investors to buy stocks and shares: both less risky and easier.

Complaints. Complaints about unit trust groups are handled by the Insurance Ombudsman. He has power to make awards up to £100,000 and, other than actuarial issues which are outside his scope, he should be able to advise and adjudicate on most matters, including for example: delays to act on instructions, failure to disclose the proper amount of commission and misleading advertising.

The Ombudsman can only intervene where a member company is involved and only after a complaint has first been taken up with the company concerned direct. For further information, contact: **The Insurance Ombudsman Bureau**, City Gate One, 135 Park Street, London SE1 9EA. T:071-928 7600.

If you have a complaint about a unit trust group which is not a member of the Ombudsman scheme, you should take up the case with LAUTRO (Centre Point, 103 New Oxford Street, London WC1A 1QH) if your complaint is about a group's marketing or selling techniques; or with IMRO (Broadwalk House, 5 Appold Street, London EC2A 2LL) if your complaint is connected with an investment management matter.

Ordinary shares listed on the Stock Exchange

Definition. Public companies issue shares as a method of raising money. When you buy shares and become a shareholder in a company, you own a small part of the business and are entitled to participate in its profits through a dividend which is normally paid six monthly.

Dividends go up and down according to how well the company is doing and it is possible that in a bad year no dividends at all will be paid. However, in good years, dividends can increase very substantially.

The money you invest is unsecured. This means that, quite apart from any dividends, your capital could be slashed in value – or if the company goes bankrupt, you could lose the lot. Against this, if the company performs well you could enormously increase your wealth.

You can buy shares via a stockbroker. Alternatively, you can go to the securities department of your bank – or to one of the new share shops being opened by some of the banks – who will place the order for you. Either way, you will be charged both commission and stamp duty which is 0.5 per cent (until stamp duty is abolished some time in 1993 or 1994).

Until then, however, when you buy shares, the company issues you with a share certificate which you or your adviser must keep, as you will have to produce it when you wish to sell all or part of your holding.

Investment trusts are companies just like ICI and Shell but, instead of making products to sell, they invest in the shares of other companies, providing a spread of risk. You can buy investment trusts through saving and investment schemes (monthly, lump sum or dividend reinvestment) which are simple, cheap, and with a choice of over 120 different trusts.

One important group of trusts is known as split capital trusts, which separate capital growth and income growth. These can be mixed and matched to meet your needs during retirement and are well worth investigating.

For a free information pack and a list of advisers who specialise in these trusts, write to **The Association of Investment Trust Companies**, Park House (6th Floor), 16 Finsbury Circus, London EC2M 7JJ.

Personal equity plan (PEP)

Anyone over the age of 18 can invest up to £6,000 a year in UK or EC shares listed on the Stock Exchange or on the Unlisted Securities Market or on a recognised stock exchange of any member state of the EC.

If you like, you can invest all the money in a unit or investment trust, provided that 50 per cent of the holdings of such trusts are in UK/EC equities. In trusts, where the holdings are below 50 per cent, the amount you can invest is limited to £1,500.

Alternatively, if you own shares in your company's 'all employee share scheme', you can transfer your holding to a PEP with all its tax advantages, provided this is within three months of your receiving the shares.

Since 1992, an additional £3,000 per annum can be invested in the shares of a single company, bringing your total maximum allowed PEP investment to £9,000 a year.

The money has to be invested through an authorised manager, for example: a stockbroker, bank, building society or financial intermediary.

Tax. PEPs are free of both income tax and capital gains tax. The normal 25 per cent tax on dividends will be claimed back on your behalf by the plan manager. Capital gains tax losses incurred on other investments cannot, however, be offset against PEP profits.

Assessment. Shares can go down as well as up. Also, some PEP managers charge pretty hefty fees. That said, a PEP looks like a good investment for almost everyone. Specially advantageous to higher rate taxpayers or those liable for capital gains tax.

Long-term lock-ups

Certain types of investment, mostly offered by insurance companies, provide fairly high guaranteed growth in exchange for your undertaking to leave a lump sum with them or to pay regular premiums for a fixed period, probably 10 years. The list includes: life assurance policies, investment bonds and some types of National Savings certificates.

Life assurance policies
Definition. Life assurance can provide you with one of two main benefits: it can either provide your successors with money when you die and/or it can be used as a savings plan to provide you with a lump sum (or income) on a fixed date.

There are three basic types of life assurance: whole life policies, term policies and endowment policies.

Whole life policies are designed to pay out on your death. In its most straightforward form, the scheme works as follows: you pay a premium every year and, when you die, your beneficiaries receive the money.

As with an ordinary household policy, the insurance only holds good if you continue the payments. If one year you did not pay and were to die, the policy could be void and your successors would receive nothing.

Term policies involve a definite commitment. As opposed to paying premiums every year, you elect to make regular payments for an agreed period: for example, until such time as your children have completed their education, say eight years.

If you die during this period, your family will be paid the agreed sum in full. If you die after the end of the term (when you have stopped making payments), your family will normally receive nothing.

Most policies, whether term or otherwise, pay the money in lump sum form. Under term assurance, it is possible, however, to arrange for the benefit to be paid out as regular income. This is known as *family income benefit*. The income payments will cease at the end of the insured term.

There is a fairly widespread view that term and whole life policies, while eminently sensible for people in their thirties or forties, are not really suitable for older people, since: on the one hand death is at some stage

Investment

inevitable; while on the other, when children grow up, there is less requirement to provide for their security.

Additionally, many people argue that when income is tight, as it often is on retirement, this is one expense that can cheerfully be dropped. While generally true, the thinking could nevertheless prove short-sighted. A major problem for many widows is that, when their husband dies, part of his pension dies with him – leaving them with a significantly reduced income. A lump sum or regular income plan could make all the difference in helping to bridge the gap. Alternatively – and for many this is a more attractive option – whole life or term can be converted into an endowment policy.

Endowment policies are essentially a savings plan. You sign a contract to pay regular premiums over a number of years and in exchange receive a lump sum on a specific date.

Most endowment policies are written for periods varying from 10 to 25 years. Once you have committed yourself, you have to go on paying every year (as with term assurance). There are heavy penalties if, after having paid for a number of years, you decide that you no longer wish to continue. According to the terms of the policy, you may receive a token lump sum based on the premiums you have paid; or you may receive nothing at all. This is especially likely to apply if you withdraw during the early years. (However, see heading 'Alternatives to surrendering a policy' on page 89)

An important feature of endowment policies is that they are linked in with death cover. If you die before the policy matures, the remaining payments are excused and your successors will be paid a lump sum on your death.

Endowment policies are a very popular way of making extra financial provision for retirement. They combine the advantages of guaranteeing you a lump sum, with a built-in life assurance proviso.

Options. Both whole life policies and endowment policies offer two basic options: with profits or without profits. Very briefly the difference is as follows:

Without profits. This is sometimes known as 'guaranteed sum assured'. What it means is that the insurance company guarantees you a specific fixed sum (provided of course you meet the various terms and conditions). You know the amount in advance and this is the sum you – or your successors – will be paid.

With profits. You are paid a guaranteed fixed sum plus an addition, based on the profits that the insurance company has made, by investing your annual or monthly payments. The basic premiums are higher and, by definition, the profits element is not known in advance. If the insurance company has invested your money wisely, a 'with profits' policy provides a useful hedge against inflation. If its investment policy is mediocre, you could have paid higher premiums for very little extra return.

Unit linked. This is a refinement of the 'with profits' policy, in that the investment element of the policy is linked in with a unit trust.

Other basics. Premiums can normally be paid monthly or annually, as you prefer.

Size of premium varies enormously, depending on the type of policy you choose and the amount of cover you want. Also, of course, some insurance companies are more competitive than others. As very general guidance, £35–£40 a month would probably be a normal starting figure. Again as a generalisation, higher premiums tend to give better value as relatively less of your contribution is swallowed up in administrative costs.

Most policies require you to fill in and sign a declaration of health. It is very important that this should be honestly completed: if you make a claim on your policy and it is subsequently discovered that you gave misleading information, your policy could be declared void and the insurance company could refuse to pay.

How to obtain. Policies are usually available through banks, insurance companies, financial intermediaries and building societies. The biggest problem for most people is the sheer volume of choice. Another difficulty can be understanding the small print: terms and conditions which sound very similar may obscure important differences which could affect your benefit.

An accountant could advise you in general terms, whether you are being offered a good deal or otherwise. However, if it is a question of choosing a specific policy best suited to your requirements, it is usually advisable to consult an insurance broker. For help in contacting a broker in your area, write to: **British Insurance and Investment Brokers' Association**, BIIBA House, 14 Bevis Marks, London EC3A 7NT. See also Chapter 6, Financial Advisers.

As general wisdom, before buying a policy it is sensible to check whether the person selling it to you is an independent adviser, or a tied agent who is restricted to selling his/her company's (or institution's) own products. You need not feel the slightest bit embarrassed to ask the individual concerned since this is a question that most people dealing in financial services expect and are happy to answer (as well as being required to do so by law).

Investment

The **Association of British Insurers** (ABI) has a number of useful booklets on life assurance. Contact ABI, 51 Gresham Street, London EC2V 7HQ. T:071-600 3333.

Tax. Under current legislation, the proceeds of a qualifying policy – whether taken as a lump sum or in regular income payments (as in the case of family income benefit) – are free of all tax.

Assessment. Life assurance is normally a sensible investment, whether the aim is to provide death cover or the benefits of a lump sum to boost your retirement income. It has the merit of being very attractive from a tax angle and additionally certain policies provide good capital appreciation. However, you are locked into a long term commitment. So, even more than most areas, choosing the right policy is very important. Shop around, take advice and, above all, do not sign anything unless you are absolutely certain that you understand every last dot and comma.

Alternatives to surrendering a policy

As already mentioned, there are heavy penalties if you surrender an endowment policy before its maturity. Some people, however, either because they can no longer afford the payments or for some other reason, wish to terminate the agreement – regardless of any losses they may make/or investment gains they sacrifice.

Instead of simply surrendering the policy to the insurance company, people in this situation have two alternative options, both of which stand to yield them a higher return than surrender. The one is to sell the policy by auction; the other to sell it outright.

Probably the best known specialist auctioneer in this field is H E Foster & Cranfield. They hold monthly auctions in London and suggest to clients a reserve price, which by definition would be higher than the surrender value – otherwise they would not accept it on their books. They charge a £50 registration fee plus commission, which is a third of the excess (they make at auction) above the surrender value quoted. While auctioneers can never guarantee a sale, auctioning a policy is a very low risk gamble, since if the policy fails to reach its reserve it can still be surrendered in the normal way. Furthermore, if the policy does not sell at auction, the £50 registration fee would not be payable. For further information, contact: **H E Foster & Cranfield**, 20 Britton Street, London EC1M 5NQ. T:071-608 1941.

If, rather than auction a policy, you prefer to sell it outright, Beale Dobie & Co. Ltd. may be able to help you. They deal in all endowment with-profits life policies (not unit linked) and say that to be of interest to them the policy: must have run at least a quarter of its life; have a maximum of 15 years to run before maturity; and must be with a leading life office. Provided these conditions are met, they will make an immediate cash offer which, if accepted by the vendor, would be paid in the same time-scale as surrender. As with Foster & Cranfield, they would not make an offer unless that offer exceeded the surrender value. For further information, contact: **Beale Dobie & Co Ltd.**, 3 The Friars, Friars Lane, Maldon, Essex CM9 6AG. T:0621 851133.

Investment bonds

Definition. This is the method of investing a lump sum with an insurance company, in the hope of receiving a much larger sum back at a specific date – normally a few years later. There are no guarantees, however, and while bonds can achieve significant capital appreciation, you could also lose a lot of money.

All bonds offer life assurance cover as part of the deal. Also, all bond proceeds are free of both basic rate tax and capital gains tax on redemption.

Companies normally charge a front end fee of around 5 per cent plus a small annual management fee, usually not related to performance.

Some financial institutions – banks, unit trusts, and others – offer investment bonds through their insurance subsidiaries. Accordingly, almost any type of financial adviser will have some knowledge of this area.

Tax. Tax treatment is very complicated, as it is influenced by your marginal income tax rate in the year of encashment. For this reason, it is generally best to buy a bond when you are working and plan to cash it after retirement.

Assessment. This investment is more likely to be attractive to the sophisticated investor, with high earnings in the years before retirement.

Investor protection

Over the past few years, we have heard a great deal about investor protection. Since the Financial Services Act there is now a set of stringent rules on businesses offering investment services and also a powerful watchdog body, namely the Securities and Investments Board (SIB). Additionally, there are a number of Self-Regulating Organisations (SROs) and Recognised Professional Bodies (RPBs), charged with the responsibility of regulating businesses that are 'fit and proper' to operate in the investment field and of monitoring their activities via 'spot checks' and other means.

The main effects of these changes are as follows:

- Investment businesses (including individuals such as accountants or solicitors giving investment advice) are not at liberty to operate without authorisation from their appropriate SRO or RPB, or from the SIB direct. Operating without such authorisation is a criminal offence.
- Businesses may either promote their own in-house investment plans (unit trusts, insurance policies and so on) *or* they must act as independent consultants and have no vested interest in any product they may recommend. The dual intention is: to enable customers to know the status of an adviser, i.e. whether he/she is: a company sales representative, a tied agent or an independent consultant; and also to ensure that those who call themselves independent consultants, or intermediaries, can legitimately offer 'best advice' by virtue of being free of commercial bias.
- Investment businesses must adhere to a proper complaints procedure with provision for customers to receive fair compensation, where appropriate.
- Unsolicited visits and telephone calls to sell investments are for the most part banned. Where these are allowed, (as in the case of unit trusts, life assurance and certain other package products), should a sale result, the customer will have a 14-day 'cooling-off period'. The cooling-off period is to give the customer time to explore other options before deciding whether to cancel the contract or not.
- There is also provision for disclosure of the following information to purchasers of life assurance products: an independent intermediary's commission, expressed as a percentage of premium; and the company's costs and expenses, expressed as a reduction in yield, to enable investors to make inter-company comparisons.

    Further changes are in the pipeline which are expected during early 1993. These should bring unit trusts within the same regulatory regime and result in certain 'key facts' being provided to investors, including: information on the penalties of early surrender, easier identification of intermediary status and the provision of a 'reason why' letter explaining the rationale on which recommendations are based.
- All intermediaries must give clients a copy of a *Buyer's Guide*, prepared by their regulatory body. The *Guide* gives the status of the intermediary, says what the buyer's rights are and what subsequent information the client should receive.

In practice, most members of the public are unlikely to require recourse to one of the regulatory organisations since, as already stated, it is the job of SROs and RPBs to authorise membership of any investment business within their appropriate sector and to establish monitoring procedures to check that the investor protection rules are being properly followed. In turn, SROs and RPBs are answerable to the Securities and Investments Board, which itself is directly accountable to the Chancellor of the Exchequer. If you need to contact SIB, the address to write to is: **Securities and Investments Board (SIB)**, Gavrelle House, 2-14 Bunhill Row, London EC1Y 8RA. T:071-638 1240.

Complaints
If you have a complaint against an authorised firm, you should in the first instance take it up with the firm concerned: you may be able to resolve the matter at this level, since all authorised firms are obliged to have a complaints procedure. If, however, you do not receive satisfaction, you can take your complaint to the regulatory body which has authorised the company. (This will be stated on the company literature.) Should you still not be satisfied, you can approach the relevant ombudsman or referee who will investigate the matter on your behalf and may even be able to get compensation for you.

Warning
Although the new investor protection legislation should improve standards and help to rid the financial services industry of cowboy operators, as the Securities and Investments Board writes in its published guide: 'All investment carries some degree of risk, whether relating to business or general economic conditions. The existence of SIB no more removes the need for investors to pay attention to where they place their money than the existence of the highway code removes the need to look before crossing the road.'

The existence of SIB and the setting up of the various SROs and RPBs does at least, however, enable you to check on the credentials of anyone purporting to be a financial adviser or trying to persuade you to invest your money in an insurance policy, bond, unit or investment trust, equity, futures contract or similar. If either they or the organisation they represent are not authorised by a relevant SRO, RPB or by SIB, you are very strongly recommended to leave well alone.

Useful reading
Self Defence for Investors; Investment Businesses: What to Do if You Need to Complain; How to Spot the Investment Cowboys and The Investors'

Compensation Scheme; these are all available free from the Securities and Investments Board (SIB).

Chapter 6

Financial Advisers

If there is one golden rule when it comes to money matters, it must be: when in doubt, ask. This applies as much if it is a term with which you are unfamiliar or whether you are wondering how best to invest your savings.

When thinking ahead to retirement planning, it is especially important to get as much advice as possible. Nearly everyone has a certain amount of leeway in budgeting for the future and the difference between an unwise choice and a sensible one could significantly affect your standard of living.

While a great deal of unnecessary mystique seems to pervade the financial services sector, questions to do with money are often genuinely more complex than they at first appear.

There may be important tax angles to consider. Phrases commonly used in conversation may, when written into a formal document, have legal implications of which you are unaware. The jargon is apt to be confusing: for example, the term 'bond' has a variety of different meanings. Another problem is the volume of propaganda. There are plenty of enticing advertisements seeming to offer the moon which, if you were to take them at face value without being totally sure that you understand the commitment, could prove a sorry mistake.

Moreover, whereas most professional advisers are extremely sound, not everyone who proffers advice is qualified to do so. Before parting with your money, it is essential to ensure that you are dealing with a registered member of a recognised institution. For information, see also 'Investor protection', pages 90-93.

Even if you have never done so before, there is no cause to feel hesitant about approaching financial advisers. Nor should you feel that because you have asked for advice, you are morally obliged to use a particular individual's services. Indeed, when it comes to investment decisions, you are strongly recommended to shop around in order to compare the many different options on offer.

As someone who may shortly be retiring, you are seen as a very attractive potential client especially if you are a member of a pension scheme with a sizeable commuted lump sum to invest.

However, before making contact, it is generally a good idea to try to sort out your priorities, for example: whether you are looking for capital growth or whether your main objective is to increase your income. Also, if you have any special plans such as helping your grandchildren or if you need several thousand pounds to improve your home, these too should be thought through in advance as they could affect the advice you receive.

A further reason for doing some advance thinking is that, whereas certain types of advisers – for example, insurance brokers – do not specifically charge you for their time, others such as accountants and solicitors charge fees by the hour. Drinking coffee in their office and musing aloud about the future delights of retirement may be a pleasant way of spending the afternoon but it can also work out to be pretty costly!

Choosing an adviser

When choosing an adviser, there are usually four main considerations: respectability, suitability, price and convenience.

Where your money is concerned, you cannot afford to take unnecessary risks. Merely establishing that an individual is a member of a recognised institution, while a basic safeguard, is insufficient recommendation if you want to be assured of dealing with someone who will personally suit you. The principle applies as much with friends, as with complete strangers.

If you are thinking of using a particular adviser whom you do not already know in a *professional* capacity, you should certainly check on their reputation and, ideally, talk to some of their existing clients. No one who is any good will object to your asking for references.

However, quite apart from their general competence, enlisting professional help is very much a question of 'horses for courses'. Just as you would hardly consult a divorce lawyer if you were planning to buy a house, so too in the financial field most practitioners have different areas of expertise. It is, therefore, important to establish that your adviser has the particular capability you require.

This issue is less of a consideration if you choose a sizeable firm, with at least four or five partners, since the likelihood is that between them they will be able to offer a mix of skills. But it can be a problem with the one or two-man band who, though outstanding generalists, may lack the specialist knowledge if you require sophisticated advice in, say, tax planning or investment strategy.

Although some people enjoy bobbing up to London to consult their solicitor, or whoever, generally speaking it makes more sense to choose a firm that is reasonably accessible.

If you live in a part of the country where the choice of financial advisers is limited, you can approach one of the organisations listed on the following pages that maintain a register of members – or alternatively, you could ask your bank manager to recommend someone suitable.

Finally, you should be aware that some specialist advisers are in the business of selling; or at least stand to gain some financial advantage from persuading you that the investments they market are best for you. In some cases, the commissions are publicly known. In others, they tend to be disguised. Also some brokers and dealers are tied agents for a specific company, so under the Financial Services Act regulations can only promote their own in-house products. To know where you stand, you should ask any agent whom he represents and if it is a single company or group, however excellent the prospect sounds, you should aim to investigate at least two or three other propositions before signing on the dotted line.

Accountants

Accountants are specialists in matters concerning taxation. If there is scope to do so, they can advise on ways of reducing your tax liability and can assess the various tax effects of different types of investment you may be considering. Likewise, they can help you with charitable covenants, the preparation of tax returns and if you are thinking of becoming self-employed or starting your own business, they will be able to assist you with some of the practicalities – such as registering for VAT and establishing a system of business accounts.

Additionally, they may be able to advise in a general way about pensions and your proposed investment strategy. Most accountants, however, do not claim to be experts in these fields and may refer their clients to stockbrokers or other advisers for these more specialised services.

If you need help in locating a suitable accountant, any of the following should be able to assist:

Institute of Chartered Accountants in England and Wales, PO Box 433, Chartered Accountants' Hall, Moorgate Place, London EC2P 2BJ.

Financial Advisers

Institute of Chartered Accountants of Scotland, 27 Queen Street, Edinburgh EH2 1LA.
Institute of Chartered Accountants in Ireland, 11 Donegall Square South, Belfast BT1 5JE. (This covers accountants in both Northern Ireland and the Republic.)
Chartered Association of Certified Accountants, 29 Lincoln's Inn Fields, London WC2A 3EE.

Complaints. Anyone with a complaint against an accountant can write to the Secretary of the Institute's Investigating Committee who, if the complaint is valid, will refer the matter to the Disciplinary Committee.

Banks

Most people need no introduction to the clearing banks since, if they have a bank account, they have probably been popping in and out of their local branch for years.

Yet despite the fact that the counter is usually well decorated with leaflets – and additionally some are apt to come in the post – many customers do not actually realise what a fully comprehensive service their bank can offer.

In addition to the normal account facilities, all the major high street banks offer (either direct or through one of their specialised subsidiaries) investment, insurance and tax planning services, as well as advice on drawing up a will, together with a host of special arrangements for small businesses.

Brief information follows on the main clearing banks but there also are other more specialised banks such as Williams and Glynn, Coutts, Hoares and overseas banks that are all part of the UK clearing system and can offer a very good service. The addresses given are those of the head office.

Barclays Bank Plc, PO Box 120, Longwood Close, Westwood Business Park, Coventry CV4 8JN. Barclays offers free banking to personal current account customers. The Barclays Bank Account, makes no charge for normal transactions whether the account is in credit or overdrawn. In addition to a range of accounts to suit a variety of personal savings requirements, financial planning services are available to customers and the public through various subsidiary companies. Included in these services are personal investment advice, investment management, unit trusts, life assurance, pensions, personal taxation, wills and trusts. You can either write to the above address, or apply through your local branch of Barclays Bank.

Lloyds Bank Plc, 71 Lombard Street, London EC3P 3BS. The Lloyds Bank Classic account offers all the facilities traditionally associated with a current account plus interest on credit balances. Classic account holders can apply for a personal overdraft. Once agreed, the first £100 is completely free – with no interest and no service charges.

For those with an income of £20,000 or more, Lloyds Bank Gold Service offers tiered credit interest at competitive rates. There is also a £250 cheque guarantee facility, plus an overdraft facility if required.

Lloyds Private Banking Ltd., Capital House, 1-5 Perrymount Road, Haywards Heath, West Sussex RH16 3SP offers a personalised service and provides independent advice on the whole spectrum of investments including assistance with taxation, wills and estate planning.

The Asset Management Service offers many features, including an investment management service and a 'Cash Sweep' facility, whereby any excess cash in your current account is automatically transferred into a high interest-earning account.

There is the Unit Trust Management Service and also the Lloyds Bank Personal Equity Plan Centre which provides clients with the opportunity of investing in leading British companies. A proportion of the investment can also be directed into unit trusts managed by Lloyds Bank Unit Trust Managers Ltd.

Lloyds Bank Insurance Services Ltd., again accommodated at Haywards Heath, offers independent advice on general insurance matters.

Midland Financial Services (Division of Midland Bank plc), Poultry, London EC2P 2BX. Offers a range of stockbroking and personal financial services which can be tailored to individual requirements.

Midland Personal Financial Services provides customers with a comprehensive choice of financial products including unit trusts, PEPs and life assurance, which are selected according to a customer's requirements by a personal financial consultant.

Midland Personal Asset Management offers a discretionary Investment Management and Estate Planning Service to clients who prefer to have a local specialist to look after their affairs on a regular basis. Clients would typically have over £100,000 to invest. The Estate Planning Service includes preparation of a will, drawing up trusts and administering customers' estates.

Midland Stockbrokers offers a share dealing and advisory service to those customers who prefer to manage their own portfolios.

Any Midland branch can arrange a meeting if you would like to discuss these services.

Financial Advisers

National Westminster Bank Plc, 41 Lothbury, London EC2P 2BP. National Westminster offers free banking to personal customers. No transaction charges are payable, even if overdrawn.

National Westminster Bank's Financial and Investment Services Department offers services to clients on a fee paying basis. You can apply at any branch of the bank or write to: Freepost, (KE 2355/2), PO Box 394, Bristol BS99 7XZ. The services include: advice on drawing up a will and the administration of an estate, an investment management service which will devise an individual investment policy for you and a personal taxation service.

National Westminster Bank offers advice on all types of insurance including life assurance and pensions. For further information, contact your local NatWest branch.

Royal Bank Of Scotland, 42 St Andrew Square, Edinburgh EH2 2YE. The Royal Bank of Scotland offers free banking for customers whose current account is in credit. There is an interest-paying current account, a high interest cheque account called the Premium Account and a high interest Gold Deposit Account.

The Bank's Trustee Division offers free advice in making a will, although the usual legal fees are applicable if you proceed. This is available to customers and non-customers and you should write to The Royal Bank of Scotland, Freepost, PO Box 31, Edinburgh EH2 OBG. You can also write to this address or approach your local branch manager for a personal tax service. The service, again available to customers and non-customers, is charged according to the complexity of the work involved.

The Royal Bank of Scotland offers investment management services through Capital House Investment Management Limited and Royal Scottish Assurance; information can be obtained from any branch of the Bank.

New high street banks

As a result of a recent change in the law, building societies have been given the choice to become plcs and to offer the same services as the high street banks. To date, the only one to do so is Abbey National.

Abbey National Plc., 215-229 Baker Street, London NW1 6XL. Abbey National offers a range of savings, mortgage and insurance products, cheque account facilities and loans for such items as home improvements, a car or money to finance a holiday.

Abbey National provides two cheque accounts: a current account which is interest bearing, with no charges, and can be opened with £1;

and a high interest cheque account which has tiered interest rates, no charges and requires a minimum balance of £1,000.

There is also: an investment account, which is a passbook savings account that can be opened with £500 and that either pays interest annually or according to a monthly plan; a tiered-rate instant saver account that can be opened with £1 (interest paid annually); and a high yield bond at £10,000+ (tiered rates of interest).

Additionally, Abbey National Financial Services (at Prestwood House, Corporation Street, High Wycombe, Bucks HP13 6PQ) offers independent financial planning for those nearing retirement or facing redundancy.

Complaints. The Banking Ombudsman acts as an independent arbiter, who aims to resolve complaints by individuals about banking services from the 30 banks which come within his orbit. These include all the main high street banks in the UK. His decisions are binding on member banks and he is empowered to award compensation of up to £100,000.

Complaints can be handled on most aspects of personal banking, including bank credit cards and other matters normally transacted through bank branches, as well as maladministration or undue delays by banks dealing with wills and trusts. However, except where there has been maladministration, the Ombudsman's powers do not extend to commercial decisions by a bank on the grant of an overdraft or loan.

The address to write to is: **The Banking Ombudsman**, Citadel House, 5-11 Fetter Lane, London EC4A 1BR. T:071-583 1395.

Insurance brokers

The insurance business covers a very wide range from straightforward policies – such as motor or household insurance – to the rather more complex areas, including life assurance and pensions. Quite apart from the confusion of the enormous choice of policies available and the importance of ensuring that you understand the conditions laid down in the small print, a further difficulty is the number of different categories of people – agents, salesmen, consultants, brokers – who may try to sell you insurance.

Unless you are already dealing with an insurance company whose advice you value, as a general rule you would be advised to consult an insurance broker. A broker should be able to help you choose the policies that are best suited to you, help you determine how much cover you require and explain any technical terms contained in the documents. He can also assist with any claims and advise you when renewals are necessary. An essential point to check before proceeding is that the firm the broker represents is registered with the Insurance Brokers Registration Council, which operates a code of conduct.

Although a condition of registration is that a broker must deal with a multiplicity of insurers and therefore be in a position to offer a comprehensive choice of policies, most companies pay insurance brokers on a commission basis; so, despite the code of conduct which emphasises that the customer's interest is paramount, it is possible that you could be offered advice that is not totally unbiased. If you are worried about this, you are perfectly entitled to ask a broker how much commission he is receiving. Generally speaking, you are safer to use a larger brokerage with an established reputation. Also, before you take out a policy, it is advisable to consult several brokers in order to get a better feel for the market.

The British Insurance and Investment Brokers Association, which represents over 3,000 insurance broking businesses, can put you in touch with a member broker in your area.

However, while commission is still the norm, over the past two or three years a small but growing number of financial advisers have switched from commission to offering a fee-based service, rather in the manner of an accountant or solicitor. This means, of course, that clients are charged an up-front fee. But against this, they are not forfeiting the often very much larger sum – deducted from their investment that the broker would have received. Because of the way some insurance companies operate, fee-charging brokers may still receive the commission in the first instance but will then – depending on the client's preference – either rebate it back to them in cash or (and this could be more sensible) re-invest it on their behalf in the product.

Until recently, the big difficulty for someone wanting to consult a fee-charging adviser was discovering those who actually offered such a service. However, the search should now be very much easier thanks to the Fee-Based Adviser Register, compiled by Money Management. Anyone wanting a list of names should write to the Register, enclosing an sae, and will receive back (free of charge) details of at least six local advisers for them to investigate.

The address is: **Money Management Fee-Based Adviser Register**, Financial Times Business Information, Greystoke Place, Fetter Lane, London EC4A 1ND. T:071-405 6969.

Complaints. If you have a complaint against a broker you should contact the UK technical officer at BIIBA, who runs a conciliation service. Write to: **British Insurance and Investment Brokers Association**, BIIBA House, 14 Bevis Marks, London EC3A 7NT. T:071-623 9043.

Another organisation that you could contact in the event of a complaint against a registered insurance broker is the Insurance Brokers Registration Council. You should write to the Registrar at: **Insurance Brokers Registration Council**, 15 St. Helen's Place, London EC3A 6DS. T:071-588 4387.

Also useful to know about is the Association of British Insurers. It represents over 450 companies (as opposed to Lloyd's syndicates or brokers), providing all types of insurance from life assurance and pensions to household, motor and other forms of general insurance. About 90 per cent of the worldwide business done by British insurance companies is handled by members of ABI.

The Association publishes a wide range of leaflets and booklets and will, if you are in dispute with one of its member companies, ensure that your complaint is dealt with at top level. There are also regional offices in: Belfast, Birmingham, Bristol, Glasgow, Leeds, Manchester, Newcastle upon Tyne, Norwich and Southampton. The head office is at: **Association of British Insurers (ABI)**, 51 Gresham Street, London EC2V 7HQ. T:071-600 3333.

Finally, there is the Insurance Ombudsman. The Ombudsman and his Council are paid for by the insurance and unit trust management companies in the scheme – over 330 belong – but maintain complete independence in all negotiations. As with the ABI, the Ombudsman can only try to settle a dispute if the company in question is within the scheme. You can find this out from: your insurance or unit trust company, your insurance broker, financial adviser, from a Citizens' Advice Bureau – or from the Insurance Ombudsman Bureau.

You can only contact the Ombudsman after you have attempted to resolve the difficulty, at the highest level, with the company itself.

The Ombudsman exists to help private policy holders or investors only and cannot take up the cudgels on behalf of commercial organisations, however small. The policy must have been written or the investment made in the United Kingdom, Isle of Man or Channel Islands. Also, the Ombudsman is powerless to act if legal proceedings have been started.

The Ombudsman has power to make awards up to £100,000 and while he can advise, adjudicate or arbitrate on most issues, some matters are outside his scope. The Ombudsman cannot assist with third party claims and with certain types of dispute concerning life assurance (for example, actuarial decisions).

You must contact the Ombudsman within six months of the insurance company's final decision on the dispute, giving the details as briefly as possible. Currently, there is no charge for the service. You may accept or reject the Ombudsman's decision. If you reject it, your right to take legal action is not affected. If you want help from the Ombudsman, you should

Financial Advisers

contact: **The Insurance Ombudsman Bureau**, City Gate One, 135 Park Street, London SE1 9EA. T:071-928 7600.

Another possible source of help is the Personal Insurance Arbitration Service which, although it cannot advise on the merits of a claim, will appoint an arbitrator to determine the matter. There is a limit on the maximum amount of awards (up to £50,000 depending on the insurer concerned). Arbitration is free of charge but the parties pay their own costs of preparing and submitting their cases. The company concerned must be a subscriber to the service. Most major insurance companies are members of PIAS or the Ombudsman scheme (see above). Write to: **Personal Insurance Arbitration Service**, Chartered Institute of Arbitrators, International Arbitration Centre, 24 Angel Gate, City Road, London EC1V 2RS. T:071-837 4483.

Other pension advisers

If you have a query to do with your pension, there are other organisations – or professional advisers – who may be able to assist.

Individuals in paid employment

If you are (or have been) in salaried employment and are a member of an occupational pension scheme, the normal person to ask is your company's personnel manager or pensions adviser – or via them, the pension fund trustees.

Alternatively, if you have a problem with your pension you could approach your union, since this is an area where most unions are particularly active and well informed.

If you are in need of specific help, a source to try could be the Occupational Pensions Advisory Service. It has a network of 360 volunteer advisers who can be contacted through Citizens' Advice Bureaux. OPAS is an independent voluntary organisation that offers help and advice on all matters concerning pension schemes (except state pensions). The service is available to anyone: scheme members, those with deferred pensions, existing pensioners and dependants. Contact: **Occupational Pensions Advisory Service (OPAS)**, 11 Belgrave Road, London SW1V 1RB. T:071-233 8080.

As part of a package of recent consumer protection measures, a Pensions Ombudsman has been appointed. You would normally only approach the Ombudsman if neither the pension scheme trustees nor OPAS are able to solve your problem.

Also, as with all ombudsmen, he can only investigate matters that come within his orbit. These are: (1) complaints of injustice caused by maladministration by the trustees or managers of an occupational or personal pension scheme; (2) disputes of fact or law with the trustees or managers. He cannot, however, investigate a complaint that is already subject to court proceedings; one that is about a State social security benefit; or a dispute that is more appropriate for investigation by another regulatory body.

As OPAS is in the same building, they will gladly refer you to the Ombudsman, where appropriate. Or you can write direct to: **The Pensions Ombudsman**, 11 Belgrave Road, London SW1V 1RB. T:071-834 9144.

Another source of help is the pensions registry and tracing service, managed by the Occupational Pensions Board, which assists individuals in need of help to trace their pension rights. Like the Ombudsman, there is no charge for the service. For further information, write to: **Registrar of Pension Schemes**, Occupational Pensions Board, PO Box 1NN, Newcastle upon Tyne NE99 1NN.

Self-employed or running a company

If you are self-employed and want to make pension arrangements, you would probably approach an insurance broker; or possibly your bank, a building society, unit trust or friendly society. However, in certain circumstances you might be better off to pay for the services of an authorised pension consultant.

The roles are fairly similar. In general, however, pension consultants would normally only be used by employers and by individuals with significant self-employment income.

There are two ways in which the services of a pension consultant are paid for: either in commission or in fees paid directly by the client to the consultant. The position as regards commission is that if advice given by the consultant results in money being invested in an institution, that institution will often pay a commission to the consultant, which may mean that there will be no direct charge to the individual. Fees need no explanation, as they are charged on broadly the same basis as any other professional fees. In order to know where you stand, it is a good idea to enquire from the outset how the consultant will expect to be paid – by you or in commission – and if a fee is involved, what this is likely to be.

Although apparently expensive, the best consultants are independent specialists who can give very valuable advice. Many of them will be members of the Society of Pension Consultants and must comply with its code of conduct.

If you contact the Society, it can supply you with a list of local members. Anyone with a complaint about a member consultant can write to the Secretary. For further information, contact: The Secretary, **Society of Pension Consultants**, Ludgate House, Ludgate Circus, London EC4A 2AB. T: 071-353 1688.

Solicitors

Solicitors are professional advisers on subjects to do with the law or on matters that could have legal implications. They can assist with: the purchase or rental of property; drawing up a will; if you are charged with a criminal offence; or if you are sued in a civil matter.

Additionally, their advice can be invaluable in vetting any important document before you sign it. A solicitor can also help with the legal formalities of setting up a business; trusts; guardianship arrangements or other agreement, where the intention is to make it binding. Likewise, a solicitor would normally be the first person to consult if you were thinking of suing an individual or commercial organisation.

If you do not have a solicitor (or if your solicitor does not have the knowledge to advise on, say, a business matter), often the best way of finding a suitable lawyer is through the recommendation of a friend or other professional adviser, such as an accountant or maybe your bank manager.

Another solution is to consult the *Solicitors' and Barristers' Directory and Diary*, available in public libraries and Citizens' Advice Bureaux, which lists the names and addresses of solicitors all over the country, together with brief details about the type of work in which they have experience.

If you want information about your rights, you could approach a Law Centre (sometimes known as a Neighbourhood or Community Law Centre). You can get the address by asking at your town hall or Citizens' Advice Bureau. Or you can write to or telephone the Law Centres Federation. The advice is free. If the matter concerns an area of law that is not dealt with by Law Centres (e.g., conveyancing, probate, divorce, commercial law), the Centre will be able to refer you to a solicitor. **Law Centres Federation**, Duchess House, 18-19 Warren Street, London W1P 5DB. T:071-387 8570.

Legal aid

If you need a legal aid solicitor (or want to find out if you are eligible for legal aid), the place to go is your Citizens' Advice Bureau.

Ask for leaflet *The Legal Aid Guide*, which will enable you to work out if you qualify for assistance. The financial limits are more generous than are generally supposed so it could be worth checking, even if you expect to be disappointed. If you are entitled to legal aid, your CAB will explain what is involved and will refer you to a legal aid solicitor. Instead of going through your CAB, if you prefer you can contact the **Legal Aid Board**, 6th Floor, 29-37 Red Lion Street, London WC1R 4PP. T:071-831 4209.

Also useful to know about is the *Solicitors Regional Directory* which, among other information, lists solicitors who do legal aid work. A copy should be available at most libraries and town halls.

Complaints

If you have a complaint against a solicitor, the Solicitors Complaints Bureau may be able to help you. It can investigate such complaints as: failure to reply to letters; delay in dealing with your case; overcharging (see below); wrongly retaining your papers; dishonesty and deception. It can also deal with complaints which allege 'inadequate professional service (IPS)', that is to say the carrying out of work by your solicitor to an unacceptably low standard, and is able to award compensation up to £1,000.

The Bureau cannot, however, give legal advice or tell a solicitor how to handle a case; nor can it investigate claims of professional negligence. The difference between inadequate professional service (IPS) and negligence is that IPS is substandard work, whereas negligence is a mistake by your solicitor which has lost you money or caused some other loss for which you may be entitled to compensation.

If you believe you have a complaint of negligence, the Bureau will normally be able to help you either by putting you in touch with a solicitor specialising in negligence claims or passing your complaint directly on to the Solicitors Indemnity Fund (where it will be dealt with like any other insurance claim). If the Bureau arranges an appointment for you with a Negligence Panellist, the panel solicitor will see you free of charge for up to an hour and advise you as to your best course of action.

If you believe that you have been *overcharged*, you should ask the Bureau to send you a copy of their leaflet *Complaints About Solicitors' Charges*, which explains the procedure for getting your bill checked, the various time limits involved and the circumstances in which you might be successful in getting the fee reduced.

You can either ring the Helpline on 071-834 8663 or 8664 or you can write requesting a copy of leaflet and helpform called *How and When*. The address to contact is: **The Solicitors Complaints Bureau**, Portland House, Stag Place, Victoria, London SW1E 5BL. T:071-834 2288.

If you are still not satisfied, you can approach the **Legal Services**

Financial Advisers

Ombudsman at 22 Oxford Court, Oxford Street, Manchester M2 3WQ. T:061-236 9532.

General queries. For queries of a more general nature, you should approach: **The Law Society**, 113 Chancery Lane, London WC2A 1PL. T:071-242 1222.

For those in Scotland and Northern Ireland. If you live in Scotland or Northern Ireland, the Solicitors Complaints Bureau will not be able to help you. Instead you should contact the Law Society at the relevant address, as follows:

The Law Society of Scotland, The Law Society's Hall, 26-28 Drumsheugh Gardens, Edinburgh EH3 7YR. T:031-226 7411.
The Law Society of Northern Ireland, Law Society House, 98 Victoria Street, Belfast BT1 3JZ. T:0232 231614.

GET MORE FROM YOUR RETIREMENT LUMP SUM

If you keep most of your money in a building society, falling interest rates will mean a drop in your standard of living. So the first priority is to maintain a high regular income.

Yet Government statistics show we are living longer than ever, so income also needs to rise to beat inflation.

Only a sensible mix of deposits and investments can deliver a rising income as well as security.

Unlike many other companies, we specialise only in retirement income planning.

And because we are independent we are free to choose the best investments from every possible source.

Send the coupon Freepost or call Freephone Knight Williams.

It'll cost you nothing to find out just how much more your lump sum could be earning for your retirement.

A MEMBER OF FIMBRA.

To Knight Williams & Company Ltd, FREEPOST 15 (WD699) London W1E 8YZ. Telephone: 071-408 1138.

Please send me details of your services to private clients.   GRG/93/GET

Name _____

Address _____

_____ Postcode _____

I am retired/plan to retire in _____ months

KNIGHT WILLIAMS
Britain's Largest Retirement Income Specialists.

HALCYON DAYS or HARD TIMES?

A happy and fulfilling retirement, as opposed to a bleak and uncertain future, is the result of careful and accurate financial planning.

Boyton Financial Services Limited (BFS) has developed a highly refined and comprehensive service that will quickly highlight potential shortfalls in your current arrangements.

And, BFS is one of the few independent firms of advisers that <u>only</u> operates on a time spent, fee charging basis.

It is never too late for you to seek our professional advice – we could make a considerable difference to your life style in the years ahead.

Telephone or write to:
BOYTON FINANCIAL SERVICES LIMITED, PO BOX 14, HALSTEAD, ESSEX, CO9 4DY.
TELEPHONE: 0787 61919

BOYTON FINANCIAL SERVICES LTD
Member of the Financial Intermediaries and Brokers Regulatory Association.

A HAPPY RETIREMENT FOR GARDENERS

Donations, deeds of covenant and legacies ensure nursing/residential accommodation, sheltered homes, benefit, grants and holidays.

Donations are urgently needed for expansion of the Society's work in Gloucestershire and Scotland.

THE GARDENERS' ROYAL BENEVOLENT SOCIETY
BRIDGE HOUSE, 139 KINGSTON ROAD,
LEATHERHEAD, SURREY KT22 7NT
TELEPHONE: 0372 373962

Children are the most vulnerable members of our society and sick or injured children are in the greatest need of our help and protection. Every year over one million children receive treatment in Britain's hospitals – more than half are under five years old. A further three million attend hospitals for accident and emergency treatment. Separation from family and friends and the disruption of their lives adds to their distress. Adults, however well prepared are apprehensive at the thought of a stay in hospital – to a small child the prospect and reality can be terrifying.

What we do Action for Sick Children was among the first organisations to recognise the problems and do something about them. In 30 years of pioneering work we have achieved some of our goals, including provision of overnight rooms for parents in some hospitals, more specifically children's wards and trained children's nurses. We talk to the Government, Health Authorities and policy makers. We provide a parent's helpline, special research and information on child health. We publish guidelines for health professionals and run conferences and seminars. We have the only centralised library in the UK on all aspects of children's welfare, medical and social care. We support over 50 branches who provide tremendous help to parents and children at a local level.

The future Our work will never be done. As long as there are sick children there will be problems for parents and professionals, both social and financial. We are entirely dependent on grants and voluntary contributions and we need your help. As an individual member you can play your part in ensuring that sick children and their families get the care and attention they deserve.

ACTION FOR SICK CHILDREN
Argyle House, 29-31 Euston Road, London NW1 2SD. Tel: 071-833 2041 Fax 071-837 2100
Chief Executive Leslie Marks BA(HONS) COSW

RETIREMENT SAVINGS
ARE YOU LOOKING FOR:

The opportunity for real growth... ☑

Balanced security.. ☑

A regular monthly cheque option... ☑

Immediate access to your money.. ☑

A bonus of up to 2.5%.. ☑

If your money is sitting in a bank, building society, or national savings account, it could be working harder. With the Personal Retirement Account, half of your investment goes into gilts or high interest building society accounts. The other half is invested by a leading City stockbroker mainly in the UK stockmarkets, giving you a perfect balance of security and the prospect of high growth. Your money isn't tied up either. You can make withdrawals at any time without delay or take a regular monthly cheque.

Taking more than the growth rate would reduce your capital over time.

Homeowners, a leading U.K. Friendly Society, currently manages over £510 million on behalf of 250,000 investors. Our objective is to beat the best building society rates.

Tax-free savings for children? Send or phone for details 0800 591139

The value of investments can fall as well as rise, and you may not recover the amount invested.

Minimum investment is £1000. Return the coupon now for full details of this hardworking, flexible investment including a bonus of up to 2.5%.

You'll be under no obligation whatsoever.

Cut the coupon now or phone or write to us quoting the reference below.

PHONE FREE 0800 591137 PHONE NOW

Please quote ref: RP1993RG   MEMBER OF LAUTRO

Send to: Homeowners Friendly Society, FREEPOST, Springfield Avenue, Harrogate, North Yorkshire HG1 5BR.

Mr/Miss/Mrs/Ms_____
BLOCK CAPITALS

Address_____

_____

Postcode_____ Tel. No._____ Date of Birth_____

HOMEOWNERS FRIENDLY SOCIETY

Chapter 7

Budget Planner

Whether you are about to retire tomorrow or not for several years, completing the following Budget Planner (even if there are a great many gaps) is well worth the effort.

If retirement is imminent, then hopefully doing the arithmetic in detail will not only reassure you but will enable you to plan your future life with the confidence of really knowing how you stand financially. Moreover, even at this stage, there is probably a variety of options available to you and just examining the figures you have written down will highlight the areas of greatest flexibility.

An imaginative tip, given to us by one of the retirement magazines, is to start living on your retirement income some six months before you retire. Not only will you see if your budget estimates are broadly correct but since most people err on the cautious side when they first retire, you will have the added bonus of all the extra money you will have saved.

If retirement is still some years ahead, there will be both more unknowns and more opportunities. When assessing the figures, you should take account of your future earnings; and perhaps more to the point, since your pension may well be based on it, what your final salary is likely to be. Also, though it may mean stinting a bit now, you should consider whether you should be paying additional voluntary contributions (AVCs) and/or making other investments.

Imprecise as they will be, the Budget Planner estimates you have made in the various income/expenditure columns should indicate whether, unless you take action now, you could be at risk of having to make serious adjustments in your standard of living.

To be on the safe side, you must assume some increase in inflation. Equally, everyone should budget for a nest egg, to pay for any emergencies or special events – perhaps a family wedding – that may come along.

Retirement Made Easy

1. Possible savings when you retire

Item	Estimated monthly savings
National insurance contributions	....
Pension payments	....
Travel expenses to work	....
Bought lunches	....
Incidentals at work, e.g. drinks with colleagues, collections for presents	....
Special work clothes	....
Concessionary travel	....
Free NHS prescriptions	....
Mature Drivers' Insurance Policy	....
Life assurance payments and/or possible endowment policy premiums	....
Other	....
TOTAL	....

N.B. You should also take into account reduced running costs, if you move to a smaller home; any expenses for dependent children that may cease; plus other costs, e.g. mortgage payments, that may end around the time you retire. Also the fact that you may be in a lower tax bracket.

2. Possible extra outgoings when you retire

Items   *Estimated monthly cost*

Extra heating/lighting bills   ....

Extra spending on hobbies and other
   entertainment   ....

Replacement of company car   ....

Private health care insurance   ....

Life/permanent health insurance   ....

Cost of substituting other perks,
   e.g. expense account lunches   ....

Out-of-pocket expenses for voluntary
   work activity   ....

Other   ....

TOTAL   ....

N.B. Looking ahead, you will need to make provision for any extra home comforts you might want; and also, at some point, of having to pay other people to do some of the jobs that you normally manage yourself. If you intend to take out a covenant for a charity, this too should be included on the list. The same applies to any new private pension or savings plan, that you might want to invest in to boost your long term retirement income.

Note on Table 3
Many people have difficulty understanding the tax system and you should certainly take professional advice if you are in any doubt at all.

However, if you fill in the table on page 115 carefully, it should give you a pretty good idea of your income after retirement and enable you to make provisional plans at least.

Remember too that you may have one or two capital sums to invest, such as:

- The commuted lump sum from your pension
- money from an endowment policy
- Gains from the sale of company shares (SAYE or other share option scheme)
- Profits from the sale of your home or other asset.

Budget Planner

3. Expected sources of income on retirement

A. *Income Received Before Tax*

State basic pension	....
Graduated pension	....
SERPS	....
Occupational pension(s)	....
Self-employed or personal pension	....
State benefits	....
Casual or other pre-tax earnings	....
Total	....
Less Personal Tax Allowance and possibly also Married Couple's Allowance	....
The new lower 20 per cent rate tax on the first £2,000 of taxable income	....
Basic Rate Tax	....
TOTAL A	....

B. *Income Received After Tax*

Dividends (gilts, unit trusts, shares, etc.)	
Bank deposit account	....
Building society interest	....
Annuity income	....
Other (incl. earnings subject to PAYE)	....
TOTAL B	....
TOTAL A + TOTAL B	....
Less Higher rate tax (if any)	....
Plus Other tax-free receipts	....
Investment Bond withdrawals	....
National Savings interest	....
Other	....
TOTAL NET INCOME	....

4. Unavoidable outgoings

Items	Estimated monthly cost
Food	....
Rent or mortgage repayments	....
Community charge/council tax	....
Repair and maintenance costs	....
Heating	....
Lighting and other energy	....
Telephone	....
TV licence/rental	....
Household insurance	....
Clothes	....
Laundry, cleaner's bills, shoe repair	....
Domestic cleaning products	....
Misc. services, e.g. plumber, window cleaner	....
Car (incl. licence, petrol etc.)	....
Other transport	....
Regular savings/life assurance	....
HP/other loan repayments	....
Outgoings on health	....
Other	....
TOTAL	....

N.B. Before adding up the total, you should look at the 'Normal Additional Expenditure' list, as you may well want to juggle some of the items between the two.

5. Normal additional expenditure

Items	*Estimated monthly cost*
Gifts	....
Holidays	....
Newspapers/books/videos	....
Drink	....
Cigarettes/tobacco	....
Hairdressing	....
Toiletries/cosmetics	....
Entertainment (hobbies, outings, home entertaining etc.)	....
Misc. subscriptions/membership fees	....
Charitable donations	....
Covenants	....
Expenditure on pets	....
Other	....
TOTAL	....

N.B. For some items, such as holidays and gifts, you may tend to think in annual expenditure terms. However, for the purpose of comparing monthly income versus outgoings, it is probably easier if you itemise all the expenditure in the same fashion. Moreover, if you need to save for a special event such as your holiday, it helps if you get into the habit of putting so much aside every month (or even weekly).

Chapter 8

Your Home

One of the most important decisions to be taken as you approach retirement is where you will live. To many people, one of the biggest attractions is the pleasure of moving home. No longer tied to an area within easy commuting distance of work, they can indulge their cherished dreams of a wisteria-covered cottage in the Cotswolds or a white-washed villa in some remote Spanish resort. While this could turn out to be everything they hoped for, and more, many people rush full steam ahead without any real assessment of the pros and cons.

It is normally sensible at least to examine the other options, even if you end up rejecting them. An obvious possibility is to stay where you are and perhaps adapt your present home to make it more suitable for your requirements. You might move in to live with family or friends. Or looking further ahead, you could consider buying or renting some form of purpose-built retirement accommodation.

Before you come to any definite decision, first ask yourself a few down-to-earth questions. What are your main priorities? To be closer to your family? To have a smaller, more manageable home that will be easier to run – and less expensive? To realise some capital in order to provide you with extra money for your retirement? To live in a specific town or village, which you know you like and where you have plenty of friends? Or to enjoy the security of being in accommodation that offers some of the facilities you may want as you become older, such as a resident caretaker and the option of having some of your meals catered?

Whatever choice you make is bound to have its advantages and drawbacks, but, if you weigh these up, you will be far less likely to take a decision which – while attractive in the short term – you may later regret.

Staying put

While there may be plenty of arguments for moving there are probably just as many for staying where you are. Moving house can be a traumatic experience at the best of times and even more so as you become older, when emotional ties are harder to break and precious possessions more painful to part with, as is usually the necessity especially when moving somewhere smaller.

Although ideally you may want to remain where you are, you may feel that your home is really too large or inconvenient for you to manage in the future. However, before you heave your last sigh of regret and put it on the market, it is worth considering whether there are ways of adapting it to provide what you want. If your house is too big, you might think about re-using the space in a better way. Would it be possible, for example, to turn a bedroom into a small upstairs study? Or perhaps you could convert a spare room into a separate workroom for hobbies and get rid of the clutter from the main living area? Equally, have you thought about letting one or two rooms? As well as solving the problem of wasted space, it would also bring in some extra income.

A few judicious home improvements invested in now could make the world of difference in terms of comfort and practicality. Many of us carry on for years with totally inefficient heating systems that could be improved relatively easily and cheaply. Stairs need not necessarily be a problem, even when you are very much older, thanks to the various types of stair lift now on the market. Even so, a few basic facilities installed on the ground floor could save your legs in years to come. Similarly, gardens can be endlessly replanned to suit changing requirements: for example, extending the areas of lawn or paving could spare you hours of exhausting weeding.

Moving to a new home

If you do decide to move, the sooner you start looking for your new home the better. With time to spare, you will have a far greater choice of properties and are less likely to indulge in any panic buying.

While a smaller house will almost certainly be easier and cheaper to run, make sure that it is not so small that you are going to feel cramped. Remember that when you are both at home, you may need more room to avoid getting on top of each other. Also if your family lives in another part of the country, you may wish to have them and your grandchildren to stay. Conversely, beware of taking on commitments such as a huge garden. While this might be a great source of enjoyment when you are in your sixties, it could prove a burden as you become older.

If you are thinking of moving out of the neighbourhood, there are other factors to be taken into account such as: access to shops and social activities, proximity to friends and relatives, availability of public transport and even health and social support services. While these may not seem particularly important now, they could become so in the future. Couples who retire to a seemingly 'idyllic' spot often return quite quickly. New friends are not always easy to make. So-called 'retirement areas' can mean that you are cut off from a normal cross-section of society and health services are likely to be over-taxed.

While retiring to the country can be glorious, city dwellers should, however, bear in mind some of the less attractive sides of rural living. Noise, for example low flying aircraft and church bells, can be an unexpected irritant. If you are not used to it, living near a silage pit or farm can also be an unpleasant experience. Prices in village shops are often higher than in city supermarkets and bus services tend to be more infrequent. Finally, would a small village or seaside resort offer sufficient scope to pursue your interests once the initial flurry of activity is over?

Even if you think you know an area well, check it out properly before coming to a final decision. If possible take a self-catering let for a couple of months, preferably out of season when rents are low and the weather is bad. A good idea is to limit your daily spending to your likely retirement income rather than splurge as most of us do on holiday.

Counting the cost
Moving house can be an expensive exercise. It is estimated that the cost is between 5 and 10 per cent of the value of a new home, once you have totted up such extras as removal charges, insurance, stamp duty, VAT, legal fees and estate agents' commission. If you plan any repairs, alterations or decorations, the figure will be considerably higher. On the other hand, if you move to smaller or cheaper accommodation you will be able to release money for other uses.

A good tip to remember is that stamp duty (which applies to all properties costing more than £30,000) is not levied on fitments such as carpets and curtains. If you are considering a purchase which includes some of these, try to negotiate a separate price for them.

When buying a new home, it is essential to have a full building (structural) survey done before committing yourself. This will cost in the region of £400 for a small terraced house but is worth every penny. In particular, it will provide you with a comeback in law should things go wrong.

If you are buying a newly built house, there are now a number of safeguards against structural defects. Most mortgagors will only lend on new homes with a National House Building Council (NHBC) warranty. The NHBC operates a 10-year warranty scheme under which the builder will remedy any defects which appear in the first two years. For the next eight years, it provides insurance against any major damage due to defects in the load bearing structure.

Many of the problems of buying or selling a house could be eased in time thanks to a logbook called *The House Diary*, which has been devised by the Northern Consortium of Housing Authorities in association with the Building Centre Trust.

Its purpose is to help owners record all the vital information about their property including such technical areas as the foundations and the roof loading, as well as more everyday concerns such as the location of the gas and electricity meters, the essentials of the central heating system and the position of water stopcocks. As well as being of help to both buyers and sellers, the information could also prove invaluable to owners planning a conversion or extension to their home.

The House Diary which costs £2.25 is available from the **Northern Consortium Of Housing Authorities**, 1 High Chare, Chester-le-Street, County Durham DH3 3PX. T:091-387 1085.

In a move that will be welcomed by many home-buyers, H.M. Land Registry has opened its doors to allow members of the public to seek information direct about the 14 or so million properties held on its register. There is a small charge for the service, details of which are explained in Leaflet no. 15 *The Open Register – A Guide to Information Held by the Land Registry and How to Obtain It*. To request a copy, write to **H.M. Land Registry**, Lincoln's Inn Fields, London WC2A 3PH; or telephone 071-405 3488.

Bridging loans

Finally, a word about bridging loans which for some unlucky people can end up costing literally thousands of pounds. Tempting as it may be to buy before you sell, unless you have the money available to finance the cost of two homes – including possibly two mortgages – you need to do your sums very carefully indeed.

To give you an idea of the sort of costs involved, banks usually charge 3 points or more over base rate plus an arrangement or administration fee on top. In other words, if bank rate is 10 per cent, the interest charged on a £100,000 loan works out at £1,083 a month; or £6,498 if it takes you six months to sell.

Although by shopping around the building societies you may get somewhat better terms, you don't need to be a mathematician to work out that if your home is on the market for more than a very short while, the payments can escalate alarmingly.

As an alternative to bridging loans, some of the major institutional estate agents operate chain-breaking schemes and may offer to buy your property at a discount: normally around 10 or 12 per cent less than the market price. In some circumstances this could be worth while but a lot of money is involved, so this is not a decision to be taken lightly.

Removals

Transporting your worldly goods from A to B is an exhausting business. Professional help can remove many of the headaches if carried out by a reputable firm.

Costs can vary considerably from around £300 to £600 or more for an average three-bedroom suburban house, depending on the type and size of furniture and the distance over which it is being moved. It pays to shop around and get at least three quotes from different removal firms. Large firms may be able to help reduce costs by arranging part or return loads. Remember, however, that the cheapest quote is not necessarily the best. Find out exactly what you are paying for and whether the price includes packing and insurance.

A useful organisation to contact is: **British Association of Removers**, 3 Churchill Court, 58 Station Road, North Harrow HA2 7SA. T:081-861 3331. They will send you a free leaflet advising you what to do when you move house and a list of approved removal firms. (Please enclose sae.)

Moving in with family or friends

This may be accommodation such as a self-contained flat or actually living together as part of the family. It may be possible to get a renovation grant from your local council to help with any conversion costs. Ask about the availability of such grants *before* any work is started.

There are many advantages to such an arrangement. While you are active, you can contribute to the household. Should you become frail or ill, help will be at hand.

Living together can also be fraught with problems, however. As a general precaution, try to work out in advance any potential conflicts. Questions worth considering include: whether you will share any meals, social life or transport; whether you will contribute in any practical ways, like baby-sitting, shopping, cleaning or looking after the house during the family's holidays; also, whether you can keep a pet and have friends to stay.

Money is also a common source of dispute. Decide whether you will have your own telephone or whether you will share one. If you will be paying rent, make it a formal arrangement exactly as if you were a normal tenant. You must agree a set figure: what it will cover, how it will be assessed in future and how it will be paid, i.e. weekly, monthly, cash or standing order. If you make a contribution towards the cost of any conversion work, work out beforehand how you would be reimbursed should the arrangement have to be terminated for one reason or another.

Living with family or friends is generally an informal arrangement. However, it is worth having a word with your solicitor or local housing advice centre about how it might affect your rights and obligations as either landlord or tenant. In particular, you should take advice before embarking on any construction work, such as a self-contained granny flat, which might affect the property's exemption from capital gains tax in the future.

Sharing with friends

Yet another possibility is to share your own home with one or two friends. For some, this can be a perfect solution but the same pitfalls as living with your family apply, so work out the arrangements carefully beforehand. Legal advice is an absolute 'must' in these circumstances. A solicitor or Housing Advice Centre will be able to explain any important points that could affect you, as will your building society or bank should you be considering actually buying a property together.

Retirement housing and sheltered accommodation

The term 'retirement' or 'sheltered' accommodation covers a wide variety of housing but generally means property with a resident warden/caretaker, an emergency alarm system, optional meals and some communal facilities such as living rooms, garden and laundry. Guest accommodation and visiting services such as hairdressers and chiropodists are sometimes also available. An increasing number of companies now offer extra care and nursing facilities in some of their developments.

Designed to bridge the gap between the family home and residential care, such housing offers continued independence for the fit and active within a secure environment. Much of it is owned and run by local authorities, housing associations and charities. However, there are also many private developments on the market, for sale or rent, at prices to suit most pockets.

As a general rule, you have to be over 55 when you buy property of this kind. While you may not wish to move into this type of accommodation just now, if the idea interests you in the long term it is worth planning ahead as there are often very long waiting lists.

Full details of the various types of sheltered accommodation, together with some addresses, are given in Chapter 14, Caring for Elderly Parents.

Making your home more practical

It is sensible to set about any home improvement plans earlier rather than later. For one thing, these are often easier to afford when you are still earning a regular salary. For another, any building work is tiresome and most people find it easier to put up with the mess when they are not living among it 24 hours a day. Thirdly, if you start early, you will enjoy the benefit that much sooner.

Insulation
When you retire, you may be at home more during the day so are likely to be using your heating more intensively. One of the best ways of reducing the bills is to get your house properly insulated. Heat escapes from a building in four main ways: through the roof, walls, floor and through loose-fitting doors and windows. Insulation can not only cut the heat loss dramatically but will usually more than pay for itself within four or five years.

Loft insulation. As much as 25 per cent of heat in a house escapes through the loft. The answer is to put a layer of insulating material, at least 150mm (6 inches) thick, between or over the roof joists. You can lay this yourself quite easily and the materials are readily available from builders merchants. If you prefer to employ a specialist contractor, contact the **National Association of Loft Insulation Contractors**, PO Box 12, Haslemere, Surrey GU27 3AH, T:0428 654011, for a list of their members.

Doors and windows. A further 25 per cent of heat escapes through single-glazed windows, half of which could be saved through double-glazing. There are two main types: sealed units and secondary sashes (that can be removed in the summer).

Compared with other forms of insulation, double glazing is expensive; however, it does have the additional advantage of reducing noise levels. There are now a number of DIY systems on the market. If using a contractor, make sure that the company you deal with is a member of the **Glass and Glazing Federation**, 44-48 Borough High Street, London SE1 1XB. T:071-403 7177.

Effective draught-proofing saves heat loss as well as keeping out cold blasts of air. It is also relatively cheap and easy to install. Compression seals are the simplest and most cost-effective way to fill the gap between the fixed and moving edges of doors and windows. For draught-proofing older sliding sash windows and doors, wiper seals, fixed with rust-proof pins and screws, need to be used. For very loose fitting frames, gap fillers that can be squeezed from a tube provide a more efficient seal between frame and surround, but this is normally work for a specialist.

If you do fit draught seals, make sure you leave a space for a small amount of air to get through, or you may get problems with condensation. If the house is not well ventilated, you should put in a vapour check to slow down the leakage of moisture into the walls and ceiling. For advice on durable products and contractors, contact the **Draught Proofing Advisory Association**, PO Box 12, Haslemere, Surrey U27 3AH. T:0428 654011.

Heat loss can also be considerably reduced through hanging heavy curtains (both lined and interlined) over windows and doors. Make sure all curtains cover the window sill or rest on the floor. It is better to have them too long than too short.

Wall insulation. More heat is lost through the walls than perhaps anywhere else in the house: it can be as much as 50 per cent. If your house has cavity walls – and most houses built after 1930 do – then cavity wall insulation should be considered. This involves injecting a type of foam, polystyrene or mineral wool into the cavity through holes drilled in the outside wall.

It is work for a specialist and therefore quite expensive, costing from around £350 for a terraced house up to £650 plus for a detached house. Against this, you could expect a typical saving of around 25 per cent on your heating bill each year so that, in most cases, the initial outlay will be recovered in four years or less. Make sure that the firm you use is on the British Standards Institution's Registered Firms List or can show a current Agrement Certificate for the system and is approved by the BBA. If using a foam fill, the material should comply with British Standard BS5617 and the installation with BS5618.

Solid wall insulation can be considerably more expensive, but well worthwhile, providing similar savings of around 25 per cent of your annual heating bill. Again, this is work for a specialist and involves applying an insulating material to the outside of the wall, plus rendering or cladding.

For further information and addresses of registered contractors, contact:

BSI Quality Assurance, British Standards Institution, PO Box 375, Milton Keynes MK14 6LL. T:0908 220908.
British Board of Agrement, PO Box 195, Bucknalls Lane, Garston, Herts WD2 7NG. T:0923 670844.
External Wall Insulation Association, PO Box 12, Haslemere, Surrey GU27 3AH. T:0428 654011 – for solid or defective walls.

Retirement Made Easy

Cavity Foam Bureau, PO Box 79, Oldbury, Warley, West Midlands B69 4BW. T:021-544 4949. All installers that belong to the Cavity Foam Bureau are registered with the BSI.
National Cavity Insulation Association, PO Box 12, Haslemere, Surrey GU27 3AH. T:0428 654011.
Eurisol UK Ltd., Mineral Wool Association, 39 High Street, Redbourn, Herts AL3 7LW. T:0582 794624.
Expanded Polystyrene Cavity Insulation Association, Waldorf Way, Denby Dale Road, Wakefield WF2 8DH. T:0924 362081.

Floor insulation. Up to 15 per cent of heat loss can be saved through filling the cracks or gaps in the floorboards and skirting. If you can take up your floorboards, a glass fibre blanket can be extremely effective when fixed underneath the joists. Filling spaces with papier mâché or plastic wool will also help especially if a good felt or rubber underlay is then laid under the carpet. Be careful, however, that you do not block up the underfloor ventilation which is necessary to protect floor timbers from dampness and rot. Solid concrete floors can be covered with cork tiles or carpet and felt or rubber underlay.

Hot water cylinder insulation. If your hot water cylinder has no insulation, it could be costing you several pounds a week in wasted heat. An insulating jacket around your hot water cylinder will cut wastage by three-quarters. Most hot water tanks now come ready supplied with insulation. If not, the jacket should be at least 80mm thick and will cost around £25. Jackets come in various sizes, so measure your cylinder before buying. Only purchase one that carries BSI's kitemark no. 5615.

Grants
There are a number of useful grants – in particular Minor Works Assistance Grant and Renovation Grant – to assist those on low income with insulation costs. See section headed 'Improvement and repair' on page 130.

Heating
It may be possible to save money by using different fuels or by heating parts of your house off different systems. This could apply especially if some rooms are only occasionally used. Your local high street gas and electricity showrooms, and also **Solid Fuel Advisory Council** office, can advise on heating systems, running costs and energy conservation, as well as heating and hot water appliances.

Buying and installing heating equipment. When buying equipment, check that it has been approved by the appropriate standards approvals board.

For electrical equipment, the letters to look for are BEAB (British Electrotechnicals Approvals Board) or CCA (Cenelec Certification Agreement), which is the European Community equivalent.

For gas appliances, either buy from a British Gas showroom where all products conform to relevant European or British Standards, or if buying elsewhere, look for the BSI kitemark. The same applies for domestic solid fuel appliances, which should be approved by the Solid Fuel Appliances Approval Scheme (see sales literature).

When looking for contractors to install your equipment, check that they are enrolled with the relevant inspection council or are members of the relevant trade association.

Electricians should be approved by the **National Inspection Council for Electrical Installation Contracting**, Vintage House, 37 Albert Embankment, London SE1 7UJ. T:071-582 7746. All approved contractors are covered by the NICEIC Guarantee of Standards Scheme: sub-standard work must be put right at no extra cost. Names and addresses of local approved contractors can be found in the NICEIC Roll of Approved Contractors kept in libraries, some CABs and electricity showrooms.

An alternative source for finding a reputable electrician is the **Electrical Contractors Association**, 34 Palace Court, London W2 4HY. T:071-229 1266. Their members are also covered by a guarantee scheme; among other benefits this guarantees that, in the event of a contractor becoming insolvent, the work will be completed by another approved electrician at the originally quoted price subject to the conditions of the scheme.

Gas appliances can either be installed by British Gas or by an installer who is also registered with CORGI. Registration is now compulsory by law. The address for CORGI is: **Council for Registered Gas Installers**, 4 Elm Wood, Chineham Business Park, Crockford Lane, Basingstoke, Hants RG24 0WG. T:0256 707060.

The relevant associations for solid fuel and oil central heating installers are respectively the **Solid Fuel Advisory Service** and the **Approved Coal Merchants Scheme** (see local telephone directory).

Additionally, the Heating and Ventilating Contractors' Association can advise on all types of central heating. All installation work done by member companies is covered by a free one-year guarantee; for other work on domestic central heating there is a code of fair trading which provides for free conciliation and low cost arbitration in the event of a dispute. There is also an optional extended warranty scheme. For further information contact the **Heating and Ventilating Contractors' Association**, ESCA House, 34 Palace Court, London W2 4JG. T:071-229 2488; or call the Home Heating Linkline (all calls charged at local rate) on 0345 581158.

Grants. If you are disabled or on a low income you may be eligible for a grant to assist with improving the heating system to your home. See 'Improvement and repair' on page 130.

Useful reading
Energy and Your Home and *Handy Hints to Save Energy in Your Home*. Extremely useful booklets, available free from the Energy Efficiency Office, Blackhorse Road, London SE99 7UB.

Tips for reducing your energy bills

Energy can be saved in lots of small ways. Taken together, they could amount to quite a large cut in your heating bills. You may find some of the following ideas worth considering:

- Set your central heating timer and thermostat to suit the weather. A saving of half an hour or one degree can be substantial. For example, by setting the thermostat at 3 degrees Fahrenheit (2 degrees centigrade) lower than last year, you could save up to 15 per cent on your heating bill.
- A separate thermostat on your hot water cylinder set at around 140 degrees Fahrenheit will enable you to keep hot water for taps at a lower temperature than for the heating system.
- If you run your hot water off an immersion heater, have a time-switch fitted attached to an Economy 7 meter so that the water is heated at the cheap rate overnight. An override switch will enable you to top up the heat during the day if necessary.
- Showers are more economical than baths as well as being easier to use when you become older.
- Reflective foil sheets put behind radiators help to reduce heat loss through the walls.
- Switch off or reduce the heating in rooms not being used.
- If you have an open fire, a vast amount of heat tends to be lost up the chimney. A wood-burning stove can help reduce heat loss as well as maximising the amount of heat you get from your wood or solid fuel in other ways. If you dislike the idea of losing the look of an open fire, there are now a number of appliances on the market that are open fronted and fit flush with the fireplace opening. Contact your local Solid Fuel Advisory Service for further

Your Home

information. If you decide to block up a fireplace, don't forget to fit an air vent to allow some ventilation.
- Some small cooking appliances can save energy in comparison with a full-sized cooker. An electric casserole or slow cooker uses only a fraction more energy than a light bulb and is economical for single households. Similarly, an electric frying pan or multi-cooker can be a sensible alternative for people living on their own. Pressure cookers and microwave ovens can save fuel and time.
- Finally, it is a good idea to get in the habit of reading your electricity and gas meters regularly. This will help you keep track of likely bills.

You might like to take advantage of the British Gas 'budget payment' plan which allows customers to spread their gas payments over the year in fixed monthly instalments, based on an estimate of their annual consumption. Estimates are periodically adjusted up or down, depending on actual meter readings. Many of the electricity companies have similar budget plans. If the idea appeals to you, you should enquire via the accounts department or customer services' number listed.

Other useful addresses
OFFER, Hagley House, Hagley Road, Birmingham B16 8QG. T:021-456 2100. Should you have any queries or complaints about electricity matters including, for example, threat of disconnection or mistakes in your bill, OFFER advises that in the first instance you should contact your local electricity company (see your electricity bill for address and telephone number).

If you are still dissatisfied you should get in touch with your OFFER regional office (the address will be on the back of your electricity bill) who, if they cannot resolve the problem, may refer it to the local consumers' committee. The committee will investigate the matter and if they agree you have a legitimate complaint will take up the cudgels on your behalf.

If you have a query or problem about gas or a gas appliance which you cannot resolve with British Gas or the appliance retailer, you can approach your regional office of the Gas Consumers Council. The Council has offices in: Birmingham, Bournemouth, Cardiff, Edinburgh, Leeds, Leicester, Letchworth, London, Manchester, Newcastle and Plymouth. For address and telephone number, see the back of your gas bill or look in the telephone directory.

Domestic Coal Consumers' Council, Freepost, London SW1P 2YZ. T:071-233 0583. The DCCC is an independent body which represents all consumers who burn solid fuel in their home. The Council is especially concerned with the supply, quality and price of solid fuel and with safety matters. If you cannot resolve a dispute with your supplier or coal merchant, contact the Approved Coal Merchants Scheme (see telephone directory) or, if this fails, you can send your complaint to the Council at the above address.

Neighbourhood Energy Action, 2-4 Bigg Market, Newcastle upon Tyne NE1 1UW. T:091-261 5677. A national charity representing organisations which draught-proof and insulate the homes of the elderly, disabled or others on low incomes at risk from the cold. People claiming income support, housing benefit, community charge benefit, council tax benefit or family credit may be able to obtain a grant for draught-proofing and loft insulation materials through the Home Energy Efficiency Scheme. For your local contact write to the address above.

Useful reading
British Gas supplies leaflets describing the services it offers for older and disabled people, including: free gas safety checks, fuel saving, paying for gas, gas safety and appliance servicing. Ask at your local gas showroom.

Age Concern publishes a useful fact sheet, entitled *Help With Heating* (free), available from Citizens' Advice Bureaux and local Age Concern branches.

Help the Aged has a 'Winter Warmth Line' on 0800 289 404 and distributes the Department of Health's free booklet *Keep Warm, Keep Well*.

Improvement and repair

Building work is notoriously expensive and can be a major deterrent to doing some of the alterations to your home that may be necessary. Before abandoning the idea, it is worth investigating whether you could take advantage of some of the various grants available.

A bank loan may be the simplest way of raising funds for most repairs and improvements. Many banks and building societies are prepared to offer interest-only mortgages to older people to cover essential repairs and improvements.

Improvement and repair grants
Improvements and structural repairs, especially to older houses, often qualify for grants from the local council as does conversion work, such as creating a granny flat. Most grants are discretionary and are more likely

to be given either if the council has a policy of encouraging improvements or if a member of the household is disabled. There are five types of grant as follows:

Renovation grant. There are six main eventualities where application for a grant might be successful: (1) to bring a property up to a standard of fitness for human habitation; (2) to replace or repair rotten or defective parts of the structure including, for example, doors, windows, walls, an ineffective damp-proof course or unsatisfactory wiring; (3) for home insulation; (4) to provide heating facilities; (5) for the provision of satisfactory internal arrangements such as improvement of a very steep or winding staircase; (6) for conversions, such as the creation of a self-contained flat.

Other than (1) which is mandatory provided the applicant is eligible for grant, all other claims are at the discretion of the council. Eligibility is means-tested and different tests apply according to whether the applicant is an owner-occupier or tenant or whether he/she is a landlord. An individual's resources are also taken into account in determining the actual amount of grant which, even if mandatory, could only make a tiny contribution to the cost of the works – or might pay for everything.

The property must have been built or converted at least 10 years before the date of application for grant. Second homes do not qualify.

Common parts grant. This is for the improvement or repair of the common parts of a building containing one or more flats. Items that normally count as 'common parts' include the roof, lift, staircase and entrance lobby. The grant is usually discretionary and can be applied for either by a landlord and/or by at least three-quarters of the occupying tenants. As with a renovation grant, the applicant's financial resources are taken into account and (where applicable) the property must have been converted at least 10 years previously.

HMO grant. This can only be applied for by a landlord and is for the improvement of Houses in Multiple Occupation; or for the conversion of a property for HMO use. Depending on the requirements, the grant may be either mandatory or discretionary. Further information is contained in Housing Booklets nos. 31 and 32 on HMOs, available from the council.

Disabled facilities grant. This is designed to adapt or provide facilities for a home (including the common parts where applicable) to make it more suitable for occupation by a disabled person. It can cover a wide range of improvements to enable a disabled person to manage more independently including, for example: work to facilitate access either to the property itself or to the main rooms; the provision of suitable bathroom or kitchen facilities; the adaptation of heating or lighting controls; improvement of the heating system.

Provided the applicant is eligible, the grant is mandatory for all the above. Discretionary grant is also available for a variety of other works where these would make a home suitable for a disabled person.

The individual must be registered (or registrable) as disabled and, as with other grants, there is a means test. Additionally, the council will want to check that the proposed work is necessary, appropriate and also reasonable according to the age/condition of the property. The grant can either be applied for by the disabled person or by a joint owner/tenant or landlord, on their behalf.

Eligibility for all the above grants depends on the validity of the proposed work and on the applicant's resources, taking into account their income and any savings over £5,000 (savings below this amount are ignored). There are different calculations according to whether an applicant is an owner–occupier or tenant – or whether he/she is a landlord. More generous criteria apply where application is on behalf of a disabled person.

How to apply. Contact the Home Improvement Section of your local council for an application form. Other applications, such as planning permission, may also be necessary; or, in the case of flats, you may need to apply jointly with other tenants.

Before making an application, you should read carefully Department of Environment booklet, *Home Renovation Grants* (available from the council) which explains the various requirements in detail and also advises of sources such as your Citizens' Advice Bureau and local Agency Service that can both help you assess your likelihood of qualifying and can advise you of any preliminary steps (such as getting estimates) you need to take. Even if they are highly optimistic of your chances of obtaining a grant, **do not start work until approval has been given to your grant application.**

Minor works assistance. In contrast to the grants described above, minor works assistance is for small but essential works to your home, including: (1) to provide or improve thermal insulation; (2) to repair, improve or adapt a property to enable individuals over 60 to remain in their own home; (3) as 2, if you have an older person coming to live with you permanently; (4) to carry out repairs to a property in a clearance area.

A grant is only available to owner-occupiers and private sector tenants (including housing association tenants) who are in receipt of income support, family credit, housing benefit or community charge benefit (or council tax benefit after April 1993).

Maximum grant is £1,000 per application, up to a total of £3,000 over three years. For further information and application form, contact your Housing Department. If there is an agency service (sometimes known as 'Care and Repair') in your area, it could be useful to ask them to help you assess the likely cost and feasibility of the work. **N.B.** Do not start on any improvement until your council has informed you that your application has been approved.

Also useful to know about is the government Home Energy Efficiency Scheme (HEES) which provides insulation grants for those on low income in special need. For further information contact: **Energy Action Grants Agency**, PO Box ING, Newcastle upon Tyne NE99 1NG; or telephone freephone 0800 181667.

Grants for the sick and disabled
Your local authority may be able to help with the provision of certain special facilities such as a stair lift, telephone installations or a ramp to replace steps. Apply to your local Social Services Department and, if you encounter any difficulties, ask for further help either from your local Disability Group, local Age Concern Group or from RADAR (Royal Association for Disability and Rehabilitation), 25 Mortimer Street, London W1N 8AB. T:071-637 5400.

Useful addresses
The Building Centre, 26 Store Street, London WC1E 7BT. T:071-637 1022. Has displays of building products, heating appliances, kitchen layouts and other exhibits and can give information about building problems. It has manufacturers' lists and other free literature you can take away and there is also a well-stocked bookshop.

Federation of Master Builders (FMB), Gordon Fisher House, 14-15 Great James Street, London WC1N 3DP. T:071-242 7583. Lists of members are available from regional offices. Warranty Scheme, which insures work in progress and gives up to five years' guarantee on completion of work, is available from some of its members.

Guild of Master Craftsmen, Castle Place, 166 High Street, Lewes, East Sussex BN7 1XU. T:0273 478449. Can supply names of all types of specialist craftsmen including, for example, carpenters, joiners, ceramic workers and restorers.

Institute of Plumbing, 64 Station Lane, Hornchurch, Essex RM12 6NB. T:0708 472791. Can provide a list of registered plumbers; sae appreciated. Also issues a free leaflet, *Always Look for the Sign of a Competent Plumber*.

The Scottish and Northern Ireland Plumbing Employers' Federation, 2 Walker Street, Edinburgh EH3 7LB. T:031-225 2255. The Federation consists of over 1,150 plumbing and domestic heating firms. It operates a Code of Fair Trading and Guarantee of Work Scheme and provides lists of local members on request.

Royal Institution of Chartered Surveyors, The RICS Information Centre, Surveyor Court, Westwood Way, Coventry CV4 8JE. T:071-222 7000. Can nominate qualified surveyors in your area who are recognisable by the initials ARICS or FRICS after their name. It also publishes a number of useful leaflets, including *What Will It Cost?* which gives guidance on various plumbing, electrical and building jobs around the house. (Send an sae.)

Royal Institute of British Architects, 66 Portland Place, London W1N 4AD. T:071-580 5533. Has a free Clients' Advisory Service which, however small your building project, will recommend up to half a dozen suitable architects. It can also supply you with useful leaflets giving advice on working with an architect.

The British Wood Preserving and Damp-proofing Association (BWPDA), No. 6, The Office Village, 4 Romford Road, Stratford, London E15 4EA. T:081-519 2588. Has over 220 member companies throughout the UK and will advise on anything to do with wood preservation and rising damp in the home.

The Building Conservation Trust, Apartment 39, Hampton Court Palace, East Molesey KT8 9BS. T:081-943 2277. Runs an exhibition centre at Hampton Court which can provide information on just about anything that can go wrong with your home. They will advise on specific technical difficulties and on organisations to contact if you have a problem.

Useful reading
Home Improvement Price Guide, £9.95 from E & F N Spon, 2-6 Boundary Row, London SE1 8HN. A comprehensive guide to cost and estimated time required for every little job around the home, whether

you hire a builder or do-it-yourself. Also describes how to choose builders, the best ways to pay and how to get planning permission and grants.

Home Improvements, a magazine published by the National Home Improvement Council, 125 Kennington Road, London SE11 6SF, T:071-582 7790, offering advice and useful addresses, price 75p (incl. p&p).

Older Home Owners – Financial Help With Repairs, free from Age Concern.

Care and repair projects

Local Care and Repair or Staying Put projects exist in an increasing number of areas to help house owners aged 50-plus repair and adapt their homes. They will help to assess your needs, get a builder, supervise the work, raise the finance, verify the estimate and check the completed job. Contact your local authority or local Age Concern branch who will be able to advise you about any such schemes in your area.

Safety in the home

Accidents in the home account for 40 per cent of all fatal accidents, resulting in nearly 5,000 deaths a year. Seventy per cent of these victims are over retirement age. The vast majority of accidents are caused by carelessness or by obvious danger spots in the home that for the most part could very easily be made safer.

Steps and stairs should be well lit with light switches at both the top and bottom. Frayed carpet is notoriously easy to trip on and, on staircases especially, should be repaired or replaced as soon as possible. All stairs should have a hand rail along the wall to provide extra support – and on both sides, if the stairs are very steep. It is also a good idea to have a white line painted on the edge of steps that are difficult to see – for instance in the garden or leading up to the front door.

It is perhaps stating the obvious to say that climbing on chairs and tables is dangerous – and yet we all do this. You should keep proper steps, preferably with a hand rail, to do high jobs in the house such as hanging curtains or reaching cupboards.

Floors can be another danger zone. Rugs and mats can slip on polished floors and should *always* be laid on some form of non-slip backing material. Remember also that spilt water or talcum powder on tiled or linoleum floors is a number one cause of accidents.

The **bathroom** is particularly hazardous for falls. Sensible precautionary measures include using a suction-type bath mat and putting handrails on the bath or alongside the shower. For older people who have difficulty in getting in and out of the bath, a bath seat can be helpful. Soap on a rope is safer in a shower, as it is less likely to slither out of your hands and make the floor slippery.

Regardless of age, you should make sure that *all medicines* are clearly labelled and throw away any prescribed drugs left over from a previous illness.

Fires can all too easily start in the home. If you have an open fire, you should always use a fireguard and sparkguard at night. The chimney should be regularly swept at least once a year and maybe more if you have a wood-burning stove. Never place a clothes horse near an open fire or heater and be careful of inflammable objects that could fall from the mantelpiece.

Upholstered furniture is a particular fire hazard, especially when polyurethane foam (which is now banned) has been used in its manufacture. If buying new furniture, make sure that it carries a red triangle label.

Portable heaters should be kept away from furniture and curtains and positioned where you cannot trip over them. Paraffin heaters should be handled particularly carefully and should *never* be filled while alight. Avoid leaving paraffin where it will be exposed to heat, including sunlight. If possible, it should be kept in a metal container outside the house.

Gas appliances should be regularly serviced by British Gas or other CORGI-registered installers. You should also ensure that there is adequate ventilation when using heaters. Never block up air vents: carbon monoxide fumes can kill. British Gas publishes a free leaflet, *Our Commitment to Your Safety*, which includes advice on how to deal with a gas leak as well as how to use your gas appliances safely and effectively.

A free gas safety check on gas appliances is available to anyone living alone who is over the age of 60 or registered disabled; or living with other people where everyone, like themselves, is either over 60 or registered disabled. If additional work needs to be done, you will receive an estimate and may be able to get help with the cost through your local Social Security office or Social Services Department. If you think you might qualify, *you must get official approval before any work is started*. You can arrange a check through your local gas showroom or by contacting your local district office (look under Gas in your local telephone directory).

More than one in three fires in the home are due to accidents with **cookers**. Chip pans are a particular hazard: only fill the pan one-third full with oil and always dry the chips before putting them in the fat. Or better still, use oven-ready chips which you just pop into the oven to cook. Pan handles should be turned away from the heat and positioned so you cannot knock them off the stove. If called to the door or telephone, *always* take the pan off the ring and turn off the heat before you leave the kitchen.

Cigarettes left smouldering in an ashtray could be dangerous if the ashtray is full. Smoking in bed is a potential killer!

Faulty **electric wiring** is another frequent cause of fires, as are overloaded power points. The wiring in your home should be checked every five years and you should avoid using too many appliances off a single plug. Ask an electrician's advice about what is the maximum safe number. Only use plugs that conform to the British Standard 1365 and it is a good idea to get into the habit of pulling the plug out of the wall socket when you have finished using an appliance, whether TV or toaster. All electrical equipment should be regularly checked for wear and tear and frayed or damaged flexes immediately replaced. Wherever possible, have electric sockets moved to waist height to avoid unnecessary bending whenever you want to turn on the switch.

In particular, **electric blankets** should be routinely overhauled and checked in accordance with the manufacturer's instructions. It is dangerous to use both a hot-water bottle and electric blanket – and never use an underblanket as an overblanket.

Electrical appliances are an increasing feature of labour-saving **gardening** but can be dangerous unless treated with respect. They should never be used when it is raining. Moreover, gardeners should always wear rubber-soled shoes or boots and avoid floppy clothing that could get caught in the equipment. For other good advice, see the leaflet *Safety in Your Garden*, available from your electricity showroom.

As a general precaution, keep **fire extinguishers** handy and make sure they are maintained in working order. They should conform to the British Standard 5423 or 5306 part 3. Many insurance companies now recommend that you install a smoke alarm as an effective and cheap early warning device.

Home security

Nine out of ten burglaries are spontaneous and take less than 10 minutes. However, there is much you can do to protect yourself. The Crime Prevention Officer attached to your local police station will come and check your security arrangements, advise you how to improve them and will also tell you whether there is a Neighbourhood Watch Scheme and how you join it. This is a free service which the police are happy to provide.

The most vulnerable access points are doors and windows, so proper precautions are essential.

Doors should have secure bolts or a five-lever deadlock, a burglar chain and a spyhole in the front door. Additionally, you might consider outside lights to illuminate night-time visitors and an answerphone system requiring a caller to identify himself before you open the door.

Windows should preferably be fitted with locks to secure them when partially open; french windows should have proper bolts. If you are particularly worried, you could also have bars fitted to the windows or install old-fashioned internal shutters which can be closed at night. An obvious point is to ensure that the house is securely locked whenever you go out, even for five minutes. Insist that official callers such as meter men show their identity cards before you allow them inside. If you are going away, even for only a couple of days, remember to cancel the milk and the newspapers. Finally, consider a time-switch (cost around £15) which will turn the lights on and off when you are away and can be used to switch on the heating before your return.

For names of reputable locksmiths, contact: **Master Locksmiths Association**, Units 4-5, Woodford Halse Business Park, Woodford Halse, Daventry, Northants NN11 6PZ. T:0327 62255.

Burglar alarms and safes

Many insurance companies will recommend suitable contractors to install burglar alarm equipment. Alternatively, contact: The **National Approval Council for Security Systems** (NACOSS), Queensgate House, 14 Cookham Road, Maidenhead, Berkshire SL6 8AJ, T:0628 37512; it operates a code of practice and will send a free list of their approved contractors in your locality who install burglar alarm systems to British Standard 4737.

If you keep valuables or money in the house, you should think about buying a concealed wall or floor safe.

Personal safety

Older people who live on their own can be particularly at risk. A number of personal alarms now available are highly effective and can generally ease your peace of mind.

A sensible precaution is to carry a 'screamer alarm', sometimes known as a 'personal attack button'. These are readily available in department stores, electrical shops and alarm companies.

A telephone can also increase your sense of security. Some families come to an arrangement whereby they ring their older relatives at regular times to check that all is well.

Your Home

Insurance

According to recent research seven out of ten householders are under-insured, some of them unknowingly but some intentionally to keep premiums lower. This could be dangerous because in the event of a mishap they could end up seriously out of pocket.

With increases in premiums up by an average 20 per cent or more compared with a year ago, many readers may feel that this is hardly the moment to be discussing any reassessment of their policy. However, there are several good reasons why this could be sensible – not least, because you may be able to obtain better value than you are getting at present.

For example, some insurance companies now offer Retired Householders Insurance Policies at substantially reduced rates, on the basis that retired people are less likely to leave their homes empty at a fixed time every day. Such policies are arranged through **Age Concern Insurance Services**, Orbital House, 85 Croydon Road, Caterham, Surrey CR3 6PD; and through **Hill House Hammond Ltd.**, Retired Householders Insurance Department, Freepost BS1162, Lewins Mead, Bristol BS1 2BR.

Additionally, many insurers offer discounts linked to the installation of proper security precautions, with extra points awarded if the householder joins a Neighbourhood Watch Scheme. Brokers adopting this approach can be contacted by writing to: **Institute of Insurance Brokers**, Higham Business Centre, Midland Road, Higham Ferrers, Northamptonshire NN9 8DW. T:0933 410003.

Another type of discount-linked policy that is becoming more popular is one that carries an excess, whereby the householder pays the first chunk of any claim – say, the first £100 or £250. Savings on premiums can be quite appreciable, so it could be worth asking your insurance company what terms they offer.

Some people pay more than they need because they unthinkingly sign their renewal policy on the dotted line quite forgetting to cancel items such as furniture or jewellery which they may have given away or sold. Equally, many forget to add new valuables they have bought or received as presents. In particular, do check that you are adequately covered for any home improvements you may have added such as a new kitchen, extra bathroom or other luxury.

An even more vital point is to ensure that your policy has not lapsed. If the insurance was originally arranged through your building society it may cease when your mortgage is paid off, in which case it will be essential for you to arrange new cover direct. Similarly, when buying for cash – for instance when moving to a smaller house – it will be up to you to organise the insurance and to calculate the rebuilding value of your home. It is advisable to get a qualified valuer to do this for you. For advice, contact the **Royal Institution of Chartered Surveyors,** 12 Great George Street, London SW1P 3AD. T:071-222 7000. They also publish a *Guide to House Rebuilding Costs for Insurance Valuations* which is updated annually.

The **Association of British Insurers,** 51 Gresham Street, London EC2V 7HQ, T:071-600 3333, will send you free leaflets on various aspects of household insurance including *Buildings Insurance for Home Owners, Home Contents Insurance* and *Claiming on Your Home Insurance Policy* which describe what policies you need and indicate the correct amount of cover. Enclose sae.

The **British Insurance and Investment Brokers Association,** BIIBA House, 14 Bevis Marks, London EC3A 7NT, T:071-623 9043, can send you a list of insurance brokers in your area.

Raising money on your home

Many retired owner-occupiers have substantial amounts of money tied up in their homes while they struggle to make ends meet on reduced incomes. One way round the dilemma is to sell up and move somewhere smaller in order to provide extra income. For those who prefer to stay put, however, there are a number of schemes that enable people to unlock capital without having to move. Generally known as Home Income Plans, these usually fall into one of two categories: mortgage annuity schemes and home reversions.

Although other types of schemes exist, these are too dangerous and should not be considered. In particular you should avoid any home income plans linked in with the following: investment bonds, roll-up loans and variable interest mortgages.

Even so-called safe income plans are not without their drawbacks. The likelihood is that you would be selling your home at a substantial discount or otherwise reducing the value of your estate. Additionally, there may be fairly hefty setting-up or arrangement charges - as well as the cost of independent legal advice which we recommend as essential.

Mortgage annuity plans
The more popular format tends to be the mortgage annuity which produces a monthly income for life while allowing you to retain ownership of the property. It works as follows: you take out a mortgage on your home and use at least 90 per cent of the money raised to buy an annuity.

Part of the income from the annuity goes to pay the interest on the loan (which is tax deductible, at basic rate only, on loans of up to £30,000), while you receive the balance as spending money each month. You still own the house and any increase in the value of the property remains with the family.

The loans are all made on a fixed interest-only basis and are repaid from the proceeds of the sale of the house (or estate) when the owner, or surviving partner, dies. Alternatively, if you decide to sell the property at an earlier date, the loan can be repaid, but the annuity will continue.

Normally, these schemes are only available to people over 70 and the older you are the better the annuity payments. If you are married, your combined ages should ideally be at least 150. As with other annuities, the longer you live the greater the benefit. If you survive only a few years, however, the amount of income you receive may nowhere near reach the lump sum you would have sacrificed to buy the annuity. As a safeguard against early death, some schemes offer a 'capital protection' policy, which can be taken in return for lower payments.

Typically, these provide that should you die within one year, only a fifth of the original loan would have to be repaid. This rises to three-fifths within three years. After four years the loan would be repayable in full from the estate.

There are other possible drawbacks including the fact that annuity payments are often fixed for life, so your return may not look so attractive if inflation and interest rates shoot up in the future.

Further information about home income plans can be obtained from the **Association of British Insurers**; and from specialist financial advisers **Hinton & Wild (Home Plans) Ltd.**, 374-378 Ewell Road, Surbiton, Surrey KT6 7BB. T:081-390 8166.

Home reversion schemes

Many people prefer a cash sum to a regular income, in which case a home reversion plan could be the answer. With these schemes, you *sell* all or part of your house – generally at a substantial discount – but retain the right to live in the house for the remainder of your life at a peppercorn rent. You are only likely to receive about 40 to 60 per cent of the market value of your property, as the price will be based on a 'sitting tenant' valuation according to your life expectancy. The proceeds from the sale are received as a lump sum or can be invested in an annuity. You would continue to be responsible for keeping the property in good repair.

While such plans provide a higher initial income than mortgage annuity schemes, they carry a number of disadvantages: the value placed on the house is frequently too low; you lose the benefit of any future increases in the value of the property and you cannot leave the house to your beneficiaries since you no longer own it. Furthermore, your options are reduced should you wish to move in the future.

New style reversion schemes. Some insurance companies have now come up with a variety of new-style home reversion schemes which aim to get over many of these problems. These schemes not only provide an immediate cash sum for elderly home owners, but also enable them to maintain a share in the future appreciation of their homes.

Before committing yourself to a reversion scheme, you are strongly advised to consult a solicitor. For further information, you might like to read: *Extra Income for Life for Elderly Home Owners*, free from Hinton & Wild (Home Plans) Ltd., *Raising Income or Capital from Your Home*, free from Age Concern England (enclose sae) or *Using Your Home as Capital*, price £4.50 from Age Concern.

Letting rooms in your home

Rather than move, many people whose home has become too large are tempted by the idea of taking in tenants. For some, it is an ideal plan; for others, a disaster. At best, it could provide you with extra income and the possibility of pleasant company. At worst, you could be involved in a lengthy legal battle to regain possession of your property.

There are three broad choices: taking in paying guests or lodgers; letting part of your home as self-contained accommodation; or renting the whole house for a specified period. In all cases, for your own protection it is essential to have a written agreement and to take up bank references, unless the let is a strictly temporary one where the money is paid in advance. Otherwise, rent should be collected quarterly and you should arrange a hefty deposit to cover any damage.

In a move to encourage more people to let out rooms in their home, the government has recently relaxed the tax rules allowing you to earn up to £62.50 a week (or £3,250 a year) free of tax. Any excess rental income you receive over £3,250 will be assessed for income tax in the normal way. For further information, see Inland Revenue booklet IR 87 *Rooms To Let*, available from any tax office.

Finally, if you have a mortgage or are a tenant yourself (even with a very long lease), check with your building society or landlord that you are entitled to sublet.

Paying guests or lodgers. This is the most informal arrangement and will normally be either a casual holiday-type bed and breakfast let or a lodger who might be with you for a couple of years.

In either case, the visitor would be sharing part of your home, the accommodation would be fully furnished and you would be providing at least one full meal a day and possibly also basic cleaning services.

There are few legal formalities involved in these types of letting and rent is entirely a matter for friendly agreement. As a resident owner you are also in a very strong position if you want your lodger to leave, since lodgers have no legal rights to stay after the agreed period.

A wise precaution would be to check with your insurance company that your home contents policy would not be affected as some insurers restrict cover to households with lodgers. Also, unless you make arrangements to the contrary, you should inform your lodger that his or her possessions are not covered by your policy.

Holiday lets. It is a good idea to register with your Tourist Information Centre and to contact the Environmental Health Office at your local council for any help and advice.

Useful reading
Want to Rent a Room? DoE leaflet, available from local libraries, Housing Advice Centres and Citizens' Advice Bureaux.

Letting part of your home. You could convert a basement or part of your house as a self-contained flat and let this either furnished or unfurnished. Alternatively, you could let a room or rooms as bed-sitters with no meals provided.

In general terms, provided you continue to live in the house yourself you will be in much the same position as if you had a lodger or paying guest. The advice about checking your home contents policy with your insurance company equally applies. The good news, however, is that the 'fair rent' system for new tenancies has been abolished and landlords can now charge market rates. For more details, see housing booklet No. 22 *Letting Rooms in Your Home*, available from Citizens' Advice Bureaux.

As a resident landlord, you have a guaranteed right to repossession of your property. If the letting was for a fixed term (e.g. six months or a year), the tenancy will automatically cease at the end of the fixed period. If the arrangement was more casual, you may have to give at least four weeks' notice in writing. The position over notices to quit will vary according to circumstances. For further information, see DoE housing booklet No. 24 *Notice That You Must Leave*.

Tax note. If you subsequently sell your home, you may not be able to claim exemption from capital gains tax on the increase in value of a flat if it is entirely self-contained. It is therefore a good idea to retain some means of access to the main house or flat, but take legal advice as to what will qualify.

Renting out your home on a temporary basis

If you are thinking of spending the winter in the sun or are considering buying a retirement home which you will not occupy for a year or two, you might be tempted by the idea of letting the whole house. To safeguard your rights, you should write the lease under the shorthold tenancy rules; see housing booklet No. 19, *Assured Tenancies*. It is essential to ask a solicitor to help you draw up the agreement.

Another useful housing booklet is *Now it's Worthwhile Being a Landlord*, available from your local housing department.

Holiday lets

Buying a future retirement home in the country and renting it out as a holiday home is another option worth considering. As well as providing you with a weekend cottage at other times of the year, it can also prove a useful and profitable investment.

There are various attractive tax advantages which an accountant would explain, together with the rules to qualify. An important condition is that the property must be available for holiday letting for at least 140 days during the tax year and be actually let for at least 70 days.

Housing benefit and community charge benefit

Provided you have no more than £16,000 in savings, you may be able to get help with your rent and community charge from your local council. You may qualify for housing benefit whether you are a council or private tenant or live in a hotel or hostel. You may qualify for community charge benefit if you have to pay a full personal community charge. The amount you get depends on your income, capital, the number of people in your household and the amount of rent and the community charge you pay. The maximum benefit you can get is 100 per cent of your eligible rent and 80 per cent of your community charge.

Applicable Amount. Your 'applicable amount' will generally be the same as the amount of income support you would be eligible for and consists of personal allowances for the members of your family, plus any premiums (i.e. additional amounts for pensioners, the disabled and so on) to which you might be entitled. As an indication of the amounts involved, a single pensioner under 75 would be deemed to need an income of £59.15 a week; a married retired couple, £91.95 (1992/93 rates). Higher

Your Home

amounts apply for disabled pensioners and those over the age of 75. Details of allowances and premium rates are contained in leaflet NI 196 from your local Social Security office.

If your income is *less* than your 'applicable amount' you will receive maximum housing benefit and community charge benefit (100 per cent rent and 80 per cent community charge) and you may be eligible for income support if your capital is less than £8,000.

If your income is *equal* to your 'applicable amount' you will also receive maximum housing benefit and community charge benefit.

If your income is *higher* than your 'applicable amount' a taper adjustment will be made: maximum housing benefit for rent will be reduced by 65 per cent of the *difference* between your income and your 'applicable amount'; and the maximum benefit for community charge will be reduced by 15 per cent of the difference between your income and 'applicable amount'.

How to claim. If you think you might be eligible for benefit (see leaflets RR 1 and CCB 1 available from any Social Security office), ask your council for an application form. They should let you know within 14 days of receiving your completed application whether you are entitled to benefit and will inform you of the amount.

If you make a claim for income support you can claim housing benefit and community charge benefit at the same time. A claim form for these is included inside the income support claim form. When completed, the form is returned to the Social Security office and they pass it on to the local authority.

If you need any help or advice in understanding the forms, ask at your Citizens' Advice Bureau or local Age Concern branch.

Useful reading
Income Related Benefits: Income and Capital and Housing Benefit and *Community Charge Benefit*, free factsheets from Age Concern.

Community charge. As most people will know, the community charge is being abolished in April 1993 and is being replaced by the new council tax. Until the change-over happens community charge and community charge benefit will continue to apply as before. For people who have difficulty in paying, a leaflet to ask for is *Help with Community Charge*.

Council tax

The council tax comes into effect on 1 April 1993.

It is based on the value of the dwelling in which you live (the property element) and also consists of a personal element – with discounts/exemptions applying to certain groups of people.

The property element. Most domestic properties will be liable for council tax including rented property, mobile homes and house boats.

The value of the property will be assessed according to a banding system, with eight different bands (A to H): ranging in England from property valued at up to £40,000 (band A) to property valued at over £320,000 (band H). In Wales, the bands run from up to £30,000 (band A) to over £240,000 (band H). In Scotland, the bands run from up to £27,000 (band A) to over £212,000 (band H).

The valuation of each property to determine in which band it falls will be administered by the Inland Revenue Valuation Office. The value set will be consistent with prices applying at 1 April 1991. Small extensions/other improvements made after this date will not affect the valuation.

New homes will be banded as if they had already been built and sold on 1 April 1991, in order not to penalise occupants of new dwellings.

Notification of the band will be shown on the bill when it is sent out in April 1993. However, if you would like the information sooner, a list showing the band for all homes in your area will be available from December 1992 at the local valuation office and the council offices. If you think there has been a misunderstanding about the valuation (or your liability to pay the full amount) you have the right of appeal.

The Personal Element. Not everyone will pay council tax. The bill will normally be sent to the owner, or joint owners, of the property; or in the case of rented accommodation, to the tenant or joint tenants; or in the case of licensed property, to the residents or joint residents.

In some cases, for example in hostels or multi occupied property, a landlord or owner may pass on a share of the bill to the tenants/residents which would probably be included as part of the rental charge.

The valuation of each dwelling assumes that two adults will be resident. The charge will not increase if there are more adults. However if, as in many homes, there is a single adult, your council tax bill will be reduced by 25 per cent.

There will also be a number of other special discounts, or exemptions, as follows:

- People who are severely mentally impaired qualify for a 25 per cent discount;
- Disabled people who require additional space will have their bill reduced to a lower band;

- People on income support should normally have nothing to pay, as their bill will be met in full by the benefit;
- Disabled people on higher rate attendance allowance need not count a full-time carer as an additional resident and therefore may continue to qualify for the 25 per cent single (adult) householder discount; exceptions are spouses/partners and parents of a disabled child under 18 who would normally be living with the disabled person and whose presence therefore would not be adding to the council tax;
- Young people over 18 but still at school will not be counted when assessing the number of adults in a house;
- Students including student nurses, apprentices and YT trainees living in halls of residence, student hostels or similar are exempted; those living with a parent or other non-student adult are eligible for the 25 per cent personal discount;
- Service personnel living in barracks or married quarters will not receive any bill for council tax.

Discounts/Exemptions applying to property

Certain property will either be exempt from council tax or will be eligible for a discount.

Discounts. Empty property (e.g. second homes) will normally get a 50 per cent discount. There are some exceptions where empty property is treated more generously – see exemptions below.

Exemptions. The most common cases of exemptions will include:

- Property in course of being built or undergoing major structural alteration/repair: the exemption will last until six months after the work is completed
- Property which has been unoccupied and unfurnished for less than six months
- Granny flats that are part of another private domestic dwelling
- Home of a deceased person: the exemption lasts until six months after the grant of probate
- Home that is empty because the occupier is absent in order to care for someone else
- Home of a person who is/would be exempted from personal community charge due to moving to a residential home or similar.

Business-cum-domestic property

Business-cum-domestic property will be rated according to usage, with the business section assessed for business rates and the domestic section for council tax. For example, where there is a flat over a shop, the value of the shop would not be included in the valuation for council tax.

Transitional arrangements
Transitional arrangements are expected to be introduced in areas including London and the South East where council tax bills might otherwise work out considerably higher than a household's community charge.

Appeals
People who feel they have been wrongly assessed for council tax have the right of appeal.

In the first instance, you should take up the matter with the valuation office (see local telephone directory). If the matter is not resolved, you can then appeal to an independent valuation tribunal. For advice and further information, contact your CAB.

Possible changes
As the council tax has not yet come into being, it is possible that the government may decide to make a number of small changes before (or even after) its introduction in April 1993.

Nearer the time, your local council will almost certainly have a leaflet explaining how you are likely to be affected and also giving more detailed information about the appeals procedure. If you need advice and help, contact your local CAB.

Council tax benefit
Council tax benefit will replace community charge benefit when the council tax is introduced in April 1993. People on income support or those on an equally low income will be entitled to rebates of up to 100 per cent of their council tax (rather than the 80 per cent maximum under community charge benefit). Although some people thought that income support benefit levels would be reduced accordingly, this is not so – and consequently many householders will have more money in their pockets.

Council tax benefit will operate in much the same way as community charge benefit i.e., with reductions in benefit for those whose income is above their applicable amount: the sum clawed back will be 20p for every £1 of excess income. Also, as with housing benefit, there will be a system of deductions for non-dependent adults sharing the same household – with special help given if they too are on a low income.

For further information, ask your local Social Security office to give you a leaflet explaining how to claim council tax benefit (leaflet number was not available at time of writing).

Useful organisations

The following should be able to provide general advice about housing and help with housing problems:

- Local authority Housing Departments
- Housing Advice or Housing Aid Centres
- Citizens' Advice Bureaux
- Local authority Social Service Departments if your problem is linked to disability
- Welfare Rights Centres if your problem, for example, concerns a landlord who does not keep the property properly maintained
- Local councillors and MPs.

Yorkshire Wildlife Trust

The County Trust for Nature Conservation for Yorkshire and North Humberside

Protecting our countryside and our environment is one of the most important issues facing us today, whoever we are, wherever we live. The wildlife and wild places of Yorkshire are probably the most varied of any in Britain, and with over 50 nature reserves the Yorkshire Wildlife Trust conserves and protects plants, animals and their habitats throughout the old county of Yorkshire.

As urban sprawl encroaches, life will be the poorer without the wildflowers and animals, the woods and moors, fields and rivers, the Trust fights to protect for this generation and our children.

Wherever you're from, but especially if Yorkshire is or was home to you, a legacy to the Trust will help preserve the beauty and variety of a countryside that will enrich the lives of your successors.

For more information please contact Stephen Suart at our Office in York.

10 TOFT GREEN, YORK YO1 1JT.
TEL: (0904) 659570

Registered in England as a Company Limited by Guarantee No. 409650
Registered Charity No. 210807 VAT No 170 391475.

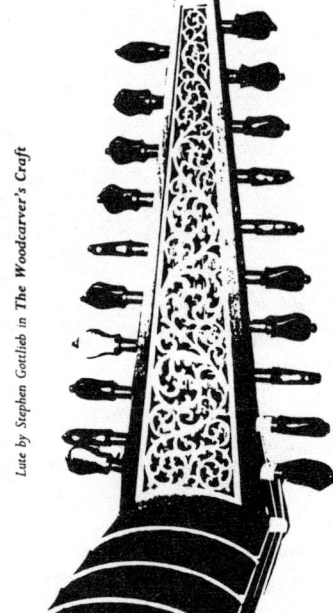

Lute by Stephen Gottlieb in The Woodcarver's Craft

Discover the best of today's crafts at the Crafts Council Gallery

Studio Glass
14 January to 7 March
Contemporary American Quilts
15 July to 22 August
The Woodcarver's Craft
9 September to 7 November

plus shop, slide library and cafe

Crafts Council   Free entry
44a Pentonville Road   Tuesdays to Saturdays 11-6
Islington London N1 9BY Sundays 2-6
Telephone 071 278 7700 Closed Mondays
(Angel Tube)   (disabled access)

ACQUIRE THE DREAM... NOT THE NIGHTMARE!!

The Daily Telegraph
GUIDE TO LIVING AND RETIRING ABROAD

'The least expensive way to avoid being caught in the rain'
MONEY WEEK

Full of essential information, practical advice and handy hints for anyone planning a move abroad.

TELEPHONE YOUR CREDIT CARD DETAILS

on 071-278 0433 (24 hour) or send a cheque/po made payable to Kogan Page for £8.99 (£1 p&p) to Kogan Page, 120 Pentonville Rd, London N1 9JN.

A lasting and living memorial to your generosity

ALMSWORTH COMMON, EXMOOR. PHOTOGRAPHY BY BRIAN HARRIS FOR CPRE

The English countryside has been the delight of countles generations - yet this very heart of our national heritage is constantly under threat from damaging development.

Working at national and local level since 1926, CPRE has played a major part in the creation and protection of National Parks, the provision of Green Belts around cities and in establishing firm planning controls. Important contributions are also being made to agricultural, forestry, water and transport policies and hedgerow protection. CPRE's success is based on solid research, constructive ideas and reasoned argument.

CPRE is ever-vigilant but its work as a small but cost-effective charity is totally dependent on public support. By making a bequest or a donation to CPRE, you can help to ensure that England's Green and Pleasant Land is enjoyed by future generations. Remember, a legacy to a registered charity like CPRE is exempt from Inheritance Tax.

REGISTERED CHARITY NUMBER 233179

If you would like further information about remembering CPRE in a will, write to David Conder, Room 12, Council for the Protection of Rural England, Warwick House, 25 Buckingham Palace Road London SW1W 0PP

PATRON HM THE QUEEN
PRESIDENT DAVID PUTTNAM CBE

What's a bequest to the RSPB worth?

The future of our wild birds and environment is under threat. Our heathlands, hedgerows and woodlands are vanishing. Our birds and other animals are disappearing with them.

A FUTURE WHERE BIRDS FLY SAFE AND FREE.

Moorlands are being destroyed, marshes drained and river beds straightened out.

Our rivers and oceans are polluted. Pesticides are endangering our wildlife, their natural habitats and food.

A FUTURE WITH POLLUTION-FREE RIVERS AND OCEANS.

The RSPB researches these situations and uses practical solutions to fight these and other threats to our environment.

We use our influence at public enquiries and press for new laws and policies to create a healthier, richer future.

But action costs money. So when you or your clients are considering a charitable bequest, please think of the RSPB.

A FUTURE FOR WOODLANDS, HEDGEROWS AND HEATHS.

Further information on the RSPB's work in protecting the future of our wild birds and environment is included in our FREE information packs.

We will gladly send you as many of these free packs as you require, including copies of the booklet on making a will, "Where there's a will there's your way", which has been specially written for the RSPB

Please write to:
Legacy Officer, Bequests (KH128), RSPB, The Lodge, Sandy, Beds SG19 2DL.
Or telephone 0767 680551.

Reg Charity 207076.

IF YOU CARE, THE RSPB WILL ACT.

Chapter 9

Leisure Activities

Whether you are looking forward to devoting more time to an existing interest, resuming an old hobby or trying your hand at an entirely new pastime, the choice is enormous.

You can do anything from basket-weaving to bridge, archery to amateur dramatics. You can join a music-making group, a Scrabble club, a photographic society or become a beekeeper. There are any number of historic homes and beautiful gardens to visit, as well as museums, art galleries, abbeys and castles.

Almost every locality now has excellent sports facilities and thanks to the Sports Council's 50-Plus campaign, there is scope for complete novices to take up bowls, golf, badminton and many others. Similarly, there are dancing and keep-fit classes, railway enthusiasts' clubs and groups devoted to researching their local history. Many of the organisations offer special concessionary rates to people of retirement age, as do a number of theatres and other places of entertainment.

This chapter should be read in conjunction with Chapter 13, Holidays, as many of the organisations listed there – such as the Field Studies Council – could apply equally well here. Those that appear in the Holiday chapter tend in the main either to offer residential courses or would probably involve most people in spending a few days away from home to take advantage of the facilities.

While every effort has been made to ensure that prices are correct, these cannot be guaranteed and those quoted should, therefore, only be taken as a guide rather than gospel. The reason is that most organisations alter their charges from time to time and since there is no set date when this happens, it is impossible to keep track.

In addition to the suggestions contained in this chapter, your library, local authority recreation department and Adult Education Institute will be able to signpost you to other activities in your area.

Adult education

Ever longed to take a degree, learn about computing, study philosophy or do a course in archaeology? Opportunities for education abound with these and scores of other subjects easily available to everyone, regardless of age or previous qualifications.

Adult Education Institutes

There is an Adult Education Institute in most areas of the country. Classes normally start in September and run through the academic year. Choice of subjects is enormous and many AEIs allow concessionary fees for students over 60. Ask at your local library for details. Or in London, buy the booklet *Floodlight* (£2), available from most bookstalls.

Council for the Accreditation of Correspondence Colleges, 27 Marylebone Road, London NW1 5JS. T:071-935 5391. If you want to study at home, the Council will give you a list of colleges which teach your chosen subject.

National Adult School Organisation, Masu Centre, Gaywood Croft, Cregoe Street, Birmingham B15 2ED. T:021-622 3400. Their 'Friendship through Discussion' groups meet in members' homes or in halls, weekly or fortnightly. They follow either a national study syllabus or topics of their own choice. Some groups organise social activities and there is also a national summer school. For further information, write to the above address, enclosing sae.

National Extension College, 18 Brooklands Avenue, Cambridge CB2 2HN. T:0223 316644. The NEC is a non-profit making body established to provide high quality home study courses for adults, details of which are listed in their free *Guide to Courses*, available on request. Many of the NEC's most able students are retired and are returning to study after many years. Cost is £50 upwards depending on which course you pick (there is a choice of over 100), with 10 per cent discount for pensioners on those costing £75 and over.

Open University, Central Enquiry Service, PO Box 200, Walton Hall, Milton Keynes MK7 6YZ. T:0908 653231. Why not take a degree or a short course through the Open University? Students are all ages – the oldest OU graduate was 92 – no academic qualifications are required and there is a vast range of subjects from which to choose.

Courses normally involve a mix of: correspondence work, radio and TV programmes, audio and video cassettes, contact with local tutors and, in some cases, also a residential school with plenty of opportunities for meeting other students.

You can study entirely at your own speed: on average people take up to six or eight years to acquire a degree. However, there is no long-term commitment and it is quite possible to sign on just for one course.

In addition to its degree studies, the Open University offers courses for 'associate' students and study packs in areas of general community and vocational interest. There are also materials designed for use by groups on such subjects as planning for retirement and working with older people. Fees range from under £10 for a study pack to £475 for a full-credit degree level course taken as an associate student. (Other courses, designed for professional and technical audiences, can be considerably more expensive.) Some local authorities will give financial assistance.

For information about opportunities for adult education in Scotland, contact: **Network Scotland Ltd.**, The Mews, Ruthven Lane, Glasgow G12 9JQ. T:041-357 1774.

University of the Third Age, U3A National Office, 1 Stockwell Green, London SW9 9JF. T:071-737 2541. U3A is a self-help movement for people no longer in paid work, offering a wide range of educational, creative and leisure activities. It operates through a national network of local U3As, which determine their own courses and social programmes according to members' interests. Individuals may join as Associates for £5 per annum. For a brochure, together with addresses of all local U3As, contact the address above enclosing a 6" x 10" sae.

Workers' Educational Association, Temple House, 17 Victoria Park Square, Bethnal Green, London E2 9PB. T:081-983 1515. WEA branches in all parts of the country offer a wide range of courses including education for retirement. There is normally a choice of part-time, day or evening classes. Your library or education authority should be able to put you in touch with your local branch. Alternatively, contact the above address.

Arts

Enjoyment of the arts is certainly no longer confined to London. Whether you are interested in active participation or just appreciating the performance of others, there is an exhilarating choice of events with many offering concessionary prices to retired people.

Regional arts boards and local arts councils
For first-hand information about what is going on in your area, contact your regional arts board; or in the case of those living in Scotland, Wales and Northern Ireland, the Arts Council. Most areas arrange an immensely varied programme with musical events, drama, arts and craft exhibitions and sometimes more unusual functions, offering something of interest to just about everyone. Many regional arts boards produce regular newsletters with details of arts events in their area. For addresses, ask at your local library.

Music and ballet
Scope ranges from becoming a Friend and supporting one of the famous 'Houses' such as Covent Garden to music-making in your own right.

Friends. If you live close enough to take advantage of the 'perks', subscribing as a Friend allows you a number of very attractive advantages including in all cases priority for bookings.

Friends of Covent Garden, Royal Opera House, Covent Garden, London WC2E 9DD. T:071-240 1200 or 071-379 7783. Friends enjoy opportunities to attend talks, recitals, study days, masterclasses, certain 'open' rehearsals and informal social events. Subject to availability, Friends can buy reduced price tickets one hour before the performance. Adult membership for a year is £37.

Friends of English National Opera, London Coliseum, St. Martin's Lane, London WC2N 4ES. T:071-836 0111 (ext.442). As a Friend, you can attend open dress rehearsals, tour backstage, go to meetings with artists working at the Coliseum, enjoy lunchtime talks and recitals and obtain reduced price tickets for many of the performances. There are also arranged trips to see the work of other companies and invitations to social events. Membership costs £23 a year (£36 for two joint members). Senior citizen rates are £19 for an individual (£30 for two joint members).

Friends of Sadler's Wells, Rosebery Avenue, London EC1R 4TN. T:071-278 6563. Friends are invited to open rehearsals, talks, demonstrations and social events with the resident and visiting companies. They also receive a regular newsletter and ticket concessions. People of retirement age can join for an annual membership of £10.

Music making
Just about every style of music is catered for, even including an orchestra for retired people. Information about local societies and other groups is

Leisure Activities

contained in the *British Music Education Year Book* and the *British Music Year Book*, both of which should be in the reference section of your library.

Handbell Ringers of Great Britain, 2 Holt Park Approach, Holt Park, Leeds LS16 7PW. T:0532 677711. Arranges rallies, concerts, workshops and lectures. To contact your local group, write to the above address, enclosing sae.

National Federation of Music Societies, Francis House, Francis Street, London SW1P 1DE. T:071-828 7320. Can provide you with addresses of some 1,300 affiliated choral societies, orchestras and music societies throughout the country. Most charge a nominal membership fee and standards range from the semi-professional to the unashamedly amateur.

Society of Recorder Players, 469 Merton Road, London SW18 5LD. T:081-874 2237. Players of all standards and ages are welcomed at the many branches. There is also an annual festival with massed playing, competitions and concerts. Annual subscription is £8.50. Branch subscriptions may differ. Write to the Society, enclosing an sae, for a list of addresses.

Television and radio audiences
If you would like to be part of the invited studio audience for a radio or television programme, you can apply to the BBC through the relevant ticket unit for London-based programmes; or for outside London, through the appropriate regional centre. The ticket unit addresses are:

The Ticket Unit,
BBC Television,
Wood Lane,
Shepherd's Bush,
London W12 7SB.

The Ticket Unit,
BBC Radio,
Broadcasting House,
London W1A 1AA.

For independent television, audience participation in programmes is the responsibility of each programme maker and requests should be channelled to the appropriate contractor for the area.

Theatre
Details of current and forthcoming productions, as well as theatre reviews, are contained in the newspapers. As general wisdom, preview performances are invariably cheaper and there are often concessionary tickets for matinees.

Listed here are one or two theatres and organisations that offer special facilities of interest, including priority booking and reduced price tickets. Also included is an association for enthusiasts of amateur dramatics.

Barbican Centre, Silk Street, London EC2Y 8DS. T:071-638 4141 (ext. 218 for information). Box Office: 071-638 8891. The Barbican Centre combines two theatres, concert hall, art gallery, concourse gallery, cinema and library. The Centre offers tours of the building, frequent free live musical events in the foyers, free exhibitions and restaurant facilities. Reduced tickets for senior citizens are available for many performances on a standby basis. For £5 a year, mailing list subscribers receive a monthly diary.

Royal National Theatre, South Bank, London SE1 9PX. T:071-928 2252 (box office). Offers backstage tours, invitations to discussion meetings, live foyer music, free exhibitions and restaurant facilities as well as its three theatres. There are group price reductions for most performances and pensioners can buy matinee seats for £8.

For details of the Mailing List Membership (£6 a year), contact **Royal National Theatre**, Mailing List, Freepost, London SE1 7BR; or ring 071-261 9256 (10 a.m. to 6 p.m., Monday to Friday).

Society of West End Theatre, Bedford Chambers, The Piazza, Covent Garden, London WC2E 8HQ. T:071-836 3193. The Society co-ordinates a scheme under which senior citizens can get substantial reductions for midweek matinee performances at many West End theatres. Look for the symbol 'M' in *The London Theatre Guide* or the *Independent* and *Guardian* listings. Senior citizens can also receive concessionary prices for evening performances or weekend matinees on a standby basis with all listings showing the symbol 'S'. Standby tickets are available approximately an hour before the performance begins.

Concessions are subject to availability; it is wise to check with the box office or Theatreline before setting off for a performance. Pensioners will need to present proof of their senior citizen status at the box office, for example, using a travel pass or pension book.

Annual subscription to the *London Theatre Guide* costs £10. Write to the Society at the above address.

The Society's *Disabled Access Guide to London West End Theatres* provides information about special facilities, access for wheelchairs, transport advice and price concessions for disabled theatregoers. Available free from West End theatres or by post from SWET (please send 36p sae).

Scottish Community Drama Association, 5 York Place, Edinburgh EH1 3EB. T:031-557 5552. The Association is the umbrella organisation for amateur dramatic societies in Scotland and offers them advice, encouragement and practical help. Individual membership (£10 a year) gives access to the Association's libraries, training courses and summer schools. The Association also runs playwriting competitions and can put you in touch with local amateur dramatic societies.

Leicester Square Ticket Booth, London. The Booth sells tickets to many West End theatres at half-price on the day of performance. It is open to personal callers only Monday – Saturday at 12 noon for matinees, 2.30 – 6.30 p.m. for evening performances. There is a service charge of £1.35. Payment in cash only.

Theatre and Concert Travel Club, PO Box 1, St. Albans, Herts AL1 4ED. T:0727 41115. The Club books theatre and concert tickets and provides discounted rail travel to the theatre as a complete package. Members receive a regular *Theatre Guide* with details of special events and exclusive offers. Annual subscription is £12. Most visits are to London but short breaks to Stratford, Bath, Edinburgh and a host of other cities can also be arranged.

Late night trains. Network South-East runs late night trains for theatre goers. For details of services, enquire at your local station.

Visual arts

If you enjoy attending exhibitions and lectures, membership of some of the arts societies offers you a number of delightful privileges.

Contemporary Art Society, 20 John Islip Street, London SW1P 4LL. T:071-821 5323. Members can take part in an extensive programme of events including: visits to artists' studios, parties at special exhibitions, day or weekend trips throughout Britain and abroad, lectures and films. Annual subscription is £15 for individuals, £20 for two people at the same address.

National Art Collections Fund, 20 John Islip Street, London SW1P 4JX. T:071-821 0404.

As a member, you enjoy: free admission to all art museums and galleries; private evening viewings; visits to historic houses not normally open to the public; regular magazine, plus a countrywide programme of social events, lectures and concerts. There are also art tours at home and abroad led by experts. Subscription is £15 per year; senior citizens, £10.

National Association of Decorative & Fine Arts Societies, 8a Lower Grosvenor Place, London SW1W 0EN. T:071-233 5433.

There are lively programmes of events including monthly lectures, museum and gallery visits, guided tours of historic houses and organised tours in the UK and abroad. Many societies have volunteer groups working in the houses and there are also church-recorder groups which make detailed records of the interiors of churches. Membership of a local society is about £15-£25 a year. Details are available from NADFAS, see above.

Tate Gallery, Millbank, London SW1P 4RG. T:071-821 1313. Recorded Information: T:071-821 7128. The gallery comprises the national collections of British painting from the 16th century to the present day and also international 20th century painting and sculpture. There are free lectures (Tuesday–Sunday) and guided tours (Monday–Friday); also special tours for disabled people by prior arrangement. Friends of the Tate enjoy free admission to all exhibitions and may bring two guests on one Thursday evening a month. They are also invited to private views and have opportunities to attend lectures at other galleries. Membership is £25 (£20 senior citizens).

Painting as a hobby

If you are interested in improving your own painting technique, rather than simply viewing the works of great masters, contact your local Adult Education Institute for details of courses in your area. Your library may have information about local painting groups, clubs and societies.

Crafts

The vast majority of suggestions are contained in Chapter 13, Holidays, variously under 'Arts and crafts' and 'Special interest holidays', the reason being that most of the organisations concerned make a feature of arranging residential courses or of organising, for example, painting holidays. However, if you are interested in a particular form of craft work and want information or advice, many of the societies and others listed in Chapter 13 should be able to help you. Herewith one or two additional possibilities.

The Basketmakers' Association, Hon. Secretary: Mrs. V E Jones, The Vineyard, Bury Green, Little Hadham, Ware, Herts SG11 2ES. T:0279 651525. Promotes better standards of design and technique in the art of basketmaking, chair seating and allied crafts. It arranges courses, demonstrations and exhibitions. Membership costs £10 (£14 family membership, two people).

Crafts Council, 44A Pentonville Road, Islington, London N1 9BY. T:071-278 7700. As well as holding exhibitions, the Crafts Council runs an information centre and reference library which can give advice on almost everything you could possibly want to know: different craft courses throughout the country, suppliers of materials, addresses of craft guilds and societies, fact sheets on business practice for craftspeople as well as details of craft fairs and markets, galleries, shops and other outlets for work.

Additionally, the Council has a slide and video library (reference only), publishes a bi-monthly magazine, *Crafts*, and maintains both an index of craftspeople and a national register of makers. Admission to the Crafts Council Gallery is free: open, Tuesday to Saturday, 11 to 6; and Sunday, 2 to 6 p.m.

The Embroiderers' Guild, Apartment 41, Hampton Court Palace, East Molesey, Surrey KT8 9AU. T:081-943 1229. Membership is open to all, beginners and experts, with an interest in embroidery and related crafts. Members can visit the collection of embroideries and lace at Hampton Court, borrow study folios and attend classes and lectures. There is also a full programme of residential weekends, seminars, exhibitions and tours in the UK and abroad; plus 140 local branches. Membership is £22.50; £14.50 for those over 60. Branches have their own subscriptions.

Open College of the Arts, Houndhill, Worsbrough, Barnsley, South Yorkshire S70 6TU. T:0226 730495. Offers courses for those wishing to acquire or improve their skills in drawing, painting, sculpture, textiles, photography, creative writing, garden design, music and art history. Average price for a year's course is about £200.

Dance/keep-fit

Clubs, classes and groups exist in all parts of the country, variously offering: ballroom, Old Tyme, Scottish, folk, ballet, disco dancing and others. Additionally, there are music and relaxation classes, aerobics and more gentle keep-fit sessions.

Many of the relaxation and keep-fit classes in particular cater for all standards and some are specially designed for older people to tone up muscles and improve their circulation while making friends in an agreeable atmosphere.

Best advice is to contact your adult education or sports centre, or alternatively the library, to find out what is available in your area. Listed here are some of the national organisations that can advise you and put you in touch with local groups. There are also some extra names in Chapter 12, Health, see 'Keeping fit' section.

The Central Council of Physical Recreation, Francis House, Francis

Street, London SW1P 1DE. T:071-828 3163/4. Will provide information on all sporting activities e.g. movement, swimming, bowls and offer advice to anyone wishing to become involved in a sport or recreation.

English Folk Dance and Song Society, Cecil Sharp House, 2 Regent's Park Road, London NW1 7AY. T:071-485 2206. There are some 570 clubs around the country which organise both regular and special events. Membership costs £18 (£27 joint membership); £9 and £15 respectively for members over 60. Contact the Society for details.

Imperial Society of Teachers Of Dancing, Euston Hall, Birkenhead Street, London WC1H 8BE. T:071-837 9967. Throughout the UK there are some 7,000 teachers offering instruction in virtually all forms of dancing. Many organise classes and events particularly for older people. Contact the Society for local names.

Keep Fit Association, Francis House, Francis Street, London SW1P 1DE. T:071-233 8898. The Keep Fit Association has a responsible attitude and emphatically does not believe in 70 year olds trying to ape Olympic gymnasts. KFA teachers have special training in working with older people. Almost all adult education centres run daytime classes, many specially geared to keeping fit in retirement. (See also 'Extend', in Chapter 12, Health.)

Royal Scottish Country Dance Society, 12 Coates Crescent, Edinburgh EH3 7AF. T:031-225 3854. The Society has members from 16 to 80-plus in its many branches and groups all over the world.

For people with disabilities

Happily, there are increasingly fewer activities from which handicapped people are debarred through lack of suitable facilities, as will be evident from many of the suggestions listed earlier in the chapter. This section, therefore, only deals with one topic not covered elsewhere, namely enjoyment of books, which for many blind or partially sighted people can be a special problem.

British Wireless for the Blind, Gabriel House, 34 New Road, Chatham, Kent ME4 4QR. T:0634 832501. Issues radios or radio-cassette recorders on free permanent loan to any registered blind person. You can apply through your local Blind Welfare Officer or voluntary association for the blind.

Calibre, Aylesbury, Buckinghamshire HP22 5XQ. T:0296 432339 (24-hour service) and 0296 81211. Calibre is a lending library of recorded

Leisure Activities

books on standard cassettes. These are available to anyone on production of a doctor's certificate certifying their 'inability to read printed books in the normal way'. There are some 3,000 titles (catalogues, price £5).

National Library for the Blind, Cromwell Road, Bredbury, Stockport, Cheshire SK6 2SG. T:061-494 0217 (24 hours). Lends books in Braille and Moon as well as music scores in Braille; post-free to individual readers.

National Listening Library, 12 Lant Street, London SE1 1QH. T:071-407 9417. Loans a special tape player and a wide range of titles to those unable to read due to disability. Annual subscription, £15.

RNIB Talking Book Service, Mount Pleasant, Wembley, Middlesex HA0 1RR. T:081-903 6666. This is a library service with more than 8,500 titles for anyone who is registered as blind or partially sighted or whose vision is such that they cannot easily read normal print. Application should be made to the local authority Social Services Department or direct to the library. The charge for the service is normally paid by members' local authorities. Special recorder machines are available on permanent loan.

Games

Many local areas have their own bridge, chess, whist, dominoes, Scrabble and other groups who meet to enjoy friendly games. Your library should have details. Alternatively, you can contact the national organisations below.

British Chess Federation, 9a Grand Parade, St. Leonards on Sea, East Sussex TN38 0DD. T:0424 442500.
English Bridge Union, Broadfields, Bicester Road, Aylesbury, Bucks HP19 3BG. T:0296 394414.
Scrabble Club Co-ordinator, 42 Elthiron Road, London SW6 4BW. T:071-731 2633.

Gardens and gardening

Courses, gardens to visit, special help for people with disabilities, how to run a gardening association . . . these and other interests are all catered for by the organisations listed.

The English Gardening School, at the Chelsea Physic Garden, 66 Royal Hospital Road, London SW3 4HS. T:071-352 4347. Short courses are held in the historic lecture room of the Chelsea Physic Garden. Cost is about £50 plus VAT per day.

Gardening for the Disabled Trust & Garden Club, Hayes Farmhouse, Hayes Lane, Peasmarsh, Nr. Rye, East Sussex TN31 6XR.

Provides practical and financial help to disabled people who want to garden actively. The annual subscription is £3 (£5 for groups), £25 for 10-year membership.

Horticultural Therapy, Goulds Ground, Vallis Way, Frome, Somerset BA11 3DW. T:0373 464782; 24-hour answerphone service for visually impaired people: 0373 467072. Helps elderly, disabled or visually impaired people to garden. It runs an advisory service by post and telephone. Members receive a quarterly magazine. There are demonstrations, workshops and meetings. The centre can also advise on special tools and where these can be obtained.

National Gardens Scheme, Hatchlands Park, East Clandon, Guildford, Surrey GU4 7RT. T:0483 211535. (For England and Wales.) The Scheme covers nearly 3,000 private gardens which are open to the public, perhaps one day a year, to raise money for charitable causes. Further information is given in the Scheme's Yellow Book, *The Gardens of England and Wales* (£2 from booksellers or £2.75 including p&p from the address above). Suitability for wheelchairs is also indicated. The organisation is always looking for new gardens. Should you wish to offer yours, however small, apply to the county organiser whose address is in one of the handbooks.

National Society of Allotment and Leisure Gardeners Ltd., O'Dell House, Hunters Road, Corby, Northants NN17 1JE. T:0536 66576. The Society encourages all forms of horticultural education and the forming of local allotment and gardening associations. Annual membership costs £6; associate membership for home gardeners, £3.50 and society membership 40p per member. This gives you access to free help and advice plus receipt of the Society's bulletin. There is also a Seeds Scheme, offering special prices.

Royal Horticultural Society, PO Box 313, Vincent Square, London SW1P 2PE. T:071-834 4333. Members receive free and reduced price tickets to gardens and shows, including the Chelsea Flower Show, and can also attend lectures and practical demonstrations both in and out of London. Membership costs £21 (1992) plus a once only enrolment fee of £5. For further information, contact the Membership Manager.

History

People with an interest in the past have a truly glorious choice of activities to sample. You can visit historic monuments, including ancient castles and stately homes; study genealogy; research the history of your local area; attend lectures and receptions.

Age Exchange Reminiscence Centre, 11 Blackheath Village, Blackheath, London SE3 9LA. T:081-318 9105. The Centre features exhibitions recording the life-styles of the 1920s and 1930s. There are also publications, depicting the period plus a year-round programme of activities including music and drama. Open Monday to Saturday, 10 a.m. to 5.30 p.m.; admission free.

British Association for Local History, Shopwyke Hall, Chichester, Sussex PO20 6BQ. T:0243 787639. The Association promotes the study of local history. It will put you in touch with your local group, give advice and invite you to seminars and courses. Annual membership (basic) is £8.

City of London Information Centre, St. Paul's Churchyard (Southside), London EC4M 8BX. T:071-260 1456. The City of London offers enough interest to occupy you for a year or longer. The Information Centre acts as a tourist office, giving advice and guidance. There are lots of free leaflets including a monthly events list.

English Heritage (Membership Department), PO Box 1BB, London W1A 1BB, T:071-973 3400. Manages over 350 historic properties. Members receive a Welcome Pack including guidebook and map, a card granting free admission plus a magazine publicising events and developments of conservation interest. Annual subscription (1992) is £15, £10.50 for senior citizens with reductions for couples.

Federation of Family History Societies, The Benson Room, Birmingham and Midland Institute, Margaret Street, Birmingham B3 3BS. An umbrella organisation for 150 societies throughout the world (90 in the UK) that provide assistance if you are interested in tracing your ancestors. Write to the administrator, Mrs. Pauline Saul, enclosing (A4) sae.

Friends of Historic Scotland, PO Box 157, Edinburgh EH3 5RA. T:031-244 3099. Membership gives you free access to 330 of Scotland's historic buildings and ancient monuments, a free directory of the sites, special guided tours and a quarterly newsletter to keep you up to date with new activities. Membership cost is £13 a year; £9 for senior citizens over 60; £13.50 for retired couples.

Historical Association, 59a Kennington Park Road, London SE11 4JH. T:071-735 3901. Brings together people of all ages and backgrounds who share an interest in and love for the past. Members receive *The Historian* and may join in a wide variety of activities such as lectures, outings, conferences and tours conducted by expert lecturers. There are over 80 local branches. Membership costs £22 a year.

Historic Houses Association (Membership), PO Box 21, Unit 7, Campus 5, The Business Park, Letchworth, Herts SG6 2JF. T:0462 675848. Friends of the HHA enjoy free entrance to nearly 300 HHA houses and gardens, get a quarterly magazine and receive invitations to lectures, concerts, receptions and other events. Membership costs £20; £30 double.

National Trust, 36 Queen Anne's Gate, London SW1H 9AS. T:071-222 9251. Exists to protect historic buildings and areas of great natural beauty in England, Wales and Northern Ireland. Membership gives you free entry to the Trust's many properties and to those of the National Trust for Scotland. Hundreds of special events are arranged each year, including guided tours, fairs and outdoor entertainments. Individual membership (1992) is £23; £15 for pensioners.

National Trust for Scotland, 5 Charlotte Square, Edinburgh EH2 4DU. T:031-226 5922. Individual membership is £22 a year; £11 for pensioners.

Society Of Genealogists, 14 Charterhouse Buildings, Goswell Road, London EC1M 7BA. T:071-251 8799. The Society promotes the study of genealogy and heraldry. Lectures are arranged and there is also a variety of annual courses, including day and weekend seminars. There is a joining fee of £7.50. Annual membership is £25; £16 for country members. Non-members may use the library on payment of a small fee.

Hobbies

Whatever your special enthusiasm, most of the organisations listed organise events, answer queries and can put you in contact with kindred spirits.

The British Association of Numismatic Societies, Secretary: P H Mernick, c/o Bush Boake Allen Ltd., Blackhorse Lane, London E17 5QP. BANS is an umbrella organisation for some 60 local societies and can put you in touch with your nearest group.

British Jigsaw Puzzle Library, 8 Heath Terrace, Leamington Spa, Warwickshire CV32 5LY. T:0926 311874. This is a lending library with puzzles exchanged by post. Subscriptions range from £26 for three months to £58 for a year. Postal charges are extra.

Leisure Activities

English Vineyards Association, 38 West Park, London SE9 4RH. T:081-857 0452. Publishes a free booklet listing vineyards you can visit and where you can sample the wine. Please enclose sae (8½" × 4½").

Miniature Armoured Fighting Vehicle Association, 15 Berwick Avenue, Heaton Mersey, Stockport, Cheshire SK4 3AA. T:061-432 7574. Provides advice and information on tanks and other military equipment, issues a bi-monthly magazine and can put you in touch with a local branch. There are meetings, displays and competitions. UK membership is £4.50 a year.

National Association of Flower Arrangement Societies of Great Britain, 21 Denbigh Street, London SW1V 2HF. T:071-828 5145. Can put you in touch with local clubs and classes.

National Philatelic Society, 107 Charterhouse Street, London EC1M 6PT. T:071-251 5040. Holds monthly Saturday meetings with auctions in London and sometimes elsewhere. Members receive a free journal and have use of the library. An advisory service can help with philatelic queries and there is an exchange packet scheme. Membership costs £17.50 a year.

Radio Society of Great Britain, Lambda House, Cranborne Road, Potters Bar, Herts EN6 3JE. T:0707 59015. The Society provides advice on how to join the one-and-a-half million amateur radio operators around the world.

Railway Correspondence & Travel Society, 97 Greenhill Road, Kettering, Northants NN15 7LN. T:0536 85575. There are regular meetings at about 30 centres and the RC&TS also organises visits, rail trips and overseas tours to see railways in other countries. Membership costs £12 a year, including a magazine.

The Royal Photographic Society, The Octagon, Milsom Street, Bath BA1 1DN. T:0225 462841. Promotes photography through meetings, lectures, workshops, conferences and exhibitions. There are also field trips and social events. Membership is open to anyone interested in photography, amateur or professional. Current annual subscription rates are £54; £32 for over-65s.

Museums

Most museums organise free lectures, guided tours, and sometimes slide shows, on aspects of their collection or special exhibitions. As with art galleries and theatres, an increasing trend is to form a group of 'Friends' who pay a membership subscription to support the museum and in return enjoy certain advantages, such as: access to private views, visits to places of interest, receptions and other social activities. Examples include:

British Association of Friends Of Museums, 548 Wilbraham Road, Manchester M21 1LB.
British Museum Society, c/o The British Museum, London WC1B 3DG. T:071-637 9983.
Friends of the Fitzwilliam Museum, Fitzwilliam Museum, Trumpington Street, Cambridge CB2 1RB. T:0223 332900.
Friends of the National Maritime Museum, Greenwich, London SE10 9NF. T:081-312 6678/6638.
Museum of the Moving Image, South Bank, London SE1 8XT. T:071-401 2636 (recorded information).
National Museum of Wales, Cathays Park, Cardiff CF1 3NP. T:0222 397951.
Friends of the National Museums of Scotland, The Royal Museum of Scotland, Chambers Street, Edinburgh EH1 1JF. T:031-225 7534.
Friends of the V & A, The Victoria and Albert Museum, London SW7 2RL. T:071-589 4040.

Nature and conservation

Many of the conservation organisations are very keen to recruit volunteers and are, therefore, listed in Chapter 11, Voluntary Work, rather than here. By the same token, many of those concerned with field studies arrange courses and other special activity interests which, because there is usually a residential content, seem more appropriate in Chapter 13, Holidays. The potential list is enormous. To give you a flavour, herewith a short 'mixed bag', highlighting a range from canals to ecology.

Amenity Organisations. If you are interested in conservation and the environment, you might like to join your local amenity society. You should be able to contact it through your public library.

British Ecological Society, Burlington House, Piccadilly, London W1V 0LQ. T:071-434 2641. The Society holds general and special interest group meetings and supports various ecological projects. Membership costs about £16 (1992), more if you wish to receive journals.

The Civic Trust, 17 Carlton House Terrace, London SW1Y 5AW. T:071-930 0914. Publishes both an *Environmental Directory* (£4 post paid) listing 300 organisations including voluntary societies; and a newsletter, *Urban Focus*, with articles on planning, architecture, transport, pollution and landscaping. Annual subscription £10.50.

The Conservation Foundation, 1 Kensington Gore, London SW7 2AR. T:071-823 8842. For those interested in conservation and protecting the environment, both rural and urban, the Conservation Foundation is a good starting point. It provides an information and legal advice service and publishes various books and guides.

Forestry Commission, 231 Corstorphine Road, Edinburgh EH12 7AT. T:031-334 0303. For information on Forestry Commission walks and trails, picnic places and visitor centres contact your local Forestry Commission office or the Public Information Division at the above address.

The Royal Society for the Protection of Birds, The Lodge, Sandy, Bedfordshire SG19 2DL. T:0767 680551. The Society promotes the conservation of wild birds and the countryside in which they live and breed. Members receive a quarterly magazine, plus free entry to 100 RSPB nature reserves. A national network of 176 groups enables members to support the Society at local level and to pursue their interest in birds, often by undertaking voluntary work on reserves. Membership costs £18 single, £22 joint and £26 family, with special rates for senior citizens.

RSNC, The Wildlife Trusts Partnership, The Green, Witham Park, Waterside South, Lincoln LN5 7JR. T:0522 544400. RSNC is a partnership of 47 local Wildlife Trusts and over 50 Urban Wildlife Groups which between them care for 1,800 nature reserves, as well as protecting our threatened countryside. By joining the Wildlife Trust for your area, you can visit the reserves or even help in their wardening and management. The Trusts run their own activities including arranging talks and organising guided walks along with many other events. Membership fee is £12. Application forms are obtainable from RSNC at the above address.

Scottish Inland Waterways Association, 139 Old Dalkeith Road, Edinburgh EH16 4SZ. T:031-664 1070. Co-ordinates the activities of local canal preservation societies and will put you in touch with your nearest group.

Wildfowl and Wetlands Trust, Slimbridge, Gloucester GL2 7BT. T:0453 890333. Aims to protect wildfowl, to conserve wetlands and to make it possible for people to observe, enjoy and learn about birds. Membership (£12) gives you free entry to all Trust centres plus receipt of the biannual magazine. Wheelchair access to reserves and hides.

Public library service

Britain's public library service is among the best in the world. It issues about 600 million books free a year, loans records and cassettes and is a source of an enormous amount of information about both local and national activities.

Many libraries have a mobile service and some also have volunteer library visitors who deliver books and materials to housebound people. Among the many facilities on offer, large print books are usually available as are musical scores, leaflets on DSS benefits, consumer information and details of local community activities.

Sport

Retirement is no excuse for giving up sport. On the contrary, it is an ideal time to get into trim. Facilities abound and, unlike people with a 9 to 5 job, you enjoy the great advantage of being able to book outside peak hours. To find out about opportunities in your area, contact your local authority recreational department, or your sports/leisure centre.

If you have any difficulties or wish to receive their *50-Plus* leaflets, contact the regional office of the Sports Council, address from: The Information Centre, **Sports Council**, 16 Upper Woburn Place, London WC1H 0QP. T:071-388 1277.

Also useful to know about is: **The Central Council of Physical Recreation**, Francis House, Francis Street, London SW1P 1DE. T:071-828 3163/4. They can provide information on all sporting activities and offer advice to anyone wishing to become involved in a sport or recreation.

Angling
The Angling Foundation, 23 Brighton Road, South Croydon, Surrey CR2 6EA. T:081-681 1242. Can advise on where to find qualified tuition, local tackle dealers and similar information, as well as supply a number of useful leaflets.

Archery
Grand National Archery Society, 7th Street, The National Agricultural Centre, Stoneleigh, Kenilworth, Warwickshire CV8 2LG. T:0203 696631. Can put you in touch with your nearest club of which there are now over 1,200 around the country. Club membership varies from approximately £25 to £75 a year, including affiliation fees.

Badminton
Badminton Association of England Ltd., National Badminton Centre, Bradwell Road, Loughton Lodge, Milton Keynes, Bucks MK8 9LA. T:0908 568822. Most sports and leisure centres have badminton courts

Leisure Activities

and give instruction, as do many Adult Education Institutes. If you need advice, or are interested in a short residential course contact the Association.

Bowling

There are many clubs all over the country and a number of local authorities may also provide facilities. Alternatively contact:

English Bowling Association, Lyndhurst Road, Worthing, West Sussex BN11 2AZ. T:0903 820222.
English Women's Indoor Bowling Association, 9 Pine Road, Whitenap, Romsey, Hants SO51 8SG. T:0794 514922.
English Women's Bowling Association, 'Darracombe', The Clays, Market Lavington, Wiltshire SN10 4AY. T:0380 813774.
English Indoor Bowling Association, 290a Barking Road, London E6 3BA. T:081-470 1237.

There are over 2,700 local clubs, many of which provide instruction for beginners. Some have reduced rates for senior citizens. A national competition for 55-plus singles and pairs is organised each year. If you decide to take up bowls, you are advised not to buy your equipment without advice from the club coach.

Clay pigeon shooting

Clay Pigeon Shooting Association, 107 Epping New Road, Buckhurst Hill, Essex IG9 5TQ. T:081-505 6221. The CPSA is an association of individual shooters and a federation of clubs. As a member you have public liability insurance of £2 million, your scores are recorded in the national averages and you can compete in national events. You also receive the Association magazine for free. Individual membership is £25 per year.

Cricket

MCC Lord's Cricket Ground, St. John's Wood Road, London NW8 8QN. T:071-289 1611. You can enjoy a conducted tour of Lord's which among other attractions includes the Cricket Museum, showing the original 'Ashes' as well as a video recording some of the great cricketing performances of the past. Price is £4.50 (£3 for pensioners) and tour times are normally at noon and 2 p.m. These times are subject to variation and you are advised to check before making a special visit (T:071-266 3825). Half-price tickets are available to pensioners for some matches.

National Cricket Association, Lord's Cricket Ground, London NW8 8QZ. T:071-289 6098. If you want to play, watch or help at cricket matches, contact your local club or send an sae to the above address. The NCA can put you in touch with your county cricket association. It also organises an over-50 County Cricket Championship.

The Foster's Oval Cricket Ground, Surrey County Cricket Club, Kennington, London SE11 5SS. T:071-582 6660. The Foster's Oval Cricket Ground is one of the main venues for test and county matches. Half-price tickets are available to pensioners for county matches and there are also special club membership rates entitling pensioners to a number of special benefits including free or reduced price entry to the members' pavilion.

Croquet
Croquet Association, Tony Antenen, Secretary, Hurlingham Club, Ranelagh Gardens, London SW6 3PR. T:071-736 3148. A growing number of local authorities as well as clubs now offer facilities for croquet enthusiasts. The Croquet Association runs coaching courses and can advise you about club membership, events, purchase of equipment and other information.

Cycling
Cyclists' Touring Club, Cotterell House, 69 Meadrow, Godalming, Surrey GU7 3HS. T:0483-417217. The CTC offers members competitive cycle and free third party insurance, free legal aid, a handbook, colour magazines, organised cycling holidays and introductions to 200 local cycling groups. There is also a veterans' section. Membership (1992/93) costs £24 a year; £16 for retired people.

Darts
British Darts Organisation Ltd., 2 Pages Lane, Muswell Hill, London N10 1PS. T:081-883 5544/5. Opportunities for playing darts can be found almost anywhere in clubs, pubs and sports centres. Contact the national body should you require further help.

Golf
English Golf Union, 1-3 Upper King Street, Leicester LE1 6XF. T:0533 553042.
Golfing Union of Ireland, Glencar House, 81 Eglinton Road, Donnybrook, Dublin 4. T:010 353 1 2694111.
Scottish Golf Union, The Cottage, 181a Whitehouse Road, Barnton, Edinburgh EH4 6BY. T:031-339 7546.

Welsh Golfing Union, Powys House, Cwmbran, Gwent. T:0633 870261.

The National Golf Unions can provide information about municipal courses and private clubs. Additionally, many adult education institutes and sports centres run classes for beginners.

Rambling
Ramblers' Association, 1-5 Wandsworth Road, London SW8 2XX. T:071-582 6878. The Ramblers' Association will be glad to put you in touch with one of its many local groups. Membership (1992) is £14 a year; £7 for the retired.

Running
The Running Sixties, 120 Norfolk Avenue, Sanderstead, Surrey CR2 8BS. T:081-657 7660. Contact: the Secretary. Membership is open to all men and women over 60 who are interested in running and the comradeship that it can engender. The programme of activities includes regular handicap runs which cater for all abilities from hares to tortoises as well as the possibility of competing in some of the major marathon events. The membership subscription is £5.

Swimming
Amateur Swimming Association, Harold Fern House, Derby Square, Loughborough, Leics LE11 0AL. T:0509 230431. Coaching and 'Learn to Swim' classes are arranged by many authorities who also make the pool available at various times of the week for older people who prefer to swim quietly and unhindered. The Association offers many award achemes to encourage greater proficiency in swimming and as an incentive to swim regularly for fitness and health. Further details on request from the ASA.

Table tennis
The Veterans English Table Tennis Society (VETTS), Harwood House, 90 Broadway, Letchworth, Herts SG6 3PH. T:0462 671191. Holds regional and national championships including singles and doubles events for over 40s, 50s, 60s and 70s. For further information, contact the Membership Secretary.

Tennis
Veterans' Lawn Tennis Association of Great Britain, c/o 26 Marryat Square, Wyfold Road, London SW6 6VA. Promotes competitions for

veterans in various age groups. The VLTA Yearbook (£1.50) lists affiliated clubs.

Veteran rowing

Amateur Rowing Association, 6 Lower Mall, London W6 9DJ. T:081-748 3632. Veteran rowing as a sport is fast growing in popularity. For those who enjoy a competitive edge, there are special races and regattas. Touring rowing is also on the increase and additionally, there is plenty of scope for those who simply want the exercise and a pleasant afternoon afloat. Nearly all clubs welcome novice veterans and membership is normally in the range of £50 to £80 a year. The A.R.A. can give information about clubs in your locality.

Wheelchair sport

British Wheelchair Sports Foundation, Harvey Road, Stoke Mandeville, Bucks HP21 9PP. T:0296 84848. Being confined to a wheelchair is no barrier to participating – and even excelling – at sport. The British Wheelchair Sports Foundation, as well as staging annual events and supporting the training of wheelchair athletes, also runs 'Sportstart' activity courses as an introduction to the challenge and excitement of sport on wheels. Included among a host of options that novice competitors can try are: basketball, table tennis, weightlifting, badminton, fencing and indoor cricket. The courses take place from Monday to Friday throughout the year and cost £65 including meals and dormitory accommodation. There is a £10 supplement for single room.

Yachting

Royal Yachting Association, RYA House, Romsey Road, Eastleigh, Hampshire SO5 4YA. T:0703 629962. There are 1,500 sailing clubs affiliated to the RYA and more than 1,000 recognised teaching establishments. Membership costs £16 a year.

Women's organisations

Although today women can participate in almost any activity on equal terms with men, women's clubs and organisations continue to enjoy enormous popularity. Among the best known are Women's Institutes, the Mothers' Union and Townswomen's Guilds.

Co-operative Women's Guild, 342 Hoe Street, London E17 9PX. T:081-520 4902. Branches throughout England and Wales organise their own programme, partly linked to a national theme, which is usually a major topical concern, such as support for carers. Branches also raise funds for a nationally agreed charity. Membership is £7.20 a year; 60p a month.

Mothers' Union, 24 Tufton Street, London SW1P 3RB. T:071-222 5533. Members of the Mothers' Union are involved in a wide range of activities which balance service to the community, learning, worship and recreation. Members who are housebound are linked through prayer circles.

National Association of Women's Clubs, 5 Vernon Rise, King's Cross Road, London WC1X 9EP. T:071-837 1434. There are 400 women's clubs. All are self-governing, choosing their own meeting times and programmes. Typical activities include: crafts, health care, music, drama and keep fit. There are visits to places of interest and many clubs arrange holiday groups in Great Britain and abroad. Some do voluntary service in their communities and a number run mutual self-help projects. Membership is £2.50 a year to head office plus a small membership fee to the local club.

National Federation of Women's Institutes, 104 New King's Road, Parsons Green, London SW6 4LY. T:071-371 9300. The WI has 310,000 members in 9,000 institutes. It offers women the opportunity to work together to improve the quality of life locally and nationally and to develop individual skills and talents. There is a college, which runs short courses, a monthly magazine and the WI markets. Membership is £9 per annum.

Women in Scotland and Northern Ireland should contact:

Scottish Women's Rural Institutes, 42 Heriot Row, Edinburgh EH3 6ES. T:031-225 1724.
Federation of Women's Institutes of Northern Ireland, 209-211 Upper Lisburn Road, Belfast BT10 0LL. T:0232 301506.

National Women's Register, 9 Bank Plain, Norwich, Norfolk NR2 4SL. T:0603 765392. Members meet in each others' homes to take part in informal discussions on subjects outside the domestic sphere. There are about 18,000 members in some 1,000 groups. Many additionally arrange social and other activities; also has a house exchange scheme and an international register of members covering 23 countries. The annual subscription is £7.50.

Townswomen's Guilds, Chamber of Commerce House, 75 Harborne Road, Edgbaston, Birmingham B15 3DA. T:021-456 3435. The Guilds have over 100,000 members who meet to exchange ideas, learn new skills and take part in a wide range of activities. There are regular monthly meetings plus a programme of local, regional and national events. Annual subscription is £7.

Other information

Public transport. One of the big gains of reaching retirement age is the availability of cheap travel. Most local authorities offer concessionary fares to senior citizens during the off-peak periods. Coaches too very often have special rates for older people and, as everyone knows, British Rail Senior Rail Cards, available to men and women over **60**, offer wonderful savings. Details of these are given in Chapter 13, Holidays.

PLAY IN MONTHS – not Years!

PIANO, ORGAN (all kinds) and PIANO-ACCORDION

Trial Lesson free without obligation

KNOW THE GREAT JOY OF MAKING MUSIC – you can learn at home, and start to play after only one lesson; no tricks or gimmicks, but constant improvement through pleasurable learning. The Klavar system will amaze you, and there is no more cost-effective way. The Klavar Music Foundation is an Educational Trust operating on a totally non-profit basis, with the aim of bringing the joy of music-making to as many people as possible. Klavar students play better after 3 months than many people can after 3 years.

From grateful letters, recently received:

"I can hardly believe it's true – to be able, now, to make my own music." "The Klavar system is continually rewarding. It is hugely appreciated, and gives many hours of enjoyment that would otherwise not be possible." "Really do appreciate the work of the Foundation, which gives so much happiness to so many people."

The Klavar system is for people of all ages. Many of our students are retired, and have at long-last realised their ambition to enjoy playing. You can discover the secret free, with absolutely no obligation. Just write or phone for details of Klavar Courses, and a Free Trial Lesson, naming your instrument please. For the cost of a stamp or phone call your life could be transformed.

**KLAVAR MUSIC FOUNDATION OF GREAT BRITAIN (GRG)
171 YARBOROUGH ROAD, LINCOLN LN1 3NQ.
Tel: 0522 523117 (24-hour answering service)**

The Redundant Churches Fund cares for over 270 churches throughout England that have architectural, historical or archaeological importance.

This church, at Old Langho in Lancashire, was one of the few churches built in Mary Tudor's reign. Much of the material came from the dissolved abbey at nearby Whalley. Vested in the Fund in 1990, the completion of repairs in 1991 was celebrated with a concert of early music.

Keeping an eye on buildings like this – where few people now live – can be an enjoyable activity for the retired.

For a list of churches in the Fund's care please write to:
**Redundant Churches Fund,
89 Fleet Street, London EC4Y 1DH.**

Chapter 10

Looking for Paid Work

Far from thinking of putting your feet up when you retire from your present job – perhaps like many other people today – one of your ambitions is to continue working in some form of paid employment. If so, then despite present unemployment levels, there could be more choices than you think, as many employers are actively seeking to recruit older people. However, before dashing off a shoal of application letters, it helps to think through some of the practicalities. Start by asking yourself a few basic questions.

Firstly, what is your main motive in wanting to work? The wish to supplement your income? The companionship? Fear of boredom? The desire for mental stimulation? The need to have a sense of purpose? Or the lurking suspicion that without a job, friends and social acquaintances will be less interested in hearing your views? The answer may well be a combination of factors but you should at least try to pinpoint your priorities to avoid drifting into a job that does not satisfy your main aims.

Another fundamental consideration is how many hours you are thinking of committing per week. A full Monday to Friday? Or just a couple of half-days? And while on the subject of time, is working a long-term goal or simply a pleasant occupation to fill in the next year or so?

What about distance? Would you be prepared to commute or are you aiming for a job that is strictly local? Was there anything, for example the travel, that you particularly disliked about your previous employment and that you are determined to avoid in your future job?

Also very much to the point, are you planning to seek an opening in a similar field, where your experience and contacts would come in useful? Or do you want to do something entirely different? And if so, were this to help, would you be willing to do a training course?

Moreover, have you considered the important economic questions? It may sound stupid when you have been working most of your life but factors such as your age, your total weekly earnings, your pension and other income, as well, of course as any out-of-pocket expenses you incur, could mean that at the end of the day the sums look rather different from what you had supposed.

Unemployment benefit. Even if you are in your sixties and already receiving an occupational or personal pension, you are entitled just like anyone else to claim unemployment benefit, although if you are over 55, the sum will be abated by the amount by which your occupational/personal pension exceeds £35. To qualify, however, you must genuinely be available for work and moreover be able to prove that you are actively seeking a job.

The current (1992/93) rates of unemployment benefit are as follows: £43.10 a week for people under State pension age; £54.15 a week for people over State pension age (i.e. 60 for women, 65 for men). A higher rate of benefit is paid to those with responsibility for dependants. For further details, see leaflet NI 12 *Unemployment Benefit* and FB 9 *Unemployed? A Guide to Benefits to Help Make Ends Meet* available from any Social Security office.

If you want to work but are not earning very much, there are two benefits which could be helpful: Disability Working Allowance and Family Credit.

Disability Working Allowance (DWA). This is a new tax-free benefit, introduced in April 1992, for people with an illness or disability who wish to work. The benefit is means-tested and additionally, to qualify you would need to work at least 16 hours a week, either as an employee or in a self-employed capacity.

The benefit amount depends on your income, savings and size of your family – but could be worth up to £42.40 for a single person and up to £58 for a couple with children. A further attraction is that DWA can be claimed by people who are over pension age. For further information and a claim form, obtain leaflet DS 703 available from your local Social Security office or from post offices.

Family Credit. This is a tax-free weekly payment for families who, despite the fact of one or both parents working, still have a low income. To be eligible for benefit, the claimant must work at least 16 hours a week and have at least one child under 16 (or under 19 if in full-time education).

Although means-tested, benefit levels are more generous than many people realise – with the average payment being around £35 a week. Additionally, in April 1992 two important improvements were made: firstly, the number of hours needing to be worked was reduced from 24 to 16 hours a week; secondly, the first £15 of any maintenance payment is now allowed free, as opposed to being counted as before in calculating Family Credit entitlement.

For further information, ask at your local Social Security office or post office for a claim pack; or telephone the Family Credit freephone number: 0800 500 222.

Assessing your abilities

Some people know exactly what they want to do. They have planned their action campaign for months, done their research, prepared a CV, followed up selective openings and are just waiting for their present employment to come to an end before embarking on a new career. But for most of us, it is not like that. Having merrily announced our intention to find a job, there comes a moment of truth when the big question is what?

Knowing what you have to offer is an essential first step. Make a list of everything you have done, both in your formal career and ordinary life, including your outside interests such as: local politics, Rotary, hobbies, voluntary work and even jobs around the home – decorating, gardening, carpentry or cooking. In particular, consider any practical or other skills, knowledge or contacts that you have acquired through these activities which may now prove useful, for example: public speaking, fund-raising, committee work, conference organisation, use of mini-computers, production know-how or fluency in a foreign language.

As a result of writing everything down, most people find that they have far more to offer than they originally realised. Add too your personal attributes and any special assets you can offer an employer. The list might include: health, organising ability, a good telephone manner, communication skills, the ability to work well with other people, use of a car and willingness to do flexible hours.

Maturity can also be a positive asset. Many employers prefer older people as being more reliable and less likely to be preoccupied with family and social demands. Also, in many small firms in particular, a senior person's accumulated experience is often rated as especially valuable.

By dint of looking at yourself afresh in this fashion, you may get a clearer idea of the sort of job that would suit you. Although there is an argument for keeping a fairly open mind and not limiting your applications too narrowly, the worst mistake you can make is to answer scores of advertisements indiscriminately – and inevitably end up with a sackload of rejections.

Talking to other people helps. Friends, family, work colleagues or business acquaintances may have useful information. It could also be sensible to consult outside experts, who specialise in adult career counselling and whose advice may be more realistic than that of friends in the context of current employment opportunities.

Job counselling

This is usually a mixture of helping you to identify your talents in a vocational sense combined with practical advice on successful job-hunting techniques. Counsellors can assist with such essentials as writing a curriculum vitae, preparing for an interview and locating job vacancies. They can also advise you of suitable training courses.

There are three services that could be helpful to adult jobseekers:

Restart programme. Everyone who has been unemployed for six months or more is offered a Restart interview at which Jobcentre staff discuss what job vacancies, training courses or other programmes might be suitable. One-week Restart courses give practical help with job-hunting, including: letter-writing and other ways of applying for a job; interview technique; information on vacancies and training opportunities available locally. For further details, contact your local Jobcentre.

Jobclubs. Open to those who have been out of work for at least six months, Jobclubs are self-help groups run by Jobcentre staff or other agencies on the Employment Department's behalf to help members who are seriously looking for work. People with disabilities do not have to meet the six-month criterion – they simply need to be out of work or in sheltered employment. Intensive counselling is given to improve job-hunting techniques, including performance at interviews. The service also includes the free use of facilities such as typing, photocopying, stationery, telephone and free postage. Entry is usually via the Restart programme. For more information contact your local Jobcentre.

Jobcentres. Although not a formal counselling service, Jobcentres are often a good starting point, as the staff will know about local vacancies and what training provision exists in the area. An increasing number of Jobcentres provide careers libraries with books, articles and leaflets on a whole range of occupations. It is often a good idea to ring beforehand and make an appointment to see the Employment Adviser.

Training opportunities

Knowing what you want to do is one thing. But before starting in a new job, you may want to brush up existing skills or possibly acquire new ones. Most professional bodies have a full programme of training events, ranging from one-day seminars to proper courses lasting a week or longer. Additionally, the Employment Department offers a number of schemes – available nationally – which may be of interest.

Open and Flexible Learning. The main purpose of the Employment Department's Open and Flexible Learning Scheme is to expand the range and flexibility of vocational education and training opportunities available to individuals of all ages. The courses are designed to increase the scope for participants to learn at a time, place and pace best suited to their own particular circumstances. For further information on the full range of open learning opportunities, ask to see a copy of the *Open Learning Directory* at your local Training and Enterprise Council (TEC).

Employment Training. This programme provides a broad range of opportunities so that individuals can be offered quality training from basic skills to high level courses leading to a recognised vocational qualification. For more details contact your local Jobcentre.

Meeting local needs. The new Training and Enterprise Councils, or TECs as they are more generally known, also offer a variety of training courses. These are specifically tailored to local employment requirements and therefore offer participants a good chance of finding a job in their area. In Scotland, the new training bodies are called local enterprise companies. For further information, together with an address and name of individual to contact, ask at your local Jobcentre.

Useful reading
Second Chances (9th Edition). A comprehensive guide to adult education and training opportunities. Price, £16.95 plus £5 p&p. Obtainable from: COIC, Employment Department, Moorfoot, Sheffield S1 4PQ.

Help with finding a job

There are four basic ways of finding a job: through contacts; by following up advertisements; by applying to an agency for suitable introductions; or by direct approaches to suitable employers. As general wisdom, the more irons you have in the fire, the better.

Make sure all your friends and acquaintances know that you are in the market for work – and include on the list your present employer, as many firms are more than happy to take on previous employees over a rush period or during the holiday season.

A possible source of useful contacts is the local chamber of commerce. Likewise, if you are a member of a Rotary Club, it can only be helpful to spread the word; and the same applies to, say, a golf club, political association where you are active, any committee you sit on or other group with which you are involved. Often the most unlikely person turns out to be the one who helps you most.

If you intend to follow up advertisements, selectivity is the name of the game. Rather than write around to all and sundry, limit your applications to those that sound genuinely promising.

As well as national and local newspapers, remember that the trade press often offers the best bet of all. Some local radio programmes broadcast a regular weekly 'job spot'; it could be useful to check when this is scheduled.

Agencies will invariably have more applicants than vacancies, except where skill shortages exist. However, most of them clearly place a fair number of people (or they would be out of business) and, as with other endeavours, keenness counts. People who simply register their name and then sit back and wait tend to be forgotten. The moral is telephone frequently to enquire what opportunities have arrived; or if you live close-by, pop into the office from time to time. Being on the spot at the right time is nine-tenths of success. A selection of agencies that specialise in appointments for people aged 50-plus is listed at the end of the chapter.

A direct approach to likely employers is another option. Study the business press and talk to your colleagues for ideas of firms that might be interested in employing someone with your abilities. Always find out who the appropriate person is to whom you should be writing – a properly addressed letter is far more likely to get noticed than one merely marked 'For the attention of the Personnel Manager'.

Regardless of whether you use contacts, advertisements or agencies – or preferably all three – a prime requirement will be to have a well presented CV.

CV Writing

This is your personal sales document. It should contain:

- Your name
- Address
- Telephone number
- Age (optional)
- Brief details of your education
- A summary of your work experience including: dates, employers, job titles and outline of responsibilities
- Other achievements
- Key outside interests

Ideally, it should not be longer than two pages of A4 and *it must be typed*.

There are a number of firms that specialise in providing assistance with the writing of CVs, who advertise their services regularly in *The Times* and other serious newspapers. While some are highly professional, a common fault tends to be the production of over-lengthy CVs, which can be definitely counter-productive. An all-purpose CV can also put off employers. Wherever possible, you should try to gear your CV specifically to the job on offer, emphasising those elements of your experience and skills that are relevant.

If you are thinking of using a specialist service, check the price first as charges can be on the hefty side. As with other purchases, you should do a bit of price comparison before making a decision. The price will normally include a batch of immaculately typed copies of your CV, ready for you to distribute.

A far cheaper option is to take advantage of the government Jobclubs, which are run by Jobcentre staff or other agencies on the Employment Department's behalf to assist those who have been out of work for six months or more (people with disabilities need only to be out of work or in sheltered employment). As part of the service, help is given with CV preparation and free facilities are provided including telephone, typewriter and photocopying equipment. Contact your Jobcentre for details.

Interview technique

If you have worked for the same employer for a number of years, your interview skills are liable to be a little rusty. It is a good idea to list all the questions you expect to be asked, (including those you hope won't be brought up) and then get a good friend to rehearse you in your answers.

In addition to questions about your previous job, be prepared for some or all of the following: what you have done since leaving employment; why, if you are now seeking a job, you retired earlier than you might have done; whether your health is good – this may take the form of a polite enquiry as to whether you would not find the hours or travelling too much of a strain; why you are particularly interested in working for them as an employer; and given the job requirements, what you think you have of special value to offer. You may also be asked what you know about the organisation. If the answer is likely to be 'very little', it could pay you to do a bit of research – such as obtaining a copy of the annual report.

Obvious mistakes to avoid are: claiming skills/knowledge that you do not possess; giving the impression that you have a series of stock answers to problems; criticising your former employer; or by contrast, drawing comparisons which could be interpreted as being faintly disparaging of the organisation where you are attending for interview.

Possibly the most difficult subject of all to come up may be the question, how much money would you expect? As a sad generalisation, most jobs for retired people – including early retirers – pay less than their previous employment, so you may have to strike a balance between what you want and the risk of pricing yourself out of the market.

Part-time openings

Another reason why the pay may appear low is that the work is part-time. For some people, of course, this is the ideal arrangement. Others may regard it as very second best. However, do not sniff at part-time work if the opportunity is available. Firstly, it is a way back into the market and many part-time or temporary assignments develop into full-time jobs in due course. This is especially true in small firms, which may of necessity be cautious about recruitment while the business is in the early development stage.

Additionally, far-reaching changes are happening in the job market, with temporary, or project-based assignments becoming increasingly common. For example, temporary computer staff are in considerable demand, as are part-time secretaries and accountancy staff. Likewise, there are part-time and other openings for older people to work in supermarkets, chain stores, hotels, conference centres and other outlets connected with the tourist industry.

The only real note of caution is that many employment rights do not apply to part-timers and those working less than 16 hours a week are particularly vulnerable, for example with regard to redundancy.

Openings via a company reference

Your employer may be able to assist with useful introductions. For example, if you are still a couple of years off retirement, you could broach the idea of seconding you to an enterprise agency or charity, where you would be helping small businesses or a worthwhile voluntary organisation in your local community. Secondment can be part time for a few hours a week or full time for anything from a few weeks to two years. It can also often lead to a new career.

Normally, only larger employers are willing to consider the idea since, as a rule, the company will continue to pay your salary and other benefits during the period of secondment. However, the concept has been gaining increasing popularity and more and more companies are giving the idea sympathetic consideration.

The major organisations that specialise in co-ordinating secondments are: Action Resource Centre, which operates nationally and is the leading consultant to companies on secondment policies and practice, as well as the main agency arranging all forms of secondment to community organisations; and Business in the Community or, in Scotland, SBC (Scottish Business in the Community) which work closely with enterprise agencies/trusts. Addresses are:

Action Resource Centre, 1st Floor, 102 Park Village East, London NW1 3SP. T:071-383 2200.
Business in the Community, 227a City Road, London EC1V 1LX. T:071-253 3716.
SBC, Romano House, 43 Station Road, Edinburgh EH12 7AF. T:031-334 9876.

Public appointments

Opportunities regularly arise for individuals to be appointed to a wide range of public bodies, such as tribunals, commissions and consumer consultative councils. Many appointments are to local and regional bodies throughout the country, including Scotland, Wales and Northern Ireland. Some are paid but many offer an opportunity to contribute to the community and gain valuable experience of working in the public sector on a part-time, expenses-only basis.

Self-nomination and the nomination of others who are willing to be considered for public appointments are always welcome. Short application forms are available from the **Public Appointments Unit**, Cabinet Office (OMCS), Horse Guards Road, London SW1P 3AL. T:071-270 6210/6217.

The Public Appointments Unit is not the only gateway to nomination and those with particular interests may also wish to make their availability known to an individual government department, or to a chairman of a public body for which they feel they have suitable qualifications.

Additionally, both the TUC and CBI are consulted on some appointments. If you are active on either, there is nothing to lose by letting it be known that you could be interested in a public appointment.

Market research

The work covers a very broad spectrum, from street or telephone interviewing to data processing, designing questionnaires, statistical analysis and sample group selection.

Many of the specialist market research agencies employ researchers and analysts on a freelance basis. However, as with other fields, supply exceeds demand so there is a certain amount of luck involved, as well of course as ability, in finding regular work.

For further details, together with a list of market research companies that employ freelance interviewers, contact: **Market Research Society**, 15 Northburgh Street, London EC1V 0AH. T:071-490 4911.

Paid work for charities

Although charities rely to a very large extent on voluntary workers, most charitable organisations of any size have a number of paid appointments. Other than social workers and other specialists that particular charities may require for their work, the majority of openings are for general managers/administrators, fund-raisers and for those with financial skills. Secretarial vacancies also exist from time to time.

Salaries have been improving but in general are still considerably below the commercial market rate. A further point is that, unlike the big company world, managers cannot expect to find a battery of support staff and must be willing to turn their hand to the more menial jobs such as adding up the petty cash and fixing the photocopier – as well as handling meetings, building up good media relations and sustaining the enthusiasm of volunteers and paid staff alike.

It is essential, therefore, that anyone thinking of applying for a job in a charity must be in sympathy with its aims and style. Agencies specialising in charity recruitment advise that it is a good idea to do a stint as a volunteer before seeking a paid appointment, as not only will this provide useful experience but will help you to decide whether you would find the work satisfying.

Most of the serious newspapers carry charity job advertisements – the *Guardian* on Wednesday is especially fertile hunting ground – as do some of the weeklies and monthlies including *Social Work Today*, *Community Care* and *New Statesman and Society*. Other possibilities are to approach a charity direct or to register with one of the agencies below.

Charity Appointments, 3 Spital Yard, Bishopgate, London E1 6AQ. T:071-247 4502. Charity Appointments helps other charities fill their key jobs, for example those of: chief executive, finance manager and fund-raiser. If you are interested in putting your name on the Charity Appointments register, you should send a CV with a brief covering letter indicating the type of job you are seeking, together with any preferences re salary or location. (Please enclose sae.)

Charity Recruitment, 40 Rosebery Avenue, London EC1R 4RN. T:071-833 0770. A specialist recruitment service aimed only at paid employment within the voluntary sector. It caters for jobs at all levels from directors and fund-raisers to secretaries and clerical staff. Details of all applicants are kept in a computer data-bank.

Charities Effectiveness Review Trust (CERT), 12 Mercer Street, London WC2H 9QE. T:071-497 2499. CERT provides a specialised consultancy service for charities, carrying out a range of activities from a general review of an organisation to assessment of a particular project. It maintains a panel of consultants, many of whom are recently retired. Members of the panel include development and programme specialists, administrators, accountants, lawyers, public relations advisers and others with appropriate skills.

Sales

If you are a whizz salesperson, you will hardly be reading this chapter. You will already have used your contacts and flair to talk yourself into a dozen jobs, with the only problem being which one to choose. Almost every commercial firm in the country is crying out for people with that particular brand of authority, charm and persuasiveness to win extra orders.

Many people who have never thought of sales could be excellent in the job, because of their specialist knowledge in a particular field combined with their enthusiasm for the subject. Educational and children's book publishers for example are often keen to recruit ex-teachers to sell their books to schools and libraries.

There is an almost insatiable demand for insurance salesmen and, having pondered the question of how to invest your pension lump sum, you will probably have some knowledge of the options as well as first-hand experience of being on the receiving end of a professional sales pitch.

Selling today is not just standing in a shop or trudging the rounds of sceptical customers. Over the past few years telephone selling has caught on in a big way and, like mail order, is used by a vast array of very different companies; so if you have a good telephone voice, this could be for you.

Additionally, many firms employ demonstrators in shops or at exhibitions for special promotions. The work is usually temporary or freelance by definition; and while pay is normally good, the big drawback is that you could be standing on your feet for long periods of the day.

The big 'beware' are firms that pay on a commission-only basis. Far from merely earning a pittance, you could end up distinctly out of pocket.

If the idea of selling appeals, either study the newspaper advertisements or, better still, approach firms direct that you reckon could make genuine use of your special knowledge. If the idea makes you quail, the likelihood is that selling is not for you. If it fires you with enthusiasm, you could actually find yourself making more money in your retirement than ever before.

Jobs in tourism

You might like to consider courier work. Holiday firms are increasingly looking to recruit people in their fifties and early sixties, in part due to the decline in the number of students but equally because they are finding that their clients often prefer having more mature people in charge.

Some jobs take you overseas, others not. Not very long ago, for example, one of Britain's biggest camping and mobile home travel companies ran a campaign to recruit around 1,000 individuals in middle life to look after visitors at their caravan and camp sites. Pay was advertised as between £80 and £105 a week, depending on the job.

It is demanding work that calls for a calm, unflappable personality. If the idea appeals, watch the classified columns for vacancies or, if there is a travel company you particularly admire, you might try approaching them direct.

If you live in a popular tourist area, there is a whole variety of seasonal work, including: jobs in hotels, restaurants, shops and local places of interest. Depending on the locality, the list might also include: deckchair attendants, play leaders for children, caravan site staff, extra coach drivers and many others.

Teaching and training skills

If you have been a teacher at any stage of your career, there are a number of part-time possibilities:

Coaching

With examinations becoming more competitive, demand has been increasing for ex-teachers with knowledge of the public examination system to coach youngsters in preparation for 'A' level, GCSE and common entrance. Contact local schools or a specialist educational consultant such as **Gabbitas, Truman & Thring Educational Trust**, 6, 7 & 8 Sackville Street, London W1X 2BR. T:071-734 0161 and 071-439 2071.

GT&T provides a wide range of recruitment and consultancy services to independent schools in Great Britain and for English-speaking schools overseas. It also maintains an extensive register of teachers seeking appointments.

It is also worth looking in the *Yellow Pages* under 'Coaching', 'Tutoring' and 'Education'.

Specialist subjects
Teachers are still in short supply in subjects such as mathematics, physical science, computer studies, craft design and technology, business studies and modern languages. People with relevant work experience and qualifications are in demand to teach or give tuition in these subjects, although some formal teaching qualification is often now required.

The **Teaching as a Career Unit (TASC)**, Elizabeth House, York Road, London SE1 7PH, T:071-925 6617, publishes a useful booklet *Switch to Teaching*, for those considering mature entry to teaching.

English as a foreign language
There has been a mini-explosion of new schools teaching English to foreign students. These tend to be concentrated in London and the major academic cities such as Oxford, Cambridge, Bath and York. The standard entry requirement is the Cambridge/RSA Examination Certificate/Diploma offered by the University of Cambridge Examinations Board which can be taken either part time or through a four-week crash course. A list of colleges offering the course can be obtained from: **University of Cambridge Local Examination Syndicate**, EFL Division, 1 Hills Road, Cambridge CB1 2EU. T:0223 61111.

Other. Adult Education Institutes and Colleges of Further Education may sometimes have part-time vacancies.

Working in the Third World

There are various opportunities for suitably qualified people to work in the developing countries of Africa, Asia, the Caribbean and the Pacific on a semi-voluntary basis. Skills most in demand include: civil engineering; mechanical engineering; water engineering; architecture; urban, rural and regional planning; agriculture; forestry; medicine; teaching English as a foreign language; maths and physics training; and economics. All air fares, accommodation costs and insurance are usually covered by the organising agency and pay is limited to a 'living allowance' based on local levels. As a general rule, there is an upper age limit of 65 and you must be willing to work for a minimum of two years. The following are the major agencies involved in this kind of work.

VSO (Voluntary Service Overseas), 317 Putney Bridge Road, Putney, London SW15 2PN. T:081-780 2266.
Skillshare Africa, Recruitment/Selection, 3 Belvoir Street, Leicester LE1 6SL. T:0533 540517.

International Co-operation For Development, Unit 3, Canonbury Yard, 190a New North Road, London N1 7BJ. T:071-354 0883.
United Nations Association International Service, Suite 3A, Hunter House, 57 Goodramgate, York YO1 2LS. T:0904 647799.

Caring for other people

There are a number of opportunities for paid work in this field. Mature women or couples are often preferred.

Fostering elderly people
An increasing number of local authorities run fostering schemes, whereby an elderly person lives with a family as an ordinary member of the household, receiving whatever care and special assistance is necessary. As with child fostering, enormous trouble is taken by social workers in matching families with their foster guest. Pay varies from one area to another but averages around £90-£130 a week for every elderly person fostered, up to a legal maximum of three per home.

Under new regulations expected to be introduced in April 1993, anyone offering a fostering service (even if it is only for one person) will be required to register with their local authority. A further change is that there will no longer be a legal maximum, as such. Instead each case will be judged on its own merits, according to the accommodation and other important practicalities.

Ask at your Social Services Department whether there is a fostering or 'boarding out' scheme to which you could contribute.

Domestic work
A number of private domestic agencies specialise in finding temporary or permanent companions, housekeepers, caretakers, emergency mothers and extra care help for elderly and handicapped people or for those who are convalescent. Many of these jobs are particularly suitable for retired people or couples. Pay generally starts at around £150 or more a week plus travelling expenses (£75 a week for caretakers). Residential jobs usually last a maximum of four weeks in any one situation. Agencies worth contacting include:

Auntie Fay Agency, Royal Albert House, Sheet Street, Windsor, Berkshire SL4 1BE. T:0753 831960.
Care Alternatives, 206 Worple Road, Wimbledon, London SW20 8PN. T:081-946 8202.
Consultus, 17 London Road, Tonbridge, Kent TN10 3AB. T:0732 355231.

Country Cousins and Emergency Mothers, 10a Market Square, Horsham, West Sussex RH12 1EU, T:0403 210415. Also branches in Plymouth and Lutterworth (Leics).
Easymind: Home Care Services, 3 Oakshade Road, Oxshott, Surrey KT22 0LF. T:0372 842087.
Universal Aunts Ltd., PO Box 304, London SW4 0NN. T:071-738 8937.

Another possibility worth pursuing is to contact the United Kingdom Home Care Association which represents over 200 member agencies and organisations that provide home care. As well as refer you to a local agency, UKHCA can advise on pay, conditions and training. For further information, contact: **UKHCA**, Premier House, Holmes Road, Sowerby Bridge, West Yorkshire HX6 3LD. T:0422 835057; or telephone 081-946 8202.

Local agencies will be listed in *Yellow Pages* under 'Domestic' or 'Domestic Staff'.

Home helps
Local authorities sometimes have vacancies for home helps, to assist disabled or elderly people in their own home by giving a hand with the cleaning, light cooking and other chores. Ask at your local Social Services Department.

Childminding
If you already look after a grandchild during the day, you might consider caring for an additional couple of youngsters. You will need to be registered with the local Social Services Department who will explain all the requirements.

Nursing
Qualified nurses may be able to find work at their local hospital or alternatively through one of the many nursing agencies. See *Yellow Pages*. Family planning clinics could also be worth approaching.

Homesitting
Homesitting means taking care of someone else's home while they are away on holiday or business trips. Mature, responsible people, usually non-smokers with no children or pets, are in demand for this type of work. More like a paid holiday, you could expect to receive anything from about £35 to £90 a week plus food and travelling expenses, depending on the

responsibilities and on the size of house or flat. It is useful to have your own car.

Firms specialising in this type of work include: **Homesitters Ltd.**, Buckland Wharf, Buckland, Aylesbury, Bucks HP22 5LQ. T:0296 630730; and **Universal Aunts**, PO Box 304, London SW4 0NN. T:071-738 8937.

Cashing in on your home interests

Cooking, gardening, home decorating, dressmaking and DIY skills can all be turned into modest money-spinners.

Cooking
Scope includes: catering other people's dinner parties, selling home-made goodies and cooking for directors' lunches. Other than top class culinary skills, requirements are: a large deep-freeze, a car (you will normally be required to do all the necessary shopping) and plenty of stamina. Notify your friends, advertise your services through the local newspapers, chamber of commerce or local businessmen's club or, if you are really serious about it, enrol with one of the specialist catering agencies. See *Yellow Pages*.

Gardening
Small shopkeepers and florists sometimes purchase flowers or plants direct from local gardeners, in preference to going to the market. Alternatively, you might consider dried flower arrangements or herbs for which there has been a growing increase in demand. However, before spending any money, check around to find out what the sales possibilities are. If you are willing to tend someone else's garden, the likelihood is that you will be inundated with enquiries. Spread the word among friends, acquaintances, local shops and in the pub. For information on all aspects of herbs including growing techniques, contact: **The Herb Society**, PO Box 599, London SW11 4RW.

Dressmaking and home decorating
If you are happy to do alterations, the chances are that you could be kept busy from dawn to dusk. Many shops are desperate for seamstresses. Likewise, many individuals and families would love to know of someone who could alter clothes, as well as dressmake properly. Perhaps to a slightly lesser extent, the same goes for curtains, chair covers and other soft furnishings. Often a good move is to approach firms selling materials for the home, who may be only too glad to put work out to you. Alternatively,

put up a card in newsagents' shops or run a small advertisement in the local paper.

DIY
Competition is more intense, as many small builders offer this service. However, elderly people often require small jobs, as do women who do not have a handy-man around the house. Advice for getting your services known is the same as for gardening.

Pubs and paying guests
Many people dream of running a pub in their retirement – and many people live to regret it. A less strenuous option which others may like is offering bed and breakfast accommodation in their own home.

Running a pub
Running a pub is more a way of life than a job and one that requires a great deal of stamina. Anything less like a quiet retirement would be hard to imagine. You are on your feet for most of the day, the hours are long and when you are not pulling pints or preparing bar snacks, you will be dealing with the paperwork plus all the other day-to-day business requirements.

You can either buy your own 'free' house outright or become the tenant of a brewery or pub-owning company. Prices vary according to the length of lease, location and so on but, as a rough guide, you would need around £20,000 in order to get started as a tenant; and between £150,000 and £250,000 – or even more – for a 'free house'. On top of all this, as with any other business, you will need to budget for operating capital.

If you are over 50, some experience of self-employment or the leisure industry is vital in order to be considered for a tenancy or long-term lease and even then, you may need to convince the company that you are not making the mistake of imagining that running a pub is a congenial way of easing into retirement.

Tenancy packages vary and may include the range of products you sell as well as repairs and decorations. As a self-employed business person, a tenant or leaseholder has responsibility for the hiring and firing of any staff, compliance with the fire regulations and with the other laws of the land. As a licensee, he is also required to know and enforce the licensing laws.

For anyone even considering a career move into the licensed trade, there are two textbooks published by the Brewers' Society which are recognised by the British Institute of Innkeeping. *Innkeeping* is the standard manual for publicans and costs £12.50. *The Complete Book of Pub Catering*, the sister volume, costs £11.95. Both books are available from Brewing Publications Ltd., 42 Portman Square, London W1H 0BB. *The Morning Advertiser*, the daily newspaper for publicans (available from newsagents), carries details of tenancies and pubs for sale, particularly in its Monday editions.

Also of interest is *Running Your Own Pub* by Elven Money, Kogan Page, £8.99.

Bed and breakfast

Tourist areas, in particular, offer scope for taking in bed and breakfast visitors. However, unless you want to make a regular business of it, it is advisable to limit the number of guests to a maximum of five otherwise you will be subject to stringent fire regulation precautions requiring special doors and other expensive paraphernalia. To be on the safe side, contact the local Environmental Health Officer (see telephone directory or enquire at the town hall) who will advise you of anything necessary you should do. You should also register with your local Tourist Information Centre. See the section headed 'Letting rooms in your home' in Chapter 8, Your Home.

Agencies and other useful organisations

Jobhunting through agencies is very much a question of luck. People can be on their books for months and months and not be sent to a single interview. Someone else can walk through the door and within 48 hours be fixed up with an ideal job.

Applicants normally greatly exceed vacancies and the majority of jobs, especially for the over-60s, tend to be on the modest side: clerical, security work, gardening, domestic services and similar.

A positive attitude helps. People are often their own worst enemy when it comes to job-hunting and sadly this is especially true of older people, who may give the impression of half expecting to be turned down on the grounds of age. While you may be asked to state your date of birth (in which case it is usually better to be honest), there is no need to volunteer the information unless requested – least of all at the start of an interview.

Equally, there is no need to limit your applications to agencies that specialise in placing older candidates. If you are serious about finding work, you need to cast your net as widely as possible. So check the *Yellow Pages* and keep an eye on the local papers for other agencies in your area.

Depending on what you are looking for, several of the following organisations may be able to help.

Jobcentres. It is easy to forget the obvious. Jobcentres have changed their image considerably over the last few years and now carry a wide range of vacancies for all levels of ability. In particular, many small firms use them for recruitment in preference to the more expensive private employment agencies.

There are around 1,000 Jobcentres throughout Great Britain which, between them, handle about 2 million vacancies a year. They also act as a gateway to many of the training courses and advisory services. See local telephone directory for address.

Other organisations

Age Concern. Age Concern runs employment bureaux for people over 60 in a few areas around the country. They deal mainly in fairly unskilled part-time work, such as: shop and office cleaning, messengers, clerks, home help for elderly people and manual jobs. Contact your local Age Concern group (see telephone directory).

Corps of Commissionaires, Market House, 85 Cowcross Street, London EC1M 6BP. T:071-490 1125. Offers full- or part-time work to ex-servicemen and women, police, prison officers, firemen, coastguards and merchant seamen. Jobs cover a fairly broad range from managerial and administrative posts to others that require the wearing of the Corps' uniform, for example: commissionaires, security staff, ushers at sporting or official events. Maximum age is normally 60 for permanent jobs; 70 for temporary work. The Corps is not an employment agency as such, but operates as a membership association and charges a fee to employers for its services. All applicants are invited to an interview and are required to provide references.

Extend, 1A North Street, Sheringham, Norfolk NR26 8LJ. T:0263 822479. Extend runs recreational exercise-to-music classes for the over-60s and for people with disabilities of all ages. The organisation is constantly looking for potential group teachers. Training courses last 8 to 12 days spread over several weeks and cost £240. There are written and practical assessments on completion. At the present time, eight training teams operate in different parts of the UK and Ireland. Details can be obtained from the above address, on enclosure of sae.

Hera Recruitment Ltd., 2 Valentine Place, London SE1 8QH. T:071-928 6141. HERA has recently expanded and now operates nationwide. Job-seekers receive a weekly bulletin of vacancies at all levels in the field of housing, from management to secretarial. HERA also offers careers counselling and training courses relevant to jobs to do with housing.

Manpower (UK) Ltd., 66 Chiltern Street, London W1A 1PR. T:071-224 6688. Manpower is the largest supplier of temporary work in the UK with 150 offices nationwide. Jobs cover a wide range from technical and skilled work to assembly, packing and similar services, as well as secretarial and other office work. Additionally, Manpower operates a placement service for qualified HGV drivers, chauffeurs and light van drivers. There may also be permanent work openings in any of these fields.

Officers' Association, Employment Department, 48 Pall Mall, London SW1Y 5JY. T:071-930 0125. The Association maintains an Employment Department which operates in conjunction with the Forces Resettlement Service. Eligibility to register is restricted to candidates who have held a commission in the armed services, who must be under 60 and currently unemployed. A wide range of vacancies is handled in industry, commerce, high technology and in the professional and charitable institutions. There are regional offices in Scotland and Eire.

OwnBase, 68 First Avenue, Bush Hill Park, Enfield, Middlesex EN1 1BN. A non-profit making organisation that provides mutual support for people who work from home. As well as a bi-monthly newsletter, Own-Base offers the opportunity of active networking via a contact list designed to help members exchange views, share skill or other resources, broaden their circle of business acquaintances and possibly find new trading openings. Membership is £17.50 a year.

Part-Time Careers Ltd., 10 Golden Square, London W1R 3AF. T:071-437 3103. Specialises in part-time secretarial jobs as well as accountancy, book-keeping and similar.

Royal British Legion Attendants Co. Ltd., 2a Rathmore Road, Charlton, London SE7 7QW. T:081-305 1218. Offers full- or part-time work for ex-servicemen and women. Uniform is required to be worn and typical jobs are for security officers, commissionaires and car park attendants. The RBLA has regional offices in Preston, Leeds, Cardiff, Cambridge and Poole.

Who has the will to help children with the greatest need?

Where the doing matters most.

For information on making a will please contact Legacies and Trusts, Barnardo's, (Ref: GRG1993), Tanners Lane, Barkingside Ilford, Essex IG6 1QG
(Tel: 081-550 8822 during office hours).

Charity Reg No 216250

How you can help shape the future...

Making a will is one of the most important things we ever do. It's a way to show friends and loved ones how much we care for them. It's also a chance to consider leaving a contribution to a cause which you believe in.

In response to the number of enquiries we receive from our supporters on this subject, Friends of the Earth has written a special guide outlining the facts you need to know when making a will.

To receive your free copy of *Promise the Earth a Brighter Future* please contact:

*Adam Laidlaw, Friends of the Earth,
Freepost, 26-28 Underwood Street, London N1 7JQ
Telephone: 071-253 4694*

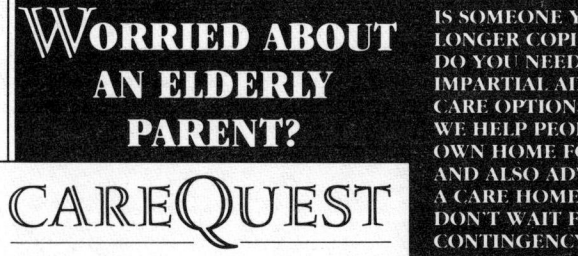

It takes WILL POWER to fight a drink or drug problem
Please add your will power by including a bequest to Turning Point in your will.
Throughout Britain men and women are fighting hard to free themselves from the grim effects of alcohol or drugs. But they can't succeed alone. They need help—and so do their friends and families. They need advice, information, counselling and support.
Founded 28 years ago, Turning Point is today the largest national charity helping people with drink, drug and mental problems. It provides residential rehabilitation, day care and street-level advice services. Last year alone, it helped over 14,000 people.
Please help Turning Point to help many thousands more—who else can they turn to?

New Loom House, 101 Backchurch Lane, London E1 1LU.
Tel: 071-702 2300
Reg. Charity No. 234887

THE ROYAL BRITISH LEGION
48 Pall Mall, London SW1Y 5JY.
Tel: 071-973 0633 Fax: 071-973 0634
Lt. Col. P.C.E. Creasy, O.B.E., General Secretary

Britain's premier ex-service organisation for the welfare of ex-service men, women and their dependents. Provides financial assistance, residential and convalescent homes, employment for disabled, free pensions advice and much more, mainly financed from the Poppy Appeal. Also provides social focus for ex-service community in branches (3,268) and clubs (975) throughout England, Wales and Ireland.

Royal Patron: H.R.H. The Princess of Wales
HEADWAY NATIONAL HEAD INJURIES ASSOCIATION

Aims to provide:

Advice and counselling centres in towns and cities

Regional rehabilitation and care training centres

Respite homes to give short term relief to long term carers

Campaigning on behalf of those sustaining long term or permanent mental and/or physical deficits

Distribution of health education literature of improved content and quality

Contributions to improve rehabilitation techniques and research programmes

DONATIONS GRATEFULLY ACKNOWLEDGED.
For further information contact:
National Head Injuries Association Limited, 7 King Edward Court, King Edward Street, Nottingham NG1 1EW
Telephone: (0602) 240800, Fax: (0602) 240432

THE BRITISH GERIATRIC SOCIETY: FOR HEALTH IN OLD AGE

Founded in 1947, we are the professional association of 1600 specialist geriatricians and other doctors concerned with the medicine of old age.

LEAVE A LEGACY OF HOPE

When you make a bequest to our Society, you will help us to:
- promote high standards of health care
- encourage the teaching of geriatric medicine
- advance research into age-related disease
- disseminate the latest scientific information
- provide information to elderly people and their carers
- prevent the abuse of elderly people in care
- inform the public about the medicine of old age
- advocate well-funded health and community care

**The British Geriatrics Society,
1 St Andrew's Place, London NW1 4LB**

For some Service men and women a posthumous award is a lifesaver.

SSAFA is an entirely voluntary and worldwide independent organisation.

Our role is to help, advise as well as comfort all members and ex-members of the Armed Forces and their families.

In the UK we have an army of 6,500 specially trained volunteers who last year gave practical help to 72,000 families.

Help that included disbursing millions of pounds to those in need.

The main source of such funds, besides various regimental charities, is charitable donations.

Such as a posthumous award, like a legacy in your will. It could pay for equipment for the disabled.

It could help a war veteran pay his heating bills.

Or provide financial help for a war widow and her family. However much you bequeath we'll see it goes towards repaying those who have sacrificed so much.

Rest assured.

For further information contact: SSAFA, Room 70, 19 Queen Elizabeth Street, London SE1 2LP.

SSAFA
THE SOLDIERS SAILORS AND AIRMEN'S FAMILIES ASSOCIATION

HELP THE HOSPICES

Help the Hospices was founded in 1984 by the Duchess of Norfolk. It has two main aims:

- To give grants to individual hospices, both voluntary and NHS, to alleviate the suffering of the terminally ill.
- To run and fund training courses on all aspects of care for the dying. Participants include doctors, nurses, chaplains and counsellors.

There are more than 170 hospices throughout the country, and more are due to open in the coming year. With inflation and increasing numbers of units needing our support, we require to increase our annual income by almost 30% merely to stand still.

The hospice movement is best summed up by a quotation from Martyn Lewis, our Vice President.

"It goes out of its way to concentrate thought and effort on the quality of each individual life, seeking to enrich a very precious time and ensuring that people do not give up but really live until the very moment they die."

Your legacy, your covenant or just a single gift will help us to maintain this high standard. Donations should be sent to:

The Duchess of Norfolk

Help the Hospices
34-44 Britannia Street
London WC1X 9JG
Telephone 071-278 5668

Reg. Charity No. 289345

HAVE YOU AN INTEREST IN THINGS NAUTICAL ?

The Sea Cadet Association invite you to consider giving some of your leisure time to assist in a variety of activities and to pass on your expertise to the youth of your local area.

The Sea Cadet Corps is a charity and relies heavily upon the generosity of the public to support and finance its activities. Perhaps you would like to become a member or next time you revise your Will you might consider a legacy?

If you have an interest in our aims and the work we do we would like to hear from you.

Please contact us at:

SEA CADET HEADQUARTERS
202 LAMBETH ROAD
LONDON SE1 7JF

Tel: 071-928-8978

The Sea Cadet Association's own square rigged brigantine T.S.ROYALIST

Chapter 11

Voluntary Work

There are probably as many different kinds of voluntary work that need to be done, as there are organisations that need your help. The range of tasks and the variety of groups are both enormous. Perhaps this is one reason why some people fear that the commitment may get out of control and that they may find themselves involved to a greater extent than they wish. Though this may be true in a few cases there are probably thousands more who, starting in a small way, find themselves caught up in the enthusiasm for their cause and immensely rewarded by the contribution they feel able to make and by the new friends that it has brought them.

As any voluntary organisation would tell you, it is far better to give just one morning a month and be reliable than to promise more time than you can spare and end up always being late or having to cancel at the last minute. Equally, as with a paid job, before you start you should be absolutely clear about all the terms and conditions.

- What sort of work is involved?
- Who will be working with you?
- What is expected?
- When will you be needed?
- Are expenses paid? What for? How much?

If you straighten all this out in the beginning there will be less chance of any misunderstandings or your secretly wishing after a few weeks that you had volunteered for something different.

Choosing the right voluntary work

It is one thing to decide that you would like to do some kind of voluntary work; quite another to discover what is available in your area and what particular outlet would suit you. For this reason we have included a list of organisations, arranged in broad categories of interest, indicating the types of activity for which they are seeking volunteers. But no such list can be complete – there are literally thousands of voluntary groups which need help in some way or other. For further information there are three other major sources to which you can turn:

REACH, 89 Southwark Street, London SE1 0HD. T:071-928 0452. Specialises in placing retired men and women with business or other professional skills in voluntary organisations, throughout Great Britain. It finds only part-time, voluntary jobs, but with out-of-pocket expenses paid. REACH is itself a registered charity and makes no charge for its services.

Scottish Core of Retired Executives, sponsored by Scottish Business in the Community, Romano House, 43 Station Road, Edinburgh EH12 7AF. T:031-334 9876. Assists both community and charitable organisations and under-resourced new small businesses. Members are retired business people who give what time they have available. If you would like to help please contact the Administrator.

Volunteer Bureaux. Usually listed in the telephone book under 'V'. Most towns have a body of this kind which seeks to match up volunteers with local organisations. Alternatively, see the *Volunteer Bureaux Directory*, which is available at most libraries.

The Volunteer Centre UK, 29 Lower King's Road, Berkhamsted, Herts HP4 2AB. T:0442 873311. Can provide information if you want to volunteer for the first time or if you are already involved and want to know more. Sae appreciated.

Citizens' Advice Bureau. Your local CAB will also have information on local needs and groups to contact.

If you have a good idea for a new voluntary project, it is worth contacting: **New Horizons Trust**, Paramount House, 290-292 Brighton Road, South Croydon, Surrey CR2 6AG. T:081-666 0201. This is a registered charity offering grants of up to £5,000 to groups of retired people who wish to start a new voluntary project, drawing on their own knowledge and experience for the benefit of their local community. To qualify, there must be at least 10 people in the group, half of whom must be over the age of 60. Schemes may improve local amenities or fill identified gaps in social services.

General

The scope of the work of the British Red Cross, WRVS and Citizens' Advice Bureaux is so broad that they almost justify a category to themselves.

British Red Cross, 9 Grosvenor Crescent, London SW1X 7EJ. T:071-235 5454. The Red Cross needs help from men and women for first aid, nursing, beauty care and welfare duties. Training is given where required. It also needs fund-raisers, publicity officers, drivers for escort work and people with teaching, clerical, administrative and management skills.

Expenses and, in a few cases, modest salaries are paid. Volunteers may give as little or as much time as they choose. Contact the local branch (under 'British' or 'Red Cross' in the telephone book) or write to the London headquarters.

Women's Royal Voluntary Service, 234-244 Stockwell Road, London SW9 9SP. T:071-416 0146. (See telephone book for your local branch.) The WRVS works with the local authority Social Services to cover almost the complete range of needs in the community. It particularly welcomes offers of help from people with time during the working day.

Activities are too numerous to list but include: meals on wheels, visiting and shopping for the elderly, helping in playgroups and organising children's holiday schemes, running canteens in prisons and courts, providing transport in rural areas, running hospital shops and assisting with catering and welfare services in emergencies. No special qualifications are required.

Citizens' Advice Bureaux deals with over 7 million enquiries a year. Apart from being an excellent source of information on other voluntary organisations needing help, the CAB itself has over 15,000 volunteer helpers working in its 1,000 or so branches throughout the country.

The work involves interviewing and advising clients on a wide range of questions from welfare benefits and legal rights to local events and community schemes. No formal qualifications are required but it is essential that the applicant is able to master and explain a considerable amount of complicated and detailed information.

Training is given (usually two days a week for about six weeks followed by a period of in-service training and appraisal) and volunteers are then expected to work a minimum of six hours a week in their Bureau. Contact the manager at your nearest CAB (see telephone directory) for further details.

Another well known organisation which functions across a more general spectrum is: **Community Service Volunteers**, 237 Pentonville Road, London N1 9NJ. T:071-278 6601. Operates a nationwide scheme called the Retired and Senior Volunteer Programme (RSVP) for people aged over 50 who want to be involved in their community. Each group plans its own activities which might include helping single parents, working with elderly people, using their business experience to advise young people starting out on their own and going into primary schools to teach craft and other skills. Area organisers provide guidance and suppport. For further details, contact Janet Atfield.

Animals

Cinnamon Trust, Poldarves Farm, Trescowe Common, Germoe, Penzance, Cornwall TR20 9RX. T:0736 850291. Seeks to relieve the problems of elderly pet owners who, owing to illness or some other emergency, are temporarily unable to care for their pets.

Animal lovers throughout the country assist either by fostering a pet in their own home or helping out on a daily basis, for example walking a dog, feeding it, cleaning out a bird cage or similar. Likewise, long-term homes are required for pets who have lost their owners. For further details, write to Mrs. Averil Jarvis at the above address (enclosing sae).

Pet Fostering Service Scotland. T:067-481 356. Provides short-term foster care for the pets of elderly people who, owing to some emergency, are temporarily unable to manage. Volunteers may either look after a pet in their own home until the owner is able to receive it back or provide some other caring service, such as walking a dog or feeding a cat or bird in its own surroundings. Food and other expenses are paid for by the owner. If you live in Scotland, have a love of pets and would like to help out in a crisis, telephone the above number.

PRO Dogs, Rocky Bank, 4 New Road, Ditton, Maidstone, Kent ME20 6AD. T:0732 848 499. PRO Dogs is a national charity which originated the PAT Dog Hospital visiting scheme. To bring both an extra interest and an outlet for petting and affection into the lives of those in institutional care, dog owners visit long-stay hospital wards and residential homes together with their pets.

An essential is that the dogs are of suitable temperament and well behaved. To participate, it is necessary to become a PRO Dogs member to be covered by their insurance scheme. Annual subscription is £10.

Royal Society for the Prevention of Cruelty to Animals, Causeway, Horsham, West Sussex RH12 1HG. T:0403 64181.

Volunteers are needed to help with fund-raising at local level. Contact headquarters for the address of your nearest branch.

Bereavement

Cruse, Cruse House, 126 Sheen Road, Richmond, Surrey TW9 1UR.

T:081-940 4818. Cruse is the national organisation for bereavement care. It provides counselling, practical help and organises social programmes to counter loneliness. Volunteers are needed in the branch offices to help in all these areas. Training for counselling is given and the work involves about half a day a week.

Children and young people

Action for Sick Children (National Association for the Welfare of Children in Hospital), Argyle House, 29-31 Euston Road, London NW1 2SD. T:071-833 2041. The Association supports sick children and their families and advocates that health services be planned to cater for their special needs. Local branches give practical help to parents and professionals in the hospitals.

Work is organised through local branches which can be contacted through the London headquarters. Although different branches may operate slightly different schemes, most will welcome voluntary help, for example:

Help with transport. Either driving, where a mileage charge is payable, or accompanying mothers with young children.

Help with volunteer play schemes, on wards or in out-patients' departments.

Help with fund-raising for more parents' and children's facilities in hospital.

Barnardo's, Tanners Lane, Barkingside, Ilford, Essex IG6 1QG. T:081-550 8822. Barnardo's provides services for children who face disability or disadvantage. Projects throughout the country include work with families, day care centres, community projects, playgroups, play buses and holiday schemes. Two major areas require help:

Fund-raising. Activities may include helping in a charity shop or with local flag-days and events. Write to the National Appeals Director at the above address.

Child care programme. This usually involves befriending a young person with a handicap, perhaps to give the mother a much-needed break. Write to the Child Care Administration Officer at the above address.

Children's Country Holidays Fund, 1st Floor (Rear), 42-43 Lower Marsh, Tanswell Street, London SE1 7RG. T:071-928 6522. Contact: The Director. The purpose is to give disadvantaged London children a country or seaside holiday, either in private homes or camps. Host families are needed as are London organisers, camp supervisors, train marshals, people to co-ordinate the travel arrangements, volunteer office helpers and fund-raisers.

The Children's Society, Edward Rudolf House, Margery Street, London WC1X 0JL. T:071-837 4299. Offers a comprehensive child care service to children and families in need. It runs nearly 160 projects which include safe houses for young runaways, family and community centres, teenage units and residential centres and special holiday projects for young people with disabilities.

Help with fund-raising is needed. There are also more than 144 charity shops, run entirely by volunteers. Contact may be made either through the London headquarters or the local office, which may be listed in the telephone book.

Save the Children, Mary Datchelor House, 17 Grove Lane, London SE5 8RD. T:071-703 5400. Volunteers are very much welcomed to assist with fund-raising and to work in SCF shops. Check the local telephone directory for the nearest branch or contact the head office.

Scout Association, Baden Powell House, Queen's Gate, London SW7 5JS. T:071-584 7030. There is a multitude of opportunities for voluntary help, either as a leader or commissioner, an administrator or committee member, or as a member of a District Scout Fellowship. Administrators have important responsibilities in the management of the property as well as for the equipment and finances of the movement. Members of the Fellowship help to organise events, contribute to training (e.g. vehicle maintenance, map reading, first aid), maintain camp-sites, raise funds, work in a Scout shop or edit a District Newsletter.

Sea Cadet Corps, 202 Lambeth Road, London SE1 7JF. T:071-928 8978. The Sea Cadet Corps is a youth organisation which offers boys and girls aged 12-18 challenging new experiences and adventure. Emphasis is placed on waterborne activities, with encouragement given to those who wish to pursue a career at sea. Units exist throughout the UK and welcome volunteer help either as administrators or specialist instructors. Details may be obtained by contacting the national headquarters above.

Volunteer Reading Help, Unit 111, The Foundry, 156 Blackfriars Road, London SE1 8EN. T:071-721 7156. The purpose of the scheme is to assist children in the age group 6 to 11 who need help and encouragement with their reading. Volunteers undertake to give two hours, twice a week during term time, by going into a local school and devoting half an hour's individual attention to three children on a regular one-to-one basis. No formal qualifications are needed but volunteers must like children, have plenty of patience, possess a sense of humour and be willing to commit themselves for at least a year. A short training of about six hours, spread over three sessions, is provided. In addition to London, the scheme operates in: Bolton, Bristol, Liverpool, Nottingham, Oxford City, Reading, Surrey, both East and West Dorset, West Kent and West Oxfordshire.

Youth Clubs UK (formerly National Association of Youth Clubs), 11 St. Bride Street, London EC4A 4AS. T:071-353 2366. Provides leisure activities for young people through a network of local associations and three divisions in Scotland, Wales and Northern Ireland. The local associations need help with administration and fund-raising. They may also be aware of particular clubs that can use assistance, for example with the accounts or maintenance work on the building. No special time commitment is required. Expenses may be paid. See telephone book for address of the nearest association or write to the London office.

Conservation

Architectural Heritage Society of Scotland, The Glasite Meeting House, 33 Barony Street, Edinburgh EH3 6NX. T:031-557 0019. Promotes the study and protection of Scottish architecture. As well as enjoying events such as talks and visits, members can play an active part in defending Scotland's threatened heritage by joining case panels for which volunteers are always needed. The work involves assessing and commenting on listed building and conservation area consent applications. Membership of the Society, which includes a free copy of its annual journal *Architectural Heritage*, is £12 a year; £18 for families (1992).

British Trust For Conservation Volunteers, 36 St. Mary's Street, Wallingford, Oxfordshire OX10 0EU. T:0491 39766. Over 600 working holidays are organised nationally and over 900 local groups run community projects at weekends and sometimes mid-week.

Membership costs £12 (£6 for retired people) and local newsletters and a national magazine, *The Conserver*, give details of events. Typical projects include planting trees, cleaning ponds, creating nature gardens, restoring footpaths, scrub clearance and woodland management. Not all of them involve heavy work but a reasonable degree of fitness is required.

Council for the Protection of Rural England (CPRE), Warwick House, 25 Buckingham Palace Road, London SW1W 0PP. T:071-976 6433. CPRE aims to protect the English countryside. Voluntary helpers act as local watchdogs within CPRE's county branches, assessing and reporting threats to the environment and sometimes representing the

Council at enquiries. There is also a need for help with fund-raising which is carried out by local groups.

Friends of the Earth, 26-28 Underwood Street, London N1 7JQ. T:071-490 1555. Friends of the Earth is one of the leading environmental pressure organisations in the UK, aiming to conserve and protect the resources of the planet.

Over 330 groups run local campaigns and fund-raising projects. These can be contacted through the London office which can also use help with the administration and with answering enquiries. Travelling expenses and a lunch allowance are paid. Most volunteers work between one and three days a week. People with scientific training may also be able to help on specific research projects.

Greenpeace, Canonbury Villas, London N1 2PN. T:071-354 5100. An international environmental protection group which campaigns against nuclear and other pollution and in favour of wild-life preservation. Part-time volunteers are needed both to help in the London office and also for fund-raising by local groups across the country.

Ramblers' Association, 1-5 Wandsworth Road, London SW8 2XX. T:071-582 6878. The aims of the Ramblers' Association are to keep footpaths open and to protect the countryside. Each of its 50 area offices needs help with administration and with walking over and checking the condition of the local footpaths. The time involved can be as much or as little as is available.

Scottish Conservation Projects Trust, Balallan House, 24 Allan Park, Stirling FK8 2QG. T:0786 79697. SCP offers training in conservation skills and opportunities to work as a volunteer for as little or as much time as you can spare. There are 7-14 day conservation projects, called 'Action Breaks', in all parts of Scotland as well as weekend and single day events. The type of work varies from conservation proper – fencing, footpath construction, small traditional building restoration and habitat management – to jobs such as office skills, cooking and driving. Volunteers are also welcomed to help with administration, fund-raising and publicity. Volunteers pay for their own fares, as well as a contribution to board and lodging (£4 a day). Annual membership, which includes subscription to the SCP magazine, is £12 (£6 for pensioners). For further information, contact Rita Crowe at the above address.

The elderly

Abbeyfield Society, 186-192 Darkes Lane, Potters Bar, Herts EN6 1AB. T:0707 44845. Volunteers working with 600 local Abbeyfield Societies nationwide acquire or build houses to provide independent accommodation for elderly people who are on their own. There are also 'extra care' schemes for elderly people who can no longer look after themselves without some help. Voluntary help needed may vary from shopping for a resident, standing in for the housekeeper, gardening, typing or organising a fund-raising event to giving specialist financial and legal advice with regard to the purchase of new Abbeyfield houses.

Age Concern England, Astral House, 1268 London Road, London SW16 4ER, T:081-679 8000; **Age Concern Scotland**, 54A Fountainbridge, Edinburgh EH3 9PT, T:031-228 5656; **Age Concern Wales**, 4th Floor, 1 Cathedral Road, Cardiff CF1 9SD, T:0222 371566; **Age Concern Northern Ireland**, 6 Lower Crescent, Belfast BT7 1NR. T:0232 245729.

The aim of Age Concern is to promote the welfare of older people. It does this by campaigning on their behalf and by organising services to meet their needs. Local groups, using over 250,000 volunteer helpers, operate all over the country and services include day care, lunch clubs, home visiting and over-60s clubs. Fund-raising activities in all their variety are also organised by the local groups which may be contacted through the central offices listed above.

Carers' National Association, 29 Chilworth Mews, London W2 3RG. T:071-724 7776. Helps those who care for elderly or infirm people. It provides a postal advisory service, campaigns for better social security benefits and domiciliary services, supports holiday and sitter-in help for carers and organises conferences. Help is needed to organise carers' groups, to enable them to meet occasionally to discuss mutual problems. Contact Jill Pitkeathley at the above address for details of your local branch.

Contact, 15 Henrietta Street, Covent Garden, London WC2E 8QH. T:071-240 0630. Contact is a way of making new friends and at the same time providing much needed companionship for lonely elderly people. Volunteers maintain a personal link by taking them once a month to have tea in the home of a volunteer host. Help is needed with driving (one Sunday a month) and/or hosting a tea-party for about 10 elderly people once or twice a year. No expenses are paid. There are about 200 Contact groups, nationwide. The name and address of the nearest local organiser can be got from the above address.

Help the Aged, St. James's Walk, London EC1R 0BE. T:071-253 0253. Aims to improve the quality of life for elderly people here and overseas. In the UK, it funds day centres and day hospitals, community transport, home safety devices, emergency alarm systems and sheltered housing. Overseas, it advises on social policy for elderly people and supports projects in combating destitution and ill-health. Volunteer help is needed to staff charity shops and to assist local organisers in their work. Contact the Personnel Manager at the above address for further details.

The family

Catholic Marriage Advisory Council, Clitherow House, 1 Blythe Mews, Blythe Road, London W14 0NW. T:071-371 1341. Aims to provide education for marriage and family life through a national network of trained marriage guidance counsellors. Help is required in running and administering the 80 local centres. For local addresses, contact the headquarters above.

Family Service Units, 207 Old Marylebone Road, London NW1 5QP. T:071-402 5175. Twenty local Units work to prevent the breakdown of family and community life by running services for disadvantaged communities, deprived families and children. They carry out welfare counselling, community work and social work with families.

The Units, which are professionally staffed, are managed by voluntary committees and help is needed on these as well as with administration and fund-raising.

Relate: National Marriage Guidance, Herbert Gray College, Little Church Street, Rugby, Warwickshire CV21 3AP. T:0788 573241. Works to support marriage and family life. There are over 160 local marriage guidance councils which offer counselling to anyone with relationship problems and also undertake education work in schools and youth clubs.

Volunteers who would like to become counsellors undertake training. There are also openings to serve on committees and help in the office. The work is most likely to appeal to people who have been previously involved with social or community activity of some kind.

Soldiers', Sailors' and Airmen's Families' Association, 19 Queen Elizabeth Street, London SE1 2LP. T:071-403 8783. SSAFA provides a welfare and advisory service for the families of service and ex-servicemen and women. There are 6,000 volunteers in over 1,000 branches throughout the UK and wherever service families are stationed.

Case workers deal with every kind of problem – domestic, financial, legal and compassionate. Training is given and although there is no minimum time commitment it is obviously critical to see a case through to the end. Help is particularly needed in inner cities. There is also a requirement for assistance in the counties and in similar-sized branches as chairman, treasurer or administrative helper. A service background may be helpful but is not necessary.

Health and handicapped people

British Heart Foundation, 14 Fitzhardinge Street, London W1H 4DH. T:071-935 0185. Funds research into the causes, prevention, diagnosis and treatment of heart disease; helps to support rehabilitation centres and also provides life-saving cardiac care equipment to hospitals and ambulance services. There are over 500 branches which assist this vital work through a wide variety of fund-raising schemes. For details of your local branch please contact head office.

Calibre, Cassette Library for the Blind and Handicapped, Aylesbury, Bucks HP22 5XQ. T:0296 432339 or 81211. This is a national lending library of recorded books on ordinary standard cassette tapes for use by 'anyone unable to read'. Volunteers are needed to help run the library, which is maintained entirely from donations. Publicity and fund-raising help are also required. Contact the General Secretary, Mr. AFC Montgomery.

Cancer Research Campaign, Cambridge House, 6-10 Cambridge Terrace, Regent's Park, London NW1 4JL. T:071-224 1333. The aim of the Campaign is to defeat cancer. It supports research at centres throughout the United Kingdom on the recommendation of its Scientific and Education Committees. Money for this is raised by about 1,000 voluntary local committees and hundreds of honorary organisers. If you would like to help, see 'Cancer Research Campaign' in the telephone directory for the address of your local group.

Help the Hospices, 34-44 Britannia Street, London WC1X 9JG. T:071-278 5668. There are nearly 200 hospices and allied organisations in the UK caring for patients of all ages with terminal illnesses. Over 30,000 people are helped each year. For many, the hospice will be their last home and the skilled care they receive will help them to die with peace and dignity.

Hospices rely on volunteers for much important work, including: acting as drivers for patients and visiting relatives, helping on wards, running the hospice shop or coffee bar, doing reception work, sitting with patients and assisting with the vital task of fund-raising. It is no exaggeration to say that without volunteers many hospices would collapse. For further information including details of local hospices, contact the above address.

Voluntary Work

Imperial Cancer Research Fund, PO Box 123, Lincoln's Inn Fields, London WC2A 3PX. T:071-242 0200. Imperial Cancer Research Fund is the largest independent cancer research institute in Europe, responsible for a third of all cancer research carried out in the UK. Help is needed in the Fund's growing network of shops (sorting, serving, pricing, ironing, mending and similar) or to assist with general office work in the regional centres. All offers of help are greatly appreciated. Look in the *Yellow Pages* for the phone number of your nearest regional centre.

Leonard Cheshire Foundation, Leonard Cheshire House, 26-29 Maunsel Street, London SW1P 2QN. T:071-828 1822. The Cheshire Foundation aims to encourage severely disabled people to live as useful and independent a life as possible. It runs over 85 residential homes in the UK and organises help for handicapped people in their own homes. There are also 185 homes in 48 overseas countries.

If there is a Cheshire Home in your area it would be grateful for all kinds of practical help. This might include driving, gardening, painting and decorating, shopping or writing letters for residents. Homes also need help with local fund-raising: jumble sales, bring-and-buy sales and similar events. The London office will give you the address of the nearest home.

Mencap (Royal Society for Mentally Handicapped Adults and Children), Holiday Services, 119 Drake Street, Rochdale OL16 1PZ. T:0706 54111. Volunteers help on holidays for people with mental handicaps. They work in small groups looking after a similar number of guests, usually for a two-week period. After the holiday, volunteering can be continued by helping at a Gateway Club, which is a leisure time youth club for people with mental handicaps, or by working at weekends at a hostel or hospital. Board and lodging on the holidays is free for volunteers and a travel allowance up to £20 is also paid.

Mental Health Foundation, 8 Hallam Street, London W1N 6DH. T:071-580 0145. Promotes research into the causes and treatment of mental illness and learning disability, supports innovative care schemes and seeks to rehabilitate those who have suffered from mental illness by encouraging new self-help projects, housing and employment schemes.

Volunteers are needed for fund-raising: either helping with the annual flag day or working in conjunction with their local committee. For further information, please write to the Director at the above address.

Mind (National Association For Mental Health), 22 Harley Street, London W1N 2ED. T:071-637 0741. Works to promote the interests of people who are diagnosed as mentally ill and campaigns for their right to lead an active and valued life in the community. MIND provides an information service and guidance on legal rights and also publishes a range of books and leaflets as well as a bi-monthly magazine.

The local associations, which can be contacted through the national office, vary in size and in the scope of their work. While all will be involved in fund-raising, their activities also include running social clubs, day centres and an advice and information service as well as offering support and help to individuals.

National Association of Leagues of Hospital Friends, 2nd Floor, Fairfax House, Causton Road, Colchester, Essex CO1 1RJ. T:0206 761227. The Association acts as a national support and advice centre for the 1,200 Leagues of Hospital Friends. Each League is autonomous and opportunities for voluntary work will therefore vary. All, however, are concerned with both service to patients and fund-raising and all need new volunteers, especially those who are at or near retirement age. The National Association will be pleased to provide addresses of local Leagues.

National Back Pain Association, 31-33 Park Road, Teddington, Middlesex TW11 OAB. T:081-977 5474. Funds research into the causes and treatment of back pain and runs a network of local self-help branches. The NBPA needs volunteers to start local branches and to provide practical help for back pain sufferers. Particular activities include: organising exercise and hydrotherapy classes, arranging talks and running social and fund-raising events. For further information, contact the Branches Officer at the above address.

Riding for the Disabled Association, Avenue R, National Agricultural Centre, Kenilworth, Warwickshire CV8 2LY. T:0203 696510. Aims to help provide opportunities for riding for disabled children and adults. You do not have to be 'horsey' to help with the administration in one of the 702 local groups or with fund-raising to support it. Legal and financial knowledge is particularly valuable in connection with the opening of new groups and with keeping the accounts.

For those with experience of horses (which may be supplemented by training courses) the main jobs are leading or walking beside the ponies while they are being ridden and accompanying parties on riding holidays. Write to the head office above for the address of your nearest group.

Royal National Institute for the Blind, 224 Great Portland Street, London W1N 6AA. T:071-388 1266. RNIB aims to help blind people lead full and independent lives. Among many other initiatives, it runs schools for blind children, provides careers advice, offers training and assists with finding suitable employment. It also manages two rehabilita-

Voluntary Work

tion centres and special homes; has a welfare advisory service; sells specially designed or adapted goods to make life easier and safer for the visually handicapped; publishes books and magazines in Braille and Moon and runs the Talking Book Library.

Help is mostly required with fund-raising: by lending a hand on flag days; or by placing and emptying RNIB collecting tins. Additionally, volunteers are needed all over the country to service talking book machines on a regular basis, two or three times a month. London office will put you in touch with your nearest local group.

St. John Ambulance, 1 Grosvenor Crescent, London SW1X 7EF. T:071-235 5231. Best known for their first aid role at public events, St. John Ambulance workers also help in hospitals and do general welfare work within the community. Scope for volunteers is hugely varied and includes such activities as vehicle maintenance, fund-raising, public relations and community work as well, of course, as first aid. For further information contact your county office or London headquarters at the above address.

Spastics Society, 12 Park Crescent, London W1N 4EQ. T:071-636 5020. Contact the Information Officer. Provides a range of services including schools, colleges and residential care homes for people with cerebral palsy. There is also a Helpline information service (0800 626216) and a monthly newspaper, *Disability Now*, as well as over 200 local groups throughout the country.

Helpers are needed particularly with transport – either driving or assisting with wheelchairs – with running open days and events put on by local groups and with fund-raising and street collections.

The Stroke Association, CHSA House, Whitecross Street, London EC1Y 8JJ. T:071-490 7999. The Stroke Association works for the prevention of stroke illnesses and helps stroke patients and their families. Volunteers visit patients in their own homes and, depending on what is required, may practise speaking, reading or help with exercises. There are also more than 500 Stroke Clubs which offer social and therapeutic support. Details of local schemes and clubs are available from the above address.

Sue Ryder Foundation, Sue Ryder Home, Cavendish, Sudbury, Suffolk CO10 8AY. T:0787 280252. Contact: Mr. K Wilkinson. Sue Ryder Homes cater for the sick and disabled of all ages. They are run fairly informally and as far as possible as family homes in the true sense of the word. Volunteers with nursing or any other appropriate skills or experience are needed for work in a variety of jobs including the general running of the homes or headquarters. Those with secretarial skills are particularly sought for weekend work. Board and lodging is provided.

Heritage and the arts

Arts Council of Great Britain, Information Unit, 14 Great Peter Street, London SW1P 3NQ. T:071-333 0100.

There is wide scope for becoming involved in the arts in a volunteer capacity. All kinds of abilities are needed from painting and other creative skills to accounting and clerical know-how. Additionally, local arts councils which seek to promote the arts in their areas especially welcome people with experience of communications and marketing. To find out about your local arts council, contact your local authority or library.

Council for British Archaeology, 112 Kennington Road, London SE11 6RE. T:071-582 0494. Various archaeological excavations take place throughout the UK, mainly from March to September. The work will probably involve lifting, stooping and wheeling barrows so is not suitable for people with bad backs. No training is necessary. A two-week stay is the average. Accommodation will vary according to the site but may be pretty basic.

Information on the various digs is given in *British Archaeological News* (£10.50 annual subscription, from the above address). The Council will also supply the address of the nearest local Archaeological Society (enclose sae).

National Trust, Heywood House, Westbury, Wiltshire BA13 4NA. T:0373 826826. Contact: Jenny Baker. The National Trust uses volunteers in many aspects of the work of conservation in the great houses open to the public and on 500,000 acres of coast and countryside properties. If you are interested, write to Jenny Baker at the address above.

The needy

Christian Aid, PO Box 100, London SE1 7RT. T:071-620 4444. Christian Aid acts on behalf of UK and Irish churches to assist some of the poorest communities in the world. It also contributes to race relations and refugee work in the UK. Volunteers are needed to help with many aspects of the work from fund-raising to development education, including assisting with emergency appeals and selling flags during Christian Aid Week. For further information, contact Brenda Nicholson at the above address.

Homelife-DGAA, Vicarage Gate House, Vicarage Gate, Kensington, London W8 4AQ. T:071-229 9341. Assists people from professional or similar backgrounds either financially or with nursing and care in a number of residential homes. Work involves general fund-raising and also visiting patients and helping to organise outings and entertainments for them.

Oxfam, Volunteers Department, Oxfam House, 274 Banbury Road, Oxford OX2 7DZ. T:0865 311311. Oxfam aims to relieve poverty, distress and suffering in any part of the world. Over 30,000 volunteers are involved in all parts of the UK: running shops, 'auditing' them for possible improvements, organising fund-raising events, helping with the administrative work in local offices or assisting with the educational or campaigning aspect of Oxfam's work. There are also openings for volunteers with bookkeeping know-how, as well as design and other display skills. Travel expenses and meals may be reimbursed, depending on the number of hours given in a day. For further information, look up your local Oxfam in the telephone directory or contact the National Volunteers' Adviser at the above address.

Royal British Legion, Aylesford, Kent ME20 7NX. T:0622 717172. Best known for its Poppy Day Appeal, the Royal British Legion exists to help ex-Servicemen and women by relieving hardship and providing services to assist the injured in rebuilding their lives. Among its many initiatives, the Legion runs convalescent and care homes, maintains sheltered workshops, provides pension counselling, organises training and operates an advice and welfare service through its 3,268 branches around the country.

Its most pressing need is to recruit more honorary Poppy Appeal Organisers and volunteers for street, or house-to-house, collections without whom none of this work would be possible. Contact your local branch (see telephone directory) or write to the Appeals Department at the above address.

Samaritans, 10 The Grove, Slough, Berks. SL1 1QP. T:0753 532713. The Samaritans aim to help the suicidal and the despairing. Much of the work is done on the telephone so that, while no special qualifications are required, good hearing, an unshockable disposition and complete reliability are essential qualities in a volunteer. Training is given – often at weekends – and those who qualify will be expected to attend further courses from time to time.

The minimum time commitment is about 12 hours a month plus a few all night duties each year. Some expenses are paid. Apart from this work, there is need for fund-raising help from anyone with a little time and a lot of enthusiasm.

Offenders and the victims of crime

Society of Voluntary Associates (SOVA), Brixton Hill Place, London SW2 1HJ. T:081-671 7833. Promotes the work of volunteers with offenders, ex-offenders, their families and young people at risk. It recruits, trains and deploys volunteers to the probation and social services. The work may be with children, in the adult literacy scheme, prison visiting or helping ex-offenders. The necessary training is given by SOVA and the volunteer then works in a Probation Service or Befrienders' Scheme.

Victim Support, 39 Brixton Road, London SW9 6DZ. T:071-735 9166. Over 350 local groups train volunteers to visit and help victims of crime. Help includes offering emotional support as well as practical advice on issues such as possible compensation, insurance claims, crime prevention and the availability of local resources. Contact the nearest group by writing to the National Office above; or apply via the local police or CAB.

Useful reading

For those with a serious interest, a guide well worth reading is *Volunteer Work*, published by the Central Bureau. It contains information on over 100 organisations recruiting volunteers in the UK and countries worldwide including organisations specifically seeking one-time executives or those on early retirement. Price £7.99 from bookshops or £8.99 (by post) from the Central Bureau, Seymour Mews House, Seymour Mews, London W1H 9PE. T:071-486 5101.

Work After Work, by Judy Kirby, £3.95 from Quiller Press, 46 Lillie Road, London SW6 1TN.

The Volunteer Centre UK, 29 Lower King's Road, Berkhamsted, Herts HP4 2AB, T:0442 873311, produces a regular magazine about volunteering from your workplace and provides pages of information on page 481 of the BBC's CEEFAX Service. There is no charge to the viewer. The Centre also publishes a pack *So You Want to be a Volunteer?*; price £4. To order publications, send sae to the above address.

Directory of Social Change, Radius Works, Back Lane, London NW3 1HL. T:071-431 1817. The Directory publishes a number of useful guides giving practical advice to those working for charities and also organises seminars and training courses in fund-raising, financial management and communications.

DO YOU CARE ABOUT ANIMALS AND THE ENVIRONMENT?

Of course you do. But young people today are brought up in a world of aggressive and negative images.

The Athene Trust produces educational materials to foster a caring, compassionate and responsible attitude to animals and the environment. We'd rather see youngsters engage in voluntary work than violence.

We help to develop caring citizens - but to reach all age groups and every school, we need your help.

Do ask us for our educational materials list or 'phone us for more details.

The Athene Trust, First Floor, 20 Lavant Street,
Petersfield Hants GU32 3EW
Tel: (0730) 68070 Fax: (0730) 60791

Registered Charity Number 295126

THERE'S SO MUCH TO BE DONE. HELP US TO DO IT.

Skillshare Africa sends skilled and experienced people to work in support of development in Botswana, Lesotho, Mozambique and Swaziland.

If you want a challenge, if you want to make a difference, if you are fit and able to carry a job through write to us now for a vacancy list and an application form.

"The peoples of southern Africa . . . will never forget those who decide to match their resources and skills to our potential and aims." *A. Casimiro, Skillshare Africa's Mozambique Field Director.*

I have technical/business/social/education/agricultural skills (delete appropriately).

Name _____

Address _____

_____

_____

Registered Office: 3 Belvoir Street, Leicester LE1 6SL, UK

Happier lives for lonely old people can be provided with Your HELP

LORD TONYPANDY asks you to help the NBFA – a small charity that gives direct help to improve the quality of life in old age which is often a time of hardship, loneliness and failing health. The NBFA supplies:

TENS machines for LONG TERM PAIN RELIEF from conditions such as Arthritis and Rheumatism. EMERGENCY ALARMS for the increasing number of people who prefer to lead an independent life and remain in their own homes and HOLIDAYS for people who could never afford one without our help.

Your legacy, donation or deed of covenant could help the NBFA to continue with much needed work.

NATIONAL BENEVOLENT FUND FOR THE AGED
65 London Wall, London EC2M 5TU
071 638 2026

Charity Reg. No. 243387

Please help MIND leave a legacy of hope...

If mental distress has afflicted you or a loved one, you will understand the tremendous importance of MIND's work.
MIND is the leading national charity dedicated to the relief of mental distress.

...remember us in your will

To obtain a legacy leaflet, write to
The Legacy Officer, MIND (NAMH), Dept. GRG
22 Harley Street, London W1N 2ED

the Camphill Village Trust

A member of the Association of Camphill Communities
Reg. Charity No: 232402

CAMPHIL

WORKING ACTIVELY
The trust has eight communities with people with learning difficulties in rural and urban areas. All need your interest and support for their growth and development.

AN ACTIVE FRIENDS GROUP
Helping with fund raising and getting involved.
If you would like to know more, please write to:

The Secretary
(GRG) Delrow House,
Aldenham, Watford, Herts WD2 8DJ.

"Tom had Health Insurance, House Insurance, Car Insurance.

If only he'd thought of making a will"

Most people with family responsibilities take great trouble to protect their loved ones.

But sadly, too many neglect to take one essential precaution.

They don't make a will. And the result can be a disaster for those they leave behind.

For a widow it can mean that financial worries are added to her grief. Without a will to protect her, the security she thought she had may turn out to be an illusion. She may even lose her home because other family members have a claim on it.

And for the whole family it can mean distressing legal proceedings over "who gets what".

Now the Red Cross has produced a booklet telling you how to protect your family by making a will.

For a free copy of Caring for the next generation, the Red Cross Guide to Wills and Legacies, simply post the coupon below to: British Red Cross, FREEPOST, 9 Grosvenor Crescent, London SW1X 7BR. Or phone David Noble on 071 235 3424 now.

Send for this FREE booklet today.

Please send me a free copy of the Red Cross Guide to Wills and Legacies (BLOCK CAPITALS PLEASE)

Mr/Mrs/Ms/Miss: _____

Address: _____

_____

_____

Postcode: _____ Tel: _____

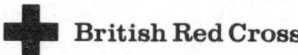 **British Red Cross**

Send to: British Red Cross, FREEPOST, 9 Grosvenor Crescent, London SW1X 7BR.   GRG2

GREYHOUNDS CAN BE ORPHANS TOO

Most greyhounds are cared for by their owners or trainers when their racing days are over. But greyhounds can be orphans too. Nearly 10,000 have been homed by the Trust but help is needed to continue this work. Your help, or legacy will provide a new life for a greyhound orphan.

Please write or telephone the NGRC Retired Greyhound Trust, 24-28 Oval Road, London NW1 7DA.
Telephone No: 071-267 9256.

AQUIRE THE DREAM... NOT THE NIGHTMARE!

The Daily Telegraph
GUIDE TO LIVING AND RETIRING ABROAD - 6th Edition
(£8.99 + £1 p&p)

'The least expensive way to avoid being caught in the rain'
MONEY WEEK

Full of essential information, practical advice and handy hints for anyone planning a move abroad.

24 HOUR BOOKLINE 071-278 0433

For credit card orders anytime... or send your cheque/p.o. (made payable to Kogan Page) to Kogan Page, 120 Pentonville Rd, London N1 9JN.

Please allow 21 days for delivery (50 days overseas).

KOGAN PAGE

The Dogs' Home Battersea

As the oldest and most famous dog rescue organisation in the world, we have launched our very first major appeal in our 130 year history, to help pay for a £2 million multi-storey kennel block we are having to build for the more than 20,000 dogs (and 800 cats) which come to us each year.

PLEASE help us with this work.
Bequests – Donations – Covenants gratefully received.
The Secretary, The Dogs' Home Battersea, 4 Battersea Park Road SW8 4AA
Telephone: 071-622 3626   Fax: 071-622 6451

Chapter 12

Health

How often have you enviously commented when meeting a recently retired friend: 'Goodness, he looks a different man. Fit, relaxed, contented – retirement must suit him.' And why not? Perhaps more than any other period since your twenties, retirement is a time for positive good health! You have more chance to be out in the fresh air and take up a favourite sport again. You won't have to rush your meals so much and, without the need for business lunches or sandwiches day after day, will probably knock off a few pounds without any effort at dieting.

A major gain is that there will be no more fighting your way to work on buses and trains, jam-packed with people all coughing and sneezing; or sitting in traffic, raising your blood pressure. Also, once free of the strains and pressures that are part of any job, you will feel less harassed, look better and, best of all, have the energy to devote to new interests and activities.

People can get aches and pains of course as they become older but, as any doctor will tell you, this is far less likely if you remain physically and mentally active.

As with anything else, however, bodies do require a modicum of care and attention if they are to function at their best and, just as cars need regular servicing, routine checks such as eye testing and dental appointments are obviously sensible.

Also moderation, middle-aged as it may sound, is generally a wiser policy than excess. Don't get it wrong! This has nothing to do with treating yourself as a premature geriatric – quite the reverse. It means enjoying small vices without paying the penalty for over-indulgence, keeping trim instead of getting out of shape and looking good when you take exercise rather than puffing like the proverbial grampus.

Health

Keeping fit

Exercise plays an important part in keeping you healthy. It tones up muscles, improves the circulation, reduces flab, helps to ward off illnesses such as heart disease and, above all, can be a great deal of fun.

The experts' motto is: little and often. For those not accustomed to regular exercise, it is essential to build up gradually.

The Sports Council runs a campaign aimed at the 50-plus age group, to encourage men and women to get back into the sporting habit. Training in a whole range of activities is available around the country, with beginners particularly welcome. Details of some of the many facilities, together with other keep-fit options, are listed in Chapter 9, Leisure Activities.

In addition to some of the more exotic choices, swimming has long been recognised as one of the best forms of exercise. Some swear that there is nothing to beat a good brisk walk. Gardening is also recommended. With the explosion of sports clubs, leisure centres and adult keep-fit classes run by local authorities, opportunities have never been better for athletes of all ability levels – and none.

Equally, emphasis on more leisurely keep-fit is also on the increase and a welcome innovation is the growing number of opportunities for older people as well as for the disabled. The town hall should be able to tell you what local provision exists. Additionally, the following organisations may be able to help you.

Extend, 1A North Street, Sheringham, Norfolk NR26 8LJ. T:0263 822479. Extend aims to enhance the quality of life for older and handicapped people by providing structured recreational movement sessions to music. For information about classes in your area please send sae.

Health and Beauty Exercise, 3rd Floor, Walter House, 418-422 Strand, London WC2R 0PT. T:071-240 8456. A national organisation whose aim is to promote fitness in an atmosphere of 'happy informality'. Emphasis is on movement and exercise to music and classes are organised in three grades: elementary, intermediate and advanced. Additionally, some areas provide special courses for elderly people with some participants aged 80 and older. Membership (including joining fee) is about £4. Classes cost from £1 upwards.

Medau Society, 8b Robson House, East Street, Epsom, Surrey KT17 1HH. T:0372 729056. Offers recreational movement classes which improve posture and muscle tone, while developing suppleness, strength and stamina. There are also special breathing exercises, designed to aid respiration and stimulate the circulation. Classes are held all over the country. For further information, send a large sae to the address above.

Relaxation for Living, 29 Burwood Park Road, Walton-on-Thames, Surrey KT12 5LH. Promotes the teaching of stress management and physical relaxation to combat strain and increase well-being. There are usually between six and ten in a class and courses run over several weeks. Prices are very roughly in the bracket £15 to £50. A correspondence course with tapes is available to those who are out of reach of a teacher. For addresses of local classes, tapes and leaflets for sale, please send large sae.

Yoga

Around half a million people in Britain regularly practise yoga as a means of improving fitness and helping relaxation. Classes are provided by a great many local authorities. There are also a number of specialist organisations. Three which arrange courses in many parts of the country are:

British Wheel of Yoga, 1 Hamilton Place, Boston Road, Sleaford, Lincs. NG34 7ES. T:0529 306851. Runs classes suitable for all levels of ability. Fees vary according to class size and area of the country but average about £20 to £25 a term. Some classes have special rates for retired people. Further details available from the secretary.

Iyengar Yoga Institute, 223a Randolph Avenue, London W9 1NL. T:071-624 3080. Runs classes at all levels, including remedial for those with medical conditions. Of special interest is the 59-plus class for people who would like to start gently. Fees begin at £2; membership is £12 a year. For further information contact the headquarters above.

Yoga for Health Foundation, Ickwell Bury, Biggleswade, Bedfordshire SG18 9EF. T:0767 27271. This is a registered charity with clubs and teachers around the country. Additionally, residential programmes are provided at the Foundation's headquarters. Cost includes full board and for five days would be around £172.50. There are also special courses for senior citizens. National membership is £11.50 a year (£16 for couples).

Sensible eating

A trim, well kept body is one of the secrets of a youthful appearance, whereas being fat and out-of-condition adds years to anyone's age. Regular exercise is one-half of the equation, sensible eating the other. Not to put too fine a point on it, more than one in five adults in Britain

Health

is obese – in other words, overweight. No one is going to fuss about two or three pounds but half a stone or more, as well as looking unsightly, starts to become a health risk. In middle-aged men in particular, it increases the possibility of a heart attack, can lead to other illnesses, makes operations more difficult – and, in older people, is one of the causes of restricted mobility.

No one should go on a serious diet without first consulting their doctor. However, medical advice is not necessary for knocking off: sweets, cakes, sticky buns, deep-fried foods, alcohol and rich sauces. Healthy foods which most people (except of course those on a special doctor's diet) can eat in almost unlimited quantities are: fruit, salad, vegetables, fish and white meat such as chicken.

Many people seeking to become more healthy eaters find it helpful to join a Weight Watchers Club. To assist those unable (or unwilling) to attend meetings, WW have introduced Weight Watchers by Mail. For further details, telephone 091-296 2200; or write to **Weight Watchers by Mail**, Freepost, Newcastle upon Tyne NE2 1BR.

As a rule chubby people tend to be those who enjoy rather too many good meals in the company of others. People living on their own, however, sometimes also get weight problems: either because they cannot be bothered to cook for themselves, so snack off the wrong kinds of food such as jam sandwiches and chocolate biscuits; or because they neglect themselves and do not take enough nourishment.

Elderly ladies, in particular, sometimes quite literally eat hardly enough to keep a bird alive and, in consequence, not only undermine their health but because of their general frailty are more susceptible to falls and broken bones. An excellent stocking filler for anyone living alone or for couples whose family has flown the nest is: *Easy Cooking for One or Two* by Louise Davies. Penguin, £4.99.

Other useful reading includes: *Eight Guidelines to a Healthy Diet*, obtainable free from: **Food Sense**, London SE99 7TT; and *Enjoy Healthy Eating*, free from the Distribution Department, Health Education Authority, Hamilton House, Mabledon Place, London WC1H 9TX.

Food safety

No discussion about food would be complete without a word or two on the subject of food safety. As most readers will know it is inadvisable for anyone to eat raw eggs, whether consumed steak tartare fashion or used in uncooked dishes such as mayonnaise and mousses. To be on the safe side, elderly people as well as the very young should probably also avoid lightly cooked eggs. Likewise, if as was the case a couple of summers ago, there is an official warning about certain seafood, then it is only common sense to refrain from eating the items in question.

However, when it comes to food poisoning, eggs and seafood are far from being the only culprits. 'Cook-chill' foods in particular, including ready-cooked chickens and pork pies, are a breeding ground for bacteria especially in the summer, when many foods – even vegetables – are liable to deteriorate more quickly.

Storage and cooking also play a major part in warding off the dangers of food poisoning. The government leaflet Food Safety (available free from Food Sense) recommends the following basic advice:

- Keep all parts of your kitchen clean
- Do not allow the temperature of chilled foods to rise above a maximum of 5°C
- Keep raw and cooked foods separate and use within the recommended dates
- Cook foods thoroughly
- Do not reheat food more than once and don't keep cooked food longer than two days.

Drink

Most doctors cheerfully maintain that 'a little bit of what you fancy does you good'. The majority of healthy adults can enjoy a drink at a party or a glass of wine with dinner without any ill effects and retirement is no reason for giving up these pleasures. Moreover, in small quantities, it can be a very effective nightcap and can also help to stimulate a sluggish appetite. However, where problems begin is when people fancy more than is good for them. Alcoholism is the third great killer after heart disease and cancer.

The condition is far more likely among those who are bored or depressed and who, perhaps almost without realising it, drift into the habit of having a drink to cheer themselves up or to pass the time when they have nothing else to do. The trouble is the habit can become insidious and, though at the beginning it does not feel that way, individuals can quite quickly start becoming dependent on drink.

Whereas most people are sensible enough to be able to control the habit themselves, others may need help. The family doctor will of course be the first person to check with for medical advice. But additionally, for those who need moral support, the following self-help groups may be the answer.

Drinkwatchers, 724 Fulham Road, London SW6 5SE. T:071-371

7477. Drinkwatchers is for those who want to cut back on alcohol and drink more sensibly – rather than abstain altogether. For addresses of local groups and handbook (£2.25), contact the headquarters above.

Alcoholics Anonymous, PO Box 1, Stonebow House, Stonebow, York YO1 2NJ. T:0904 644026. AA has around 2,800 autonomous groups all over the country, designed to help those with a serious alcohol problem learn how to abstain. Sufferers assist each other in trying to kick the habit which is made easier by meeting others with the same problem. Meetings take two forms. Some are for members only, where everyone is anonymous and participants can discuss their feelings in strictest confidence. Others are open to relatives and friends, where discussion of the wider family problems is welcomed. Membership is free, although a collection is taken towards the cost of renting meeting rooms. For addresses of local groups, see telephone directory.

Al-Anon Family Groups UK & Eire, 61 Great Dover Street, London SE1 4YF. T:071-403 0888 (24-hour confidential service). Offer support and understanding where a relative or friend's drinking is causing concern. There are over 1,080 groups throughout the UK and Eire. Please write or telephone for details of local meetings.

Smoking

Any age is a good one to cut back on smoking or preferably give it up altogether. The gruesome facts are that smokers are 20 times more likely to contract lung cancer. They are at more serious risk of suffering from heart disease, particularly coronary thrombosis; and additionally are more liable to chronic bronchitis as well as various other ailments.

Most people agree that is easier to give up completely than attempt to cut back since, as every smoker knows after the first cigarette of the day, you can always think of a thousand excuses for lighting another. Aids to will-power include: travelling in non-smoking carriages in the train; leaving your cigarettes behind when you go out; not buying cigarettes for guests to smoke in your home, which they leave but you take; and refusing as a personal point of honour to cadge off friends. Working out how much money you could save in a year and promising yourself a holiday or other reward on the proceeds could help. Thinking about your health in years to come should be an even more convincing argument.

Dozens of organisations concerned with health publish leaflets giving the facts, including the harm you can do to non-smokers. To list just a few, you can obtain literature from:

Coronary Prevention Group, 102 Gloucester Place, London W1H 3DA. Enclose large sae with 18p stamp.

Retirement Made Easy

BUPA Medical Centre, 300 Gray's Inn Road, London WC1X 8DU.
Ash, 109 Gloucester Place, London W1H 3PH.
Quitline, 102 Gloucester Place, London W1H 3DA. T:071-487 3000. Offers information, advice and counselling for smokers and ex-smokers alike. Lines are open from 9.30 a.m. to 5.30 p.m., weekdays.

Aches, pains and other abnormalities

There is nothing about becoming 50, 60 or even 70 that makes aches and pains an inevitability. Age in itself has nothing to do with the vast majority of ailments. However, a big problem is that many people ignore the warning signs when something is wrong, on the basis that this symptom or that is only to be expected as one becomes older. More often than not, treatment when a condition is still in its infancy can either cure it altogether or at least help to delay its advance.

The following should always be investigated by a doctor, to be on the safe side:

- Any pain which lasts more than a few days
- Lumps, however small
- Dizziness or fainting
- Chest pains, shortness of breath or palpitations
- Persistent cough or hoarseness
- Unusual bleeding from anywhere
- Unnatural tiredness or headaches
- Frequent indigestion
- Unexplained weight loss.

Health insurance

An increasing number of people are covered by private health insurance or provident schemes during their working lives. If you wish to continue this benefit, and you are unable to remain in your company scheme after retirement, you will normally be welcomed as an individual client by most of the main groups provided you are under 70 (or in some cases, older) when you join.

Even if you have not previously been insured, it is not too late to consider doing so. Firstly, because a number of low-cost schemes for older people have recently been introduced; secondly because, since April 1990, tax relief is allowable on private health insurance payments for people aged 60 and over. Provided the scheme is a qualifying policy (permanent health insurance plans, i.e. those that pay a cash benefit of more than £5 a night, do not qualify), the tax relief is given to whoever actually makes the payment: the individual concerned or their grown-up children (or other relative/friend) buying insurance on their behalf.

Health

Similar to mortgages, basic-rate relief will be deducted at source; while higher rates of relief, where these apply, will be given by adjustment of individual pay codes.

Terms and conditions vary but all the major health insurance groups offer to pay all or the greatest part of the costs of in-patient accommodation, treatment and medical fees as well as out-patient charges for specialists, X-rays and similar services. However, as with all types of insurance, the small print matters, so look carefully at all the plans available before selecting the scheme that best suits your needs.

The major organisations that offer private health insurance include:

BUPA, Provident House, Essex Street, London WC2R 3AX. T:071-353 5212.
Private Patients Plan, PPP House, Upperton Road, Eastbourne, East Sussex BN21 1LH. T:0323 410505.
Western Provident Association Ltd., Rivergate House, 70 Redcliffe Street, Bristol BS1 6LS. T:0272 225771.
Bristol Contributory Welfare Association, Bristol House, 40-56 Victoria Street, Bristol BS1 6AB. T:0272 293742.
Exeter Hospital Aid Society, 5-7 Palace Gate, Exeter, Devon EX1 1UE. T:0392 75361.

If you would welcome advice in selecting a plan, you might like to contact **The Private Health Partnership**. They will send you a questionnaire and then help you match your key requirements to the most suitable scheme. There is a charge of £5 (plus VAT). For further information, telephone helpline: 0532 788855.

Private patients – without insurance cover
If you do not have private medical insurance but want to go into hospital as a private patient, there is of course nothing to stop you doing so provided your doctor is willing and you are able to pay the bills. The choice is between the private wings of NHS hospitals, hospitals run by charitable or non-profit-making organisations (such as the Nuffield Hospitals) and those run for profit by private companies.

Health screening
Prevention is better than cure and most of the provident associations offer a screening service to check general health and to provide advice on diet, drinking and smoking if these are problem areas. Centres are usually available to members of insurance schemes and others alike.

BUPA. There are 28 BUPA health screening centres up and down the country. These are located in: London, Birmingham, Blackpool, Bournemouth, Brentwood, Bristol, Bushey, Cambridge, Cardiff, Colchester, Croydon, Edinburgh, Gatwick, Glasgow, Harpenden, Leeds, Leicester, Lincoln, Maidstone, Manchester, North Cheshire, Norwich, Nottingham, Portsmouth, Scarborough, Sutton Coldfield, Wirral and Worcester. For further details, see relevant telephone directory; or call BUPA on 0800 800455.

PPP. PPP have medical centres in London, Manchester, and Southampton and accredited arrangements with hospitals throughout the country. For further information, contact: Customer Services, PPP Medical Centre, 99 New Cavendish Street, London W1M 7FQ. T:071-637 8941.

WPA. Centres are located in: Birmingham (T:021-441 1212); Bristol (T:0272 225771); Harrogate (T:0423 562276); Leicester (T:0533 551318); London (T:071-495 4880) and Reading (T:0734 502757).

BCWA. Offers a rebate of £14 for a health check at an approved medical centre and £7 for breast screening.

National Health Service. The NHS offers several different screening services of particular relevance to those aged 50-plus. Two are especially for women and the others are more general. Firstly, all adults are entitled to regular 'life-style' check-ups, giving you a relaxed opportunity to discuss any health problem that may be worrying you; to seek advice if, for example, you are trying to lose weight; and to have one or two simple tests such as checking your blood pressure. Individuals over 75 are now offered a special health assessment cum check-up every year, which can either be done in your own home or at the practice premises. As well as general health, attention will be devoted to such matters as failing eyesight, hearing difficulties, trouble with your feet and similar problems.

The special women's tests are to screen for cancer of the cervix and breast. These are now available in all parts of the country. All women between 20 and 64 years will be offered a smear test at least every five years; and all women between 50 and 64 years will be invited for screening by breast X-ray every three years. (Women over 64 can request a mammography test every three years.)

You should automatically receive invitations for screening if you are registered with a GP. If not, ask your GP for details or enquire at your local health authority.

For further information, see leaflets *The Cervical Smear Test – Why You Need It* and *NHS Breast Screening – The Facts*, both obtainable from: The Health Education Authority, Publication Unit (Dept WH), Hamilton House, Mabledon Place, London WC1 9TX. T:071-383 3833.

Health

Hospital cash plans

These schemes provide a cash sum for every night the insured person spends in hospital. Premiums range from 30p to £2.60 a week and payments vary between £8 and £40 a day. By buying multiple premiums, you can build up quite a significant sum which can be used to substitute for loss of earnings or to meet additional bills such as transport costs for family visits.

All benefits are tax free. Most schemes operate strict age limits and the majority will not accept contributions from individuals over the age of 65. The one or two that do normally reduce the benefits by approximately 33 per cent.

About 30 organisations offer such schemes. A full list can be obtained from: **British Health Care Association**, 24a Main Street, Garforth, Leeds LS25 1AA. T:0532 320903.

National Health Service

Most readers will need no introduction to the National Health Service. However, there are one or two scraps of information that you may not know – or possibly have forgotten – that may come in useful around retirement.

Choosing a GP

If you move to a new area, you will need to find a new doctor. The best way is normally by recommendation; otherwise you can write to the **Family Health Services Authority (FHSA)**, see telephone directory, for details of all NHS doctors practising in the area. The information should include: names, addresses, sex and type of qualifications along with essential practice information such as surgery hours, services provided and arrangements for emergencies and night calls. Additionally, all GPs must now have practice leaflets, available at their premises, with details about the service including for example whether there is an appointments system.

Having selected a doctor, you should take your medical card to the receptionist in order to try to get your name registered. This is not automatic as, firstly, there is a limit to the number of patients any one doctor can accept. Also, some doctors prefer to meet potential patients before accepting them on their list.

If you want to change your GP, you go about it in exactly the same way. You do not need to give a reason for wanting to change and you do not need to ask anyone's permission.

Two useful publications to read are:

233

Retirement Made Easy

- *The NHS Reforms and You*
- *You and Your GP*

Available free from any health centre.

Benefits

People over retirement age or in receipt of income support are entitled to free prescriptions. Additionally, certain other groups, including for example people who suffer from a specified medical condition, have automatic entitlement to free NHS prescriptions. Those on low incomes may also be entitled to free prescriptions. Claims should be made on Form AG1, obtainable from any Benefits Agency office. For further details, see the following leaflets obtainable from GPs, chemists, post offices and Benefits Agency offices:

- AB 11 *Help with NHS Costs*
- P 11 *NHS Prescriptions*

Those on income support may also get free dental treatment, free eye tests, a voucher towards the cost of glasses and help with fares to hospital.

Those below retirement age, who require a lot of prescriptions could save money by purchasing 'a season ticket'. This costs £19.40 for four months; or £53.50 for a year. A season ticket will work out cheaper if you are likely to need more than five prescription items in four months, or more than 14 items in 12 months. Obtain Form FP 95 (EC 95 in Scotland) from a post office, chemist, Benefits Agency office or your Family Health Services Authority.

If you are on income support and are disabled, you are entitled to certain premiums on top of your ordinary income support allowance. There are three rates: £17.80 (single); £25.55 (couple) for the generally disabled; and £32.55 (single and couples where only one is disabled) for the severely disabled.

Various *social security benefits* are also available to those with special problems because of illness. These include:

- *Invalidity Benefit*, see Leaflet NI 16A
- *Attendance Allowance*, see Leaflet NI 205
- *Sickness Benefit*, see Leaflet NI 16
- *Disability Living Allowance*, see Leaflet DS 704
- *Disability Working Allowance*, see Leaflet DS 703

All the above leaflets are obtainable from any social security office. For further details see Chapter 14.

Of interest to the Asian community is a guide entitled *Disability Rights*

Health

which gives details of State benefits and local authority services, variously in: Hindi, Punjabi, Gujerati, Urdu and Bengali. Free from ASRA Ltd., 155 Kennington Park Road, London SE11 4JJ.

Going into hospital

Stories abound of people who wait months and months for an operation because of shortage of beds. But while waiting lists for a hernia or hip replacement may stretch from here to eternity in one area, hospitals in another part of the country may have spare capacity. Many patients are unaware that they can ask their doctor to refer them to a surgeon anywhere in Britain.

Finding out which hospitals have beds has become very easy. The College of Health operates a telephone helpline service to advise which hospitals have the shortest waiting lists for particular operations. The list includes: general surgery, orthopaedic, ear, nose and throat, gynaecology, ophthalmology, oral surgery, urology, cardiac surgery, neurosurgery and plastic surgery.

Either you or your doctor can telephone the helpline, which is open Monday to Friday, between 10 a.m. and 4 p.m. The number to ring is: 081-983 1133.

Before you can become a patient at another hospital, your GP will need to agree to your being referred and may also need to check that money can be allocated from the district budget; but with more and more doctors becoming fundholders, the bureaucracy is fast diminishing.

As well as the helpline, the College of Health publishes a useful booklet *Going Into Hospital* (£2), available from: **The College Of Health**, 21 Old Ford Road, London E2 9PL. T:081-983 1225.

Those likely to need help on leaving hospital should speak to the hospital social worker, who will help make any necessary arrangements.

Help is sometimes available to assist patients with their travel costs to and from hospital. This applies: if you receive income support or family credit; get a war or MOD disablement pension; or if you have to travel an exceptionally long way to get to hospital, as could be the case if you live in the Isles of Scilly or the area covered by Highlands and Islands Enterprise. Claims for help with travelling costs can also be made on the grounds of low income. For detailed information, see leaflet H11 *NHS Hospital Travel Costs*.

If you go into hospital, you will continue to receive your State pension as normal for six weeks. After that, it will be reduced.

If you have any complaints while in hospital, in the first instance you should speak to the specially appointed officer within the hospital who is there to deal with complaints; or if the matter is more serious, you should write to the general manager of the hospital. In turn they may refer your complaint to the Regional Director of Public Health. If you are still unhappy, you can take the matter up with the Health Service Ombudsman – see addresses and other information below.

Complaints

One of the important new rights contained in the Patient's Charter is the right to have any complaint about NHS services investigated and to receive a full and prompt written reply from the senior person in authority.

If you have a complaint about a GP, dentist, optician or chemist, you should contact your local Family Health Services Authority (or in Scotland, your local Health Board). The address should be on your medical card. Alternatively, look in the telephone directory or ask at your Citizens' Advice Bureau. Complaints should be made in writing and submitted within the proper time limits (see below).

If you have a complaint about a health authority matter, you can either complain to the Chief Executive of the Health Authority direct or you can ask your local Community Health Council (in Scotland, Local Health Council) to help you. The address is listed under 'Community' in the telephone directory.

If you are still dissatisfied, then the Health Service Ombudsman (known formally as the Health Service Commissioner) might be able to help. His job is to investigate complaints of failure in service or maladministration by health authorities of the NHS. He cannot, however, take up legal causes on a patient's behalf nor investigate complaints about a clinical judgement. Addresses to write to are:

Health Service Commissioner for England, Church House, Great Smith Street, London SW1P 3BW. T:071-276 2035.
Health Service Commissioner for Wales, 4th Floor, Pearl Assurance House, Greyfriars Road, Cardiff CF1 3AG. T:0222 394621.
Health Service Commissioner for Scotland, 2nd Floor, 11 Melville Crescent, Edinburgh EH3 7LU. T:031-225 7465.

If you have a complaint you should get on to the matter fairly speedily while events are still fresh in your mind. Time limits require you to register complaints with Family Health Services Authorities within 13 weeks of the incident. If you delay, you may find that your complaint is out of time and that no one will be able to help you. (Ocasionally, provided there is an extremely good reason, the time limit may be extended.)

As a last resort, you can make your complaint formally in writing to the Secretary of State, Department of Health, Richmond House, 79 Whitehall, London SW1A 2NS.

Rather than proceed through the formal channels described above, an alternative approach – which does not prevent you from also applying to the Ombudsman or to anyone else – is to get in touch with **The Patients Association**, 18 Victoria Park Square, Bethnal Green, London E2 9PF. T:081-981 5676. This is an independent advice centre which offers guidance to patients in the event of a problem with the health service. The Association also publishes a selection of useful leaflets and a directory of self-help groups.

Eyes

It is advisable to have your eyes checked every year or two. You will not have to pay if: you or your partner are receiving income support or family credit; if you are registered blind or partially sighted; are prescribed complex lenses; are diagnosed as having diabetes or glaucoma, or if you are over 40 and are a close relative of someone with glaucoma; (i.e. parent, child, brother or sister); or if you are a patient of the Hospital Eye Service.

Even if you do not belong to any of these groups but are on a low income, you may be entitled to a voucher to help pay for the test. To find out whether you qualify for assistance, you should fill out claim form AG1 which you can obtain from Social Security offices, hospitals and opticians together with an envelope addressed to the Health Benefits Unit in Newcastle. You should hear from the Unit within a few weeks and if you qualify for help you will receive a certificate AG2 or AG3 entitling you to a voucher. Wait until you hear before having a sight test, as it is difficult to claim the money back afterwards.

People with mobility problems can arrange a domiciliary visit to have their eyes examined at home. For some time this has been free for those with an AG2 certificate. Since November 1991 people with a (partial help) AG3 certificate can use the benefit towards a private home visit by their optician.

The going rate for sight tests if you do have to pay is about £15. Many opticians, however, charge less for people who are retired or run special promotions at various times of the year. Even if this is not advertised in the window, you have nothing to lose by asking before booking an appointment.

As you probably know, you do not need a doctor's referral to have your eyes tested. Simply book an appointment with a registered ophthalmic optician or ophthalmic medical practitioner. If you qualify for free testing, remember to take your AG2 or AG3 certificate with you to give to the optician. The sight test should establish whether or not spectacles are required and should also include an eye examination to check for signs of injury, disease or abnormality.

Whether you have to pay or not, the optician must either give you a prescription identifying what type of glasses you require or alternatively give you a statement confirming that you have no need of spectacles. The prescription is valid for two years. If you do not use it straight away, you should keep it carefully so that it is handy when you need to use it. When you do decide to buy spectacles or contact lenses, you are under no obligation to obtain them from the optician who tested your eyes but can buy them where you like.

The voucher system also applies to the purchase of spectacles. If you are on a low income or if you require exceptionally powerful lenses, you are likely to qualify for a voucher to help towards the cost of your glasses or contact lenses. The cash value of the voucher, which currently (1992/93) ranges from £23.70 to £110, will depend on your circumstances and optical prescription: it might be sufficient to pay for your spectacles outright or it may only make a small contribution towards the cost. Part of the equation will depend on the frames you choose. You will not be tied to any particular glasses: you can choose specs that cost more than the value of the voucher and pay the difference yourself. For further details, together with an application form, see leaflet G11 *NHS Sight Tests and Vouchers for Glasses*, obtainable from any optician or health centre. People who are registered blind are entitled to a special tax allowance of £1,080 a year.

A great deal of practical help can be obtained by contacting the Royal National Institute for the Blind. In addition to giving general advice and information it can supply a range of special equipment, details of which are listed in a free catalogue. For information, contact the **Royal National Institute for the Blind**, 224 Great Portland Street, London W1N 6AA. T:071-388 1266.

Also useful, all the main banks will provide statements in Braille; and Barclaycard now also issues credit card statements in Braille, on request. There is no extra charge for these services.

BT has introduced a free directory enquiry service for blind and disabled customers. To use the service you first need to register with BT who will issue you with a personal identification number. For further information, call the free Linkline on: 0800 800 150.

See also Chapter 9 'Leisure Activities' (pages 162-3) about libraries and other facilities.

Health

Feet

Many people forget about their feet until they begin to give trouble. Corns and bunions if neglected can become extremely painful, and ideally everyone, especially women who wear high heels, should have chiropody treatment from early middle age or even younger.

Chiropody is available on the National Health Service without referral from a doctor being necessary but facilities tend to be very over-subscribed, so in many areas it is only the very elderly or those with a real problem who can get appointments.

Private chiropodists are listed in the *Yellow Pages*. Alternatively, you can write to the Society of Chiropodists which is the professional association for State registered chiropodists, for a list of local names. The address to contact is: **Society of Chiropodists**, 53 Welbeck Street, London W1M 7HE. T:071-486 3381.

Hearing

As they grow older, a great many people suffer some deterioration in their sense of hearing. Should you begin to have difficulty in hearing people speak clearly or find that you are having to turn up the television, it is probably worth having a word with your doctor.

Your GP may refer you to a consultant who will advise whether a hearing aid would be helpful and, if so, will prescribe one that is suitable.

You can either obtain a hearing aid and batteries free on the NHS or you can buy them privately. Either way, you may like to read a booklet entitled *How to Use Your Hearing Aid* (HA1), available free from hearing aid centres.

There are many other aids on the market that can make life easier. BT, for example, has a variety of special equipment from louder bell tones to flashing light systems. You can either try out the gadgets at one of BT's Aids Centres or dial the operator and ask for Freephone Telecom Sales, who will advise about local shops where you can see the equipment.

Additionally, there are a number of specialist organisations that can give you a lot of help, both as regards hearing aids and other matters.

British Association of the Hard Of Hearing, 7-11 Armstrong Road, London W3 7JL. T:081-743 1110 (voice and minicom). The BAHOH, which administers the Sympathetic Hearing Scheme publishes a selection of practical leaflets, including: *Choosing a Hearing Aid, Getting Used to a Hearing Aid* and *Lip Reading*, as well as information for the family on better communication with the hard of hearing. The Association also has about 200 local social clubs throughout the UK. Membership is £7 a year.

Retirement Made Easy

Royal National Institute for Deaf People, 105 Gower Street, London WC1E 6AH. T:071-387 8033 (voice); 071-388 6038 (QWERTY 300 Baud); 071-383 3154 (minicom). Publishes a comprehensive range of free leaflets including: *Aids to Daily Living; Hearing Aids: Questions and Answers; Visual Doorbell Systems* and *Questions About Tinnitus*. The RNID also sells environmental aids and publishes a monthly magazine, annual subscription, £8.

British Deaf Association, 38 Victoria Place, Carlisle CA1 1HU. T:0228 48844; Voice/DCT: 0228 28719. The BDA aims to help those who are profoundly deaf or who use British Sign Language as their preferred language. Branches organise social activities in most cities and towns. The Association also arranges holidays both in this country and overseas.

Teeth

Everyone knows the importance of having regular dental check-ups. Many adults, however, slip out of the habit which could result in their having more trouble with their teeth as they become older.

Dentistry is one of the treatments for which you have to pay, unless you have a low income. Charges are based on 75 per cent of the cost up to a maximum of £225. If you are receiving income support or believe you may be entitled to reduced charges because your income is very low get leaflet D11 *NHS Dental Treatment* (from any NHS dentist or Social Security office) which explains the eligibility conditions. If you think you qualify, you should obtain forms AG5 and AG1 from your local Social Security office and return them, when completed, to the address indicated. Sometimes, although treatment is not free, you may get help towards the cost of dentures should these be necessary.

Even though most people have to pay for treatment under the NHS, going as an NHS patient is normally cheaper than going as a private patient. To avoid any nasty surprises when the bill comes along, ask your dentist from the start whether or not you will be treated under the NHS. This also applies to the hygienist, should you need to see one.

Personal relationships

Retirement is a bit like getting married again. It involves a new life style, fresh opportunities and inevitably, as with marriage, a few adjustments for both husband and wife to make. He will have to accustom himself to no longer going to a regular job. She will have to start thinking about another meal to prepare and may possibly feel that she will have to reorganise her domestic or working routine. Alternatively, of course, it

Health

may be the other way round with the wife giving up her job and the husband, who has long acted as household chef, sighing at the prospect of a regular gourmet lunch to produce.

After years of perhaps hardly seeing each other for more than a few hours a week except for weekends, suddenly almost the whole of every day can be spent together. He may feel hurt that she does not appear more delighted. She may feel guilty about wanting to pursue her normal activities especially if, as more and more women are, she is still working after her husband has retired. Even in the most loving marriages, the first weeks of retirement – for either partner – can produce tensions, which may even affect their sex life, that neither had anticipated.

Normally with good will and understanding on both sides any difficulties are quickly resolved and an even deeper, more satisfying relationship develops. However, for some couples it does not work out so easily and it may be helpful to seek skilled guidance.

Relate: National Marriage Guidance, Herbert Gray College, Little Church Street, Rugby CV21 3AP. T:0788 573241. Offers a counselling service to people who are experiencing difficulties in their marriage or other personal relationships. Their clients are all ages. Some have been married twice or even three times. Many are in the throes of actually seeking a divorce but are trying to prevent the bitterness that can develop. Some come for advice because of upsets with their stepchildren. Others may have sexual problems. Often, the emphasis is not on a particular crisis but instead because couples are seeking to make their marriage more positively enjoyable, as at retirement.

Relate offers counselling in some 400 places around the country. See local telephone directory under 'Relate' or 'Marriage Guidance' or contact the national headquarters above. There is no charge for the service but contributions are very much welcomed.

The address for Scotland is: **Marriage Counselling Scotland**, 26 Frederick Street, Edinburgh EH2 2JR. T:031-225 5006.

The Catholic Marriage Advisory Council offers a similar service for those who are having problems with their marriage. Addresses are: **Catholic Marriage Advisory Council for England and Wales**, Clitherow House, 1 Blythe Mews, Blythe Road, London W14 0NW. T:071-371 1341; for Scotland, 196 Clyde Street, Glasgow G1 4JY. T:041-204 1239; for Ireland, All Hallows College, Drumcondra, Dublin 9. T:0103 53137 1151.

Depression

Depression can be first cousin to marriage and other relationship problems. It is fairly common after bereavement, can be caused by worries or may occur after an operation. Sometimes too, as a number of retired people find, it develops as a result of loneliness, boredom or general lack of purpose. Usually people come out of it of their own accord: either as time heals sorrow or the scars of a relationship that has gone wrong; or in the case of those who are temporarily bored and fed up, as they find new interests and outlets for their talents.

If the condition persists for more than a few days, a doctor should always be consulted as depression can create sleeping difficulties as well as affect the appetite and lead to an overall feeling of physical malaise. The sufferer can be caught in a vicious circle of being too listless to enjoy anything, yet not having done enough during the day to be able to sleep at the proper time.

Another reason for consulting a doctor is that depression may be due to being physically run down, as after 'flu, and all that is required is a good tonic – or perhaps a holiday.

Sometimes, however, depression persists and it may be that rather than medicines or the stimulus of a new activity, individuals may feel they need to talk to someone outside the family circle who has a deeper understanding of what they are experiencing. There are several organisations that may be able to help.

Depressives Associated, PO Box 5, Castletown, Portland, Dorset DT5 1BQ. T:081-760 0544 (answerphone). This is a self-help organisation, run by people who themselves have suffered from the effects of depression at some stage of their lives. There are local groups across the country, where individuals can meet to provide mutual support and advice. For further information, write to the headquarters enclosing a 9" x 7" sae or phone the above number for information pack.

The Samaritans, 10 The Grove, Slough, Berkshire SL1 1QP. T:0753 532713. The Samaritans are available at any time of the day or night, every single day of the year. They are there to talk or listen for as long as an individual needs or wants to be able to speak to another person. Although most people think of the Samaritans as being a telephone service for those who feel they may be in danger of taking their own lives, anyone who would like to can visit their local branch. You do not need to feel positively suicidal before contacting the Samaritans; if you are simply very depressed, they will equally welcome your call. The service is free and completely confidential. To find your local branch, look in the telephone directory under 'S'.

Mind, 22 Harley Street, London W1N 2ED. T:071-637 0741. Mind is a national charity that aims to help both individuals who are mentally ill and also their families. There are local groups throughout the country

Health

as well as day centres, social clubs, friendship schemes and self-help projects. Services also include counselling and Mind publishes a large range of pamphlets and books. For further information, either contact your local branch (see telephone directory) or the above address.

Some common afflictions

Quite probably you will be one of the lucky ones and the rest of this chapter will be of no further interest to you. It deals with some of the more common afflictions, such as back pain and heart disease, as well as with disability. However, if you are unfortunate enough to be affected, or have a member of your family who is, then knowing which organisations can provide support could make all the difference in helping you to cope.

Arthritis and rheumatism
Arthritis Care, 18 Stephenson Way, London NW1 2HD. T:071-916 1500. Has over 500 branches offering practical support including transport and social activities as well as a visiting service for housebound people. Arthritis Care also provides specially adapted holiday centres and self-catering units, runs a residential home and publishes various free leaflets and booklets. Membership is £3 a year.

The Arthritis & Rheumatism Council, St. Mary's Gate, Chesterfield, Derbyshire S41 7TD. T:0246 558033. Publishes a number of free handbooks including: *A Guide to Arthritis; Marriage, Sex and Arthritis; Gout; Pain in the Neck; A New Kneejoint.* Send a 9" x 6" sae.

Back pain
Four out of five people suffer from back pain at some stage of their lives. While there are many different causes, doctors agree that much of the trouble could be avoided through correct posture, care in lifting heavy articles, a firm mattress and chairs that provide support in the right places.

The Back Shop, 24 New Cavendish Street, London W1M 7LH. T:071-935 9120. A shop and mail order business that sells medically approved products that help to prevent back trouble or may provide relief for those who suffer. For a mail order catalogue, send a large (A4) sae.

National Back Pain Association, 31-33 Park Road, Teddington, Middlesex TW11 0AB. T:081-977 5474. Funds research into the causes and treatment of back pain and also publishes a range of free leaflets and fact sheets to help back pain sufferers. There are local branches around the country which organise talks, lectures and exercise classes as well as social activities and fund-raising events. Membership is £10. For further information, write enclosing a large sae.

Cancer
One of the really excellent trends in recent years is a far greater willingness to talk about cancer. Quite apart from the fact that discussing the subject openly has removed some of the dread, increasingly one hears stories of people who have made a complete recovery. Early diagnosis can make a vital difference. Doctors recommend that all women should undergo regular screening for cervical cancer and women over 40 are advised to have a routine mammography to screen for breast cancer at least once every three years. Computerised cervical screening systems for women aged 20 to 64 and breast cancer screening units for women aged 50 to 64 already exist in many parts of the country and are planned to be available nationwide by the end of 1993. Anyone with a lump or swelling, however small, should waste no time in having it investigated by a doctor.

There are a number of excellent support groups for cancer sufferers. Rather than list them all, we have only included two as BACUP, as well as its own services, can act as an information service about other local cancer support groups.

BACUP (British Association of Cancer United Patients), 3 Bath Place, Rivington Street, London EC2A 3JR. T:071-613 2121 – Cancer Information Service. For those outside London, Freeline 0800 181199. BACUP has three main aims: to provide information to help cancer patients and their relatives; to offer them emotional support and practical advice; and to help patients talk about their illness with doctors and family. As well as answering enquiries, it publishes a comprehensive range of free booklets, including information about different types of cancer and about practical problems such as hair care and diet. Additionally, BACUP publishes a newspaper for patients and their families and also runs a one-to-one counselling service, staffed by trained volunteer counsellors. Telephone number for this service is 071-696 9000.

Breast Care and Mastectomy Association, 15-19 Britten Street, London SW3 3TZ. T:071-867 8275. Helplines: London (9.30 a.m. to 4.30 p.m.) 071-867 1103; Glasgow (9.30 a.m. to 4.30 p.m.) 041-353 1050; Edinburgh (9 a.m. to 12.30 p.m.) 031-458 5598. Offers free help, information and support to women with breast cancer or other breast-related problems. In particular, the Association operates a nationwide volunteer network, putting women in touch by telephone, visits or via local groups with others who have had a similar experience. The Association also publishes a number of free booklets and offers a free breast prostheses fitting service, by appointment.

Chest and heart diseases
The earlier sections on smoking, diet, drink and exercise list some of the most pertinent 'dos and don'ts' that can help to prevent heart disease. The advice is not to be taken lightly.

Latest statistics from the Office of Health Economics reveal that English death rates from heart disease are among the highest in the world. Although middle age is identified as the peak danger period, about one man in four over the age of 65 is at risk of suffering a heart attack and the evidence suggests that women are fast beginning to catch up with men.

Useful reading
You and Your Heart, free from the Coronary Prevention Group, 102 Gloucester Place, London W1H 3DA. T:071-935 2889. Enclose a large sae with 18p stamp.

Free leaflets on heart disease and related problems are available from the British Heart Foundation, 14 Fitzhardinge Street, London W1H 4DH. T:071-935 0185.

Diabetes
Diabetes can be diagnosed at any age, although it is common in the elderly and especially among individuals who are overweight.

British Diabetic Association, 10 Queen Anne Street, London W1M 0BD. T:071-323 1531. Offers a comprehensive information and advisory service for all diabetics and their families covering such subjects as: diet and recipes, exercise, insurance, employment, driving and travel. There are over 400 local groups which offer support and also hold regular meetings and social activities; contact head office for details. BDA membership costs £10 (£2 for reduced rate members) per year.

Migraine
The cause of migraine is unknown but the most common trigger factor is stress, particularly anxiety and tension. Certain foods such as chocolate, cheese and citrus fruits as well as alcohol may precipitate attacks in some people.

The Migraine Trust, 45 Great Ormond Street, London WC1N 3HZ. T:071-278 2676. Offers a service to sufferers including helpline, free literature pack and regular newsletters. It also publishes a booklet called *Understanding Migraine* (£1.95). Membership costs £10 a year.

Osteoporosis and menopause problems

Osteoporosis is more commonly known as the 'brittle bone' disease, which causes loss of height, spine curvature and broken limbs and kills more women than cancer of the breast, cervix and uterus combined. If often starts around the onset of the menopause when the body begins to lose calcium more rapidly and at least one in four women are affected in some way.

The National Osteoporosis Society, PO Box 10, Radstock, Bath BA3 3YB. T:0761 432472. Offers help, support and advice on all aspects of osteoporosis and publishes a free leaflet about this ailment (send sae). Membership, which is optional but which would entitle you to free newsletters as well as attendance at annual meetings, is £10.

Women's Health Concern (WHC), 83 Earl's Court Road, London W8 6EF. T:071-938 3932. WHC offers advice and counselling to women with gynaecological and hormonal disturbance problems, in particular with the menopause and proper use of HRT. It runs a telephone counselling service and also sees patients face to face at its centres in Cardiff and London. As a charity, WHC charges no fee but donations are very much appreciated.

Stroke

Over 100,000 people in the UK suffer a stroke each year. Prevention is similar to the prevention of heart disease.

The Stroke Association, CHSA House, Whitecross Street, London EC1Y 8JJ. T:071-490 7999. Works to prevent stroke illness and to help stroke patients and their families. It produces a wide range of publications and provides advice to individuals through its London office and regional centres. The Volunteer Stroke Service helps speech-impaired stroke sufferers through home visits and more than 500 stroke clubs provide social and therapeutic support. A free information pack and details of local groups are available from the London office above.

AIDS

If you are concerned about the possibility of AIDS and do not feel able to consult your doctor, there are a number of helpful organisations to which you can turn for advice, including:

National Aids Helpline. T:0800 567123.
Healthline, T:081-681 3311. It has 14 tapes on different aspects of AIDS. Hours are 4 p.m. to 8 p.m., weekdays.

Health

Terrence Higgins Trust Ltd. Helpline: 071-242 1010. Hours are 3 p.m. to 10 p.m. every day.

London Friend. T:071-837 3337. This is a befriending and counselling agency for 'gay' and bi-sexual men and women. It has branches in most major cities in the UK. Details of these can be obtained from the above number. The helpline is open every evening between 7.30 p.m. and midnight. There is a special women's line, on Tuesday and Thursday evenings from 7.30 p.m. to 10 p.m., call 071-837 2782. London Friend also runs a number of social support groups and offers face-to-face counselling where requested.

'Health-Lines' or 'AIDS-Lines', as they are sometimes called, have been set up in a number of local areas. Ask telephone directory enquiries for the number of your nearest centre.

Gum Clinics. Genito-urinary-medicine clinics exist in all NHS hospitals. You can get telephone numbers from your local health authority. Or look in the telephone directory under 'Venereal' or 'Sexually transmitted diseases'.

Disability

Disability is mainly covered in Chapter 14, Caring for Elderly Parents, so if you or someone in your family has a problem, you may find the answer you need there. In this section, we list some of the key organisations that can help you and include one or two other points that may be useful for younger people.

Local authority services
Social Services Departments (Social Work Department in Scotland) provide many of the services which people with disabilities may need, including:

- Practical help in the home, perhaps with the support of a home help
- Adaptations to your home, such as a ramp for a wheelchair or other special equipment for your safety
- Meals on wheels
- Provision of day centres, clubs and similar
- Issue of orange badges for cars driven or used by people with a disability (in some authorities this is handled by the Works Department or by the Residents' Parking Department)

Retirement Made Easy

- Advice about other transport services or concessions that may be available locally.

In most instances, you should speak to a social worker who will either be able to make the arrangements or signpost you in the right direction. He/she will also be able to tell you of any special facilities or other help provided by the authority.

Occupational therapists, who can advise about special equipment and help teach someone with a disability through training and exercise how best to manage, also come within the orbit of the Social Services Department.

Health care
Services are normally arranged either through a GP or the local authority health centre. Key professional staff include:

- Health visitors: qualified nurses who, rather like social workers, will be able to put you in touch with whatever specialised services are required
- District nurses: will visit patients in their home
- Physiotherapists: use exercise and massage to help improve mobility, for example after an operation
- Medical social workers: employed at hospitals and will help with any arrangements before a patient is discharged.

Employment
The Disablement Resettlement Officer helps and advises people looking for work and can also give information about any available grants, for example towards the cost of fares to work and for special equipment that may make work life easier. Ask at your nearest Jobcentre.

Community charge
If someone in your family has a disability, you may be able to claim a reduction on your community charge – or council tax, when this comes in in April 1993. If you have an orange badge on your car, you may get a rebate for a garage. You would normally apply to the *Housing Benefits Officer* but different councils employ different officers to deal with this. Either ask a councillor or enquire at the town hall whom you should approach.

Equipment
If you have temporary need of, say, a wheelchair, you will normally be

able to borrow this from the hospital or your local British Red Cross branch. If you want equipment including aids for the home on a more permanent basis, the best source of information is the Disabled Living Foundation Equipment Centre where all sorts of equipment can be seen and tried out by visitors. Qualified therapists are on hand to demonstrate the material and to give advice. An appointment is essential to enjoy the most benefit from a visit. Contact: **Disabled Living Foundation**, 380 Harrow Road, London W9 2HU, T:071-289 6111.

If it is not possible for you to come to London, the Disabled Living Foundation will be able to recommend a centre nearer your home.

Another extremely useful organisation to contact for advice on equipment and home adaptations is RADAR - see 'Helpful organisations' below.

Finally, BT supplies more than 70 aids to enable handicapped people to use the telephone more easily. These are illustrated in a booklet entitled *BT Guide for People Who Are Disabled or Elderly*. For further information, dial 100 and ask the operator for Freephone Sales.

Helpful organisations
Fount of all knowledge on almost every topic to do with disability is:

Royal Association for Disability and Rehabilitation (RADAR), 25 Mortimer Street, London W1N 8AB. T:071-637 5400. It can give advice across a very wide spectrum including: statutory and voluntary services, access and mobility issues, holidays, employment and housing.

RADAR produces many useful publications and also helps with the *National Key Scheme for Toilets for Disabled People*. About 300 local authorities throughout the country have fitted standard locks to their loos – and issue keys to disabled people – so that the facilities can be used by them, even when these would normally be locked against vandalism. RADAR supplies keys at a charge of £3.75 for those who are unable to obtain an NKS key in their own locality. There is also a *National Key Scheme Guide*, listing the location of NKS toilets throughout the UK; price is £3 including p&p.

Look After Your Heart, Lay Project Centre, Christ Church College, Canterbury, Kent CT1 1QU, the address to contact for details of the Health Education Authority's 'Look After Yourself' programmes which include safe exercise, sensible eating, stress management and simple relaxation techniques.

Age Well, Age Concern England, Astral House, 1268 London Road,

London SW16 4ER. T:081-679 8000. Offers a programme of activities to promote positive attitudes to health in later life.

Disability Scotland, Princes House, 5 Shandwick Place, Edinburgh EH2 4RG. T:031-229 8632. A national voluntary organisation for people throughout Scotland with disabilities. The Information Department answers queries by letter or telephone; or alternatively, visitors are welcome at Princes House.

Health Education Board for Scotland, Health Education Centre, Woodburn House, Canaan Lane, Edinburgh EH10 4SG. T:031-447 8044. Can provide leaflets and information on all aspects of positive health; has an excellent library and also runs courses and conferences on topics related to health in retirement.

Disability Action, 2 Annadale Avenue, Belfast BT7 3JR. T:0232 491011. Provides a forum for disability organisations in Northern Ireland, as well as practical help and information for individuals. Among other services, there is a driving school for disabled people, a monthly diary of events and a range of free fact sheets. Contact the Information Officer.

Wales Council for the Disabled, Information Service, Llys Ifor, Crescent Road, Caerphilly, Mid Glamorgan CF8 1XL. T:0222 887325. Offers a similar service for people in Wales.

DIAL UK (National Association of Disablement Information and Advice Lines), Park Lodge, St. Catherine's Hospital, Tickhill Road, Balby, Doncaster, South Yorkshire DN4 8QN. T:0302 310123. Offers a free and confidential information and advice service and also produces a number of free publications including *New Beginnings*, a booklet for newly disabled people. Information about local groups which operate in England, Wales, Scotland and Northern Ireland can be obtained by telephoning the above number.

Motability, Customer Services Department, Gate House, West Gate, Harlow, Essex CM20 1HR. T:0279 635666. A registered charity, set up to assist recipients of the higher rate mobility component of disability living allowance (formerly mobility allowance) get maximum value for money when obtaining a car or wheelchair. Motability can provide you with a list of manufacturers with whom they have negotiated special discounts. They also offer hire purchase facilities and can sometimes give help from their charitable fund to meet costs that are not covered by the allowance.

Useful reading
Health and Healthy Living: A Guide for Older People. Department of Health booklet, obtainable by dialling freephone 0800 555777 or by writing freepost: Healthy Living, Freepost, Bristol B83 3YY.

Disability Rights Handbook. A complete guide to rights, benefits and services for all people with disabilities and their families. Very clearly written and set out, it is an invaluable source of information. Price is £6.95 including p&p. Available from Disability Alliance Era, 1st Floor East, Universal House, 88-94 Wentworth Street, London E1 7SA.

Home Warmth for the Aged Benevolent Fund

COLD KILLS THE OLD

Objects of the HWA
The relief of hardship and suffering among poor, aged persons by the provision of heating appliances, fuel, bedding and clothing. To take steps to reduce the appalling number of deaths each winter as a direct result of cold, the most vital step being to provide home warmth.
The HWA was set up to save life and can provide heating appliances, bedding and clothing, or make grant-in-aid from its Welfare Fund in dire emergency.
The HWA co-operates with industry in the testing of new appliances under the eye of the local general practitioner. It is grateful to family doctors for their close co-operation. They provide reports, ideas and suggestions based upon the individual needs of the aged which fall into several medical categories.
DONATIONS, LEGACIES ETC. URGENTLY NEEDED.
Contact: H.W.A. General Secretary,
Sea Haze, Gorsethorn Way, Fairlight, East Sussex TN35 4BQ. Telephone: Hastings 813515

Q. WHO HELPS THE CARERS OF ALZHEIMER'S DISEASE SUFFERERS?
A. ALZHEIMER'S DISEASE SOCIETY
  – Links families through membership
  – Has a network of 300 support groups and branches
  – Provides literature, a monthly newsletter and information on aids, services and other resources
  – Encourages the provision of services for diagnosis and assessment, day care and sitting services
Q. WHAT IS ALZHEIMER'S DISEASE?
A. It is the commonest form of Dementia affecting ¾ million people in U.K. alone, and is quoted as the 4th largest killer disease. 1 in 5 of the over 80's can suffer and in some instances as young as 30 or 40 years of age.
CAN YOU HELP US TO SUPPORT THE SUFFERERS AND THEIR CARERS OF THIS TRAGIC DISEASE?
For further information, please contact:
Paula Dawe—Appeals Officer
ALZHEIMER'S DISEASE SOCIETY
158-160 Balham High Road, London SW12 2BN
Tel: 081-675 6557/8/9/0
Registered Charity No. 296645

Ami can't see the sights of London

Blindness prevents little Ami from seeing and enjoying many of the pleasures that surround us every day. However children like Ami can still set their sights on a happy future with the special education and equipment that only money can help provide. So please support us today.

GREATER LONDON FUND FOR THE BLIND
The Geranium – Symbol of 70 years giving to the Blind
Room B8, Freepost 3, London W1E 1EZ. Tel: 071-262 0191 or 071-723 1677.
Reg. No. 240566

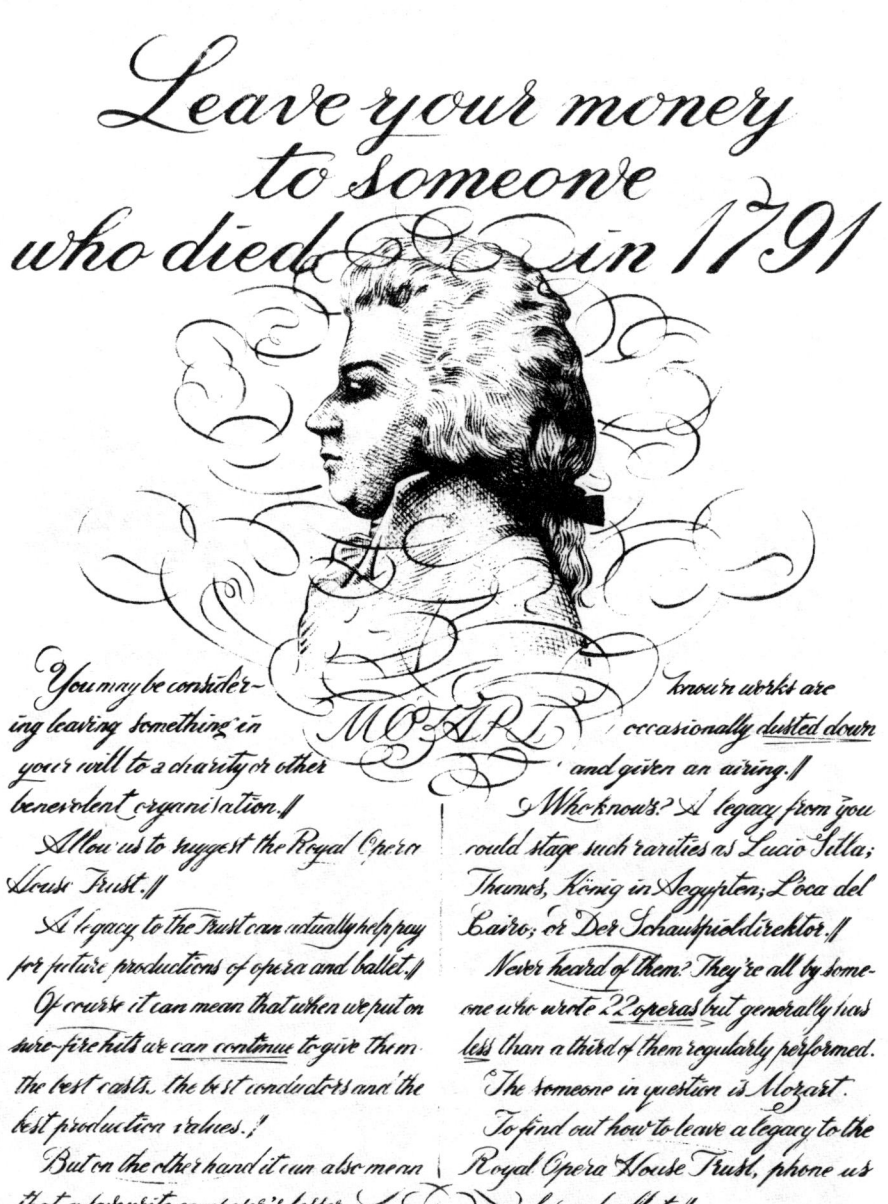

Sick children need the support and love only a family can give, especially when they are seriously ill in hospital. Unfortunately children with life threatening diseases often have to travel a long way from home in order to get the best treatment possible.

The Sick Children's Trust enables families to stay in close contact by providing 'Homes from Home' near hospitals. Each year these enable over 1000 families to stay together at a time of great stress.

Since its creation ten years ago, the Sick Children's Trust has opened four 'Homes from Home' in London and is planning two more this year, in Canterbury and Leeds.

Please help us to help more families.

10 Guildford Street, London WC1N 1DT.
Tel: 071-404 3329
Registered Charity No. 284416

"HOME FROM HOME" APPEAL
If your child was seriously ill wouldn't you want to be near?

Majestic Mountains Rushing Rivers
 Idyllic Islands Wonderful Wildlife
Unforgettable Memories...
 ...of Scotland
Your Legacy can help SCP
Save This for Your Grandchildren
Ask your Solicitor TODAY
or Write for details to:

Scottish Conservation Projects Trust
FREEPOST, Stirling FK8 2BR
Tel: 0786 479697

Charity Ref No. SCO14077

HELPING THE SUICIDAL AND DESPERATE

The Samaritans

Always there at the end of the line

In planning your new life in retirement can you spare a few hours each week to help someone come to terms with their life? The Samaritans seek volunteers from those about to retire and from those recently retired to help maintain a 24-hour listening and befriending service at their 186 branches throughout the UK and Ireland.

Preparation classes for this work are held at frequent intervals. If you would like to know more about becoming a volunteer, or a Friend to help with raising funds, please write to:
The Samaritans, Room V,
10 The Grove, Slough SL1 1QP.

The Dogs' Home Battersea

As the oldest and most famous dog rescue organisation in the world, we have launched our very first major appeal in our 130 year history, to help pay for a £2 million multi-storey kennel block we are having to build for the more than 20,000 dogs (and 800 cats) which come to us each year.

PLEASE help us with this work

Bequests – Donations – Covenants gratefully received

The Secretary, The Dogs' Home Battersea,
4 Battersea Park Road SW8 4AA
Telephone: 071-622 3626
Fax: 071-622 6451

A HOLIDAY WITH A DIFFERENCE
A RAMBLERS HOLIDAY

Walking holidays in small parties with a Ramblers leader- easy ones, moderate ones, tough ones.
Walking holidays with cookery lessons - walking holidays for lovers of birds and flowers. Walking holidays for vegetarians. A whole range of holidays suitable for people of 50+ (and 60+): a walking centre on Lake Buttermere in Britain's Lake District. Departures mainly by air and a few by coach or join us at the centre.
A mouth watering variety of holidays all rather different from the general run of package holidays but mostly with a walking base....many people find their greatest difficulty is choosing which one - our 1993 programme has over 100 different tours some 1,200 departures all graded to illustrate their ease or difficulty.

A programme is yours on request, just call, write or fax us.
RAMBLERS HOLIDAYS Ltd.
Box 43, Welwyn Garden, AL8 6PQ
Tel: 0707 331133 Fax:0707 333276
ABTA 50940   IATA   CAA-ATOL990
Established 1946

BRITISH WHEELCHAIR SPORTS FOUNDATION
GUTTMANN SPORTS CENTRE

WHEELPOWER

OUR AIM: is to improve the quality of life for men, women and children in wheelchairs by striving for excellence in competition and recreational sport.

WE ORGANISE AND FUND National Games for Men, Women and Children.
The World Stoke Mandeville Wheelchair Games.
Participation of British Teams in Paralympic Games and other International Sports Events.
Maintenance and Improvements to the Guttmann Sports Centre.

We rely entirely on the generosity of companies, trusts and individual donations. If you'd like to find out more about us, please call us on 0296 84848 or write to The British Wheelchair Sports Foundation, Harvey Road, Stoke Mandeville, Buckinghamshire HP21 9PP.

Chapter 13

Holidays

Holidays can be even better when you retire! You do not have to plan months ahead in order to fit in with colleagues. You can avoid the peak periods which are almost invariably more expensive and crowded. You can also enjoy real flexibility, in a way that is usually not possible when you are working, by taking several mini breaks when you feel like it or going away for an extended period.

Additionally, one of the great things about retirement is the availability of concessionary prices, including in particular the possibility of cheaper fares and reduced charges for hotel accommodation.

Apart from these benefits, the fact of being retired makes very little difference. You can ride an elephant in India, take a caravan around Europe, sail on the Norfolk Broads, go bird-watching in Scotland, combine a holiday with a special interest such as painting or music, enrol for summer school, exchange homes with someone in another country or sign on for a working holiday, such as voluntary conservation activity or home-sitting, for which you get paid.

The choice is literally enormous. The list of suggestions which follows is by no means exhaustive. You can go to any travel agent and collect further ideas by the dozen. However, the two main criteria we adopted in deciding which, among the thousands of possibilities, to include, were: variety and holidays which, one way or another, offer some special attraction or specifically cater for those aged 50 and above.

Some of the options verge on the exotic, with prices to match; others are extremely reasonable in cost. There are suggestions which are only suitable for the really fit and active; at the other extreme, there are a number of inclusions which would only be of interest to individuals in need of special care. Some of the choices may strike you as mad, risky, humdrum, too demanding – or simply not your style. But retirement is a time for experimentation and trying something entirely different is half the fun.

Holidays

For ease of reference, entries are listed under such headings as 'arts and crafts', 'sport', 'self-catering holidays' and so on. Inevitably, some organisations criss-cross several sections but to avoid repetition, the majority are only featured once in what, hopefully, is the most logical place.

At the end of the chapter, there is a general information section with brief details about insurance, concessionary fares and other travel tips. Prices and some of the other detailed information, while accurate at the time of writing, may be slightly out of date as programmes change (sometimes at very short notice) and it is impossible to keep track. The intention is to provide an indication of fairly typical events together with an idea of price bracket.

Art appreciation

The choice ranges from visiting classical Turkey to a four-day tour of the Lake District. You might also investigate the many music and drama festivals held around the country.

British Museum Tours, 46 Bloomsbury Street, London WC1B 3QQ. T:071-323 8895. The British Museum organises cultural tours, accompanied by their own specialist lecturers, to visit the sites of some of the great civilisations of the past such as the Splendours of Upper Egypt (10 days, £980). Parties are limited to a maximum of 25 people and hotels are normally of a high standard.

National Association of Decorative & Fine Arts Societies, 8a Lower Grosvenor Place, London SW1W 0EN. T:071-233 5433. An organisation of over 250 fine arts societies that arranges tours at home and abroad to places of interest to its members. Recent trips have included: Artistic Genoa (seven nights, £775) and a tour of the Lake District (four nights, £250).

Prospect Music & Art Tours Ltd., 454-458 Chiswick High Road, London W4 5TT. T:081-995 2163. Prospect operates cultural tours within Europe, the Americas and the Middle East. Holidays are led by experienced art historians. 1992 tours included: Cezanne to Chagall (six nights, £845) and Classical Turkey (12 nights, £1,395). Prices include transport; accommodation; some meals; admission charges; and the services of a tour leader.

Specialtours, 81a Elizabeth Street, London SW1W 9PG. T:071-730 2297. Arranges holidays for tour groups from the National Art Collections Fund and other prestigious societies. 1993 plans include among

257

others visits to Czechoslovakia, Greece, India, Italy and Russia. Prices, which start from about £700, include flight, hotels and meals, travel within the country, guides, entrance fees and insurance.

Arts and crafts

The focus here is on taking courses or just participating for the pleasure, rather than viewing the works of others. The choice includes wood carving and other crafts, painting and music. Further suggestions are also given in Chapter 9, Leisure Activities.

Artscape Painting Holidays, Suite 4, Hamlet Court Business Centre, 18 Hamlet Court Road, Westcliff-on-Sea, Essex SS0 7LX. T:0702 435990. Runs tutored painting holidays in Britain, Belgium, Italy, Austria, Crete, France and the USA and also art appreciation tours to Europe and New York. Prices range from £355 to £1,950 for a week covering accommodation, tutoring and meals (1992 rates).

Benslow Music Trust, Little Benslow Hills, Hitchin, Herts SG4 9RB. T:0462 459446. Benslow Music Trust offers weekend and other courses throughout the year for amateur players and singers. The programme covers a huge range from chamber music to jazz. The standard fee for a weekend course is £67.50 with full board or £52.50 non-resident.

Crafts Council, 44A Pentonville Road, Islington, London N1 9BY. T:071-278 7700. Keeps a list of organisations that run their own short craft courses or that can help you in tracking down what you want.

Summer Music, 22 Gresley Road, London N19 3JZ. T:071-272 5664. Despite its name, Summer Music organises a series of music weekend courses throughout the year, for among others: cello, guitar, string quartets and choirs. There is also an eight-day summer school in Berkshire and a Christmas house party for singers and string players. A weekend with full board costs about £75.

West Dean College, West Dean, Chichester, West Sussex PO18 0QZ. T:0243 63301. Organises short residential courses in arts, crafts and music – variously lasting a weekend, five or seven days. A typical programme includes: stained glass, calligraphy, textile design, woodcarving, picture framing, upholstery, blacksmithing, jewellery and many more. Prices, which include board and lodging, range from about £115 for a weekend to £275 for a five-day course.

Holidays

Coach holidays

Some of the coach companies organise holidays proper, as distinct from simply offering a mode of transport. Advice note from other holidaymakers: before embarking on a lengthy coach tour, try a few shorter excursions to see how you cope with the journey. Some people swear by the comfort, others find coach travel very exhausting.

Frames Rickards Coach Tours, 11 Herbrand Street, London WC1N 1EX. T:071-837 3111. Operates a wide range of coach tours in the UK. Prices cover: travel; full breakfast and dinner; rooms with private bath or shower and all sightseeing. 1992 examples include: Irish Experience, six days from £395; Devon and Cornwall, three days from £190; English Lakes, four days from £245.

National Express, 4 Vicarage Road, Birmingham B15 3ES. T:021-456 1122. Offers a network of coach services to 1,500 destinations in the United Kingdom and a wide choice of inclusive package holidays. For example in 1992: three- to eight-day holidays in Edinburgh, Blackpool, Wales and the South Coast cost between £71 and £306 including travel, hotels and most meals. There is also a range of Breakaways in Europe. Over-60s with a senior citizens' coach card are entitled to 30 per cent discount on all National Express services. Contact the above address or your local National Express/Caledonian Express office or agent for details.

Field studies

The number and variety of courses arranged by National Parks and Field Centres almost deserve a special publication of their own. In addition to wildlife studies, the choice, which varies from one centre to another includes: archaeology, landscape painting, spinning and weaving, ecology, folklore, yoga, silk screen printing and many others.

Council for National Parks, 246 Lavender Hill, London SW11 1LN. T:071-924 4077. The Council is the national charity concerned with promoting and protecting the 11 National Parks of England and Wales. 'Friends' support the work of the Council and keep in touch with park issues and events.

The minimum subscription (£10) entitles you to receive the Friends' magazine plus a newspaper which give visitor information and details of the many courses and other activities in the parks.

Field Studies Council (GRG), Central Services, Preston Montford, Montford Bridge, Shrewsbury SY4 1HW. T:0743 850674. The Council manages 10 Field Centres around the country offering a wide variety of courses, details of which are publicised in their free brochure. Most courses last for a week (Friday to Friday) and the average cost is from about £210 which includes tuition, full board and lodging plus transport during the course. Weekends are from around £90.

The Council also organises courses overseas, of which a few examples planned for 1993 include: Flowers of Morocco, Birds of Hungary and The Canadian Rockies. Membership of the Field Studies Council, which is optional, costs £8 a year.

Scottish Field Studies Association, Kindrogan Field Centre, Enochdhu, Blairgowrie, Perth PH10 7PG. T:0250 881286. The Centre runs a range of courses in natural history and the countryside. Examples include: Mountain Flowers, Fungi and Highland Birds. Cost is about £210 for a week including tuition, board and lodging.

Historical holidays

Holidays with a particular focus on history are becoming increasingly popular. The choice includes: battlefield and other overseas tours, exploring historic parts of Britain and the highly imaginative 'production' at Kentwell Hall.

Historical Association, 59a Kennington Park Road, London SE11 4JH. T:071-735 3901. Organises tours with expert lecturers, lasting variously between four and nine days. Examples include: Cornwall (£540); Fife and Tayside (£380); Lancashire and Cumbria (£400). All prices are approximate. Overseas trips are also arranged. Membership costs £22 a year.

Kentwell Hall, Long Melford, Suffolk CO10 9BA. T:0787 310207. Every summer Kentwell Hall recreates a living panorama of what life was like during the Tudor period. Participants are required to provide their own costumes and to enter into the role of a character living at the time. The event lasts for four weeks and participants can stay for one or more complete weeks. The only cost is the provision of a suitable costume. All meals are provided free and there is camping space available. Alternatively, you can book into one of the many local bed and breakfast hotels.

Major and Mrs. Holt's Battlefield Tours Ltd., 15 Market Street, Sandwich, Kent CT13 9DA. T:0304 612248. Battlefield Tours offers over 60 different destinations. All tours are accompanied and include: the Western Front of WW1 (from £199 for three days); Malaysia (£1,823); Munich (£398); the Falkland Islands; American Civil War; the Peninsular

Holidays

Campaigns of Wellington; and many more. Guest lecturers and local experts are used.

The company belongs to AITO (the Association of Independent Tour Operators) and is fully bonded for travellers' protection.

About one-third of travellers are ladies. Most tours are half board in good hotels with private bathrooms. Special tours can be arranged for groups and there is an annual reunion.

Should you wish to visit a particular grave, the **Commonwealth War Graves Commission**, 2 Marlow Road, Maidenhead, Berkshire SL6 7DX, will tell you where it is.

People interested in making a pilgrimage to war graves or battlefields should contact **The Royal British Legion**, The Pilgrimage Department, The Royal British Legion Village, Aylesford, Maidstone, Kent ME20 7NX. T: 0622 716182. The Pilgrimage Department is the recognised authority in this field and each year visits are organised to about 30 different countries in the Far East, Africa and Europe. Approximate prices, which include all travel, full board, accommodation in a good standard hotel and excursions (including a non-denominational Service of Remembrance in one of the Commonwealth War Graves Commission Cemeteries) are from £90 for a two-day pilgrimage to Belgium; £285 for a six-day visit to northern Germany; and £1,500 for a nine-day pilgrimage to Burma.

Under the government's War Widows Grant-in-Aid Scheme, run by the Legion, war widows can apply for a government grant to cover seven-eighths of the cost of one visit.

Language courses

If you are hoping to travel more when you retire, being able to speak the language when abroad will greatly add to your enjoyment. Quickest and easiest way to learn is in the country itself, perhaps either taking a course or living with a local family as a paying guest. Helpful organisations include:

The British Institute of Florence, Palazzo Lanfredini, Lungarno Guicciardini 9, 50125 Florence, Italy. T:(from England) 010-39 55 284031.
En Famille (Overseas), The Old Stables, 60b Maltravers Street, Arundel, West Sussex BN18 9BG. T:0903 883266.
Eurocentres, 56 Eccleston Square, London SW1V 1PQ. T:071-834 4155.
Estudio General Luliano, c/o John Galleymore, 25 High Street, Portsmouth PO1 2LZ. T:0705 824095.

Goethe Institut, PO Box 800727, D-8000 München 80, Germany. T:010-49 89 41 868200.

A recommended buy is *Study Holidays*, price £7.95 from bookshops; or by post £8.95 from the Central Bureau, Seymour Mews House, Seymour Mews, London W1H 9PE. T:071-486 5101. Just about everything you need to know on language and study courses all over Europe, including those where language learning is part of wider studies on art, literature and civilisation. The guide also offers practical information on accommodation and travel.

Other people's homes

Living in someone else's home for free is one of the cheapest ways of enjoying a holiday. There are two ways of arranging this. You can exchange your home with another person, in this country or abroad. The onus is on you to select a suitable property and to decide whether the person with whom you are swapping is likely to care for your home properly. The alternative is to become a homesitter and, for a modest payment, mind someone else's property while they are away.

Home exchange

Unless you are lucky enough to hear about someone through personal recommendation, probably the easiest method of finding a swap (and of advertising your own home) is through a specialised directory. In most cases, this is not an introduction service as such. The exchanges are normally arranged direct between the two parties concerned, who agree the terms between themselves. Some people even exchange their cars and pets.

Organisations you might contact include:

L'entente Cordiale Bureau (ECB), Dunstown, Mintlaw, Grampian AB42 7UJ, Scotland. T:0779 82249. For France.

Green Theme International, Little Rylands Farm, Redmoor, Nr Bodmin, Cornwall PL30 5AR. T:0208 873123. For Australia, New Zealand, the USA, Africa and various parts of Europe.

Home Base Holidays, 7 Park Avenue, London N13 5PG. T:081-886 8752. Mainly the USA.

Homelink International, Linfield House, Gorse Hill Road, Virginia Water, Surrey GU25 4AS. T:0344 842642. Directory listings cover around 35 countries. Readers of our Guides are offered a free copy of a book called *Trading Places*, which discusses everything you need to know

Holidays

when considering a home exchange holiday (normal retail price, £8.95). To receive a copy, contact the above address and just mention the *Good Retirement Guide*.

Intervac International Home Exchange, 6 Siddals Lane, Allestree, Derby DE3 2DY. T:0332 558931. Covers around 50 countries worldwide.

Worldwide Home Exchange Club, 13 Knightsbridge Green, London SW1X 7QL. T:071-589 6055. Around 35 countries including many American listings.

Homesitting

Retired people are generally considered ideal. Homesitting means that you provide a caretaking service and get paid for doing so. Duties variously involve: light housework, plant watering, care of pets and sometimes tending the garden. First class references are naturally required. Organisations to contact include:

Homesitters, Buckland Wharf, Buckland, Aylesbury, Bucks HP22 5LQ. T:0296 630730.
Universal Aunts, PO Box 304, London SW4 0NN. T:071-738 8937.

Overseas travel

Many of the big tour operators make a feature of offering special holidays designed for the over 55s. For up-to-date details, you should check the brochures.

Explore Worldwide Ltd., 1 Frederick Street, Aldershot, Hants GU11 1LQ. T:0252 344161. Takes small groups of people on off-beat holidays where traditional ways of life still persist. Accommodation is usually fairly simple. Highly trained leaders accompany every tour. Prices vary according to destination and length of holiday, ranging from about £395 for 15 days in the Dordogne to £2,205 for 20 days in Brazil, Paraguay and Peru.

Portland Holidays, 218 Great Portland Street, London W1N 5HG. T:071-388 5111 or Manchester: 061-236 9966. Holidays in Spain, Majorca, Malta, Tenerife and Cyprus. November–April for one to four weeks, for over-55s, arranged under Portland's Home and Away programme. Entertainments and afternoon tea are included in the price which is from £148 for a week's full board.

Thomson Young At Heart, Greater London House, Hampstead Road, London NW1 7SD. T:071-387 9321. Short and long-stay winter sunshine holidays in hotels and apartments for people over 55, accompanied by special Young at Heart representatives.

Motoring holidays abroad

Many organisations are now offering 'packages' for the motorist which include ferry crossings, accommodation and insurance. These are obtainable from the AA, RAC and some ferry companies – for example, Sealink and Hoverspeed – as well as a number of other operators. The following short selection should give you an idea of the more typical options.

Automobile Association, PO Box 128, Copenhagen Court, New Street, Basingstoke RG21 1DT. T:0256 20123. The AA's shops can arrange a continental motoring holiday tailored to suit your requirements including ferry bookings, AA 5-star service and accommodation. Prices vary enormously according to time of the year and how luxuriously you want to stay. Alternatively, instead of fixed bookings, you can go as you please using the AA's driveaway France and Europe service to help discover typically regional hotels. For further details, ask at your nearest AA shop or contact the above address.

RAC Travel Services, RAC House, Brighton Road, South Croydon, Surrey CR2 6XW. T: freephone 0800 550055. As well as providing a range of travel insurances including Eurocover Motoring Assistance (to ensure cover for the car) and Eurocover Personal Protection (cover for travellers), the RAC offers a wide choice of holidays in France: variously in villas, cottages, hotels, apartments and mobile homes. Prices start from £305 for a self-catering apartment or villa, for one week in low season, which includes the ferry crossing to Boulogne. Wine-tasting and other activity holidays are also available. For a copy of the holiday brochure call freephone: 0800 220290.

Tips when motoring abroad. All basic common sense but, given the tales of woe one hears, many holiday-makers forget the obvious precautions:

- Have your car thoroughly serviced before you go;
- Take the following with you: a tool kit, manual for your car, a rented spares kit, a gallon can, a mechanic's light which plugs into the cigarette lighter socket and at least one extra set of keys;
- Always lock your car and park it in a secure place overnight (nearly 75 per cent of luggage thefts abroad are from cars).

Unless you are taking one of the packages which include insurance, you should contact your insurance company or broker well ahead of time to arrange special insurance cover.

ABI leaflet *Motoring Abroad* summarises the essentials you need to know when taking your car overseas. Obtainable free from the **Association of British Insurers**, 51 Gresham Street, London EC2V 7HQ, T:071-600 3333.

A further possibility is to contact the RAC overseas travel department which, in addition to providing insurance has facilities for helping you if you become stranded. Non-members are welcomed by both the AA and RAC. Another well-recommended organisation is **Europ Assistance**, 252 High Street, Croydon, Surrey CR0 1NF. T:081-680 1234.

Advice from seasoned travellers is to have information about garages, spare parts and the legal rules of the country through which you are driving.

If instead of taking your own car, you plan to hire a car or motor scooter overseas, you will probably have to buy special insurance at the time of hiring the vehicle. Make sure that this is properly comprehensive and that at very least it gives you adequate third party cover. If in any doubt, you would be recommended to seek advice from the local motoring organisation as to the essential requirements - including any foreign words or terms you particularly need to understand before signing.

Retreats

Some people want to have no more than peace and quiet for a few days. Two organisations that may be of interest are:

The Hen House, Hawerby Hall, North Thoresby, Lincolnshire DN36 5QL. T:0472-840278. This is a women's holiday and retreat centre offering all the usual facilities of a good hotel. Special events throughout the year include courses on: Growing Old Disgracefully (four days, £225), Writing a Novel (long weekend, £166) and a Retreat (£166); prices quoted are for full board. The house is also available for women at all times for a general holiday or break, at a cost of about £32 a night for dinner, bed and breakfast.

The National Retreat Association, Liddon House, 24 South Audley Street, London W1Y 5DL. T:071-493 3534. The NRA's annual journal *The Vision* gives details of 160 retreat houses in Britain and Ireland, together with their programmes. Accommodation is simple and costs are relatively low.

Another publication listing more than 200 retreats in the UK, Ireland and France is *The Good Retreat Guide* by Stafford Whiteaker (Rider, £9.99).

Retirement Made Easy

Saga – in a class of its own

Saga Holidays Ltd, Saga Building, Freepost, Folkestone, Kent CT20 1BR. T:Reservations: 0800 300500; Brochures: 0800 300456. Saga specialises in holidays for over-60s and offers a varied choice of options both in Britain and overseas. The list includes: coach tours, cruises, short breaks, long-stay winter holidays and multi-centre touring vacations plus a selection of special interest holidays including, for example, dancing, fitness, bridge and bowls.

There are also holidays for single travellers as well as flight-only travel to Australia and Canada for people wishing to visit family and friends. The majority of holidays are courier assisted although a new service, Travel by Design, allows more independent travellers to choose their own itinerary. Accommodation is variously in hotels, self-catering apartments and college halls of residence (all single rooms).

Prices are too varied to quote, other than the fact that Saga gives attractive reductions on cruise fares of most of the great lines including P & O and Cunard. For further information, obtain Saga brochures: *Travellers World, Europe and the Mediterranean, Great British Collection, Universities and Study Breaks, Cruise Book and Special Interest Selection*, available from the Folkestone address above.

Self-catering and other low-budget holidays

If you cannot quite manage to survive on a tenner a day, some of the suggestions in this section need hardly cost you very much more. This applies especially if you are camping, caravanning or renting very simple accommodation with friends. The list includes: farm cottages, hostels, university accommodation, forest cabins and other rentals of varying degrees of sparseness or comfort. There are also one or two hotels that offer specially attractive rates.

British Universities Accommodation Consortium, Box 811, University Park, Nottingham NG7 2RD. T:0602 504571. Contact: Carole Formon, General Secretary. Over 50 universities provide bed and breakfast and self-catering accommodation during the student vacations. BUAC publishes a brochure describing facilities, booking periods, rates and details of study and activity holidays.

Camping & Caravanning Club, Greenfields House, Westwood Way, Coventry CV4 8JH. T:0203 694995. Sites all over Britain are listed in the annual *Your Place in the Country* and in the *Big Sites Book* which are sent to all members along with an Ordnance Survey map and free copies of the monthly magazine *Camping and Caravanning*. The Club also offers a full foreign touring service including reservations on continental sites. Senior citizen members pay reduced site fees on club sites. Membership costs £23 plus £4 joining fee.

CampusHotels, PO Box 808, Edinburgh EH14 4AS. T:031-449 4034. The Scottish Universities Accommodation Consortium, which is marketed under the name of CampusHotels, provides holiday letting in Scotland's eight universities. Average cost of bed and breakfast is about £20 a night.

English Country Cottages Ltd., Grove Farm Barns, Fakenham, Norfolk NR21 9NB. T:0328 864041 (brochures). T:0328 851155; (bookings – all UK).
Welsh Country Cottages. T:0328 851341 (brochures).
Country Cottages In Scotland. T:0328 864011 (brochures).

The 'cottages' range enormously in size, style and location and are variously capable of sleeping between 2 and 22. Many are available all the year round with low out-of-season prices and short-break arrangements from September to May. Apply for the free brochure which gives full details and pictures of all properties.

Everymann Holidays, 20a Duke Street, Douglas, Isle of Man. T:0624 629914. Everymann runs special cheap offer holidays in May, June and September on the Isle of Man for people over 55. They include return fare, either bed and breakfast or half board in hotel or guest house and discount entry to many entertainments. Cost is from about £118 a week.

Farm Holiday Bureau UK Ltd., National Agricultural Centre, Stoneleigh Park, Warwickshire CV8 2LZ. T:0203 696909. Many farms take paying guests, let holiday cottages or run sites for tents or caravans. *The Farm Holiday Bureau Guide: Stay on a Farm* contains information on over 1,000 good value farm holidays all over Great Britain and Northern Ireland. Bed and breakfast facilities are normally from about £12 upwards. Many farms provide an evening meal, if required. Self-catering cottages start at around £100. The *Guide* is available from the Bureau; also bookshops and Tourist Information Centres, £5.95.

Forestry Commission, 231 Corstorphine Road, Edinburgh EH12 7AT. T:031-334 0303. Lets modern forest cabins and holiday houses in Scotland, Cumbria, North Yorkshire and Cornwall. These sleep from two to six people and cost from about £100 a week per cabin in low season. They are also available for shorter periods and weekends.

HEAC Ltd., 36 Collegiate Crescent, Sheffield S10 2BP. T:0742

Retirement Made Easy

683759. HEAC is a network of 60 colleges and polytechnics nationwide that let residential accommodation in the vacation periods. Charges start from about £11 for bed and breakfast; £35 per person, per week for a self-catering apartment.

Holiday Club Pontin's, PO Box 100, Sagar House, The Green, Eccleston, Chorley, Lancs PR7 5QQ. T:0257 452452. Holiday Club Pontin's offers full board and self-catering holidays at 20 locations in the UK, including one in the Channel Islands and one in Southern Ireland, five of which are for adults only.

Full details can be found in their summer brochure together with special rates, early booking benefits and details of retirement planning holidays. During 1992, full board holidays were from around £149 per person including VAT; self-catering, from around £189 per chalet for four including VAT. Reservations: 0772 621621.

Landmark Trust, Shottesbrooke, Maidenhead, Berkshire SL6 3SW. T:0628 825925. The Trust owns buildings of special architectural interest all over Britain, available for rent. Sample prices are: £243 per week for a four-bed mill in Derbyshire, during April; £561 per week for a six-bed castle in Wales, in May or October. There is a fully illustrated Handbook, obtainable from the above address (£7.50).

M P Associates, 262a Wellingborough Road, Northampton NN1 4EJ. T:0604 230505. Specialises in low-cost, long winter holidays (three or four months) in Spain, Portugal and Tenerife. Accommodation varies from one-bed apartments to four-bed villas. Rents are reasonably nominal but in exchange visitors are expected to maintain the properties as they would their own homes. For further details, send large sae (41p).

National Trust Holiday Cottages. The National Trust has a wide range of holiday cottages and houses in many areas of England, Wales and Northern Ireland. A brochure is available from major National Trust Shops or by writing to PO Box 101, National Trust Warehouse, Melksham, Wiltshire SN12 8EA. Please enclose 75p to cover p&p costs.

For cottages in Scotland, contact National Trust for Scotland, 5 Charlotte Square, Edinburgh EH2 4DU.

Scottish Farmhouse Holidays, 51 Drumtenant, Ladybank, Fife KY7 7UG. T:0337 30451. Over 80 farms and crofts in all areas of Scotland which take guests for two nights or longer. The cost is from £17 per night for dinner, bed and breakfast or from £13 per night bed and breakfast. Free brochure available.

Youth Hostels Association, Trevelyan House, 8 St. Stephen's Hill,

St. Albans, Herts AL1 2DY. T:0727 55215. **Scottish YHA**, 7 Glebe Crescent, Stirling FK8 2JA. T:0786 51181. Despite the name, most hostels welcome people of all ages. Membership (1992) is £8.90 a year or £100 for life membership. This gives you access to 240 hostels in England and Wales and to 5,300 more throughout the world.

Beds are usually in single-sex dormitories with communal washrooms. Most have a lounge and many have recreational facilities and a shop. Most provide meals and also self-catering facilities. Overnight charges vary according to the facilities and location, from £4.70 to £11.60, excluding breakfast. The YHA Guide describes the hostels in England and Wales (£4.99). Membership of the Scottish YHA gives you the same access to hostels.

P.S. Watch The Sunday Newspapers. From about early January, the classified section begins to fill up with advertisements for rentals both in this country and overseas. Later in the season, this is the column to watch for slashed prices and other last minute bargains.

Special interest holidays

This is the longest section – and a real mixed bag. It includes weekend courses and more formal summer schools, between them offering a huge range of subjects. It also includes holidays in the more conventional sense, both in Britain and abroad, but with the accent on a hobby such as: bridge, folk dancing, photography, model making and other pastimes. They are impossible to categorise other than alphabetically because many of the organisations offer a veritable bran-tub of choices.

Architectural Tours, 90-92 Parkway, London NW1 7AN. T:071-267 6497. If you are seeking a de luxe holiday, Architectural Tours are probably not for you. While the accommodation is described as 'of a comfortable standard', the company's priority is to arrange imaginative study tours for people with a real interest in architecture. There is a British as well as overseas programme, with most tours lasting between three days and a week. Groups are kept fairly small and all are led by expert guides.

Countrywide Holidays, Birch Heys, Cromwell Range, Manchester M14 6HU. T:061-225 1000. Aims to provide warm hospitality, comfortable accommodation and sensible prices for guided walking and special interest holidays throughout the year.

Holidays in Britain range in cost from about £150 in winter to £250 in summer including full board and coach outings. People of pension age are offered reductions on some holidays at the company's country houses during the winter. There are also bargain offers on travel for those using British Rail. Holidays abroad include walking in Canada, USA and Europe, with prices starting from about £300.

HF Holidays Ltd., Imperial House, Edgware Road, London NW9 5AL. T:081-905 9556. HF Holidays offers walking and special interest holidays in a wide range of locations throughout Britain and abroad. The choice of activities includes, among others: golf, bridge, bowls, ballroom dancing, yoga, painting, photography, music making and birdwatching.

There are also discovery coach tours and Fellowship Weeks, with organised excursions, for those who want a more leisurely holiday. Fellowship Weeks start from £219; a week's walking in Swanage from £225; and a week in Austria from £372 (all full board).

Holiday Club Pontin's, PO Box 100, Sagar House, The Green, Eccleston, Chorley, Lancs PR7 5QQ. T:0257 452452. Organises hobby holidays at the majority of their locations. These include such activities as: darts, snooker, badminton, bridge, bowling, model making, music, dancing and retirement planning. Prices (1992) for full board range from about £149 including VAT per person per week; self-catering from around £179 including VAT per four-person chalet per week. Group discounts are available on request. Reservations: 0772 621621.

National Institute of Adult Continuing Education (NIACE), 19b De Montfort Street, Leics LE1 7GE. T:0533 551451. Special interest weekend and summer school courses are offered by many colleges and universities throughout the country. Choice of subjects is enormous ranging from yoga to astronomy, creative writing to video techniques. Prices vary very roughly from about £20 to £30 a night, including full board and tuition. Probably the easiest way to find out what is available is to obtain a copy of *Time to Learn*, published twice a year by NIACE. Price £3.95 including p&p.

Old Rectory, Fittleworth, Pulborough, West Sussex RH20 1HU. T:07988 2306. The programme is especially tilted at those approaching retirement age with the aim of creating new interests and opportunities. Typical courses, which last three to seven days, include: painting, calligraphy, embroidery, singing, clock repair, bell ringing, book binding and languages. Prices range from about £80 for two nights to £248 inclusive for a week.

Vegi-Ventures, 17 Lilian Road, Burnham-on-Crouch, Essex CM0 8DS. T:0621 784285. A holiday tour company that specialises in catering for vegetarians, offering an attractive range of destinations in Britain, Europe and wider afield. Accommodation is chosen very much with the food in mind and is variously in hotels, special guest houses and villas with own cook. A flavour of 1992 holidays includes: Christmas House Party in Norfolk (three nights, from £85); a week's walking and sightseeing in Czechoslovakia including full board (seven nights, £195); three weeks 'journey of a lifetime' in Peru with tour guide and half board (£885). Flights are willingly arranged but are not included in prices quoted above.

Useful reading
Let's Do It, published by Charles Letts in association with the English Tourist Board, £3.95 from all good bookshops and Tourist Information Centres or by post from Charles Letts & Co., Letts of London House, Parkgate Road, London SW11 4NQ.

Sport

Holidays with on-site or nearby sporting facilities exist all over the country. However, if sport is the main objective of the holiday, it is often more difficult to know where to apply. The list that follows is limited to organisations that can advise you about organised residential courses or that offer facilities themselves.

For wider information, see Chapter 9, Leisure Activities, which lists some of the many national sports associations.

Sports Council, 16 Upper Woburn Place, London WC1H 0QP. T:071-388 1277. The Council publishes *Sport for All*, a free guide to coaching courses and activity holidays (please enclose A4 sae). Tuition is available on all courses. Some of the centres are suitable for people with a disability and many welcome beginners. Cost varies according to accommodation, the activity you choose and how long you stay: this can be a weekend or longer.

The programme covers a huge range, including (among the more leisurely): archery, fishing, bird watching, orienteering, shooting, pool/billiards and table tennis. Some of the centres also run arts and crafts courses alongside the more active pursuits.

Scottish Sports Council, Caledonia House, South Gyle, Edinburgh EH12 9DQ. T:031-317 7200. The Council runs three national sports centres which offer courses for the 50-plus age group. There are outdoor sports like hill-walking and skiing at Glenmore Lodge in the Cairngorms and watersports at the Cumbrae centre in Ayrshire. The Inverclyde centre offers two and five day Sportbreak holidays with instruction.

YMCA National Centre, Lakeside, Ulverston, Cumbria LA12 8BD. T:05395 31758. Runs adventure holidays suitable for all ages including a special programme entitled '50-plus Activity'. Choice of activities includes, among many others: rock climbing, canoeing, orienteering, archery, country crafts and fell walking. There are also excursions to places of interest as well as talks and films in the evening. The accommodation is in twin bedded or single rooms with toilet and shower en suite. Cost for four nights inclusive of full board and programme is £152.55.

Cycling

Cycling for Softies, Susi Madron's Cycling Holidays Ltd., 2 & 4 Birch Polygon, Rusholme, Manchester M14 5HX. T:061-248 8282. Offers 7 to 14 night holidays in France, cycling between small country hotels, with terrain varying from very easy to quite a few hills. The cost (£350-£750) includes: ferry or air fares, transfer to hotel, dinner, bed and breakfast, bicycles, equipment and information packs.

Cyclists' Touring Club, Cotterell House, 69 Meadrow, Godalming, Surrey GU7 3HS. T:0483 417217. Organises cycling tours in Britain and overseas and can also provide a great deal of extremely helpful information for cyclists wishing to organise their own holiday, including advice on accommodation and scenic routes. Organised UK cycle tours cost about £100 a week with hostel accommodation or £170 a week bed and breakfast with evening meal. Overseas tours vary but examples include: two weeks in France, about £500; two weeks in Czechoslovakia, about £400; 19 days in South Africa, about £1,000.

The CTC also offers: free third-party and competitive cycle insurance, free legal aid, a handbook and introductions to local cycling groups. Membership (1992/93) costs £24 a year; £16 for retired people.

British Rail. Cycles are carried free on many trains. It is necessary to check as certain lines, e.g. Intercity, require advance registration for which a charge is made. The service is described in British Rail leaflet *Bike it by Train*. Available from railway stations.

Rambling

Ramblers Holidays Ltd., PO Box 43, Welwyn Garden, Herts AL8 6PQ. T:0707 331133. Organises guided walking tours at home and abroad, ranging in choice from just four or five hours a day relatively gentle exercise to maybe nine hours a day hard mountain trekking. There is a huge choice of destinations including New Zealand, North America, China, the Far East and most of Europe. Prices start from £165 for a week in Britain inclusive of all meals and VAT; and from about £300 for a week in Europe including flights and half board.

Holidays

Waymark Holidays, 44 Windsor Road, Slough SL1 2EJ. T:0753 516477. Spring and summer walking holidays in many parts of Europe and wider afield. Accommodation in hotels and guesthouses. Cost for half board is from about £475 for two weeks, depending on the country and time of year. Cross-country skiing holidays also offered during the winter.

Wine tasting

Wine-tasting holidays are becoming more popular every year. The best guided tours ensure plenty of variety with a mix of visits, talks, convivial meals, free time for exploring and memorable tastings. Specialist tour operators include:

Arblaster & Clarke, 104 Church Road, Steep, Petersfield, Hants GU32 2DD. T:0730 266883.
World Wine Tours Ltd., 69-71 Banbury Road, Oxford OX2 6PE. T:0865 310344.

Working holidays

There is scope for volunteers who would like to engage in a worthwhile project during their holidays. Activities vary from, for example, helping with handicapped people to conservation work. In order to avoid repetition, only a couple of suggestions are listed here. For more information and ideas, see Chapter 11, Voluntary Work.

British Trust for Conservation Volunteers, 36 St. Mary's Street, Wallingford, Oxfordshire OX10 0EU. T:0491 39766. Anyone, from 16 to 75, who is prepared for hard work can become a conservation volunteer. BTCV organises over 600 conservation working holidays each year. Projects usually last a week and the work can vary from creating wildlife habitats to improving access to the countryside. Cost is around £28 a week including food and accommodation. Membership: £6 for retired people; £12, ordinary members; £17, family membership.

Scottish Conservation Projects Trust, Balallan House, 24 Allan Park, Stirling FK8 2QG. T:0786 79697. Contact: Rita Crowe. SCP offers training in conservation skills and opportunities to work as a conservation volunteer for as much or as little time as you can spare. There are 7 to 14-day projects called Action Breaks as well as weekend and single day events. Type of work varies from conservation proper – drystone dyking, fencing, historic building restoration and habitat management – to jobs such as office skills, cooking and driving. Cost of Action Breaks is £4 a day, plus your fare. All participants are required to join the Trust.

Retirement Made Easy

TOC H, 1 Forest Close, Wendover, Aylesbury, Bucks HP22 6BT. T:0296 623911. Organises short residential projects throughout the year in Britain and Germany, normally lasting between a weekend and three weeks. Scope for volunteers includes running playschemes, activities with disabled people, conservation and manual work. There is a £5 registration fee; accommodation and food, however, are usually free. The projects programme, available from the above address, is published in March and September.

Useful reading
Working Holidays. Contains information on thousands of paid and voluntary seasonal opportunities, in 70 countries, for people of all ages. Comprehensive details on each country cover: entry regulations, work and residence permits, medical insurance and passport requirements plus travel, accommodation and tourist information. Price £6.95 from bookshops or (by post £8.80) from the **Central Bureau**, Seymour Mews House, Seymour Mews, London W1H 9PE. T:071-486 5101.

Holidays for singles

Many people would rather not go on holiday if it means travelling alone. Until recently single people, especially women over 50, were virtually ignored by the holiday industry. Over the past two or three years however, the outlook has been improving considerably. Many of the 'special interest holidays' listed on pages 269 to 271 are ideal for those without a partner, as are some of the 'working holidays' – see section above and also in Chapter 11, Voluntary Work. Additionally one or two organisations are now springing up that cater specifically for solo holiday-makers.

Odyssey International, 21 Cambridge Road, Waterbeach, Cambridge CB5 9NJ. T:0223 861079. Odyssey is a nationwide club, with members aged 17 to 80, which can put you in touch with a like-minded travel companion, whether you are planning a short break or long, either in England or overseas.

There are also a number of organised weekend breaks and other holidays which are focused around an activity such as walking trips, cycling or painting. Prices for weekend breaks start at £40. Odyssey also operates a members' advice line for budgeting and other queries. A year's membership subscription is £20.

Travel Companions (UK) Ltd., 110 High Mount, Station Road, London NW4 3ST. T:081-202 8478. An organisation for individuals aged 30 to 75 seeking a congenial companion with whom to go on holiday. All applicants complete a form listing their special interests, the type of destination they have in mind, as well as other requirements, and Travel Companions will then put them in contact with like-minded people. All personal information is handled in strict confidence. Travel Companions emphasises that it is not a dating service and makes the point that people often prefer to travel with someone of their own sex. Cost is £40, entitling you to at least three introductions a year.

Travelmate, 18 Cavendish Road, Bournemouth BH1 1IF. T:0202 558314. Travelmate is an introduction service for travellers. Members seeking a holiday companion are sent a list of possible individuals, who approximately fit their requirements according to age, sex and planned destination. A minimum of six introductions is guaranteed. Annual membership costs £25.

Holidays for those needing special care

Over the past few years, facilities for infirm and disabled people have at last been improving. More hotels are providing wheelchairs and other essential equipment. Transport has become easier. Specially designed self-catering units are more plentiful and of a higher standard. As a result, many people with disabilities can now travel perfectly normally, stay where they please and participate in the entertainment and sightseeing without disadvantage. This section lists general sources of advice plus one or two organisations that arrange special care holidays.

Travel and other information

If you need help getting on and off a train or plane, inform your travel agent in advance. Arrangements can be made to have staff and, if necessary, a wheelchair available to help you at both departure and arrival points. If you are travelling independently, you should ring the airline and/or local station master: explain what assistance you require, together with details of your journey in order that facilities can be arranged at any interim points, for example if you need to change trains.

A couple of useful free leaflets are *British Rail & Disabled Travellers*, available from mainline stations, and *Care in the Air – Advice for Handicapped Airline Passengers*, from: Air Transport Users Committee, 2nd Floor, Kingsway House, 103 Kingsway, London WC2B 6QX. T:071-242 3882.

Highly recommended are two very comprehensive books, published by RADAR. Both are annual guides to accommodation and facilities available to disabled holidaymakers: one deals with the UK, the other with travel overseas.

Retirement Made Easy

Holidays in the British Isles, £4.50; *Holidays and Travel Abroad*, £3. Available from W.H. Smith or direct from: Royal Association for Disability and Rehabilitation, 25 Mortimer Street, London W1N 8AB.

Two other helpful books, both published by the AA, are: *AA Travellers' Guide for the Disabled*, £3.50 (free to members at AA shops); and *The World Wheelchair Traveller*, £3.95. Obtainable from AA shops and booksellers.

A useful organisation to contact could be: **The Holiday Care Service**, 2 Old Bank Chambers, Station Road, Horley, Surrey RH6 9HW. T:0293 774535; Minicom: 0293 776943. This is a central information and advice service on holiday opportunities in the UK and abroad for elderly and disabled people and their companions. The service is free. Details are available on transport, attractions and possible sources of financial help, together with a range of leaflets listing inspected hotels that offer accessible accommodation. The HCS also organises low-cost holidays for people with special needs through the Tourism For All Holidays Scheme.

If rather than simply being pointed in the right direction you are looking for an agency that can make all the practical arrangements for you, get on to **ATS Travel** (28 Church Street, Old Dagenham, Essex RM10 9UR. T:081-593 5509) which specialises in organising tailor-made holidays for people with disabilities.

Among other services, they will arrange the journey from door to door, book suitable accommodation according to your requirements, organise the provision of special equipment and generally take care of any other details to make your holiday as enjoyable and trouble-free as possible.

Also worth knowing about is **Carefree Holidays**, 64 Florence Road, Northampton NN1 4NA, T:0604 34301. This is a tour operator, offering package holidays (mainly within the UK and Europe) that has built up a reputation for the quality of its service in assisting older retired and disabled travellers.

Many local Age Concern branches are a mine of information. They can often put individuals in touch with organisations that assist with, say, transport; or that organise special care holidays, as do a number of Age Concern branches themselves. Age Concern England also publishes a free fact sheet *Holidays for Older People*.

Another source to contact is your local Social Services Department. Some local authorities arrange holidays or give financial help to those in real need.

Examples of special holidays
John Grooms Association for Disabled People, 10 Gloucester Drive,

Holidays

London N4 2LP. T:081-802 7272. Provides a variety of holiday accommodation including two award-winning hotels, self-catering flats, bungalows and caravans and also a holiday centre in South Wales, offering 24-hour care.

Winged Fellowship Trust, Angel House, 20-32 Pentonville Road, London N1 9XD. T:071-833 2594. Caters for people who would not otherwise have a holiday because of their physical disability, in well-staffed, purpose-built centres. There are plenty of activities including theatre outings and other excursions. The Fellowship also organises holidays abroad. Cost is from about £160 per week.

Many voluntary organisations and others provide special holidays for those with a particular disability.

Arthritis Care, 18 Stephenson Way, London NW1 2HD. T:071-916 1500. Runs five holiday centres and 14 self-catering units adapted for people with arthritis. Holiday centre accommodation available to members costs £40-£135 a week; units £40-£100 depending on the time of year. Specialist holidays include painting weeks, whist, scrabble and ornithology. Family weeks are also a feature.

British Diabetic Association, 10 Queen Anne Street, London W1M 0BD. T:071-323 1531. Advice on holidays is given and foreign travel guides are available for various destinations.

Royal National Institute for the Blind, 224 Great Portland Street, London W1N 6AA. T:071-388 1266. Has four seaside hotels, specially catering for blind and partially sighted people. Additionally, RNIB can provide advice about suitable hotels, self-catering holidays, accommodation in London, outdoor activity and educational holidays.

Multiple Sclerosis Society of Great Britain & Northern Ireland, 25 Effie Road, London SW6 1EE. T:071-736 6267. Runs several holiday homes throughout the UK. Additionally, some local branches have adapted self-catering accommodation for family holidays.

National Trust for the Welfare of the Elderly, 33 Hook Road, Goole, North Humberside DN14 5JB. T:0405-763149.
Parkinson's Disease Society, 22 Upper Woburn Place, London WC1H 0RA. T:071-383 3513.
Stroke Association, CHSA House, Whitecross Street, London EC1Y 8JJ. T:071-490 7999.

Tourist Boards

England's Regional Tourist Boards and the Scottish and Wales Tourist Boards are the main sources of information for all aspects of holidays in their areas. They can advise about: accommodation, transport, highlights to see, special events and festivals, sporting facilities, special interest holidays – in short, almost everything you could possibly want to know. All produce excellent leaflets and guide books.

Insurance

Even the best-laid holiday plans can go wrong. It is therefore only sensible to take out proper insurance cover before you depart. Holiday insurance should cover you for:

- Personal accident leading to injury or death
- Medical expenses including: hospital treatment, cost of ambulance, emergency dental treatment plus expenses for a companion, who may have to remain overseas with you should you become ill (see 'Medical insurance' page 280)
- Additional hotel and repatriation costs resulting from injury or illness
- Loss of deposit or cancellation: check what emergencies or contingencies this covers
- Cost of having to curtail your holiday because of serious illness in the family
- Compensation for inconvenience caused by flight cancellations or other travel delays
- Cover for baggage and personal effects and for emergency purchases should your baggage be delayed
- Cover for loss of personal money
- Personal liability cover, should you cause injury to another person or property
- Extra insurance in respect of your car, if you are taking it abroad (see 'Motoring abroad' page 264); or fully comprehensive insurance cover (which you may need to purchase while on holiday) if you are planning to hire a car or motor scooter overseas.

When assessing the insurance you are being offered, it pays to do a bit of mental arithmetic. Although at first glance the sums look enormous, the likelihood is that should you have to claim you will end up being out of pocket. A sum of £750 or even £1,000 in respect of lost baggage might well be insufficient if, as well as your clothes, you had to replace your watch, camera and other valuables.

A recent checklist in the Consumers' Association magazine *Which?* suggested the following guidelines in respect of the amount of cover holidaymakers should be looking for in their policy:

Cancellation or curtailment of holiday: the full cost of your holiday, as well as the deposit and any other charges paid in advance.

Money and belongings: up to £1,500.

Delayed baggage: £75 for emergency purchases in case luggage is lost en route and arrives late.

Delayed departure: £20 per hour after the first 12 hours; and full cost of your holiday if you cancel after the first full 24 hours' delay.

Personal liability: up to £1 million (£2 million for the USA).

It is essential that you take the insurance documents with you, as losses or other claims must normally be reported immediately. You will also be required to quote reference number and/or other details, given on the docket. Failure to report a claim within the specified time limit could nullify your right to compensation.

Be sure to get a receipt for any special expenses you incur – extra hotel bills, medical treatment, long-distance phone calls and so on. You may not get all the costs reimbursed but if your insurance covers some or all of these contingencies, you will need to produce evidence of your expenditure.

The **Association of British Insurers** (51 Gresham Street, London EC2V 7HQ, T:071-600 3333) publishes a free leaflet on holiday insurance, explaining the key points you should know in simple language.

The **Association of British Travel Agents** (55-57 Newman Street, London W1P 4AH, T:071-637 2444) operates a code of conduct for all travel agents and tour operators who are members of ABTA and also runs a consumer advisory service for holidaymakers on how to seek redress if they are dissatisfied with their travel company.

ABTA's code of conduct has recently been revised and with it a number of new rules, offering greater protection to travellers, have come into force. In particular, if you have an accident (e.g. trip over a frayed carpet and break your ankle in the hotel or get food poisoning at a local restaurant), your tour operator must now accept responsibility with you in making a claim and pay the legal expenses involved (up to a limit of £5,000) – even though the mishap was not due to any negligence on their part.

Medical insurance

This is one area where you should never skimp on insurance. Although many countries now have reciprocal arrangements with Britain for emergency medical treatment, these vary greatly both in quality and generosity. Some treatments are free, as they are on the National Health Service; others, even in some EC countries, may be charged for as if you were a private patient.

Department of Health leaflet *Health Advice for Travellers Anywhere in the World* (T4) explains what is entailed and what forms you should obtain. In particular you should get a Form E111 which is a certificate entitling you to free or reduced-cost emergency treatment in most European Community countries. An application form is contained in the T4 leaflet. You can pick up a copy at any main post office which will process the paperwork and stamp your Form E111 for you on the spot.

However, even the very best reciprocal arrangements may not be adequate in the event of a real emergency; and they certainly will not cover you for any additional expenses you may incur, such as: the cost of having to prolong your stay; extra hotel bills if a companion has to remain with you; special transport home, should you require it, and so on.

Additionally, since in an emergency you may need or want private treatment, you would be advised to insure for this – even if you are going to a country where good reciprocal arrangements exist.

As a general rule of thumb, the further from Britain you are going the higher the cover you need. This applies especially to Third World countries, where the risk of falling ill is greater and where medical facilities away from the big towns may be basic in the extreme; and also to America, where the cost of medical treatment is literally astronomic. *Which?* recommends the following levels of cover: £250,000 for Europe; £1 million for all other parts of the world.

Most insurance companies impose various terms and let-out clauses as a condition of payment. You should read these very carefully because, whereas some are obviously sensible, others may be very restrictive or, for whatever reason, you may not be able to satisfy the requirements: for example, if you have a chronic heart condition.

Although there is no upper age limit if you want to take out medical insurance, many companies request a note from a qualified medical practitioner stating that you are fit to travel if you are over 75.

Another common requirement is that the insured person should undertake not to indulge in any dangerous pursuits, which is fine in theory but in practice (depending on the company's interpretation of 'dangerous') could debar you from any activity that qualifies as 'strenuous'.

Holidays

Travel and other concessions

Buses, coaches, some airline companies and especially the railways offer valuable concessions to people of retirement age. Some of the best-value savings which are available to anyone aged 60 are provided by British Rail. These include:

Senior Railcards. These cost £16 and entitle you to: one-third off cheap day and standard day returns, standard single and return tickets; Savers and Supersavers returns and also Rail Rover tickets; first class single and return tickets; and one-day Travelcards subject to a minimum fare. Discounts are also available on through rail/sea bookings to the Isle of Man, Isle of Wight and Northern Ireland.

Disabled Person's Railcard. This costs £12 and entitles the holder and companion accompanying him/her to reduced rates by train. Details and conditions are described in the British Rail brochure.

Network Cards. These normally cost £12 (£15 for two people) but are available to anyone aged 60 or over for £8 (£10 for two). They are available only in South-East England. They give a one-third reduction on most standard fares after 10 a.m., Monday to Friday, (any time at weekends or bank holidays). Up to four adults (including the cardholder/s) can travel at a discount and up to four children can travel with them for £1 each.

Rail Europe Senior Cards. Available to retired persons from age 60 who are also BR Senior Railcard holders. They cost £5 and entitle you to savings of up to 30 per cent on 1st and standard/2nd class full fares from London to most parts of Europe.

Reductions on cross-Channel jetfoils, seacats and ships are only allowed if these services are part of rail/sea combined tickets to or from the Continent.

Rail Europe Senior Cards can be obtained from selected British Rail stations, British Rail International appointed travel agencies or from the International Rail Centre, Victoria Station, London SW1V 1JY (telephone enquiries: 071-834 2345; credit card telephone: 071-828 0892).

Buses and coaches

There are often reduced rates for senior citizens on long-distance buses and coaches. For example, discounts of 33 per cent apply on National Coaches on both ordinary and Rapide services.

Airlines

From time to time some airlines offer attractive discounts to older travellers. The terms and conditions vary, with some carriers offering across-the-board savings and others limiting them to selected destinations. Likewise, in some cases the qualifying age is 60; in others, it is a couple of years older. A particular bonus is that concessions are often extended to include a companion travelling at the same time.

These discounts are not particularly widely advertised and may well not be suggested by airline staff, often because they do not know a passenger's age. Best advice is to ask your travel agent at time of booking what special discounts, if any, are available.

Overseas

Many countries offer reductions to retired holidaymakers, for example, on: internal flights, coach travel, entry to museums and galleries, day excursions, sporting events and other entertainment. As in Britain, provisions are liable to change and for up-to-date information probably the best source to contact is the national tourist office of the country to which you are travelling.

Air Travel Advisory Bureau. T:071-636 5000. Advises on low-cost fares to all parts of the world. If you are looking for good-value fares, it is well worth giving them a ring rather than shopping around. The Bureau can also provide information on hotels, villa rentals and car hire. There is a free helpline which advises on all aspects of travel including visas, passports, inoculations and so on.

Health tips for travellers

Most are plain common sense – but worth repeating for all that.

- Remember to pack any regular medicines you require: even familiar branded products can be difficult to obtain in some countries.
- Take a mini first aid kit, including: plaster, disinfectant, tummy pills and so on. If you are going to any under-developed country, it is advisable to consult your doctor as to what pills (and any special precautions) you should take.
- One of the most common ailments among British travellers abroad is an overdose of sun. In some countries, it really burns, so take it easy, wear a hat and apply plenty of protective lotion.
- Travelling is tiring and a sudden change of climate more debilitating than most of us admit: allow plenty of time during the

Holidays

first couple of days to acclimatise before embarking on an activity programme that would exhaust a 17-year-old.
- Have any inoculations or vaccinations well in advance of your departure date.
- The other big travellers' woe is 'Delhi belly', which unhappily can apply in most hot countries, including Italy and Spain. Beware the water, ice, salads, seafood, ice cream and any fruit which you do not peel yourself. Check with your doctor.
- Always wash your hands before eating or handling food, particularly if you are camping or caravanning.
- When flying, wear loose clothes and above all comfortable shoes as feet and ankles tend to swell in the air. On long journeys, it helps to drink plenty of fruit juice and remember the warning that 'a drink in the air is worth two on the ground'. If you have a special diet, inform whoever makes your booking: most airlines, especially on long-distance journeys, serve vegetarian food.
- Finally, the old favourite, don't drink and drive.

Keep fit and have a wonderful holiday!

Chapter 14

Caring for Elderly Parents

Most of us sooner or later have some responsibility for the care of elderly parents. Although an increasing number of people live well into their eighties and beyond, the vast majority manage with a little help to remain in their own homes rather than go into residential care. While there is no hiding the fact that with a very elderly person this can impose strains, most families cope exceedingly well. Moreover, since the evidence shows that this is the undoubted preference of most older people themselves, the main bias of this chapter is towards helping aged parents remain as independent as possible.

Knowing what facilities are available, what precautions you can take against a mishap occurring and whom you can turn to in an emergency can make all the difference, both to you and to parents who may fear becoming a burden.

A basic choice for many families is whether parents should move in with them or continue to live on their own. While the decision will depend on individual circumstances, in the early days at least the majority choice on all sides is generally in favour of 'staying put'. Although later in the chapter we cover sheltered housing, which some people see as the best of all worlds, an alternative solution to any move may be simply to adapt the home to make it safer and more convenient.

Ways of adapting a home

Many even quite elderly people will not require anything more complicated than a few general improvements, such as: better lighting, especially near staircases; a non-slip mat and grab-rail in the bathroom; safe heating arrangements; and perhaps the lowering of some kitchen and other units to place them within easy reach.

Another plan worth considering is to convert a downstairs room into a bedroom and bathroom, in case managing the stairs should later become a difficulty. These and other common-sense measures are covered in more detail in Chapter 8, Your Home.

For some people, however, such arrangements are not really sufficient. In the case of a physically handicapped or disabled person, more radical improvements will usually be required. Far from presenting a major problem as used to be the case, today these are normally fairly easy to organise.

Local authority help
Local authorities have a legal duty to help people with disabilities and, depending on what is required and the individual's ability to pay, may assist with the cost.

Your parents can either approach their GP or contact the Social Services Department direct. A sympathetic doctor will be able to: advise what is needed; supply any prescriptions such as for a medical hoist; suggest which unit or department to approach; and can make a recommendation to the Housing Department, should rehousing be desirable.

The Social Services Department may be able to supply kitchen, bathroom and other aids for the home, arrange an appointment with an occupational therapist and support an application for a housing grant, should major adaptations be required.

If only relatively small changes are necessary, e.g. a hand-rail on the stairs or ramp for a wheelchair, the occupational therapist may arrange for these to be done by the local authority. This can take months, however, so if your parents cannot wait and want the work done privately, the occupational therapist will give you names of local firms.

Care and repair schemes
Also known as 'Staying Put' schemes, these are voluntary and/or local authority projects aimed at helping older home owners to repair and adapt their homes. They help to assess your needs, get a builder, supervise the work, raise the finance, verify the estimate and check the completed job. Your local Age Concern branch should be able to advise.

Housing grants
There are several grants available, in the event of more substantial adaptations being required. The three most likely to be of interest are: renovation grant, disabled facilities grant and minor works assistance. All are means-tested and most types of work for which grant is given are at the discretion of the council, so it is very important not to commence any work until grant application has been approved.

More detailed information is given in Chapter 8, Your Home (see section headed 'Improvement and repair grants', page 130). Also, it could be useful to contact your local Citizens' Advice Bureau, Age Concern branch or Agency Service (sometimes known as 'Care and Repair') who would be able to advise you of any preliminary steps you need to take, such as obtaining estimates, before completing the application form.

Other sources of help
The Disabled Living Foundation, 380-384 Harrow Road, London W9 2HU. T:071-289 6111. DLF runs an *Equipment Centre* where aids of all kinds can be demonstrated and tried out by visitors. The range includes: special equipment for the bathroom, kitchen, bedroom and living room; hoists, wheelchairs and gadgets to assist reading and writing. None are for sale but the Centre can provide information on suppliers and prices.

DLF is staffed by therapists who show visitors round and discuss individual needs. It is advisable to make an appointment as the Centre is sometimes closed to the public for the running of training courses.

The Royal Association for Disability and Rehabilitation (RADAR), 25 Mortimer Street, London W1N 8AB. T:071-637 5400. RADAR can help and give advice across a very wide spectrum, including: statutory and voluntary services, access and mobility issues, holidays, employment and housing. It publishes a useful monthly bulletin and can supply names and addresses of the many Disabled Living Centres (similar to the Disabled Living Foundation) which are now being established throughout the country.

Both the **British Red Cross** and **Age Concern** (see local telephone directory) may loan equipment in the short term and may also be able to advise on local stockists.

Homecraft Supplies Ltd., Sidings Road, Low Moor Industrial Estate, Kirkby-in-Ashfield, Notts NG17 7JZ. T:0623 754047. Stocks a very wide variety of practical equipment to help older people cope with everyday life including: walking aids, bed raisers, kitchen aids, special gardening utensils and other leisure items. There is also a mail order service, telephone: 0623 757955.

Keep Able, Fleming Close, Park Farm, Wellingborough, Northants. NN8 3UF. A mail order service with gadgets galore from shower chairs to needle threaders to make life easier for disabled and elderly people. The catalogue is extremely well laid out and there is an advice line – telephone 0933 679426 – to answer queries or assist with choosing a product to meet customers' particular requirements. Those lucky enough to live within convenient reach of Brentford can visit the Keep Able Centre and examine the vast range of equipment on offer. The address is: 2 Capital Interchange Way, Brentford, Middlesex TW8 0EX. T:081-742 2181.

REMAP, Hazeldene, Ightham, Sevenoaks, Kent TN15 9AD. T:0732 883818. Can often help to design or adapt goods to suit individuals, where there is no commercially available product to meet their particular needs.

The Centre for Accessible Environments, 35 Great Smith Street, London SW1P 3BJ. T:071-222 7980. Runs an architectural advisory service and can recommend local architects with experience of designing for people with disabilities. When writing, you should give broad details of the type of work required.

BT supplies some 70 devices to assist those with hearing difficulties, visual handicap, impaired mobility and other problems that make using a telephone more difficult. For details see the *BT Guide for People who are Disabled or Elderly*, available from local BT offices. A home visit can sometimes be arranged for those who are housebound. For further information, dial 100 and ask the operator for Freephone Sales.

Other helpful sources of advice include:

Disability Scotland, Princes House, 5 Shandwick Place, Edinburgh EH2 4RG. T:031-229 8632.

Wales Council for The Disabled, Information Service, Llys Ifor, Crescent Road, Caerphilly, Mid Glamorgan CF8 1XL. T:0222 887325.

Disability Action, 2 Annadale Avenue, Belfast BT7 3JR. T:0232 491011.

Alarm systems

Alarm systems have become very much more widespread in recent years. The knowledge that help can be summoned quickly in the event of an emergency is not only reassuring in its own right but in practical terms can enable many elderly people to remain independent far longer than would otherwise be sensible.

Some local authorities have alarm systems that now allow people living in their own homes to be linked to a central control. To find out whether your parents' local authority operates such a system, contact the Social Services Department.

Commercial firms

A number of firms install and operate alarm systems. Price, installation cost and reliability can vary quite considerably. For general advice plus a list of suppliers, contact the Information Service, **Disabled Living Foundation**, (see page 286).

Community alarms

Telephone alarm systems operated on the public telephone network can be used by anyone with a direct telephone line. The systems link into a 24-hour monitoring centre and have a pendant which enables help to be called even when the owner is some distance from the telephone. Grants may sometimes be available. For further information, contact: The Community Alarms Department, **Help the Aged**, St. James's Walk, London EC1R 0BE or telephone 071-253 0253.

Main local authority services

Quite apart from any assistance with housing, local authorities supply a number of services which can prove invaluable to an elderly person. The two most important are meals on wheels and home helps. Additionally, there are social workers and various specialists concerned with aspects of health.

As from April 1993, the start date for Community Care, responsibility for helping to assess and co-ordinate the best arrangements for individuals will be handled by the local authority Social Services Department instead of, as before, partially through Social Security offices. The switch should reduce much of the existing bureaucracy and time-wasting in having to deal with different offices.

Meals on wheels

The meals on wheels service is sometimes run by local authorities direct and sometimes by voluntary organisations, such as the Women's Royal Voluntary Service or the British Red Cross, acting as their agents. As you will know, the purpose is to deliver a hot lunch to individuals in their own home. Different arrangements apply in different areas and schemes variously operate from two to seven days a week. Cost also varies: from about 35p to £1.75 a day, with the norm about £1. For further information, contact the Social Services Department or your local Citizens' Advice Bureau.

Home helps

Local authorities have a legal obligation to run a home help service to help frail and housebound elderly people with such basic household chores as shopping, tidying up, a little light cooking and so on. In many areas the service is overstretched, so the amount of help actually available varies considerably. In some authorities, people are means-tested on their ability to pay; in others the service is free. Sometimes there is a charge per number of visits; sometimes a flat rate weekly charge, ranging from about £1 to £10. Apply through the Social Services Department. Some of the larger authorities have a special telephone number which may be listed either as 'Home Help Services' or 'Domiciliary Services'.

Specialist helpers

Local authorities employ a number of specialist helpers, variously based in the Social Services Department or Health Centre, who are there to assist.

Social workers. Normally the first people to contact if you have a problem. They can put you in touch with the right person if you require a home help, meals on wheels, have a housing difficulty or other query and are not sure whom to approach. You should ring the local Social Services Department; in Scotland, this is normally referred to as the Social Work Department.

Occupational therapists. Have a wide knowledge of disability and can assist a handicapped person via training, exercise, or access to aids, equipment or adaptations to the home. Ring the Social Services Department.

Health visitors. Qualified nurses with broad knowledge both of health matters and of the various services available through the local authority. Rather like social workers, health visitors can put you in touch with whatever specialised facilities are required. Contact through the local Health Centre.

District nurses. Fully qualified nurses who will visit a patient in the home: change dressings, attend to other routine nursing matters, monitor progress and help with the arrangements if more specialised care is required. Contact through the Health Centre.

Physiotherapists. Use exercise and massage to help improve mobility and strengthen muscles, for example after an operation or to alleviate a crippling condition. Normally available at both hospitals and health centres.

Medical social workers. In the old days, used to be known as almoners. Are available to consult if patients have any problems – whether practical or emotional – on leaving hospital. MSWs can advise on coping with a disablement, as well as such practical matters as transport, after-care and other immediate arrangements. Work in hospitals and an appointment should be made before the patient is discharged.

Key voluntary organisations

Voluntary organisations complement the services provided by statutory health and social services in making life easier for elderly people living at home. The range of provision varies from area to area but can include:

- Lunch clubs
- Day centres and clubs
- Aids such as wheelchairs
- Transport
- Good neighbour schemes
- Advice and information
- Holidays and short-term placements
- Friendly visiting
- Odd jobs and decorating
- Gardening
- Prescription collection
- Family support schemes.

The particular organisation providing these services depends on where you live but the Citizens' Advice Bureau will be able to advise you whom to contact. The following are the key agencies:

Age Concern Groups may provide any or all of the voluntary services listed above. Most groups recruit volunteers to do practical jobs and provide friendship. They also give advice and information and when necessary refer enquirers to a more appropriate agency. Their addresses and telephone numbers are in the local phone book. Alternatively you can telephone **Age Concern Greater London** (T:071-737 3456) for London addresses; or contact the national headquarters for addresses outside the capital:

Age Concern England, Astral House, 1268 London Road, London SW16 4ER. T:081-679 8000.

Headquarters in Scotland, Wales and Northern Ireland are:

Age Concern Scotland, 54A Fountainbridge, Edinburgh EH3 9PT. T:031-228 5656.

Age Concern Wales, 4th Floor, 1 Cathedral Road, Cardiff CF1 9SD. T:0222 371566.

Age Concern Northern Ireland, 6 Lower Crescent, Belfast BT7 1NR. T:0232 245729.

Women's Royal Voluntary Service runs a number of invaluable services:

- Meals on wheels
- Lunch clubs
- Day centres
- Crisis support for 24-48 hours

- Day and night sitting
- Books on wheels
- Transport
- Home visiting
- Shopping outings
- Children's holiday schemes.

Look in the phone book for the address of the local office or contact the national headquarters: **Women's Royal Voluntary Service**, 234–244 Stockwell Road, London SW9 9SP. T:071-416 0146.

British Red Cross supplies some important services to elderly people. The principal ones available from most branches include:

- Acting as a link between hospital and home (before admission and after discharge)
- Visiting
- Escorting sick, handicapped or frail people when travelling
- Loaning equipment for sick or convalescent patients at home, e.g. wheelchairs and commodes
- After-care and home visiting (including practical help in such tasks as hair washing, shopping, changing library books)
- Sitting-in with elderly people and those with disabilities
- Providing transport for the housebound
- Organising stroke clubs
- 'Signposting' sick people and those with disabilities towards the statutory or voluntary services from which their needs may best be met
- Beauty care service for patients with long term illness.

The following activities are also carried out by the Red Cross in co-operation with or on behalf of statutory authorities:

- Clubs
- Lunch clubs
- Day centres
- Christmas shopping
- Holidays and holiday homes for the handicapped.

To contact your local British Red Cross branch, see telephone directory, or write to: **The British Red Cross**, 9 Grosvenor Crescent, London SW1X 7EJ. T:071-235 5454.

St. John Ambulance comprises 60,000 volunteers who help in hospitals and may sometimes visit people at home to assist with, say, the shopping or by providing transport to and from hospital. In some areas loan of equipment such as wheelchairs, can be arranged. Sometimes, too, there are courses for carers. To get in touch, contact the *County* headquarters,

Retirement Made Easy

see telephone directory or contact: **St. John Ambulance**, 1 Grosvenor Crescent, London SW1X 7EF. T:071-235 5231.

Other sources of help and advice

Counsel and Care for the Elderly, Twyman House, Lower Ground Floor, 16 Bonny Street, London NW1 9PG. T:Casework (10.30 a.m. – 4 p.m.) 071-485 1566; Appeals 071-485 4513. Provides a free, confidential advisory service, which is used by thousands of elderly people and their relatives each year. There is also a range of factsheets and limited funds are available to help with an exceptional needs payment.

Central Council for Jewish Social Service, 221 Golders Green Road, London NW11 9DW. T:081-458 3282. CCJSS is an umbrella organisation for Jewish social services in the country and has over 40 affiliated member organisations. It publishes a *Directory of Jewish Social Services*, listing facilities throughout the UK. Price is £4.

Services for elderly Jewish people in London and the South East are carried out by **Jewish Care**, located at the same address as the Central Council above. Principal facilities include: kosher meals service, day centres plus a number of residential homes.

Outside London, contact:

Leeds Jewish Welfare Board, 311 Stonegate Road, Leeds LS17 6AZ. T:0532 684211.
Manchester Jewish Blind Society, Nicky Alliance Day Centre, 85 Middleton Road, Crumpsall, Manchester M8 6JY. T:061-740 0111.
Brighton & Hove Jewish Welfare Board, c/o 2 Modena Road, Hove, East Sussex BN3 5QJ. T:0273 722523.
Merseyside Jewish Representative Council, Shifrin House, 433 Smithdown Road, Liverpool 15. T:051-733 2292.

Civil Service Retirement Fellowship, 1b Deals Gateway, Blackheath Road, London SE10 8BW. T:081-691 7411. Runs a home visiting service for those who are housebound or living alone and has an extensive network of local groups throughout the country offering a wide range of social activities for retired civil servants and their families.

The Forces Help Society and Lord Roberts Workshops, 122 Brompton Road, London SW3 1JE. T:071-589 3243. In association with SSAFA, provides help to retired people who have served at any time in HM Forces. This may typically include advice on pensions and benefits or the provision of a grant for a special need, which the Society may sometimes be able to arrange.

The Society also has two residential homes, maintains cottages for ex-servicemen and their wives and has holiday accommodation for use by ex-service people in need.

For further information, write to the above headquarters or contact the Society's local representative, whose name and address is obtainable from post offices, libraries and Citizens' Advice Bureaux.

Transport

The difficulty of getting around is often a major problem for elderly and disabled people. The Department of Transport produces the following useful directory of services and is also responsible for running MAVIS.

Voluntary and Community Schemes Directory. Lists details of hundreds of transport schemes around the country helpful to elderly and/or disabled people, including those needing to use a wheelchair. The information is held on a computerised database and is therefore constantly being updated. Individuals can request the entire directory or simply the section relevant to the area in which they live. Obtainable free from the Disability Unit, Room S10/21, Department of Transport, 2 Marsham Street, London SW1P 3EB. T:071-276 5257.

Mobility Advice And Vehicle Information Service (MAVIS), Transport & Road Research Laboratory, Old Wokingham Road, Crowthorne, Berkshire RG11 6AU. T:0344 770456. MAVIS is an information service advising on all aspects of mobility – in particular, problems associated with driving. Its services include assessment of elderly motorists wishing to return to driving after a stroke or other disabling illness and advice on low-cost adaptations to relieve the pain of arthritic joints or other conditions that make driving uncomfortable. While general information is free, charges for the more specialised services are as follows: full assessment of individuals who have suffered a disablement, £50; consultation and advice on car adaptations or vehicle familiarisation, £30.

See also under both 'Mobility Allowance' and 'Disability Living Allowance', in the section headed 'Benefits and allowances', page 298.

Driving licence renewal at age 70

All drivers aged 70 are sent a licence renewal form and have to pay a £6 fee to have their licence renewed. The licence has to be renewed (and £6 paid) at least every three years. Depending on the individual's health, including in particular their eyesight, the driver might be sent a new form to complete after only one or two years. If this applies, the form must be completed honestly but no extra charge will be made.

Temporary living-in help

Elderly people living alone can be more vulnerable to 'flu and other winter ailments. They may have a fall or, for no apparent reason, go through a period of being forgetful and neglecting themselves. In the event of an emergency or if you have reason for concern – perhaps because you are going on holiday and will not be around to keep a watchful eye – engaging living-in help can be a godsend. Most agencies tend inevitably to be on the expensive side, although in the event of a real problem often represent excellent value for money. A more unusual and interesting longer-term possibility is to recruit a Community Service Volunteer.

Community Service Volunteers, 237 Pentonville Road, London N1 9NJ. T:071-278 6601. CSV matches full-time helpers with individuals and families who need a high degree of support. The volunteers, who are mostly between 16 and 35, are untrained and work for periods of 4 to 12 months. In general they provide practical assistance in the home including, for example: shopping, light cooking, tidying up, attending to the garden and sometimes also decorating jobs.

Usually a care scheme is set up through a social worker, who supervises how the arrangement is working out. Volunteers are placed on a one month's trial basis. There is an annual retainer of £1,620 that can be paid in monthly instalments (in case of real financial need, the local authority might pay). Other charges include: fares; accommodation; full board or a weekly food allowance of £25; pocket money of around £21 a week; plus one week's paid holiday, after four months. Contact your parents' local Social Services Department; or approach CSV direct, at the address given above.

Agencies

Most of the agencies listed specialise in providing temporary help, rather than permanent staff. Charges vary, but in addition to the weekly payment, there is normally an agency booking fee. As a rule payment is gross, so your parents will not be involved in having to work out tax or national insurance.

Auntie Fay Agency, Royal Albert House, Sheet Street, Windsor, Berkshire SL4 1BE. T:0753 831960.
Consultus, 17 London Road, Tonbridge, Kent TN10 3AB. T:0732 355231.
Country Cousins Employment Bureau, 10a Market Square, Horsham, West Sussex RH12 IEU. T:0403 210415.

Caring for Elderly Parents

Easymind: Home Care Services, 3 Oakshade Road, Oxshott, Surrey KT22 0LF. T:0372 842087.
Universal Aunts Ltd., PO Box 304, London SW4 0NN. T:071-738 8937.

For a further list of agencies, see *Yellow Pages* under heading 'Domestic' or 'Domestic Staff'.

Nursing care

If one of your parents needs regular nursing care, their doctor may be able to arrange for a community or district nurse to visit them at home. This will not, of course, be a sleeping-in arrangement but simply involves a qualified nurse calling round when necessary.

If you want more concentrated home nursing you will have to go through a private agency. Both *Consultus* and *Easymind* (see above) can sometimes supply trained nurses. Additionally, there are many specialised agencies, which can arrange daily or resident nurses on a temporary or longer term basis. One of the best known, with 115 branches throughout the UK, is the **British Nursing Association**, North Place, 82 Great North Road, Hatfield, Herts. AL9 5BL. T:0707 263544. (See local telephone directory for branch addresses.)

Some private health insurance policies cover home nursing. A good example is Western Provident Association's 'Welcome Home' scheme, which is designed to provide short-term nursing care for older people after a stay in hospital. Cover can be bought for a week, three weeks or 35 days with subscriptions ranging – according to the number of hours' nursing – from £44.15 to £223 a year. To qualify, patients must be under the age of 85 and must have spent at least four nights in hospital. Also a doctor must confirm that home nursing is necessary and claims cannot be made within the first three months of the policy being taken out. For further information, contact: **The Welcome Home Nursing Scheme**, WPA, BS 481 Freepost, Bristol BS1 6GT. T:0272 221166.

A problem for many elderly people is that the amount of care they need is liable to vary according to the state of their health and other factors including, for example, the availability of neighbours and family. Whereas after an operation the requirement may be for someone with basic nursing skills, a few weeks later the only need may be for someone to act as a companion – or simply to pop in for the odd hour during the day to cook a hot meal and check all is well. An organisation well worth knowing about is the:

United Kingdom Home Care Association, Premier House, Holmes

Road, Sowerby Bridge, West Yorkshire HX6 3LD. T:0422 835057; or 081-946 8202. It represents over 200 agencies throughout the country specialising in providing care for elderly and/or handicapped people. All requirements are catered for including temporary and permanent posts, residential, daily, overnight and hourly work. UKHCA runs a helpline which can advise on the different types of service, including likely charges, and can also refer enquirers to a local member agency committed to upholding the Association's Code of Practice.

Emergency care for pets

For many elderly people a pet is a most important part of their lives, providing companionship and fun as well as stimulating them into taking regular outdoor exercise. But in the event of the owner having to go into hospital or due to some other emergency being temporarily unable to care for their pet, there can be real problems including concern for the welfare of the animal and considerable distress to the owner.

To overcome these problems, two highly imaginative schemes have been set up, one operating throughout the UK and the other just in Scotland. Depending on what is required, volunteers will either simply feed or exercise the animal or will care for it in their own home until the owner can manage again.

Cinnamon Trust, Poldarves Farm, Trescowe Common, Germoe, Penzance TR20 9RX. T:0763 850291. As well as the above services, Cinnamon also offers permanent care for pets whose owners have died or who can no longer keep them as a result of having been admitted into a residential home. Emergency services can be called 24 hours a day. The Trust makes no charge but donations, or a bequest, are very much appreciated.

Pet Fostering Service Scotland. T:067-481 356. The focus is on temporary care. The only charges are the cost of pet's food, litter – in the case of cats – and any veterinary fees that may be incurred during fostering.

Practical help for carers

If your parent is still fairly active – visits friends, does his/her own shopping, enjoys some hobby which gets him/her out and about – the strains and difficulties may be fairly minimal. This applies particularly if your home lends itself to creating a granny flat, so everyone can retain some privacy and your parent can continue to enjoy maximum independence. However, this is not always possible and in the case of an ill or very frail person far more intensive care may be required.

If you have to go out to work, need time to attend to other responsibilities or quite understandably feel that if you are to remain human you must have time for your own interests, it is important to know what help is available and how to obtain it.

The many services provided by local authorities and voluntary agencies, described earlier in the chapter, apply for the most part equally to an elderly person living with their family as to one living alone. If there is nothing in the list that solves a particular problem you may have, it is sensible to talk to the Citizens' Advice Bureau and Social Services Department, as there may be some special local facility that could provide the solution.

In particular, you might ask about *day centres* and *clubs*. Activities and surroundings vary, so you might wish to investigate. However, a responsible person will always be in charge and transport, to and from the venue, is often provided. You could also ask the local Age Concern group and WRVS. These organisations will be able to tell you about the possibility of *voluntary sitters*: people who come in and stay for a few hours (or sometimes overnight) to prevent an elderly person being on their own.

In response to the government's Community Care scheme, most areas now have, or are planning, *respite care facilities* to enable carers to take a break from their dependants from time to time. Depending on the circumstances, this could be for just the odd day or possibly for a week or two to enable carers who need it to have a real rest. For further information, contact your local health or Social Services department.

Another service well worth knowing about is Crossroads. This is a national organisation which arranges for attendants to care for very frail or disabled people in their own home, while the regular carer is away. They will come in during the day, or stay overnight, as necessary. There is no charge but donations are welcomed. Demand for the service is very high, so priority is given to those in greatest need. The Citizens' Advice Bureau should be able to give you the address of the local branch. Alternatively, you could contact: **Crossroads**, 10 Regent Place, Rugby, Warwickshire CV21 2PN. T:0788 573653.

Holidays

There are various schemes to enable families with an elderly relative to go on holiday alone or simply to enjoy a respite from their caring responsibilities.

A number of local authorities run *fostering schemes*, on similar lines to child fostering. Elderly people are invited to stay in a neighbour's home

Retirement Made Easy

and live in the household as an ordinary family member. Lasting relationships often develop. There may be a charge or the service may be run on a voluntary basis (or be paid for by the local authority). Schemes are patchy around the country. The Citizens' Advice Bureau and Social Services Department will advise you if anything exists.

Some voluntary organisations organise *holidays for older people* to give relatives a break. Different charities take responsibility according to the area where you live: the CAB, Volunteer Bureau or the Social Services Department should know who you should approach.

Another solution is a *short stay home*, which is residential accommodation variously run by local authorities, voluntary organisations or by private individuals which cater specifically for elderly people. Again, the Social Services Department and CAB should be able to advise.

If, as opposed to general care, proper medical attention is necessary, you should consult your parent's GP. Many *hospitals and nursing homes* offer short-stay care arrangements as a means of relieving relatives and a doctor should be able to help organise this for you.

Fount of almost all knowledge on anything to do with caring and set up specifically to assist those with responsibility for an elderly relative is:

Carers' National Association, 29 Chilworth Mews, London W2 3RG. T:071-724 7776. The CNA has branches throughout the United Kingdom and provides a thorough-going information service. It can advise on: the statutory services; housing adaptations; where to obtain special equipment; holiday and other relief services. It also circulates a bi-monthly newsletter, giving up-to-date information on developments including current rates of grants and allowances. Supporters of the Association can be enrolled as carer or associate: £3 a year.

Useful reading
Caring for Someone?, published by the Benefits Agency. Available free from main post offices.
Taking Good Care, £6.95 published by Age Concern.
Help at Hand: The Home Carers' Survival Guide, by Jane Brotchie. Price £6.95 from Plymbridge Distributors Ltd., Estover Road, Plymouth PL6 7PZ (cheques payable to Plymbridge Ltd.).

Benefits and allowances

There are a number of benefits/allowances available to those with responsibility for the care of an elderly person and/or to elderly people themselves.

Entitlements for carers

Home responsibilities protection. A means of protecting your state pension if you are unable to work because of the necessity to care for an elderly person. For further details, see under 'State pensions' at the start of Chapter 3 or ask for leaflet NP 27 at any Social Security office.

Invalid care allowance. Women up to the age of 60 and men up to 65 who do not work other than very part-time hours because of the need to care for a severely disabled person (i.e. someone who gets Attendance Allowance, Constant Attendance Allowance or, since April 1992, the two higher care components of the new Disability Living Allowance) may qualify to receive ICA. You do not need to be related to the person and equally, you do not need to live at the same address. Current ICA payment (1992/93) is £32.55 a week and counts as taxable income. Carers in receipt of income support, housing benefit, community charge benefit or council tax benefit receive a special £11.55 premium on top of the normal ICA, which continues to be paid for eight weeks if the carer's role ceases.

To be eligible for ICA, it is necessary to spend at least 35 hours a week looking after a severely disabled person. Claimants may earn up to £40 a week after deduction of reasonable expenses without loss of benefit. For further details, together with a claim form, obtain claim pack DS 700 from any Social Security office.

Entitlements for elderly/disabled people

More generous income tax allowances. Both the personal allowance and the married couple's allowance are increased when an individual becomes 65; and are raised again after their 75th birthday. Details of the increases, and how these are calculated, are explained in the 'Tax' chapter, pages 57-8. See also Inland Revenue leaflets IR 81 *Independent Taxation – A Guide for Pensioners* and IR 80 *Independent Taxation – A Guide for Married Couples*, available from any tax office.

Attendance Allowance. This is paid to people aged 65 or over who are severely disabled, either mentally or physically, and have needed almost constant care for at least six months. An exception to the six months' waiting period is made in the case of those who are terminally ill, who can now receive the allowance without having to wait.

There are two rates of allowance: £43.35 a week for those needing 24-hour care; and £28.95 for those needing intensive day or night-time care. The allowance is tax free and is paid regardless of income (except where income support is already paid to a severely disabled person living in a private nursing or residential care home). For further details, together with a claim form, obtain leaflet DS 702 from your local Social Security office.

Disability Living Allowance (DLA). Disability Living Allowance is a new benefit for people disabled before the age of 65. It replaces both the Mobility Allowance and Attendance Allowance, combining them in one, to make claiming easier and faster. It also gives help to some 300,000 people who did not previously qualify but who require some assistance in helping them to cope with their daily needs.

The level of benefit depends on how severely disabled an individual is – with the highest rate going to those needing 24-hour care. There are two rates for the mobility part of the allowance and three rates for the care component. The top and middle rates are based on the same rules as those applying to Attendance Allowance and the old Mobility Allowance; and the bottom rate in each case goes to people who were not eligible before DLA came into existence.

The higher rate mobility element is £30.30 a week; and the new lower rate, which for the first time includes people suffering from severe mental handicap who need supervision in getting around, is £11.55.

The three rates for the care element are: higher rate, £43.35; middle rate, £28.95; new lower rate, £11.55.

Disability Living Allowance is tax free and is paid regardless of income (except when Income Support is already paid to a severely disabled person living in a private nursing or residential care home). Except in the case of people who are terminally ill and can receive DLA immediately, there is a normal qualifying period of three months.

For further information see leaflet DS 704, obtainable from any post office, Citizens' Advice Bureau or Social Security office. The leaflet contains a reply slip, which you should complete and return as soon as possible in order to obtain the necessary claim pack. The pack includes a questionnaire with space for you to explain how the disability is making your life more difficult.

Mobility Allowance. As explained in the above paragraph (see Disability Living Allowance), Mobility Allowance has been discontinued as a separate benefit and has now been absorbed as part of DLA. The mobility element of DLA is designed to help people with a severe disablement to be more mobile and can be used towards a car, taxis or in any other way that best suits the individual's needs. Eligibility is restricted to those who become unable or virtually unable to walk before the age of 65; and to people, including the deaf-blind and those with a severe mental handicap, who are unable to go out alone and need a companion to accompany them. Depending on the degree of handicap, benefit may either be at the higher rate of £30.30 a week or at the new lower rate of £11.55. Although claims cannot be accepted after an individual has reached 66, the benefit then continues to be paid for life.

Cold Weather Payments. These are designed to give particularly vulnerable people extra help with heating costs during very cold weather. The scheme automatically covers anyone of pension age who is in receipt of income support. Payment is made by post as soon as the temperature in an area is *forecast* to drop – or actually drops – to zero degrees Celsius (or below) for seven consecutive days. The amount paid is £6 a week and those eligible should receive it without having to claim. In the event of a problem, contact your local DSS office.

Financial assistance

A number of charities give financial assistance to elderly people in need. These include:

Homelife-DGAA, Vicarage Gate House, Vicarage Gate, London W8 4AQ. T:071-229 9341. Provides grants to enable people to remain in their own home. Also runs both residential and nursing homes.

Guild of Aid for Gentle People, 10 St. Christopher's Place, London W1M 6HY. T:071-935 0641. Can assist those 'of gentle birth or good education' who want to stay in their own home and who cannot call on any professional/trade body. The Guild will also consider long-term help with fees in residential and nursing homes.

Independent Living Fund, PO Box 183, Nottingham NG8 3RD. T:0602 290423. This is a charitable trust fund established in March 1988 with government backing for a period of five years. It can provide assistance to enable severely disabled people to pay for domestic or personal help in order to remain in their own home. To qualify, applicants must either be living on their own or with someone who is unable to provide all the care they need and must be receiving the higher rate of Attendance Allowance. To apply, request Form ILF 100 from the above address.

Invalids-at-Home Trust, Mrs Sarah Lomas, 17 Lapstone Gardens, Kenton, Harrow HA3 0EB. T:081-907 1706. A small trust which aims to help long-term invalids and people who are substantially handicapped remain in their own home by making modest grants for the provision of special equipment and other badly needed items. Assistance is normally limited to those who are without entitlement to any equivalent statutory benefit.

Royal United Kingdom Beneficent Association (RUKBA), 6 Avonmore Road, London W14 8RL. T:071-602 6274. Provides life-time annuities to persons in need from a professional or similar background. It is sometimes also possible to obtain help with residential home fees.

Soldiers', Sailors' and Airmen's Families Association (SSAFA), 19 Queen Elizabeth Street, London SE1 2LP. T:071-403 8783. Assistance is restricted to those who have served in the armed forces and their families. Grants (the average is about £100) can be made to meet immediate need including rent, wheelchairs and similar essentials. Contact via the local branch is preferred (see local telephone directory for address or ask at Citizens' Advice Bureau).

The Royal Agricultural Benevolent Institution, Shaw House, 27 West Way, Oxford OX2 0QH. T:0865 724931. Supports retired or disabled farmers, farm managers and their families who are in need. Assistance includes a wide range of grants, help towards fees in residential, convalescent and nursing homes and advice on government assistance.

Wireless for the Bedridden Society, 159A High Street, Hornchurch, Essex RM11 3YB. T:0708 621101. Loans on a permanent basis radios and televisions to elderly housebound people who cannot afford sets. Application should be made through a health visitor, social worker or officer of a recognised organisation.

Useful reading
For other sources of financial help, ask your library for: *A Guide to Grants for Individuals in Need*, published by the Directory of Social Change; also *The Charities Digest*, published by the Family Welfare Association.

Special accommodation

Retired people who need particular support may choose or need to move to accommodation where special services are provided. This can either be sheltered housing or a residential home. Both terms cover an enormous spectrum, so anyone considering either of these options should make a point of investigating the market before reaching a decision.

An all too common mistake is for people to anticipate old age long before it arrives and to move into accommodation that is either too small or quite unnecessarily 'sheltered', years before they have need of the facilities. By the same token, some individuals buy or rent sheltered housing with a minimum of support services, only to have to move a few months later because they need rather more help than is available.

Choosing the right accommodation is critically important, as it can make all the difference to independence, life style and general well-being. It can also of course lift a great burden off families' shoulders to know that their parents are happy, comfortable, in congenial surroundings and with help on tap, should this be necessary.

Sheltered housing

As a general description, sheltered housing is usually a development of independent, purpose-designed bungalows or flats within easy access of shops and public transport. They generally have a warden, an alarm system for emergencies and often some common facilities, such as: a garden, possibly a launderette, a sitting room and a dining room with meals provided for residents, on an optional basis, either once a day or several days a week.

Residents normally have access to all the usual range of services – home helps, meals on wheels – in the same way as any other elderly person.

Sheltered housing is available for sale or rental, variously through private developers, housing associations or local authorities. It is occasionally also provided through gifted housing schemes; or on a shared ownership basis.

Sheltered housing for sale

Flats and houses are usually sold on long leases (99 years or more) for a capital sum, with a weekly or monthly service charge to cover maintenance and resident care services.

Should a resident decide to move, the property can usually be sold on the open market, either through the developer or an estate agent, provided the prospective buyer is over 55 years of age. Most developers impose a levy of 1 per cent of the sale price for checking the credentials of incoming residents, irrespective of whether the property is sold through them. Look carefully at any schemes that enable you to buy the property at a discount as many such schemes entitle the developer to retain a proportion of the equity on resale.

Occupiers normally have to enter into a management agreement with the housebuilder and it is important to establish exactly what the commitment is likely to be before buying into such schemes. Factors that should be considered include: who the managing agent is; the warden's duties; what the service charge covers; the ground rent; the arrangements for any repairs that might prove necessary; whether there is a residents' association; whether pets are allowed; what the conditions are with regard to reselling the property – and the tenant's rights in the matter.

Prices. The range of prices is very wide – between approximately £25,000 and £250,000 – depending on size, location and type of property. Weekly service charges vary between roughly £12 and £25, with £18-£22 being the norm.

The service charge usually covers: the cost of the warden, alarm system, maintenance, repair and renewal of any communal facilities (external and internal) and sometimes the heating and lighting costs. It may also cover insurance on the building (but not the contents). A particular point to watch is that the service charge tends to rise annually, sometimes well above the inflation level. Be wary of service charges that seem uncommonly reasonable, as these are often increased sharply following purchase. Owners of sheltered accommodation have the same rights as other leaseholders and charges can therefore be challenged in the courts.

A further safeguard is the Sheltered Housing Code operated by the **National House Building Council** (Chiltern Avenue, Amersham, Bucks HP6 5AP. T:0494 434477), which has now become mandatory for all registered housebuilders. The Code, which applies to all new sheltered dwellings in England and Wales registered on or after 1 April 1990, has two main requirements: (a) that every prospective purchaser should be given a Purchaser's Information Pack (PIP), clearly outlining all essential information that they will need to enable them to decide whether or not to buy; (b) that the builder and management organisation enter into a formal legal agreement giving purchasers the benefit of the legal rights specified in the Code. An independent advice and conciliation service is also planned through Age Concern.

For those on lowish incomes, it may also be possible to get housing benefit to meet some or all of the service charge. The local authority Housing Department will advise on this.

The following organisations can provide information about sheltered housing for sale:

Sheltered Housing Services, 8-9 Abbey Parade, North Circular Road, London W5 1EE. T:081-997 9313. Independent company offering information and advice on most current sites and resales from a choice of over 1,500 locations. Cost of making an enquiry, plus up-dating service for up to two years, is £4.50.

Sheltered Housing Advisory and Conciliation Service (SHACS), Walkden House, 3-10 Melton Street, London NW1 2EJ. T:071-383 2006. Offers guidance on points to check before signing any purchase agreement. Will also help anyone with problems living in private sector sheltered housing.

Useful reading
A Buyer's Guide to Sheltered Housing, published by Age Concern England/National Housing and Town Planning Council, price £2.50. An excellent guide to the sort of questions you should ask before committing yourself. Also useful information on the financial aspects of buying a sheltered home. Available from Age Concern England.

Retirement Homes & Finance, price £1.30 from newsagents or (£2 including p&p) direct from the publishers Selwood Press Ltd., Unit 1, Raans Road, Amersham, Bucks HP6 6LX. T:0494 432433. A bi-monthly magazine giving up-to-date information on everything to do with the retirement homes market, including details of all new schemes and an invaluable Retirement Property Index of all current developments throughout the UK showing: county, town, developer, price range, size, type of facilities, service charges, completion date and any other special features.

Rented sheltered housing

This is normally provided by local authorities, housing associations and certain benevolent societies. As with accommodation to buy, quality varies.

Local authorities. This is usually only available to people who have resided in the area for some time. There is often an upper and lower age limit for admission and prospective tenants may have to undergo a medical examination, since as a rule only those who are physically fit are accepted. Should a resident become infirm or frail, alternative accommodation will be found. Apply to the local Housing or Social Services Department or via a Housing Advice Centre.

Housing associations. Housing associations supply much of the newly built sheltered housing. Rents, which may sometimes be inclusive of service charge, vary very roughly from £45 to £100 a week. In case of need, income support may be obtained to help with the cost.

Before signing an agreement, a point you should be aware of is that some charitable housing associations, including the Abbeyfield Society, offer a licensee arrangement which does not provide the same security of tenure as some other tenancy agreements. Where this is the case, you are strongly advised to have the proposed contract checked by a lawyer to ensure you properly understand your rights – and those on the other side.

Citizens' Advice Bureaux and Housing Departments often keep a list of local housing associations. You can look in the *Yellow Pages* telephone directory. Or alternatively, you can contact either Age Concern or the Housing Corporation, at the following addresses:

Retirement Made Easy

Age Concern England, Astral House, 1268 London Road, London SW16 4ER. Has a complete list of housing associations. Letters should be addressed to the Housing Information Officer and a large sae enclosed.

Housing Corporation, 149 Tottenham Court Road, London W1P 0BN. T:071-387 9466. Will send you a list of their regional offices who will be able to supply you with addresses of housing associations in their area. For Scotland, Wales and Northern Ireland, contact:

Housing for Wales, 25-30 Lambourne Crescent, Llanishen, Cardiff CF4 5ZJ. T:0222 747979.
Scottish Homes, Thistle House, 91 Haymarket Terrace, Edinburgh EH12 5HE. T:031-313 0044.
Northern Ireland Federation of Housing Associations, Carlisle Memorial Centre, 88 Clifton Street, Belfast BT13 1AB. T:0232 230446.

A few of the very many housing associations include:

The Abbeyfield Society, 186-192 Darkes Lane, Potters Bar, Herts EN6 1AB. T:0707 44845; and 2 Torphichen Place, Edinburgh EH3 8DU. T:031-228 5258. Abbeyfield has nearly a thousand supportive houses providing independent accommodation, a resident housekeeper and main meals of the day. Also over 30 houses providing 24-hour 'extra care' facilities.

Anchor Housing Association, Anchor House, 269a Banbury Road, Oxford OX2 7HU. T:0865 311511. Provides over 22,000 flats for older people who for health or other pressing reason urgently need sheltered housing. There are also special Anchor Housing-with-care flats for very frail people who need more help with everyday living. Applicants must have strong links with the area.

Cecil Houses (Inc.), 2 Priory Road, Kew, Richmond, Surrey TW9 3DG. T:081-940 9828. Runs several hostels and residential care homes in the Central London, Surrey, Ealing and Teddington areas. Current charges are from £99 a week for full board and lodging. There is a round-the-clock warden service and care assistance in all the homes.

Hanover Housing Association, Hanover House, 18 The Avenue, Egham, Surrey TW20 9AB. T:0784 438361. Provides managed sheltered accommodation through its regional and area offices in Durham, Oldham, Ipswich, Wimbledon, Horsham, St. Neots, Shipley, Nailsea, Winchester and Dudley. Applicants must have some connection with the area to which they are applying.

Servite Houses, 125 Old Brompton Road, London SW7 3RP. T:071-

370 5466. Over 4,000 flatlets with resident warden in and around London, the West Midlands and Merseyside. Rent (including service charges) is about £50 per week. There are also a number of 'extra care' schemes for frail elderly people. Servite is expecting to move around Easter 1993. Mail and phone calls will be forwarded/transferred in the normal manner.

Benevolent societies. These all cater for specific professional and other groups.

Royal British Legion Housing Association, St John's Road, Penn, High Wycombe, Bucks HP10 8JF. T:0494 813771. Over 350 sheltered housing schemes mainly for ex-service men or women and/or their dependants, with nearly 13,000 units.

Soldiers', Sailors' and Airmen's Families Association (SSAFA), 19 Queen Elizabeth Street, London SE1 2LP. T:071-403 8783. Works with the Abbeyfield Society to provide sheltered accommodation for retired ex-service people.

Teachers' Benevolent Fund, Hamilton House, Mabledon Place, London WC1H 9BE. T:071-465 0499. Sheltered unfurnished accommodation for active retired state schoolteachers and their dependants. Mid-day meal offered. Additionally, full residential care is provided in three homes variously, in Elstree, Stoke-on-Trent and near Birmingham.

Alternative ways of buying sheltered accommodation
For those who cannot afford either to buy into sheltered housing outright or through a mortgage, there is a variety of alternative payment methods:

Shared ownership and 'Sundowner' schemes. Part-ownership schemes are now offered by a number of developers. Would-be residents who must be over 55 years part-buy/part-rent, with the amount of rent varying according to the size of the initial lump sum. Residents can sell at any time but they only recoup that percentage of the sale price which is proportionate to their original capital investment, with no allowance for any rental payments made over the intervening period.

'Investment' and gifted housing schemes. Some charities and housing associations operate these schemes (sometimes called 'leasehold schemes'), for which a capital sum is required to obtain sheltered accommodation. This usually takes the form of an interest-free loan, which is returnable on leaving or when the owner dies.

Gifted housing schemes differ in that an individual *donates* his/her property to an association (usually a registered charity) in return for being housed and, if necessary, cared for in either their own home or in one of the charity's sheltered homes. The attraction is that the owner can remain in his or her own property with none of the burden of its upkeep.

However, it is advisable to consult a solicitor before signing anything, because such schemes have the big negative of reducing the value of the owner's estate with consequent loss for any beneficiaries.

One of the better known organisations to offer both kinds of scheme is the charity, **Help the Aged**, Housing and Care Division, St. James's Walk, London EC1R 0BE. T:071-253 0253.

Almshouses
The term 'almshouse' describes sheltered housing for elderly people of reduced means, which is administered by a charitable trust. It is estimated that there are now about 2,500 groups of almshouses providing about 30,000 dwellings. Rents are not charged but there may be a maintenance contribution towards upkeep and heating.

A point you should be aware of is that, similar to Abbeyfield and some other charitable housing associations, many almshouses offer a licensee arrangement which does not provide the same security of tenure as some other tenancies. Where this is the case, it is strongly advised to have the proposed agreement checked by a lawyer or other expert to ensure you understand exactly what your rights are.

For further information, write to: **The Almshouse Association**, Billingbear Lodge, Wokingham, Berkshire RG11 5RU. T:0344 52922.

Housing for ethnic groups
ASRA Greater London Housing Association, 155 Kennington Park Road, London SE11 4JJ. T:071-820 0155. Provides sheltered housing for Asian elderly, single women and families.

ASRA Leicester, 58 Earl Howe Street, Highfield, Leicester LE1 0DF. T:0533 558121. Offers a similar service to the above.

Very sheltered schemes
A number of organisations which provide sheltered accommodation (including Abbeyfield, Servite Homes and the Salvation Army) also have *extra care* sheltered housing, designed for those who can no longer look after themselves without assistance in their own rooms. Priority would normally be given to existing tenants but others can apply. Cost is in the region of £155 a week; and about £240 in London. Although expensive, it is cheaper than most private residential homes and often more appropriate than full-scale nursing care.

A possible problem is that tenants of some of these schemes do not have security of tenure and could therefore be asked to leave if more intensive care were required. Further information should be obtainable from the various regional offices of the **Housing Corporation**, 149 Tottenham Court Road, London W1P 0BN.

Residential homes

There may come a time when it is no longer possible for an elderly person to manage without being in proper residential care. The accommodation usually consists of a bedroom plus communal dining rooms, lounges and gardens. All meals are provided, rooms are cleaned and staff are at hand to give whatever help is needed. Most homes are fully furnished, though it is usually possible to take small items of furniture. Except in some of the more expensive private nursing homes, bathrooms are normally shared. Proper nursing care is not usually included.

Homes are run by private individuals (or companies), voluntary organisations and local authorities. All private and voluntary homes should be registered with the Social Services to ensure minimum standards. Any unregistered home should not be considered.

No home should ever be accepted 'on spec'. It is very important that the individual should have a proper chance to visit it and ask any questions. Before reaching a final decision, it is a good idea to arrange a short stay to see whether the facilities are suitable and pleasant.

Private homes. Private rest homes tend to be smaller than those run by councils, taking from 5 to 30 people. They will normally continue to look after residents even when frail, although it may be necessary at some point to arrange transfer to a nursing home or hospital. Fees cover an enormous range starting from £175 a week to over £1,000.

Voluntary rest homes. These are run by charities, religious bodies or organisations that exist to care for retired members of certain professions, trades and crafts. Eligibility may also be determined by age, background or religion, depending on the criteria of the managing organisation. Fees start at around the £175 mark with top charges about £350 – and even higher for Greater London.

In cases of need, the local Social Services Department may assist with the fees; if they refuse, individuals can then apply to the Department of Social Security (DSS) for income support (see 'Financial assistance', page 311).

Local authority homes. These are sometimes referred to as 'Part III Accommodation'. In theory, any local resident who needs care and attention (but not nursing care) is eligible. In practice, there are often waiting lists and, except in an emergency, individuals normally have to wait a few months before being offered a place.

If someone does not like the particular accommodation suggested, they can turn it down and wait for another offer.

Weekly charges are set by each local authority, with the average cost being about £225. Regardless of income, there is a minimum fee of £43.30. In cases of need, the local authority may pay the balance. Alternatively, it may be possible to claim income support (see 'Financial assistance', page 311).

Nursing homes

Nursing homes provide medical supervision and fully qualified nurses, 24 hours a day. Most are privately run with the remainder being supported by voluntary organisations. All nursing homes must be registered with the local Health Authority which keeps a list of what homes are available in the area.

Private. Average fees are between £250 and £450 a week; in London, they start at around £350 – rising in some of the plusher nursing homes to over £1,000 weekly. In exceptional cases, district health authorities may help to meet the cost for a patient for whom there is no other suitable facility and income support from the Department of Social Services is available for qualifying patients. For information contact: **The Registered Nursing Home Association**, Calthorpe House, Hagley Road, Edgbaston, Birmingham B16 8QY. T:021-454 2511.

Voluntary organisations. There are normally very long waiting lists and beds are often reserved for those who have been in the charity's rest home. Charges in Greater London start at around £270. Social Services Departments will sometimes help with the fees in an emergency or if there is no other suitable facility. Voluntary organisations which run residential and nursing homes include: British Red Cross; Crossways Trust Ltd.; Friends of the Elderly and Gentlefolk's Help; Homelife-DGAA; Jewish Care; Quaker Social Responsibility and Education; Royal United Kingdom Beneficent Association; Women's Royal Voluntary Service; Catholic Old People's Homes.

Community Care. As from April 1993, the start date for Community Care, responsibility for helping to assess and co-ordinate the best arrangements for individuals needing residential or other care will pass from the DSS to the local authorities. From a practical point of view, this means that instead of approaching your local Social Security office, you should contact the Social Services Department. As well as helping to work out what services are most appropriate and get these organised, the Department will also streamline the financial arrangements for individuals qualifying for help.

Financial assistance
Provided individuals do not have savings of more than £8,000, income support is often available to help meet the cost of residential care and nursing home accommodation. For more information, see leaflet IS 50 *Income Support: Help for People Who Live in Residential Care Homes or Nursing Homes* from your local DSS office. Age Concern also publishes some useful factsheets: *Local Authorities and Residential Care* and *Income Support for Residential Homes and Nursing Care*.

Further information
Key sources of information about voluntary and private homes are: the *Charities Digest* (available in libraries, Housing Aid Centres and Citizens' Advice Bureaux) and the *Directory of Private Hospitals and Health Services* (available in libraries). Also useful, *Residential Care: Is it for Me?* Published by HMSO; price £2.95.

Elderly Accommodation Counsel, 46a Chiswick High Road, London W4 1SZ. T:081-995 8320. Has a nationwide computer register with details of all types of accommodation suitable to meet the needs of retired or elderly people including very sheltered housing, residential care, nursing homes and hospices. Use of the service costs £5 (fee waived in cases of limited income).

Grace, 35 Walnut Tree Close, Guildford, Surrey GU1 4UL. T:0483 304354. Provides a comprehensive advisory service for elderly people seeking private residential or nursing home accommodation. Grace advisers personally match accommodation with a client's needs, using detailed information from their computerised database. Experienced representatives assess homes annually and on change of ownership. A search fee of £23 is requested with details of exact requirements.

Social Services Departments keep lists of both voluntary and private homes.

Some special problems

A minority of people, as they become older, suffer from special problems which can cause great distress. Because families do not like to talk about them, they may be unaware of what services are available so may be missing out both on practical help and sometimes also on financial assistance.

Hypothermia
Elderly people tend to be more vulnerable to the cold. If the body drops below a certain temperature, it can be dangerous because one of the symptoms of hypothermia is that sufferers no longer actually feel cold. For this reason, during a cold snap it is very important to check up regularly on an elderly person living alone.

A useful source of help is the **Winter Warmth Line**, run by Help the Aged. This is a freephone advice service which – as well as offering practical information on beating the cold – can, if there is a particular problem, refer you to a relevant help agency in your area. The telephone number is 0800 289404. Help the Aged also distributes a useful Department of Health booklet *Keep Warm, Keep Well*, available free by calling the Winter Warmth Line.

Insulation can play a large part in keeping a home warmer and cheaper to heat. There are various grants available to assist with this. See heating and insulation sections in Chapter 8, Your Home.

Additionally, elderly and disabled people in receipt of income support who have savings of £3,000 or less can get help with heating costs during a particularly cold spell. See paragraph 'Cold Weather Payments' on page 301.

Incontinence
Incontinence can cause deep embarrassment to sufferers as well as inconvenience to relatives. A doctor should always be consulted, as it can often be cured or at least alleviated by proper treatment. To assist with the practical problems, many local authorities operate a laundry service which collects soiled linen, sometimes several times a week. In many areas the service is free and the person to talk to is the Health Visitor or District Nurse (telephone your local Health Centre) who will be able to advise about this and other facilities.

The Disabled Living Foundation runs a confidential advisory service on incontinence (Mondays) and also has couple of useful publications on the subject. For further information, contact: the Continence Adviser, **Disabled Living Foundation**, 380-384 Harrow Road, London W9 2HU. T:071-289 6111.

Dementia
Sometimes an elderly person can become confused, forgetful, suffer severe loss of memory or can have violent mood swings and at times be

abnormally aggressive. It is important to consult a doctor as soon as possible as the cause may be due to depression, stress or even vitamin deficiency, all of which can be treated and often completely cured.

If dementia is diagnosed, it is usually a good idea to talk to the Health Visitor, as she will know about local support services and can also arrange appointments with other professionals, such as the Community Psychiatric Nurse.

The charity, MIND, can often also help. Addresses to contact are:

MIND (National Association for Mental Health), for England, 22 Harley Street, London W1N 2ED. T:071-637 0741; for Wales, 23 St. Mary Street, Cardiff CF1 2AA. T:0222 395123.
Scottish Association for Mental Health, Atlantic House, 38 Gardners Crescent, Edinburgh EH3 8DQ. T:031-229 9687.
Northern Ireland Association for Mental Health, Beacon House, 80 University Street, Belfast BT7 1HE. T:0232 328474.

Another helpful organisation is: **Alzheimer's Disease Society**, for England and Wales and Northern Ireland, 158-160 Balham High Road, London SW12 9BN. T:081-675 6557; **Alzheimer's Scotland**, 33 Castle Street, Edinburgh EH2 3DN. T:031-225 1453. The Society publishes *Caring for the Person with Dementia* (£2.50 including p&p) and has local groups throughout the country: for addresses and other information, contact the London or Edinburgh office.

WORRIED ABOUT AN ELDERLY PARENT?

CARE OPTIONS FOR THE ELDERLY
3 ORWELL ROAD, BARRINGTON, CAMBRIDGE CB2 5SE
TELEPHONE (0223) 872884

IS SOMEONE YOU CARE ABOUT NO LONGER COPING ON THEIR OWN? DO YOU NEED INDEPENDENT, IMPARTIAL ADVICE ABOUT ALL THE CARE OPTIONS, AND WHAT THEY COST? WE HELP PEOPLE TO STAY IN THEIR OWN HOME FOR AS LONG AS POSSIBLE, AND ALSO ADVISE ON HOW TO CHOOSE A CARE HOME. DON'T WAIT FOR A CRISIS, MAKE SOME CONTINGENCY PLANS NOW. RING US FOR A BROCHURE, OR TO ARRANGE A MEETING.

CAREQUEST
CARE OPTIONS FOR THE ELDERLY

In the next 20 years the number of people over the age of 85 will increase by almost two-thirds. This means that many entering their "Third Age" will spend part of it caring for an elderly relative.

Where to go for help and advice? The social work department of the local authority is a good starting place, but although "Care in the Community" is an excellent concept, resources are limited. For those with savings in excess of £8,000, there is little on offer other than the invaluable "Attendance Allowance". Age Concern has branches in most towns, and is an excellent source of local intelligence.

A new independent advisory and counselling service has been set up by "CareQuest". They offer a face to face meeting at which the individual's circumstances, preferences, and financial options can be considered in detail, and a plan of action proposed. They offer impartial advice for a fee, and are not associated with any service provider.

Most people who are gradually losing independence, would rather stay in their own home for as long as possible. With appropriate aids and adaptations, and part-time or full-time care this should be possible. Eventually a residential or nursing home may be the solution. CareQuest can advise on how to adapt the home, arrange staffing at home, or choose residential care. They can also recommend financial advisors to plan the funding of care.

Carequest is based in Cambridge, covering East Anglia and the northern Home Counties, but they also see clients in London.

Westgate House, 3 Orwell Road, Barrington, Cambs. CB2 5SE
Telephone/Fax/Answerphone (0223) 872884

CECIL HOUSES
Caring homes for the old and young

Founded in 1926, Cecil Houses provides residential care homes and sheltered flats for elderly men and women and direct access hostels for homeless women.

Cecil Houses provides very special personal care to all its residents and we rely heavily on the support of the community to fund our work.

A legacy or donation will help us, for more information please contact:
The Director, Cecil Houses,
2a Priory Road, Kew, Richmond, Surrey, TW9 3DG.
Tel: 081-940 9828.

Chapter 15

No One is Immortal

In Bali death is celebrated with glorious processions, merry-making and days of feasting. In Western society, we go to the other extreme. Many couples never even discuss death or the financial practicalities, in the subconscious belief perhaps that to do so would be tempting fate. For the same reason, many people put off making a will or rationalise that it does not really matter, since in any case their possessions will eventually go to their family. However, as every widows' organisation would testify, a great deal of heartbreak and real financial worry could be avoided if husbands and wives were more open with each other.

Wills

Anyone who is married, has children or is over the age of 35 should make a will. At very least, should anything happen, this will ensure that their wishes are known and properly executed. But also very important, it will spare their family the legal complications that arise when someone dies intestate. A major problem if someone dies without leaving a will is that the surviving husband or wife will usually have to wait very much longer for badly needed cash. There will be no executor. Also, the individual's assets will be distributed according to a rigid formula, which may be a far cry from what he or she had intended.

Making a will

You have three choices: you can do it yourself; you can ask your bank to help you; or you can use a solicitor.

Doing it yourself
Homemade wills are not generally recommended. People often use ambiguous wording which, while perfectly clear to the individual who has written it, may be less patently obvious to others. This could result in the

donor's wishes being misinterpreted and could also cause considerable delay in settling the estate.

You can buy forms from W.H. Smith and other stationers which, while helpful, are not perfect and still leave considerable margin for error. Alternatively you could purchase the *Which?* Action Pack entitled *Make Your Will*, which, in addition to a number of forms, contains guidance on inheritance tax and other helpful information. The text is based on the law as it applies in England and Wales and is therefore not pertinent to residents of Scotland and Northern Ireland.

For individuals with sight difficulties, RNIB has produced a comprehensive guide to making or changing a will which is available in large print size, Braille and on tape, as well as in standard print size. This is obtainable free by contacting Hilary Partridge at RNIB, 224 Great Portland Street, London W1N 6AA. T:071-388 1266.

Two witnesses are needed and an essential point to remember is that beneficiaries cannot witness a will; nor can the spouses of any beneficiaries. In certain circumstances, a will can be rendered invalid. A sensible precaution for anyone doing it themselves is to have it checked by a solicitor or by a legal expert from the Citizens' Advice Bureau.

Banks

Advice on wills and the administration of estates is carried out by the trustee companies of most of the major high street banks.

In particular, the services they offer are: to provide general guidance, to act as executor and to administer the estate. They will also introduce clients to a solicitor and keep a copy of the will – plus other important documents – in their safe, to avoid the risk of their being mislaid. Additionally, banks (as solicitors) can give tax planning and other financial guidance, including advice on inheritance tax. Some banks will draw up a will for you.

Solicitors

Solicitors offer to: draw up a will, act as executors and administer the estate. Like banks, they will also of course hold a copy of your will in safe keeping. If you do not know a solicitor, you can ask your bank or the Citizens' Advice Bureau. Or you can write to the **Law Society**, 113 Chancery Lane, London WC2A 1PL. T:071-242 1222.

Charges

These can vary enormously, depending on the size and complexity of the will. A basic will could be as little as £50 or the cost could run into many hundreds of pounds. Always ask for an estimate before proceeding. Remember too that professional fees carry 17.5 per cent VAT.

Solicitors charge according to the time they spend on a job, so although the actual work may not take very long, if you spend hours discussing your will, or changing it every few months, the costs can escalate considerably.

Legal aid
Legal aid is available to certain groups of people for making a will. These include, among one or two other categories: people aged over 70, people with a mental disorder and those who are blind, deaf or have no speech. Additionally, to qualify, they will need to satisfy the financial criteria. For further information enquire at your CAB.

Executors
You will need to appoint at least one executor to administer your will. An executor can be a beneficiary under the estate and can be a member of your family or a friend whom you trust to act impartially, always provided of course that he/she is willing to accept the responsibility. Or, and this is generally advisable for larger estates, you could appoint your solicitor or bank.

The fees will be additional. They are not paid at the time of making the will but instead come out of the estate. Pretty significant sums could be involved, so the advice on obtaining an estimate is, if anything, even more relevant. In certain instances, banks can be more expensive; in others, solicitors. The only way to discover is to get an estimate from each.

Banks publish a tariff of their charges. Solicitors render bills according to the time involved; so, although it is impossible for them to be precise, they should nevertheless be able to give a pretty accurate assessment – at least at the time of quoting. Both banks' and solicitors' fees may increase during the interval between their being appointed and fulfilling their duties as executor.

Other points
Wills should always be kept in a safe place – and their whereabouts known. The most sensible arrangement is for the solicitor to keep the original and for the bank to have a copy.

A helpful initiative devised by the Law Society is a mini-form, known as a Personal Assets Log. This is for individuals drawing up a will to give to their executor or close relatives. It is, quite simply, a four-sided leaflet with space to record the essential information: name and address of solicitor; where the will and other important documents – for example, share certificates and insurance policies – are kept; the date of any codicils and so on. Logs should be obtainable from most solicitors.

Wills may need updating in the event of an important change of circumstances, for example: a divorce, remarriage or the birth of a grandchild. An existing will becomes invalid in the event of marriage or remarriage and should be revised. Any changes must be by codicil (for minor alterations) or by a new will, and must be properly witnessed.

Partners who wish to leave all their possessions to each other should consider including 'a survivorship clause' in their wills, as an insurance against the intestacy rules being applied were they both to be involved in the same fatal accident.

If you have views about your funeral, it is sensible to write a letter to your executors explaining your wishes and to lodge it with your will. If you have any pets, you may equally wish to leave a letter filed with your will explaining what arrangements you have made for their immediate/long-term welfare. The charity PRO Dogs provides special cards for this purpose for owners to complete, obtainable from: **PRO Dogs**, National Head Office, Rocky Bank, 4 New Road, Ditton, Maidstone, Kent ME20 6AD. T:0732 848499.

Money worries – and how to minimise them

Most people say that the first time they really think about death, in terms of what would happen to their nearest and dearest, is after the birth of their first baby. As children grow up, requirements change but key points that any family man or woman should consider – and review from time to time – include life insurance and mortgage protection relief.

Both husbands and wives should have **life insurance cover**. If either were to die, not only would their partner lose the benefit of their earnings, they would also lose the value of their services: home decorating, gardening, cooking and so forth.

Most banks and building societies urge homeowners to take out **mortgage protection schemes**. If you die, the loan is paid off automatically and the family home will not be repossessed. Banks also offer **insurance to cover any personal or other loans**. This could be a vital safeguard to avoid leaving the family with debts.

Many people worry about **funeral costs**. These can vary, according to different parts of the country, from £700 to £1,250 or even more depending on the choice of coffin and other arrangements. Although you may well hear of cheaper estimates, these are normally exclusive of disbursements which have to be made to the vicar and others.

As a way of helping, a number of insurance companies offer savings plans to cover funeral costs and while these could be sensible, a drawback is that you are budgeting today against an unknown cost in the future.

A rather different type of scheme, which overcomes the uncertainties and is growing in popularity, is the pre-paid funeral plan which is designed so you pay all the costs in advance, so sparing your family the worry of finding the money at the time.

One such scheme is the Guaranteed Funeral Plan offered by **Chosen Heritage**, which is available through Age Concern. Another is **Perfect Assurance**, which is a 'bespoke' policy tailored to individual requirements, offered by: National Association of Funeral Directors, 618 Warwick Road, Solihull, West Midlands B91 1AA. T:021-711 1343.

Those in receipt of income support may qualify for a payment from the Social Fund to help with funeral costs. For details of eligibility and how you claim, see Leaflet D 49, *What To Do After a Death*, obtainable from any Social Security office. If the matter is urgent, make a point of asking for Form SF 200.

A very real crisis for some families is the need for immediate money while waiting for the estate to be settled. At least part of the problem can be overcome by couples having a **joint bank account**, with both partners having drawing rights without the signature of the other being required. Sole-name bank accounts and joint accounts requiring both signatures are frozen.

For the same reason, it may also be a good idea for any savings or investments to be held in the joint name of the couple. However, couples who have recently made any changes – or were planning to do so – as a result of independent taxation could be advised to discuss this point with a solicitor or qualified financial adviser. Additionally, an essential practical point for all couples is that any financial and other **important documents should be discussed together** and understood by the wife as well as by the husband. Even today, an all too common saga is for widows to come across insurance policies and other papers, which they have never seen before and do not understand – often causing quite unnecessary anxiety. A further common-sense 'must' is for both partners to **know where important papers are kept**. Best idea is either to lock them, filed together, in a home safe; or to give them to the bank to look after.

If someone dies, **the bank manager should be notified as soon as possible**, so he can assist with the problems of unpaid bills and help to work out a solution until the estate is settled. The same goes for the **suppliers of essential services**: gas, electricity, telephone and so on. Unless they know the situation, there is a risk of services being cut off if there is a delay in paying the bill. Add too any credit card companies, where if bills lie neglected, the additional interest could mount up alarmingly.

Retirement Made Easy

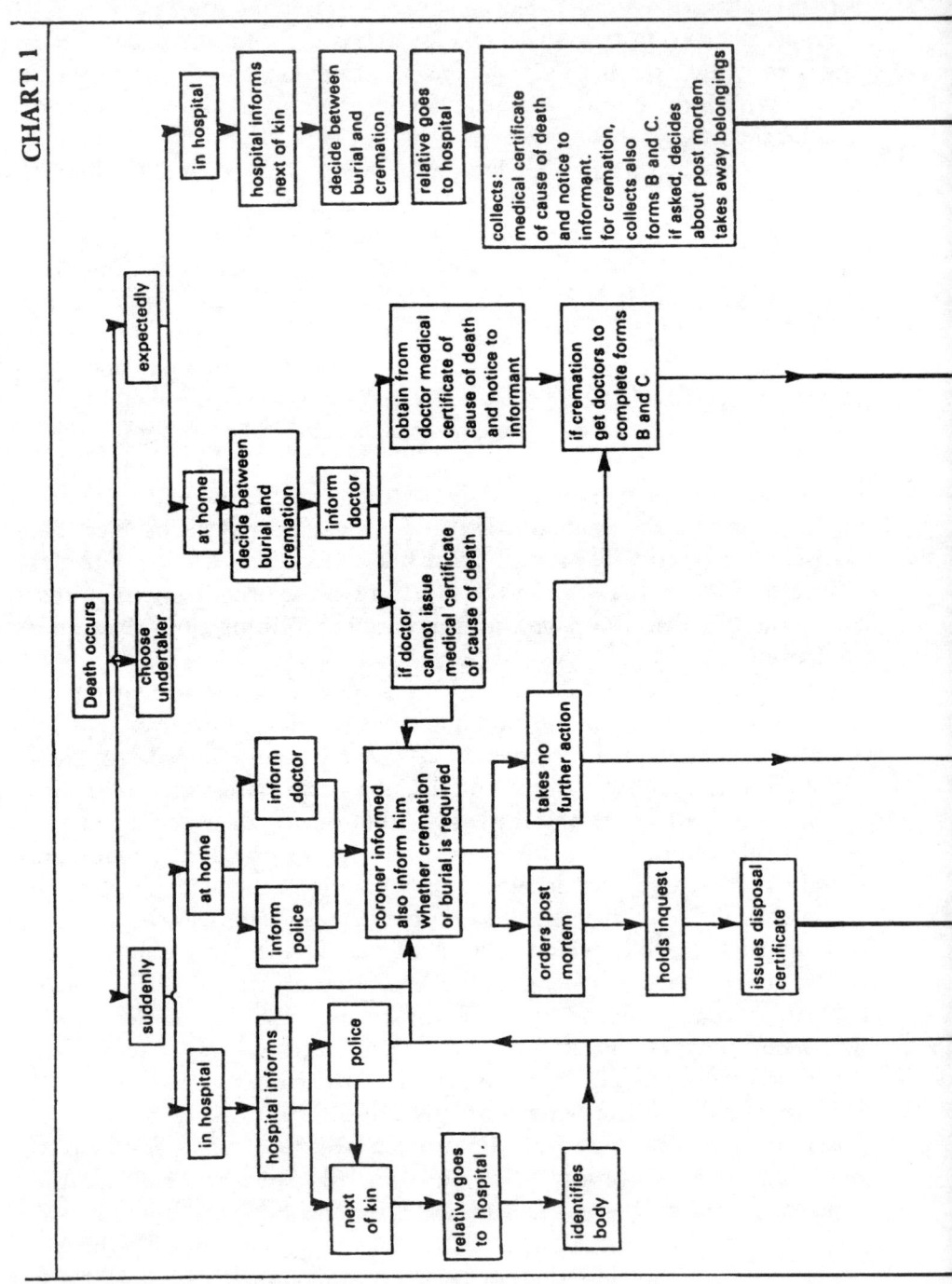

CHART 1

No One is Immortal

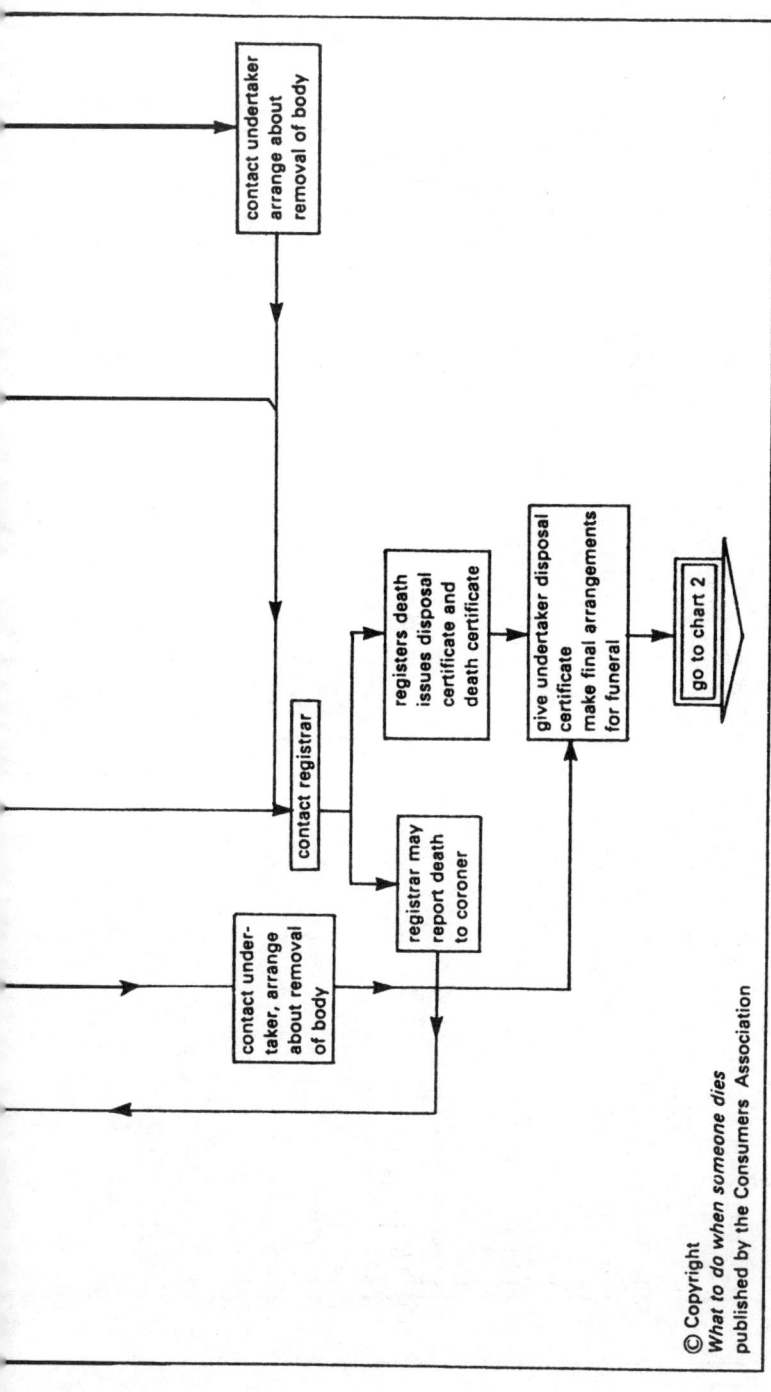

© Copyright
What to do when someone dies
published by the Consumers Association

Retirement Made Easy

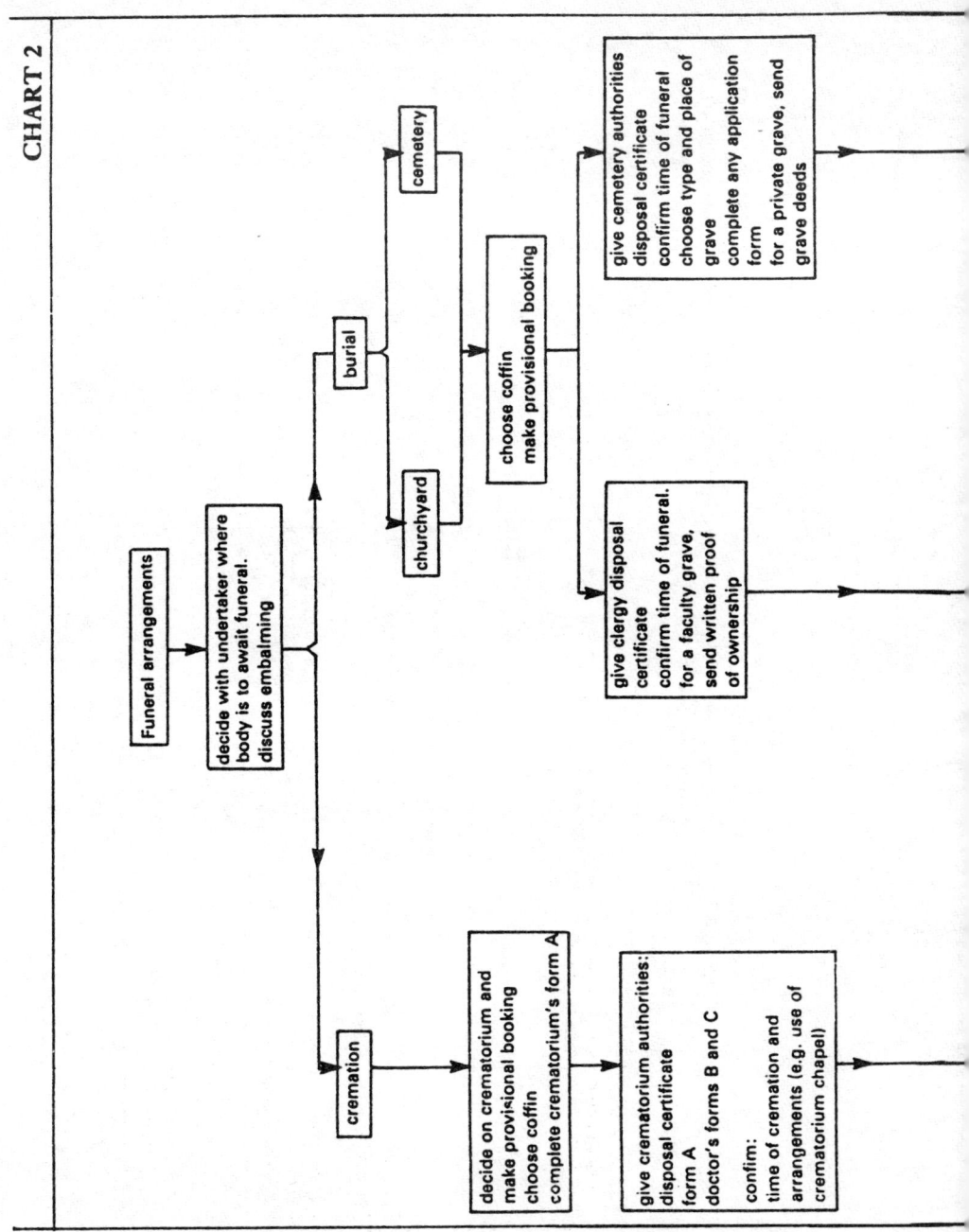

CHART 2

No One is Immortal

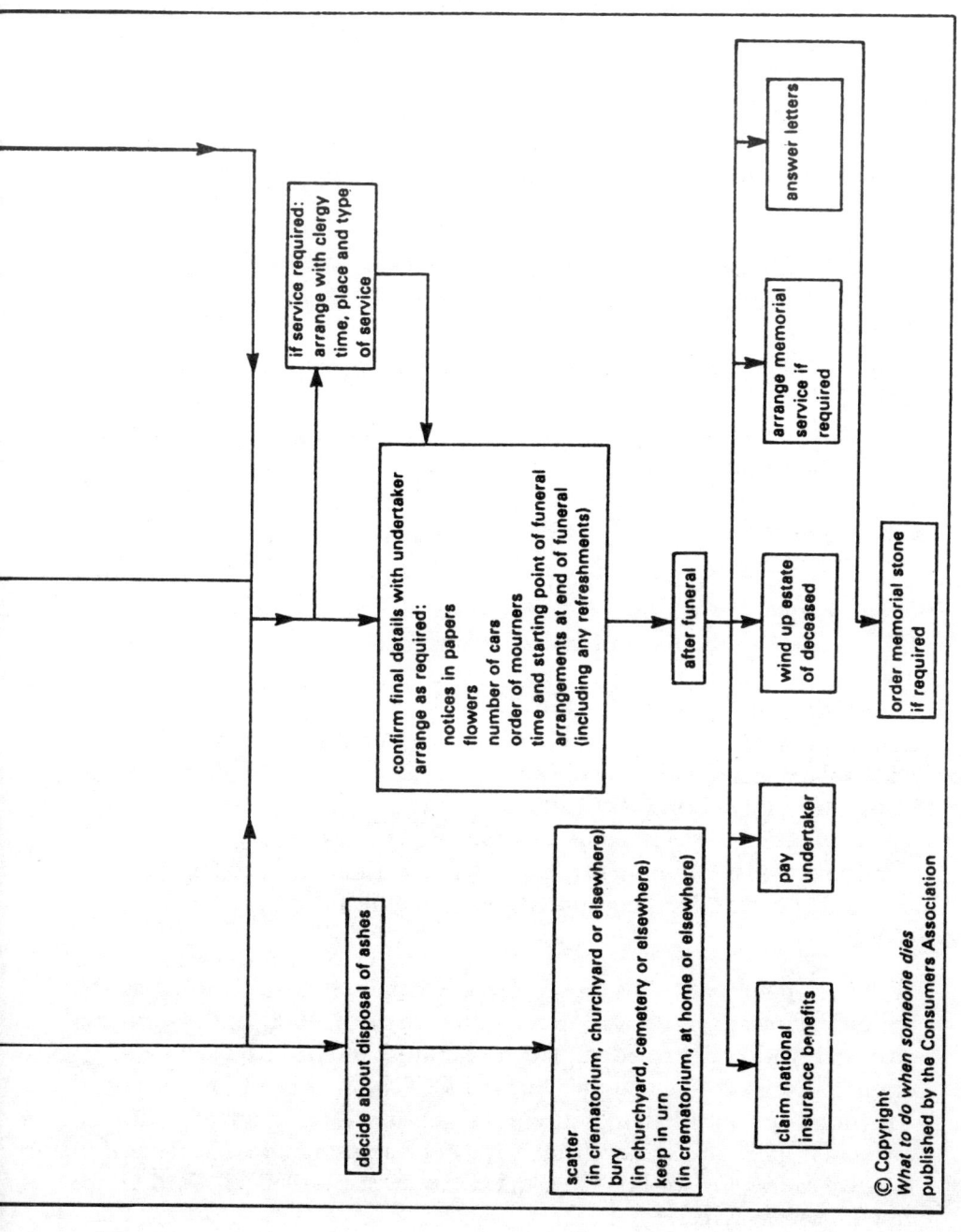

What to do when someone dies

There are formalities to be observed and arrangements to be made. The two charts on pages 320 to 323, published by courtesy of Consumers' Association, whose book, *What To Do When Someone Dies*, provides a fund of practical information, illustrate what action is required.

The first chart deals with the period immediately after death; the second, with the necessary arrangements for a funeral.

Useful reading
What To Do When Someone Dies and *Make Your Will* Action Pack; £9.99 each. Available from Consumers' Association, Gascoyne Way, Hertford X, SG14 1LH.

What To Do After a Death. Free booklet from your local Social Security office.

Making Your Will and *Arranging a Funeral*, free factsheets from Age Concern England (enclose sae).

State benefits, tax and other money points

Some extra financial benefits are given to widows and, in more limited circumstances, to widowers. Several take the form of a cash payment. Others come in the form of a relief against tax.

Benefits paid in cash

There are three important cash benefits to which widows may be entitled: widows' payment, widows' pension and widowed mother's allowance. To claim these, fill in Form BW 1, obtainable from any Social Security office. You will also be given a questionnaire (BD 8) by the Registrar. It is important that you complete this as it acts as a trigger to speed up payment of your benefits. All leaflets quoted are obtainable from any Social Security office.

Widows' payment. This has replaced what used to be known as the widows' allowance. It is a tax-free lump sum of £1,000, paid as soon as a woman is widowed provided that: (1) her husband had paid sufficient NI contributions (2) she is under 60; *or* (3) if she is over 60, her husband had not been entitled to retirement pension. Her claim will not be affected if she is already receiving a State pension, *provided this is based on her own contributions*. For more information, see leaflet NP 45 *A Guide to Widows' Benefits*.

Widowed mother's allowance. This is paid to mothers with at least one child for whom they receive child benefit. The value is £54.15 a week.

The allowance is usually paid automatically. If, for some reason, although eligible, you do not receive it, you should inform your local Social Security office. See leaflet NP 45.

Child dependency addition. This is a payment of £10.85 a week for each dependent child except for the eldest, for whom payment is only £9.75. The reason for the lower payment is because the eldest (or only) child is already receiving an extra pound in child benefit. Information about child dependency addition is included in leaflet NP 45.

Widows' pension. There are various levels of widows' pension: the full rate which is described immediately below, and age-related widows' pension, which is described in the following paragraph.

Full-rate widows' pension is paid to widows who are between the ages of 55 and 59 inclusive when their husband dies; or when they cease to receive widowed mother's allowance. The weekly amount is £54.15, which is the same as the retirement pension received by a single person. Widows' pension is normally paid once you have sent off your completed form BW1; so if for any reason you do not receive the pension after about three weeks, you should enquire at your local Social Security office. Prior to April 1988, younger widows from the age of 50 qualified for the full rate. If you were already receiving this, your benefits are not affected by the age change and you can continue claiming the full benefit even though you may not yet be 55. For further information, see leaflet NP 45.

Age-related widows' pension. This is a pension for younger widows, who do not qualify for a full widows' pension. It is payable to a widow who is aged between 45 and 54 inclusive, when her husband dies; or when her widowed mother's allowance ceases to be paid. Rates depend on age and vary from £16.25 for 45-year-olds to £50.36 for those aged 54. As with full-rate widows' pension, the qualifying ages were changed in April 1988. Widows already receiving age-related pension prior to this date are not affected. For further information, see leaflet NP 45.

Retirement pension. Once a widow reaches age 60, she may choose whether to continue with her widows' pension or whether to receive retirement pension. After her 65th birthday, she no longer has a choice and will get retirement pension. If she is over 60 when her husband dies, she will usually receive a retirement pension rather than a widows' pension. If at the time of death the couple were already getting the State retirement pension, the widow will be entitled to her husband's share of their joint pension, if this is higher than her own.

An important point to remember is that a widow may be able to use her late husband's NI contributions to boost the amount she receives. See leaflets NP 46 *A Guide to Retirement Pension* and FB 6 *Retiring? Your Pension and Other Benefits*. **N.B.** A widower getting a retirement pension at less than the full rate may be able to use his late wife's NI contributions to get more pension.

Problems. As you will probably know, pension payments – including widows' pension – are dependent on sufficient NI contributions having been paid. Your Social Security office will inform you if you are not eligible. If this should turn out to be the case, you may still be entitled to receive income support, family credit, housing benefit or a grant or loan from the social fund – so ask. If you are unsure of your position or have difficulties, ask at your Citizens' Advice Bureau who will at least be able to help you work out the sums and inform you of your rights.

Particular points to note

- Most widows' benefits are taxable. However, the £1,000 lump sum widow's payment is tax free, as are war widows' pensions and the child dependency allowance.
- A reduced rate of benefit may be paid if there are any gaps in the husband's national insurance record.
- There is no widowers' pension. However, on retirement, a widower can substitute part of his late wife's contribution record for his own if this would be more beneficial.
- A widower with dependent children will receive child benefit; and normally also the £5.85 a week one-parent benefit for the first child.
- Men and women widowed after April 1979 will normally be able to inherit their spouse's additional pension rights, if he/she contributed to SERPS; or at least half their guaranteed minimum pension, if they were in a contracted-out scheme. Additionally, where applicable, all widows are entitled on retirement to half the graduated pension earned by their husband. Likewise, a widower can receive on retirement half the graduated retirement benefit based on his late wife's contributions.
- Widows who remarry, or live with a man as his wife, cease to receive widows' pension. They will, however, continue to receive a retirement pension if they remarry when they are aged 60 or over. A widow who has cohabited and loses her entitlement to a widows' pension will, if the cohabitation ends, be entitled to claim it again.

Tax and tax allowances
Widows and widowers receive the normal single person's tax allowance of £3,445 a year. If they have dependent children, they should also claim the additional personal allowance of £1,720 for single parents. A widower is entitled to continue claiming the married couple's allowance until the end of the tax year in which his partner dies.

Widow's bereavement allowance. This is an extra allowance, worth £1,720 a year at current rates, specially given to widows to assist them over the first difficult period. The only qualification is that a widow's late husband must have been entitled to the married couple's tax allowance at the time of his death. The allowance is given from the date she became widowed up to the second 5 April following her bereavement. Both widows and widowers are also entitled to any unused portion of the married couple's allowance in the year of their partner's death.

Useful Inland Revenue leaflets. These are available from any tax office.

IR 91:	*A Guide for Widows and Widowers*
IR 90:	*Independent Taxation: A Guide to Tax Allowances and Reliefs*
IHT 3:	*An Introduction to Inheritance Tax*
IR 45:	*Income Tax and CGT – What Happens When Someone Dies.*

Advice. Many people have difficulty in working out exactly what they are entitled to – and how to claim it. The Citizens Advice Bureau is always very helpful. Additionally, Cruse and the National Association of Widows (see below) can also assist you.

Organisations that can help

Problems vary. For some, the hardest thing to bear is the loneliness of returning to an empty house. For others, money problems seem to dominate everything else. For many older women in particular, who have not got a job, widowhood creates a great gulf where for a while there is no real sense of purpose. Many widowed men and women go through a spell of feeling enraged against their partner for dying. Most are baffled and hurt by the seeming indifference of friends, who appear more embarrassed than sympathetic.

In time, all these feelings soften, problems diminish and individuals are able to recapture their joy for living with all its many pleasures. Talking to other people who know the difficulties from their own experience can be a tremendous help. The following organisations not only offer opportunities for companionship but also provide an advisory and support service.

Cruse, Cruse House, 126 Sheen Road, Richmond, Surrey TW9 1UR. T:081-940 4818. This is a national organisation for anyone who has been bereaved, with over 185 branches throughout Britain. It offers a counselling and advice service, including visiting the bereaved in their own home where there is a local branch. Additionally, Cruse publishes a wide range of informative leaflets.

The branches organise their own programmes which typically include: meetings with a speaker, theatre outings, rambles and dances. There is a monthly newsletter. National membership is £10 a year. Addresses of local branches can be obtained by contacting the headquarters above.

National Association of Widows, 54-57 Allison Street, Digbeth, Birmingham B5 5TH. T:021-643 8348. The Association is a national voluntary organisation which offers a free and confidential advice and information service. Its many branches provide a supportive social network for widows throughout the country. Membership is £5 a year.

Many professional and other groups offer a range of services for widows and widowers associated with them. Equally, many local **Age Concern** groups offer a counselling service. Trade unions are often particularly supportive, as are Rotary Clubs, all the armed forces organisations and most benevolent societies.

YOU'RE NOT A NURSE
YOU'RE NOT A DOCTOR
YOU'RE NOT A SCIENTIST...

...SO HOW CAN YOU HELP TO CURE A CHILD'S LEUKAEMIA?

You could play a vital role in helping to save the lives of many leukaemia sufferers, both children and adults, by remembering The Anthony Nolan Bone Marrow Trust in your will.

Every year, there are thousands of sufferers of leukaemia and related diseases, for whom a bone marrow transplant is the only hope.

However, as the patients' and the donors' bone marrow must be compatible, it is necessary for us to continue enlisting volunteer donors to further build upon what is now Europe's largest Register of Potential Bone Marrow Donors, providing Matched Unrelated Donors for transplants every week.

For each volunteer there is an expensive process of testing and tissue typing; demand for our services is increasing all the time and in turn, there is an ever-increasing need of funds to support both continued research and the continuing development of the Register.

Please help, your contribution could be **a legacy for life**.

For further information, please contact:

**THE ANTHONY NOLAN BONE MARROW TRUST,
THE ROYAL FREE HOSPITAL, POND STREET,
HAMPSTEAD, LONDON NW3 2QG
TEL: 071-431 5306**
Registered Charity No. 803716

The Anthony Nolan Bone Marrow Trust is Europe's largest register of 190,000 volunteer bone marrow donors.

IF YOU'VE FOUGHT HEART DISEASE YOU'LL APPRECIATE WHAT A LEGACY TO THE BRITISH HEART FOUNDATION CAN DO.

Research funded by the British Heart Foundation has helped save lives and improve the quality of life for many patients and families. Sadly, with 110,000 people dying prematurely from heart disease every year, there's still a lot to do. To continue our work we rely solely on your generosity. Leaving a legacy is one of the best ways you can help. If you would like to know more about the British Heart Foundation and how your legacy could help generations to come, please write to: British Heart Foundation, 14 Fitzhardinge Street, London W1H 4DH. Tel: 071-935 0185.

Reg. Charity No. 225971

TAKE HEART. WE'RE HERE.

British Heart Foundation

LET'S PUT IT STRAIGHT...

- **NAME:** Scoliosis or curvature of the spine.
- **VICTIMS:** World-wide problem, over 2000 affected every year within the U.K. alone.
- **SYMPTOMS:** If untreated it can cause a disabling condition — leading to respiratory diseases and premature death.
- **REMEDY:** With your help we can further the ability to detect the disease in its early stages, practise the best methods of treating it and ultimately discover the cause.
- **ACTION:** Remember Scoliosis when writing your will or making a donation to charity.

The British Scoliosis Foundation
incorporating
The Phillip Zorab Scoliosis Research Fund
Westwinds, Stanley Avenue, Beckenham, Kent BR3 2PU
Tel: 081-650 5244   Fax: (081-650 5244)   Charity No. 803772

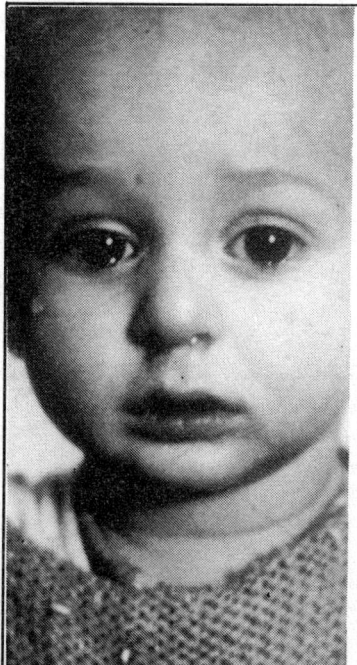

TAKING THE AID DIRECT

"On one floor there were 50 children, all suffering from malnutrition. Children aged 6 months only weighed 10 pounds. On another floor there were 40 babies suffering from severe respiratory diseases. The doctor showed me babies that would not survive for more than a few days unless they received antibiotics. I cannot describe the look on the faces of the doctors and nurses when they realised that all the drugs and equipment they sought were actually on the lorry."

FTC volunteer delivering emergency aid

Your legacy will make the continuation of this work possible

FEED THE CHILDREN
1 PRIORY AVENUE, CAVERSHAM, READING,
BERKSHIRE RG4 7SE TEL: 0734 464444
REGISTERED CHARITY NO. 803236

FORGET ABOUT FUNERAL COSTS!

- Chosen Heritage provides a guaranteed funeral when required, at any point in the future, **from as little as £695** inclusive.
- Chosen Heritage spares trouble and expense for your family.
- Chosen Heritage gives you peace of mind, knowing that all the arrangements are made and paid for.

Thousands of people have joined the Chosen Heritage scheme so they can forget about funeral costs. These are **not insurance policies** but a practical way to make arrangements in advance.

Simply return this coupon for your **FREE BROCHURE** or call **now** on **FREEPHONE 0800 525 555.**

Absolutely no obligation. No salesman will call. Completely confidential.

RECOMMENDED BY
AGE Concern

selected 'Best Buy' in recent survey

**CHOSEN HERITAGE
FREEPOST
EAST GRINSTEAD RH19 1ZA**
CUSTODIAN TRUSTEE, BARCLAYS BANK PLC

Please send me your brochure:

Name _____

Address _____

_____

_____ Postcode _____

WHEN A DEAF CHILD TALKS, OUR WORK SPEAKS FOR ITSELF

The **ELIZABETH FOUNDATION** Family Centre in Portsmouth provides vital early detection of deafness, as well as education and support, for both parents and their deaf children. This help is also given to parents Nationally through our Correspondence and Advisory Course. All our services are FREE to parents of deaf children and are funded from voluntary donations.

WE are special.

YOU can do something special.

Remember **US** in your will.

THE ELIZABETH FOUNDATION FOR DEAF CHILDREN

Dept. GRG Southwick Hill Road Cosham PORTSMOUTH PO6 3LU
Tel: (0705) 372735 Fax: (0705) 326155
Registered Charity No. 293835

MOST CHILDREN WALK AND TALK FOR FREE. SOME ONLY DO IT WITH MONEY.

I CAN students and pupils overcome all sorts of disabilities. But it costs a lot of time, experience and money.

We've got an endless amount of time and over 100 years of experience. But money is in shorter supply.

Why not suggest I CAN when drawing up your clients' wills?

Every penny goes towards educating for independence.

I CAN, 10 Bowling Green Lane, London EC1R 0BD. Tel: 071-253 9111.

'I CAN'
INVALID CHILDREN'S AID NATIONWIDE

Reg. Charity No. 210031. Patron HM the Queen. President: HRH The Princess Margaret, Countess of Snowdon.

GIVE GENEROUSLY TO SAVE SIGHT

Every year in the U.K. thousands of people go blind. Successful eye research can save sight. In 1991, the sight of 2,000 people was saved as a result of successful corneal transplant operations using corneas from our Eye Bank.

Your legacy or donation can help run the Eye Bank and develop much needed research into the causes and treatment of eye diseases and the prevention of blindness.

Sight is precious, please be generous.

NATIONAL EYE RESEARCH CENTRE
Bristol Hospital, Lower Maudlin Street, Bristol BS1 2LX. Tel: 0272 290024
(Registered Charity 294087)

HALCYON DAYS or HARD TIMES?

A happy and fulfilling retirement, as opposed to a bleak and uncertain future, is the result of careful and accurate financial planning.

Boyton Financial Services Limited (BFS) has developed a highly refined and comprehensive service that will quickly highlight potential shortfalls in your current arrangements.

And, BFS is one of the few independent firms of advisers that only operates on a time spent, fee charging basis.

It is never too late for you to seek our professional advice – we could make a considerable difference to your life style in the years ahead.

Telephone or write to:
BOYTON FINANCIAL SERVICES LIMITED, PO BOX 14, HALSTEAD, ESSEX, CO9 4DY.
TELEPHONE: 0787 61919

BOYTON FINANCIAL SERVICES LTD
Member of the Financial Intermediaries and Brokers Regulatory Association

When you're dying the last thing you want is excuses

working for *your* rights — your right to treatment — **your right to live**

NATIONAL KIDNEY FEDERATION
caring for kidney patients

6 Stanley Street, Worksop S81 7HX
Tel: 0909 487795 Fax: 0909 481723
Registered Charity No 278616
DONATIONS AND BEQUESTS MOST GRATEFULLY RECEIVED

Erskine Hospital needs to raise more than £1 million in public donations every year to provide medical care and special facilities for our many disabled residents.

That's why it's so important that people remember us when they make a will.

Legacies or bequests should be made available to The Princess Louise Scottish Hospital (Erskine Hospital), Bishopton, Renfrewshire. Correspondence to Treasurer I.W. Grimmond, B.Acc, C.A. at the hospital.
Telephone 041-812 1100.   **ERSKINE**

IT'S MIGHTIER THAN THE SWORD.

WHAT IS PSORIASIS?

ALTHOUGH much is known about the triggers and the course of this skin disease which affects approximately ONE AND A HALF MILLION PEOPLE IN THE UNITED KINGDOM, to date, it has not been possible to solve the mystery of the basic causes. HELP US in our fight to find a cure or control for this distressing condition by leaving us something in your Will for Research.

MORE and More Research is being done and interest is high in the Laboratories. Over the last two years the Psoriasis Association has given over a QUARTER OF A MILLION POUNDS to Research Projects in various centres.

Further details of Research Supported and of other aspects of our work can be obtained from:-

MRS. LINDA HENLEY, National Secretary,

The

PSORIASIS

Association   Registered Charity No. 257414
Milton House, 7 Milton Street, Northampton, NN2 7JG
Tel: (0604) 711129 Fax: (0604) 792894

A charity that doesn't want your money.

We can't expect it. We have no right to it. Because we're neither high-profile nor fashionable, you might not even know us.

The best we can hope for is that you find out more about us. About the crucial work we do with children, young people and adults who have learning difficulties. About the awful problems that simple phrase disguises.

And when you know more about us, if you want to help, all we ask is that you consider leaving us something in your Will. Something for those who are just learning to live.

Please write or phone and let us send you our literature.

**1st Floor, Princess House,
105-107 Princess Street,
Manchester M1 6DD
Tel: 061 236 5358**

Rathbone
Helping people with Learning Difficulties

EVERY YEAR WE TAKE MORE PEOPLE UNDER OUR WING

Be they aircrew or ground staff. Be they ex-RAF or serving RAF members. Be they their spouses or their dependent children.

We help them overcome financial difficulties caused through no fault of their own.

Last year we helped in 16,000 ways to the tune of an average of over £21,000 for every day of the year, including Christmas day. This amounts to £7.99 million. This year, we'll need to be there for many more people and even more next year.

By sending us a donation now and by remembering us in your Will you will help ensure that we are.

COMRADES IN ARMS SHOULD BE COMRADES IN ALMS

To: The Royal Air Force Benevolent Fund, 67 Portland Place, London W1N 4AR. Tel: 071-580 8343. Ext 257. Or in Scotland: 20 Queen Street, Edinburgh EH2 1JX

☐ I would like to make a donation of £_____ by postal order/cheque (delete as applicable)
☐ Please charge my Access/Visa/American Express/Diners Club Number
⬚⬚⬚⬚⬚⬚⬚⬚⬚⬚⬚⬚⬚⬚⬚⬚ Expiry date ___/___
☐ Please send details of making a legacy/covenant
☐ Please send information on making a Will

NAME
ADDRESS
POSTCODE
SIGNATURE

MRG92

Charity Reg No. 207327

THE ROYAL AIR FORCE BENEVOLENT FUND

THE ROYAL SCHOOL FOR DEAF CHILDREN MARGATE
200th ANNIVERSARY 1792 - 1992
Patron: Her Majesty Queen Elizabeth the Queen Mother

A proper start in life . . .

We are more than just a school for the deaf – nearly half of our pupils have other handicaps too. Hearing children know hundreds, perhaps thousands of words when they start school. At Margate the children are lucky if they know a few dozen. They are profoundly deaf – to most noises, to almost all speech. A proper start in life for those youngsters would be cheap at any price.

We also have a unit that caters especially for the multiple handicapped profoundly deaf and the deaf/blind.

There are two units outside the main school that are for the over 16 year olds. These cater for work and life skills programmes and training in independent living. A third unit of six self-contained flats allows some to experience independence whilst help is near at hand.

To continue providing these specialised facilities requires a constant income from donations and legacies. Please help us to help them gain a PROPER START IN LIFE.

Registered Office: Victoria Road, Margate, Kent CT9 1NB.
Telephone: Thanet 227561
REGISTERED CHARITY No: 325109

Leave a legacy to The Salvation Army

Every day, we care for more than 10,000 people in the UK alone. We are a friend to the helpless, the lonely and the desperate.

We provide comfort and <u>practical support</u> worldwide – community centres, homes for children and the elderly, and essential emergency services.

If you are making a will, please think of the needy, and the vital help The Salvation Army can give to them.

Thank you

H1

The Salvation Army, Dept. LA20, 101 Queen Victoria Street, London EC4P 4EP. Telephone 071-236 5222.

Trusting him to do it for himself every day will be even more painful.

Any parent whose child suffers from diabetes dreads their child's first day at school.

Suddenly the two or more daily insulin injections that they need just to stay alive will become the child's responsibility.

It's a constant worry for thousands of parents in this country.

There are over a million people in the UK who suffer from diabetes.

And recent reports show the incidence of diabetes in children under 15 has nearly doubled since 1975. (British Medical Journal, 1991, 302: p.443-7.)

The British Diabetic Association is the UK's biggest single contributor to diabetes research.

Please help us by sending a donation, joining the BDA or remembering us in your will. Then hopefully finding a cure won't be such a painful process.

To the BDA, 10 Queen Anne Street, London W1M 0BD. Tel: 071-323 1531. A charity helping people with diabetes and supporting diabetes research.
I enclose a cheque/postal order* payable to the BDA £ _____
Debit my Access/Visa* Card by the amount of £ _____
Card Number
GRG/01/BS   Expiry Date
Please send me more information and membership details ☐
Name _____
Address _____
_____
Signature _____
*Delete which is applicable   Reg. Charity No. 215199

BRITISH DIABETIC ASSOCIATION

Index

'*add*' after a page number indicates that the organisation's address is included in that reference.
References in italics indicate tables.

Abbey National plc 99-100 *add*
Abbeyfield Society 209-10 *add*, 306
accident prevention *see* safety
accountants 96-7
aches and pains 230
Action Resource Centre 185-6 *add*
additional pension (SERPS) 24-5, 44-5, 51
additional personal tax allowance 59
Additional Voluntary Contributions (AVCs) 32-3
adult education 154-5
Adult Education Centres/Institutes 6, 154
advisers *see* financial advisers
age
 addition to state pension 25, 325
 personal tax allowance 57
 widow's pension 325
 working after normal retirement 2, 16-17
Age Concern 196, 276, 286, 306, 319, 328
 Age Well 249-50
 national headquarters 210 *add*s, 290

 publications 4, 130, 135, 142, 145, 298, 305, 324
Age Concern Greater London 290 *add*
Age Concern Insurance Services 139 *add*
Age Exchange Reminiscence Centre 165 *add*
Age Well 249-50 *add*
agencies
 domestic 191-2, 294-5
 employment 183, 195-7
AIDS 246-7
AIDS-Lines 247
air, travelling by 282
Air Transport Users Committee 275 *add*
Air Travel Advisory Bureau 282
Al-Anon Family Groups 229 *add*
alarm systems
 burglar 138
 personal 287-8
alcohol problems 228-9
Alcoholics Anonymous 229 *add*
allowances 20
 carers' 298-9
 community charge benefit 145, 248
 council tax benefit 148-9, 248
 elderly/disabled 179, 299-301
 family credit 179-80

341

health service 234-5
housing benefit 144-5
income support 26
tax 56-9, 299
widows and widowers 58-9, 324-6
unemployment benefit 179
Almshouse Association 308 *add*
almshouses 308
Alzheimer's Disease Society 313 *add*
Alzheimer's Scotland 313 *add*
Amateur Rowing Association 174 *add*
Amateur Swimming Association 173 *add*
amenity organisations 168
Anchor Housing Association 306 *add*
angling 170
Angling Foundation 170 *add*
animal-related voluntary work 205
annuities 74-5
Approved Coal Merchants Scheme 127
Arblaster & Clarke 273 *add*
archery 170
Architectural Heritage Society of Scotland 208 *add*
Architectural Tours 269 *add*
ARP Over 50 7 *add*
art appreciation holidays 257-8
arthritis 243, 277
Arthritis Care 243 *add*, 277
Arthritis & Rheumatism Council 243 *add*
arts boards and councils 156, 216
Arts Council of Great Britain 216 *add*
arts-related activities 155-62
holidays 257-8
voluntary work 216

Artscape Painting Holidays 258 *add*
ASH (Action on Smoking & Health) 230 *add*
ASRA (Asians Sheltered Residential Accommodation) Greater London Housing Association 308 *add*
ASRA Leicester 308 *add*
ASRA Ltd 235 *add*
Association of British Insurers (ABI) 89 *add*, 102, 140, 141, 265, 279
Association of British Travel Agents (ABTA) 279 *add*
Association of Investment Trust Companies (AITC) 85 *add*
ATS Travel 276 *add*
attendance allowance 299-300
Auntie Fay Agency 191 *add*, 294
Automobile Association (AA) 264 *add*, 276
AVCs (Additional Voluntary Contributions) 32-3
average earnings pension schemes 31-2

back pain 243-4
Back Shop 243 *add*
BACUP (British Association of Cancer United Patients) 244 *add*
badminton 170-71
Badminton Association of England Ltd 170-71 *add*
ballet-related activities 156
Banking Ombudsman 100 *add*
banks 97-100
accounts with 319
wills 316
see also mortgages
Barbican Centre 158 *add*

Index

Barclays Bank plc 97 *add*
Barnardo's 206 *add*
Basketmakers' Association 160 *add*
bathroom safety 135-6
BBC Radio 157 *add*
BBC Television 157 *add*
BCWA (Bristol Contributory Welfare Association) 231 *add*, 232
Beale Dobie & Co Ltd 89-90 *add*
bed and breakfast, offering 195
benefits *see* allowances
benevolent societies, housing provision 307
Benslow Music Trust 258 *add*
bereavement
  allowance 327
  coping with 327-8
  voluntary work 205-6
blind people 238, 316
  books and tapes for 162-3
  holidays for 277
  voluntary work for 214-15
blind person's tax allowance 59
Bonds and Stock Office 82 *add*
bowling 171
Breast Care and Mastectomy Association 244-5 *add*
Brewing Publications Ltd 195 *add*
bridging loans 121-2
Brighton & Hove Jewish Welfare Board 292 *add*
Bristol Contributory Welfare Association (BCWA) 231 *add*, 232
British Association of Cancer United Patients (BACUP) 244 *add*
British Association of Friends of Museums 168 *add*
British Association of the Hard of Hearing 239 *add*
British Association for Local History 165 *add*
British Association of Numismatic Societies 166 *add*
British Association of Removers 122 *add*
British Board of Agreement 125 *add*
British Chess Federation 163 *add*
British Darts Organisation 172 *add*
British Deaf Association 240 *add*
British Diabetic Association 245 *add*, 277
British Ecological Society 168 *add*
British Gas 127, 129, 130, 136
British Health Care Association 232 *add*
British Heart Foundation 212 *add*, 245
British Institute of Florence 261 *add*
British Insurance and Investment Brokers Association (BIIBA) 75 *add*, 88, 101, 140
British Jigsaw Puzzle Library 166 *add*
British Museum Society 168 *add*
British Museum Tours 257 *add*
British Nursing Association 295 *add*
British Rail 272, 275, 281
British Rail Senior Rail Card 281
British Red Cross 204 *add*, 286, 291
British Standards Institution (BSI) 125 *add*, 127
British Trust for Conservation Volunteers 208 *add*, 273
British Universities

343

Accommodation Consortium 266 *add*
British Wheel of Yoga 226 *add*
British Wheelchair Sports Foundation 174 *add*
British Wireless for the Blind 162 *add*
British Wood Preserving and Damp-proofing Association 134 *add*
BSI Quality Assurance 125 *add*
BT 238, 239, 249, 287
budget planning 1-2, 10-20, 111-17
   budget planner chart 19, 112-17
Building Centre 133 *add*
Building Conservation Trust 134 *add*
building societies 79-80
   see also mortgages
Building Societies Association 79-80 *add*
Building Society Ombudsmen 80 *add*
BUPA 231 *add*, 231-2
   Medical Centre 230 *add*
burglar alarms 138
buses, travelling by 281
Business in the Community 186 *add*
businesses, selling family 67

Calibre 162-3 *add*, 212
Camping and Caravanning Club 266-7 *add*
CampusHotels 267 *add*
cancer 244
   related voluntary work 212, 213
Cancer Research Campaign 212 *add*

capital gains tax (CGT) 65-8, 82, 143-4
Care Alternatives 191 *add*
care and repair projects 135, 285
Carefree Holidays 276 *add*
carers
   benefits 298-9
   holidays for 297-8
   practical help for 296-7
Carers' National Association 210 *add*, 298
caring for elderly parents *see* elderly, caring for the
caring work 191-3
cars, buying 18-19
Catholic Marriage Advisory Council 211 *add*, 241
Cavity Foam Bureau 126 *add*
Cecil Houses (Inc) 306 *add*
Central Bureau 218 *add*, 262, 274
Central Council for Jewish Social Service 292 *add*
Central Council of Physical Recreation 161-2 *add*
Centre for Accessible Environments 287 *add*
CGT (capital gains tax) 65-8, 82
charities
   paid work for 187-8
   see also voluntary work
Charities Effectiveness Review Trust (CERT) 187 *add*
Charity Appointments 187 *add*
Charity Recruitment 187 *add*
Chartered Association of Certified Accountants 97 *add*
Cheques Act 1992 20
chess 163
chest diseases 245
child dependency addition to widow's allowance 325

Index

childminding 192
children, voluntary work with 206-8
Children's Country Holidays Fund 206-7 *add*
Children's Society 207 *add*
chiropody 239
Chosen Heritage 319
Christian Aid 216 *add*
Christmas bonus, state pensioners 28-9
Cinnamon Trust 205 *add*, 296
Citizens' Advice Bureaux 105, 106, 143, 203, 204
City of London Information Centre 165 *add*
Civic Trust 168 *add*
Civil Service Retirement Fellowship 292 *add*
clay pigeon shooting 171
Clay Pigeon Shooting Association 171 *add*
coach, travel by 281
coach holidays 259
coaching 189-90
cold weather payments 301
College of Health 235 *add*
common parts grants 131
Commonwealth War Graves Commission 261 *add*
Community Care 310-11
community charge benefit 145, 248
Community Service Volunteers 204-5 *add*, 294
company pension schemes 29-35, 45, 46-7
composite rate tax 62-3
COMPS (contracted-out money purchase schemes) 36
conservation activities 168-9
voluntary work 208-9

Conservation Foundation 169 *add*
Consultus 191 *add*, 294
Consumers' Association 324 *add*
Contact 210 *add*
Contemporary Art Society 159 *add*
contracted-out money purchase schemes (COMPS) 36
cooking, as paid work 193
Co-operative Women's Guild 174-5 *add*
CORGI (Council for Registered Gas Installers) 127 *add*, 136
Coronary Prevention Group 229 *add*, 245
corporation tax 70-71
Corps of Commissionaires 196 *add*
Council for the Accreditation of Correspondence Colleges 154 *add*
Council for British Archaeology 216 *add*
Council for National Parks 259 *add*
Council for the Protection of Rural England (CPRE) 208-9 *add*
Council for Registered Gas Installers (CORGI) 127 *add*, 136
council tax 145-8
council tax benefit 148-9, 248
councils, local *see* local authorities
Counsel & Care for the Elderly 292 *add*
Country Cottages in Scotland 267
Country Cousins and Emergency Mothers 192 *add*, 294
Countrywide Holidays 269-70 *add*

crafts activities 160-61
   holidays 258
Crafts Council 160-61 *add*, 258
cricket 171-2
croquet 172
Croquet Association 172 *add*
Crossroads 297 *add*
Cruse 205-6 *add*, 328
CV writing 183-4
cycling 172, 272
Cycling for Softies 272 *add*
Cyclists' Touring Club 172 *add*, 272

dance-related activities 161-2
darts 172
day centres 297
deaf people, assistance for 239-40
death 315-28
   benefits and tax 324-7
   helpful organisations 327-8
   money worries 318-19
   procedure 320-23, 324
   wills 68-9, 315-18
decorating work 193-4
dementia 312-13
dental treatment 240
Department of Employment see Employment Department
Department of the Environment leaflets 132, 143
Department of Health 235, 236 *add*, 251, 280
Department of Social Security (DSS) 27, 28 *add*, 29
   other advice 20, 179, 234, 299, 319, 324
   overseas branch 71 *add*
   pensions leaflets 23, 24, 28, 45, 52
Department of Transport 293 *add*

dependants, pension increase for 26, 325
deposit accounts 77-80
depression 241-3
Depressives Associated 242 *add*
diabetes 245, 277
DIAL UK (National Association of Disablement Information and Advice Lines) 250 *add*
dieting 227
Disability Action 250 *add*, 287
Disability Alliance (ERA) 251 *add*
Disability Living Allowance (DLA) 300
Disability Scotland 250 *add*, 287
Disability Working Allowance (DWA) 179
Disabled Living Foundation 249 *add*, 286, 288, 312
disabled people 247-51
   activities for 162-3, 164, 174
   adapting houses for 285-7
   benefits 179, 299-301
   facilities grants 131-2, 133
   holidays 275-7
   related voluntary work 212-16
   transport 275-6, 281, 293
   see also blind people; deaf people
Disabled Persons Railcards 281
disablement resettlement officers 248
district nurses 289
divorced wives, pensions 51-2
DIY work 194
Domestic Coal Consumers' Council 129-30 *add*
domestic work 191-2
drama-related activities 157-9
Draught Proofing Advisory Association 125 *add*
dressmaking work 193-4

Index

drink problems 228-9
Drinkwatchers 228-9 *add*
driving licence renewal 293
DSS *see* Department of Social Security

E & F N Spon 134 *add*
early leavers, pension schemes 33-5
early retirement, and pensions 27
Earnings Rule 27
Easymind: Home Care Services 192 *add*, 294
eating sensibly 226-7
Elderly Accommodation Counsel 311 *add*
elderly, caring for the 3, 191, 284-313
    adapting houses for 284-7
    alarm systems 287-8
    benefits 299-301
    financial assistance 301-2
    key voluntary organisations 290-93
    live-in help 294-6
    local authority services 288-90
    pets 296
    practical help for carers 296-9
    special accommodation 302-11
    special problems 311-13
    transport 293
    voluntary work with 209-11
electrical appliances, safety 136, 137
Electrical Contractors Association 127 *add*
Embroiderers' Guild 161 *add*
Employment Department 182 *add*
Employment Training programme 182
En Famille (Overseas) 261 *add*

endowment policies 87-90
energy, tips for reducing bills 128-9
Energy Action Grants Agency 133 *add*
Energy Efficiency Office 128 *add*
English Bowling Association 171 *add*
English Bridge Union 163 *add*
English Country Cottages Ltd 267 *add*
English Folk Dance and Song Society 162 *add*
English as a foreign language 190
English Gardening School 163 *add*
English Golf Union 172 *add*
English Heritage 165 *add*
English Indoor Bowling Association 171 *add*
English Vineyards Association 167 *add*
English Women's Bowling Association 171 *add*
English Women's Indoor Bowling Association 171 *add*
equipment, help for disabled 248-9
equities, investing in 82-6
Estudio General Luliano 261 *add*
ethnic groups, housing for 308
Eurisol UK Ltd 126 *add*
Eurocentres 261 *add*
Europ Assistance 265 *add*
Everymann Holidays 267 *add*
executors of wills 317
exercise, need for 225
Exeter Hospital Aid Society 231 *add*
Expanded Polystyrene Cavity Insulation Association 126 *add*

expenditure
    extra on retirement 12-13, *113*
    moving house 120-21
    normal additional 14, 117
    pre-retirement 16-19
    unavoidable 13-14, 116
Explore Worldwide 263 *add*
Extend 196 *add*, 225
External Wall Insulation Association 125 *add*
eyes, care of 237-8

family businesses, selling 67
Family Credit 179-80
Family Health Services Authorities 233 *add*
family members, moving in with 122-3
family-related voluntary work 211-12
Family Service Units 211 *add*
Farm Holiday Bureau UK Ltd 267 *add*
Federation of Family History Societies 165 *add*
Federation of Master Builders (FMB) 133 *add*
Federation of Women's Institutes of Northern Ireland 175 *add*
Fee-based Adviser Register 101 *add*
feet, care of 239
field studies 259-60
Field Studies Council 259-60 *add*
50-Forward 7 *add*
final salary pension schemes 31
finance
    death of relative 318-19
    help for elderly people 301-2, 311
    organising own 1-2, 10-20, 111, *112-17*

raising money on home 14-15, 16, 140-42
financial advisers 94-107
    choosing 95-6
Financial Services Act 90
fire extinguishers 137
fire hazards 136-7
fixed interest securities 80-82
flat rate pension schemes 32
food 226-7
    safety 228-9
Food Sense 227-8
Forces Help Society and Lord Roberts Workshops 292-3 *add*
Forestry Commission 169 *add*, 267 *add*
Foster's Oval Cricket Ground 172 *add*
fostering elderly people 191, 297-8
Frames Rickards Coach Tours 259 *add*
friends
    moving in with 122-3
    sharing with 123
Friends of Covent Garden 156 *add*
Friends of the Earth 209 *add*
Friends of English National Opera 156 *add*
Friends of the Fitzwilliam Museum 168 *add*
Friends of Historic Scotland 165 *add*
Friends of the National Maritime Museum 168 *add*
Friends of the National Museums of Scotland 168 *add*
Friends of Sadler's Wells 156 *add*
Friends of the V & A 168 *add*
funeral costs 318-19

Index

Gabbitas, Truman & Thring Educational Trust 189 *add*
games 163
Gardening for the Disabled Trust & Garden Club 164 *add*
gardens and gardening 163-4
　safety 137
　as work 193
gas appliances 127, 136
Gas Consumers' Council 129
general practitioners, choosing 233-4
genito-urinary medicine clinics (GUM) 247
gifted housing schemes 307-8
gilt-edged securities (gilts) 80-82
Glass and Glazing Federation 124 *add*
Goethe Institut 262 *add*
golf 172-3
Golfing Union of Ireland 172 *add*
Grace 311 *add*
graduated pension scheme 25, 51
Grand National Archery Society 170 *add*
grants, home improvement 126, 128, 130-33, 285-6
Green Theme International 262 *add*
Greenpeace 209 *add*
Guild of Aid for Gentle People 301 *add*
Guild of Master Craftsmen 133 *add*
GUM (genito-urinary medicine) clinics 247

'half test' 50
Handbell Ringers of Great Britain 157 *add*
handicapped people *see* disabled people

Hanover Housing Association 306 *add*
HE Foster & Cranfield 89 *add*
HEAC Ltd 267-8 *add*
health 2-3, 224-51
　AIDS 246-7
　common afflictions 230, 243-6
　depression 241-3
　disability 247-51
　eyes 237-8
　feet 239
　food and drink 226-9
　hearing 239-40
　insurance 230-33
　keeping fit 161-2, 225-6
　National Health Service 233-7
　personal relationships 3-5, 240-41
　related voluntary work 212-16
　smoking 229-30
　teeth 240
　tips for travellers 282-3
Health and Beauty Exercise 225 *add*
Health Education Authority 227 *add*, 232
Health Education Board for Scotland 250 *add*
health insurance 230-31
　hospital cash plans 233
health screening 231-2
Health Service Commissioners 236 *add*s
health visitors 289
Healthline 246
hearing 239-40
heart diseases 245
heating 126-30, 136
Heating and Ventilating Contractors' Association 128 *add*

Help the Aged 130, 210-11 *add*, 288, 308
   Winter Warmth Line 312
Help the Hospices 212 *add*
Hen House 265 *add*
HERA Recruitment Ltd 196-7 *add*
Herb Society 193 *add*
heritage, voluntary work 215
HF Holidays Ltd 270 *add*
Hill House Hammond Ltd 139 *add*
Hinton & Wild (Home Plans) Ltd 141 *add*, 142
hire purchase 19
Historic Houses Association 166 *add*
Historical Association 165-6 *add*, 260
history-related activities 164-6
   holidays 260-61
HM Land Registry 121 *add*
HMO (Houses in Multiple Occupation) grants 131
hobbies 166-7
Holiday Care Service 276 *add*
Holiday Club Pontin's 268 *add*, 270
holiday lets 143
holidays 256-83
   concessions 281-2
   for disabled 275-7
   to give carers a break 297-8
   health tips 282-3
   home exchange 262-3
   insurance 278-81
   overseas 263-5
   for singles 274-5
   special interest 257-62, 265-74
   tourist boards 278
Home Base Holidays 262 *add*
home decorating 193-4

Home Energy Efficiency Scheme (HEES) 133
home exchange 262-3
home helps 192, 288-9
home improvements 18, 119, 124-35
   care and repair projects 135, 285
   for elderly and handicapped 284-7
   grants 126, 128, 130-33, 285-6
   heating 126-30
   insulation 124-6
home income plans 140-42
home interests, paid work using 193-4
Home Responsibilities Protection (HRP) 22, 50, 299
home reversion schemes 141-2
Homecraft Supplies Ltd 286 *add*
Homelife-DGAA 216-17 *add*, 301
Homelink International 262-3 *add*
homes and housing 3, 118-49
   capital gains tax 66-7
   insurance 139-40
   investing proceeds from selling
   letting rooms/whole home 15-16, 66, 142-3, 144
   moving to new 3, 14-15, 118, 119-22
   moving to family or friends 122-3
   raising money on 14-15, 16, 140-42
   safety 135-7
   security 137-8
   sheltered 123, 303-9
   staying put 118-19
   tax and benefits 144-9

Index

useful organisations 149
working from 66
see also home improvements
Homesitters Ltd 193 *add*, 263
homesitting 192-3, 263
Horticultural Therapy 164 *add*
hospital, going into 235-6
hospital cash plans 233
Houses in Multiple Occupation (HMO) grants 131
housing associations 305-7
housing benefit 144-5
Housing Corporation 306 *add*
Housing for Wales 306 *add*
housing grants 126, 128, 130-33, 285-6
HRP (Home Responsibilities Protection) 22, 50, 299
hypothermia 312 *add*

Imperial Cancer Research Fund 213 *add*
Imperial Society of Teachers of Dancing 162 *add*
improving homes see home improvements
IMRO (Investment Management Regulatory Organisation) 84 *add*
income
  boosting 14-17
  expected sources of 13, *113-15*
  extra 20
income support 26
income tax 55-9, 69-70
  allowances 56-9, 299
  post-war credits 64-5
  tax relief 59-60
incontinence 312
Independent Living Fund 301 *add*
independent taxation 69-70

inheritance tax 68-9
Inland Revenue (IR)
  leaflets 58, 60, 62, 63, 64, 70, 71, 142, 299, 327
  mistakes 63
  Special Post War Credit Claim Centre 65 *add*
Institute of Chartered Accountants
  England and Wales 96 *add*
  Ireland 97 *add*
  Scotland 97 *add*
Institute of Insurance Brokers 139 *add*
Institute of Plumbing 134 *add*
insulation 124-6
insurance
  holiday 278-81
  home 139-40
  medical 60, 230-31, 233, 280
insurance brokers 100-103
Insurance Brokers' Registration Council 101, 102 *add*
Insurance Ombudsman Bureau 84 *add*, 102-3
International Co-operation for Development 191 *add*
International Rail Centre 281 *add*
Intervac International Home Exchange 263 *add*
interview technique 184-5
invalid care allowance 299
invalidity addition to pension 25
Invalids-at-Home Trust 301 *add*
investment 17, 35-6, 73-93
  annuities 74-5
  equities 82-6
  fixed interest securities 80-82
  long-term lock-ups 86-90
  protection 90-93
  sources of funds 73
  strategy 74

351

tax 62
types of pension policy 45-6
variable interest accounts 77-80
investment advisers *see* financial advisers
investment bonds 90 *add*
investment housing schemes 307
Investment Management Regulatory Organisation (IMRO) 84 *add*
investment trusts 85
Iyengar Yoga Institute 226 *add*

job agencies 183, 195-7
job counselling 181
Jobcentres 181, 196
Jobclubs 181
jobs, obtaining 2, 16-17, 178-97
　agencies and other organisations 183, 195-7
　applying for 183-5
　assessing own abilities 180-81
　counselling 181
　help with finding 182-3
　possible areas 185-95
　training 181-2
John Grooms Association for Disabled People 276-7 *add*

Keep Able 286-7 *add*
Keep Fit Association 162 *add*
keeping fit 161-2, 225-6
Kentwell Hall 260 *add*

Land Registry 121 *add*
Landmark Trust 268 *add*
language courses 261-2
LAUTRO (Life Assurance and Unit Trust Regulatory Organisation) 84 *add*
Law Centres 105
Law Centres Federation 105 *add*

Law Society
　England and Wales 107 *add*, 316
　Northern Ireland 107 *add*
　Scotland 107 *add*
Leeds Jewish Welfare Board 292 *add*
legal aid 105-6, 317
Legal Aid Board 106 *add*
Legal Services Ombudsman 106-7 *add*
Leicester Square Ticket Booth 159 *add*
leisure activities 3, 153-76
　for disabled 162-3, 164, 174
　special interest 155-76
L'Entente Cordiale Bureau 262 *add*
Leonard Cheshire Foundation 213 *add*
letting rooms 15-16, 66, 142-3
libraries 169-70
life assurance policies 86-90, 318
living-in help 294-5
Lloyds Bank plc 98
local arts councils 156
local authorities
　home improvement grants 131, 132
　homes 309-10
　services for disabled 247-8
　services for elderly 285, 288-90
　sheltered housing 305
locks, for doors and windows 138
lodgers 15-16, 66, 142-3
London Friend 247
long-term (investment) lock-ups 86-90
Look After Your Heart 249 *add*
low-budget holidays 266-9
lump sums 46-8

Index

maintenance payments, tax relief 60
Major & Mrs Holt's Battlefield Tours Ltd 260-61 *add*
Manchester Jewish Blind Society 292 *add*
Manpower (UK) Ltd 197 *add*
Market Research Society 187 *add*
market research work 186-7
Marriage Counselling Scotland 241 *add*
marriage guidance 211, 241
married couple's tax allowance 57-8
Master Locksmiths Association 138 *add*
MCC Lord's Cricket Ground 171 *add*
meals on wheels 288
Medau Society 225-6 *add*
medical insurance 60, 230-31, 233, 280
medical social workers 289-90
MENCAP (Royal Society for Mentally Handicapped Adults and Children) 213 *add*
menopause problems 246
Mental Health Foundation 213 *add*
Merseyside Jewish Representative Council 292 *add*
Midland Financial Services 98 *add*
migraine 245
Migraine Trust 245 *add*
MIND (National Association for Mental Health) 213-14 *add*, 242, 313
Miniature Armoured Fighting Vehicle Association 167 *add*
Minor Works Assistance grant 132-3

Mobility Advice and Vehicle Information Service (MAVIS) 293 *add*
Mobility Allowance 300-301
money see finance
Money Management Fee-based Adviser Register 101 *add*
money purchase pension schemes 31
mortgage annuity plans 140-41
mortgages 15, 19, 130, 318
 tax relief 59-60
Motability 250 *add*
Mothers' Union 175 *add*
motor insurance 264-5
motoring holidays 264-5
moving house 3, 14-15, 118, 119-22
MP Associates 268 *add*
Multiple Sclerosis Society 277 *add*
Museum of the Moving Image 168 *add*
museums 167-8
music-related activities 156-7, 258

NACOSS (National Approval Council for Security Systems) 138 *add*
National Adult School Organisation 154 *add*
National AIDS Helpline 246
National Approval Council for Security Systems (NACOSS) 138 *add*
National Art Collections Fund 159 *add*
National Association of Decorative & Fine Arts Societies 159-60 *add*, 257
National Association of Disablement Information

353

and Advice Lines (DIAL UK) 250 *add*
National Association of Flower Arrangement Societies of Great Britain 167 *add*
National Association of Funeral Directors 319 *add*
National Association of Leagues of Hospital Friends 214 *add*
National Association of Loft Insulation Contractors 124 *add*
National Association for Mental Health (MIND) 213-14 *add*, 242, 313
National Association of Widows 328 *add*
National Association of Women's Clubs 175 *add*
National Back Pain Association 214 *add*, 243-4
National Cavity Insulation Association 126 *add*
National Cricket Association 171-2 *add*
National Express 259 *add*
National Extension College 154 *add*
National Federation of Music Societies 157 *add*
National Federation of Women's Institutes 175 *add*
National Gardens Scheme 164 *add*
National Health Service 232, 233-7
National Home Improvement Council 135 *add*
National House Building Council (NHBC) 120-21, 304 *add*
National Inspection Council for Electrical Installation Contracting 127 *add*
National Institute of Adult Continuing Education 270 *add*
National Insurance (NI) 21-2, 49-50
National Library for the Blind 163 *add*
National Listening Library 163 *add*
National Museum of Wales 168 *add*
National Osteoporosis Society 246 *add*
National Philatelic Society 167 *add*
National Retreat Association 265 *add*
National Savings 75-7
National Savings Stock Register (NSSR) 82
National Society of Allotment and Leisure Gardeners Ltd 164 *add*
National Trust 166 *add*, 216
National Trust Holiday Cottages 268 *add*
National Trust for Scotland 166 *add*
National Trust for the Welfare of the Elderly 277 *add*
National Westminster Bank plc 99 *add*
National Women's Register 175 *add*
nature-related activities 168-9
needy, voluntary work for the 216-17
Neighbourhood Energy Action 130 *add*
Network Cards (rail) 281

Index

Network Scotland Ltd 155 *add*
New Horizons Trust 203 *add*
new-style reversion schemes 142
NI *see* National Insurance
Northern Consortium of
    Housing Authorities 121 *add*
Northern Ireland Association for
    Mental Health 313 *add*
Northern Ireland Federation of
    Housing Associations 306
    add
NSSR (National Savings Stock
    Register) 82
nursing care 295-6
nursing homes 310-11
nursing work 192

Occupational Pensions Advisory
    Service (OPAS) 37, 38 *add*,
    103
Occupational Pensions Board 38
    add
occupational therapists 248, 289
Odyssey International 274 *add*
offenders, working with 218
OFFER (Office of Electricity
    Regulation) 129 *add*
Office of the Building Societies
    Ombudsmen 80 *add*
Officers' Association 197 *add*
Official Error Concession (IR) 63
Old Rectory 270 *add*
Open College of the Arts 161 *add*
Open and Flexible Learning
    Scheme 182
Open University 6 *add*, 154-5
ordinary shares 84-5
osteoporosis 246
overseas holidays 263-5, 282
overseas payment of pensions 71
OwnBase 197 *add*
Oxfam 217 *add*

painting 160, 258
Parkinson's Disease Society 277
    add
Part-Time Careers Ltd 197 *add*
part-time jobs 185
partially sighted people *see* blind
    people
Patients Association 237 *add*
paying guests 142-3, 195
pension advisers 103-5 insurance
    brokers 100-103
pensions 21-54
    living abroad 71
    lump sums 46-8
    pre-retirement action 37-9
    private 29-35
    protection 39
    questions about 35-7
    self-employed and personal
        39-46, 60
    state 21-9
    women 22, 48-54, 325-6
    working after 27-8, 48
Pensions Ombudsman 38-9 *add*,
    103-4
PEPs (personal equity plans) 85-6
Perfect Assurance 319
personal allowances (tax) 56-7,
    59, 299
Personal Assets Log 317-18
personal equity plans (PEPs) 85-6
Personal Insurance Arbitration
    Service 103 *add*
personal pension schemes 39-46
    lump sums 46-8
    types of investment policies
        45-6
personal relationships 3-5, 240-41
personal safety 138
Pet Fostering Service Scotland
    205 *add*, 294
pets, care of 296, 318

physiotherapists 289
planning for retirement *see* budget planning
Plymbridge Distributors Ltd 298 *add*
Portland Holidays 263 *add*
post-war credits 64-5
PPP *see* Private Patients Plan
PRA *see* Pre-Retirement Association
Pre-Retirement Association of Great Britain & Northern Ireland 5-6 *add*
pre-retirement courses 5-7
Private Health Partnership 231
private medical insurance 60
private nursing homes 310
private patients 231
Private Patients Plan (PPP) 231 *add*, 232
private rest homes 309
PRO Dogs 205 *add*, 318
Prospect Music Art & Art Tours Ltd 257 *add*
protected rights, pensions 43-4
public appointments 186
Public Appointments Unit 186 *add*
public libraries 169-70
pubs, running 194-5

Quitline 230 *add*

RAC Travel Services 264 *add*
RADAR (Royal Association for Disability and Rehabilitation) 133, 249 *add*, 275-6, 286
radio programme audiences 157
Radio Society of Great Britain 167 *add*

rail, travelling by 159, 272, 275, 281
Rail Europe Senior Cards 281
Railway Correspondence & Travel Society 167 *add*
Ramblers' Association 173 *add*, 209
Ramblers' Holidays Ltd 272 *add*
rambling 173, 272-3
REACH 203 *add*
Recognised Professional Bodies *see* RPBs
reduced rate NI contributions 22, 49-50
reduced rate pensions 23-4
regional arts boards 156
Registered Nursing Homes Association 310 *add*
Registrar of Pension Schemes 38 *add*, 104
Relate: National Marriage Guidance 211 *add*, 241
'relating back' 43
relationships, personal 3-5, 240-41
Relaxation for Living 226 *add*
REMAP 287 *add*
removals 122
renovation grants 131
rented sheltered housing 305-7
renting out
 rooms 15-16, 66, 142-3
 whole house 66, 144
repairs *see* home improvements
residential homes 309-10
respite care facilities 297
Restart programme 181
retirement housing *see* sheltered housing
retreats 265
rheumatism 243

Index

Riding for the Disabled Association 214 *add*
RNIB *see* Royal National Institute for the Blind
rowing 174
Royal Agricultural Benevolent Institution 302 *add*
Royal Association for Disability and Rehabilitation *see* RADAR
Royal Bank of Scotland 99 *add*
Royal British Legion 217 *add*
    Pilgrimage Department 261 *add*
Royal British Legion Attendants Co Ltd 197 *add*
Royal British Legion Housing Association 307 *add*
Royal Horticultural Society 164 *add*
Royal Institute of British Architects 134 *add*
Royal Institution of Chartered Surveyors 134 *add*, 140
Royal National Institute for the Blind (RNIB) 214-15 *add*, 238, 277, 316 Talking Book Service 163 *add*
Royal National Institute for Deaf People 240 *add*
Royal National Theatre 158 *add*
Royal Photographic Society 167 *add*
Royal Scottish Country Dance Society 162 *add*
Royal Society for Mentally Handicapped Adults and Children (MENCAP) 213 *add*
Royal Society for the Prevention of Cruelty to Animals 205 *add*

Royal Society for the Protection of Birds 169 *add*
Royal United Kingdom Beneficent Association (RUKBA) 302 *add*
Royal Yachting Association 174 *add*
RPBs (Recognised Professional Bodies) 90, 91, 92
RSNC, the Wildlife Trusts Partnership 169 *add*
running 173
Running Sixties 173 *add*

safes 138
safety
    food 227-8
    home 135-7
    personal 138
Saga Holidays Ltd 266 *add*
sales work 188-9
Samaritans 217 *add*, 242
Save the Children 207 *add*
savings on retirement 11-12, 17-19, *112*
SBC (Scottish Business in the Community) 186 *add*
Scottish Association for Mental Health 313 *add*
Scottish Business in the Community (SBC) 186 *add*
Scottish Community Drama Association 158-9 *add*
Scottish Conservation Projects Trust 209 *add*, 273
Scottish Corps of Retired Executives (SCORE) 203 *add*
Scottish Farmhouse Holidays 268 *add*
Scottish Field Studies Association 260 *add*

Scottish Golf Union 172 *add*
Scottish Homes 306 *add*
Scottish Inland Waterways Association 169 *add*
Scottish and Northern Ireland Plumbing Employers' Federation 134 *add*
Scottish Retirement Council 6 *add*
Scottish Sports Council 271 *add*
Scottish Women's Rural Institutes 175 *add*
Scottish YHA 269 *add*
Scout Association 207 *add*
Scrabble Club Coordinator 163 *add*
Sea Cadet Corps 207 *add*
secondments 185-6
Section 226 pension policies 40-41
Securities and Investments Board (SIB) 90, 91, 92
security, home 137-8
self-catering holidays 266-9
self-employed people
 pensions 35, 39-46, 60, 104-5
 tax 71
Self-Regulating Organisations *see* SROs
Selwood Press Ltd 305 *add*
Senior Railcards 281
separated wives, pensions 52
SERPS (State Earnings-Related Pension Scheme) 24-5, 44-5, 51
Servite Houses 306-7 *add*
sex life 4
SHACS (Sheltered Housing Advisory and Conciliation Service) 304 *add*
shared ownership 307
shares 84-5

sheltered accommodation 123, 303-9 extra care 308-9 rented 305-7
Sheltered Housing Advisory and Conciliation Service (SHACS) 304 *add*
Sheltered Housing Code 304
Sheltered Housing Services 304 *add*
SIB (Securities and Investment Board) 90, 91, 92
single parent's tax allowance 59
singles' holidays 274-5
Skillshare Africa 190 *add*
smoking 229-30
Social Fund 26-7
Social Services (Work) Departments 247-8
social workers 289
Society of Chiropodists 239 *add*
Society of Genealogists 166 *add*
Society of Pension Consultants 104-5 *add*
Society of Recorder Players 157 *add*
Society of Voluntary Associates 218 *add*
Society of West End Theatre 158 *add*
Soldiers', Sailors' and Airmen's Families Association 211-12 *add*, 302, 307
solicitors 105-7, 316
Solicitors Complaints Bureau 106 *add*
Solid Fuel Advisory Council 126, 127
Spastics Society 215 *add*
special accommodation for the elderly 123, 302-11
special care, holidays for those needing 275-7

358

Index

special interest holidays 269-71
Special Post-War Credit Claim
    Centre 65 *add*
Specialtours 257-8 *add*
split capital trusts 85
sporting activities 170-74
    holidays 271-3
Sports Council 225, 271 *add*
SROs (Self-Regulating
    Organisations) 90, 91, 92
St Catherine's House 52 *add*
St John Ambulance 215 *add*,
    291-2
state benefits *see* allowances
State Earnings-Related Pension
    Scheme (SERPS) 24-5,
    44-5, 51
state pensions 21-9, 48-54
    additional (SERPS) 24-5, 44-5,
        51
    basic 23-4
    claiming 27-9
    deferring 25-6
    widow's 52-4, 325
    working after retirement age 27
'Staying Put' schemes 135, 285
Stock Exchange 84-5
Stroke Association 215 *add*, 246,
    277
strokes 246, 277
Sue Ryder Foundation 215-16
    add
Summer Music 258 *add*
'Sundowner' schemes 307
swimming 173

table tennis 173
Talking Book Service (RNIB)
    163 *add*
taper relief 68
Tate Gallery 160 *add*
tax 55-71

allowances 56-9, 299
annuities 75
capital gains 65-8, 82, 143-4
corporation 70
health insurance 230-31
income 55-9, 69-70
independent 69-70
inheritance 68-9
on investments 62
    equities 84, 85, 89, 90
    fixed interest 81-2
mistakes 63
mortgages 59-60
pensions 29, 60, 71
post-war credits 64-5
rebates 63-4
reclaiming 63
rental income 16
value-added tax 70
widows and widowers 327
Tax Exempt Special Savings
    Accounts (TESSAS) 77, 78,
    79
tax-free income 61-2
tax offices, leaflets 45, 67-8, 69,
    70
tax relief 59-60
Teachers' Benevolent Fund 307
    add
teaching 189-90
Teaching as a Career Unit 190
    add
teeth, care of 240
television programme audiences
    157
tennis 173-4
Terrence Higgins Trust Ltd 247
TESSAs (Tax Exempt Special
    Savings Accounts) 77, 78, 79
Theatre and Concert Travel Club
    159 *add*
theatre-related activities 157-9

Third World, working in the
    190-91 *add*
Thomson Young at Heart 263-4
    add
TocH 274 *add*
tourist boards 271, 278
tourist work 189
Townswomen's Guilds 175-6 *add*
training 181-2
    as paid work 189-90
Training and Enterprise Councils
    (TECs) 182
transport and travel 159, 176,
    272, 281-2, 293
    elderly and disabled 275-6
    insurance 278-80
Travel Companions (UK) Ltd
    274-5 *add*
Travelmate 275 *add*
trustees, pension fund 38

unemployment benefit 179
Unit Trust Association 83-4 *add*
unit trusts 83
United Kingdom Home Care
    Association (UKHCA) 192
    add, 295-6
United Nations Association
    International Service 191 *add*
Universal Aunts Ltd 192 *add*,
    193, 263, 294
University of Cambridge Local
    Examination Syndicate 190
    add
University of the Third Age 155
    add

Value added tax (VAT) 70
variable interest accounts 77-80
Vegi-Ventures 270-71 *add*
veteran rowing 174
Veterans English Table Tennis
    Association (VETTS) 173
    add
Veterans' Lawn Tennis
    Association of Great Britain
    173-4 *add*
Victim Support 218 *add*
victims of crime, voluntary work
    with 218
visual arts activities 159-60
voluntary-run nursing homes 310
voluntary rest homes 309
voluntary sitters 297
voluntary work 2, 202-18
    choosing 202-3
volunteer bureaux 203
Volunteer Centre UK 203 *add*,
    218
Volunteer Reading Help 207-8
    add
VSO (Voluntary Service
    Overseas) 190 *add*

Wales Council for the Disabled
    250 *add*, 287
Waymark Holidays 273 *add*
Weight Watchers by Mail 227 *add*
Welcome Home Nursing Scheme
    295 *add*
Welsh Country Cottages 267
Welsh Golfing Union 173 *add*
West Dean College 258 *add*
Western Provident Association
    Ltd (WPA) 231 *add*, 232
wheelchair sport 174
widowed mother's allowance
    324-5
widows
    benefits 58-9, 324-5,
    pension rights 52-4, 325
widow's bereavement allowance
    58-9, 326
widows' payment 324

Wildfowl and Wetlands Trust 169 *add*
wills 68-9, 315-18
wine-tasting holidays 273
Winged Fellowship Trust 277 *add*
Winter Warmth Line 312
Wireless for the Bedridden Society 302 *add*
women
  organisations for 174-6
  pensions 22, 48-54
  tax for married 57-8, 69-70
  see also widows
Women's Health Concern (WHC) 246 *add*
Women's Royal Voluntary Service (WRVS) 204 *add*, 290-91
work *see* jobs, obtaining; self-employment; voluntary work

Workers' Educational Association (WEA) 6 *add*, 155
working holidays 273-4
World Wine Tours 273 *add*
Worldwide Home Exchange Club 263 *add*
WPA *see* Western Provident Association

yachting 174
YMCA National Centre 271-2 *add*
yoga 226
Yoga for Health Foundation 226 *add*
young people, voluntary work with 206-8
Youth Clubs UK 208 *add*
Youth Hostels Association 268-9 *add*

List of Advertisers

Alzheimer's Disease Society 252
Anthony Nolan Bone Marrow Trust 329
Association of Investment Trust Companies 72
Athene Trust 219

Barnardos 198
Boyton Financial Services Ltd 109
Breakthrough Trust xv
British Association of the Hard of Hearing x
British Diabetic Association 339
British Geriatrics Society for Health in Old Age 200
British Heart Foundation 330
British Red Cross 222
British Scoliosis Research Foundation 331
British Union for the Abolition of Vivisection xvi
British Veterinary Association Animal Welfare Foundation xxxii
Brooke Hospital for Animals viii
British Wheelchair Sports Foundation 255

Camphill Village Trust 221
CareQuest 314
Carers National Association x
Cecil Houses 314
Children Nationwide xxiii
Chosen Heritage Ltd 332
Commercial Union 8
CPRE 151
Crafts Council 150

De Paul Trust vi
Dogs' Home Battersea 255
Dove Healthcare Ltd v

Elizabeth Foundation for Deaf Children 333

Family Holiday Association viii
Feed the Children 331
Flatroof Company ii

Friends of the Earth 198

Gardeners' Royal Benevolent Society 109
Greater London Fund for the Blind 252

Headway National Head Injuries Association 199
Help the Hospices 201
Home Warmth for the Aged Benevolent Fund 252
Homeowners Friendly Society 110

Invalid Children's Aid Nationwide 367

King Edward VII's Hospital for Officers ii
Klavar Music Foundation of Great Britain (GRG) 177
Knight Williams 108

Leonard Cheshire Foundation 366
Leukaemia Care vi

Mental After Care Association x

National Association for Mental Health 221
National Association for the Welfare of Children in Hospital 109
National Benevolent Fund for the Aged 221
National Canine Defence League xv
National Eye Research Centre 335
National Kidney Federation 335
NGRC Retired Greyhound Trust 223
Nuffield Hospitals vii

Open University xxxii

Prince and Princess of Wales Hospital viii
Princess Louise Scottish Hospital 335
Psoriasis Association 336

Queen Elizabeth's Foundation for Disabled People vi

Ramblers Holidays Ltd 255
Rathbone Society 336
Redundant Churches Fund 177
Royal Air Force Benevolent Fund 337
Royal British Legion 199
Royal London Society for the Blind 9
Royal Opera House Trust 253
RSPB 152
Royal School for Deaf Children Margate 338

Advertiser's Index

Royal Scottish Agricultural Benevolent Society xxiii
Royal Society of Medicine vii

St Andrew Animal Fund Ltd ii
Salvation Army 338
Samaritans 254
Scottish Conservation Projects Trust 254
Scottish Society for the Prevention of Cruelty to Animals xii
Sea Cadet Association 201
Sick Childrens Trust 254
Skillshare Africa 220
Soldiers' Sailors' and Airmen's Families Association 200

Titan Travel Ltd xxiv
Turning Point 199

W I Carr (Investments) Ltd xviii

Yorkshire Cancer Research Campaign xx
Yorkshire Wildlife Trust 150

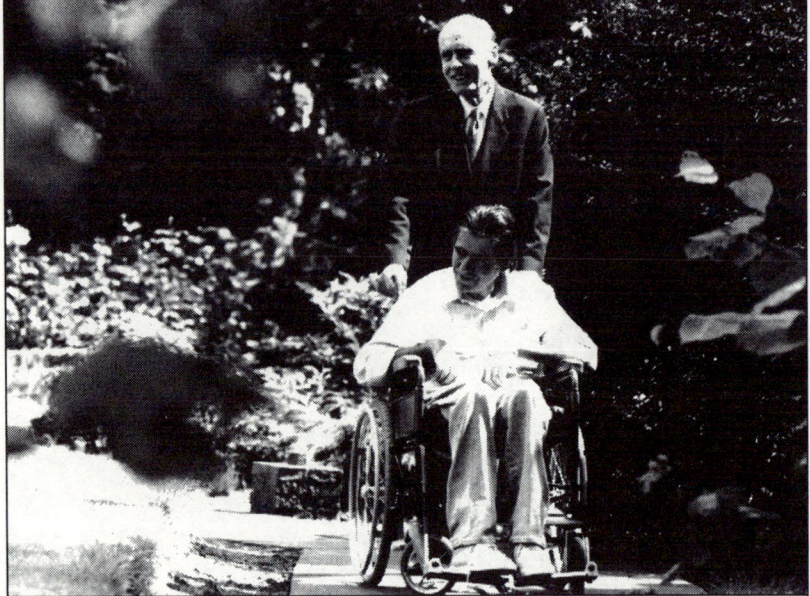

Photo: Courtesy of The Scotsman, Edinburgh

Offering choice and opportunity to people with disabilities

- Leonard Cheshire Foundation established over 40 years ago by Group Captain Lord Cheshire, V.C., O.M., D.S.O., D.F.C.
- Promotes the care, general well-being and rehabilitation of people with physical, mental and learning disabilities
- Over 85 Cheshire Homes in the UK and 185 in 50 countries overseas
- 33 UK Family Support Services providing day to day care for people with disabilities in their own homes
- Range of services including day care and respite care, allowing a break for relatives and a holiday for the person with the disability

PLEASE SUPPORT
THE LEONARD CHESHIRE
FOUNDATION AND HELP US
CONTINUE OUR WORK

*For further information,
please call Peter Tomlinson
on 071 828 1822
or write to
26-29 Maunsel Street
London SW1P 2QN*

Reg. Charity No. 218186

To: Rosemary Brown
Reward Retirement Services
Enterprise Dynamics Ltd.
9 Savoy Street
London WC2R 0BA

Tel: 071–379 6515
Fax: 071–379 3230

From: ....
....
....
....
....

Suggestions:
....
....
....
....
....
....
....
....
....
....
....
....
....